Student's Solutions Manual
for use with

FIFTH EDITION

BUSINESS MATHEMATICS
IN CANADA

F. Ernest Jerome

McGraw-Hill Ryerson

Toronto Montréal Boston Burr Ridge, IL Dubuque, IA Madison, WI New York
San Francisco St. Louis Bangkok Bogotá Caracas Kuala Lumpur Lisbon London
Madrid Mexico City Milan New Delhi Santiago Seoul Singapore Sydney Taipei

Student's Solutions Manual
for use with
Business Mathematics in Canada
Fifth Edition

ISBN: 0-07-0921741

1 2 3 4 5 6 7 8 9 10 CP 0 9 8 7 6 5

Printed and bound in Canada

Vice President, Editorial and Media Technology: Patrick Ferrier
Executive Sponsoring Editor: Lynn Fisher
Developmental Editor: Maria Chu
Senior Production Coordinator: Madeleine Harrington
Printer: Canadian Printco

To the Student:

Welcome to the study of applications of mathematics to business. Chances are that you already have some understanding of a number of the topics to which mathematics will be applied. Even when a topic is unfamiliar, it is rarely abstract. Consequently, your intuition can assist your learning and guide your reasoning.

The **Student's Solutions Manual** contains solutions to *odd-numbered* Exercise problems, Review Problems, and Concept Questions, plus solutions to *all* problems in the Self-Test Exercises. Except for the Concept Questions, numerical results for these problems are also provided in the back of the text.

There is no substitute for doing problems in order to discover and remedy deficiencies in your understanding. To derive the greatest benefit from using this manual, you should first make a serious attempt to solve a problem *before* looking at its solution. If 10 minutes pass without progress in your solution, it is unlikely you will achieve a break-through in the next 10 or 15 minutes. You should first cover the solution in this manual and then expose it line-by-line until you discover your "sticking point" or error. Then return to your own solution and attempt to complete it. By this procedure, you are much more likely to identify the gap in your understanding, and to retain the knowledge or insight gained in overcoming your "sticking point."

Part A on the CD-ROM supplied with the text discusses "How to Succeed in Business Mathematics." You should read this guide during the first or second week of your course, and review it every two or three weeks to reinforce good work and study habits until they become second nature. A general approach for solving word problems is discussed in Section 2.4 of the text.

I sincerely hope this manual assists you in productive learning of business mathematics.

F. Ernest Jerome

Table of Contents

Table of Contents (*continued*)

1 Review and Applications of Basic Mathematics

Exercise 1.1

1. $20 - 4 \times 2 - 8 = 20 - 8 - 8 = \underline{\underline{4}}$

3. $(20 - 4) \times 2 - 8 = 16 \times 2 - 8 = 32 - 8 = \underline{\underline{24}}$

5. $20 - (4 \times 2 - 8) = 20 - (8 - 8) = \underline{\underline{20}}$

7. $54 - 36 \div 4 + 2^2 = 54 - 9 + 4 = \underline{\underline{49}}$

9. $(54 - 36) \div (4 + 2)^2 = 18 \div 6^2 = 18 \div 36 = \underline{\underline{0.5}}$

11. $\dfrac{8^2 - 4^2}{(4 - 2)^3} = \dfrac{64 - 16}{2^3} = \dfrac{48}{8} = \underline{\underline{6}}$

13. $3(6 + 4)^2 - 5(17 - 20)^2 = 3 \times 10^2 - 5(-3)^2 = 3 \times 100 - 5 \times 9 = 300 - 45 = \underline{\underline{255}}$

15. $[(20 + 8 \times 5) - 7 \times (-3)] \div 9 = (20 + 40 + 21) \div 9 = 81 \div 9 = \underline{\underline{9}}$

Concept Questions (Section 1.2)

1. You must retain at least one more figure than you require in the answer. To achieve four-figure accuracy in the answer, you must retain a minimum of <u>five figures</u> in the values used in the calculations.

3. We want seven-figure accuracy in the answer. Therefore, values used in the calculations must be accurate to at least <u>eight figures</u>.

5. Any value that represents a count of discrete units, such as the number of months in a year, is an example. Prescribed payments or values (in contrast to calculated payments or values that have been rounded) are known with perfect accuracy. For example, the GST rate of 7% and a prescribed monthly payment of $10 may be treated as numbers having complete accuracy.

Exercise 1.2

1. $\frac{7}{8} = \underline{\underline{0.875}} = \underline{\underline{87.5\%}}$

3. $\frac{47}{20} = \underline{\underline{2.35}} = \underline{\underline{235\%}}$

5. $-\frac{35}{25} = \underline{\underline{-1.4}} = \underline{\underline{-140\%}}$

7. $\frac{25}{1000} = \underline{\underline{0.025}} = \underline{\underline{2.5\%}}$

9. $2\frac{2}{100} = \underline{\underline{2.02}} = \underline{\underline{202\%}}$

11. $\frac{37.5}{50} = \underline{\underline{0.75}} = \underline{\underline{75\%}}$

13. $\frac{5}{6} = \underline{\underline{0.8\overline{3}}} = \underline{\underline{83.\overline{3}\%}}$

15. $7\frac{7}{9} = \underline{\underline{7.\overline{7}}} = \underline{\underline{777.\overline{7}\%}}$

Exercise 1.2 *(continued)*

17. $\frac{10}{9} = 1.\overline{1} = 111.\overline{1}\%$

19. $-\frac{7}{270} = -0.0\overline{259} = -2.\overline{592}\%$

21. $11.3845 \approx 11.38$

23. $0.5545454 \approx 0.5545$

25. $1.0023456 \approx 1.002$

27. $40.09515 \approx 40.10$

29. $\frac{1}{6} = 0.16667 = 16.667\%$

31. $\frac{1}{60} = 0.016667 = 1.6667\%$

33. $\frac{250}{365} = 0.68493 = 68.493\%$

35. $\frac{0.11}{12} = 0.0091667 = 0.91667\%$

37. $\$92\left(1 + 0.095 \times \frac{112}{365}\right) = \$92 \times 1.02915 = \$94.68$

39. $\$454.76\left(1 - 0.105 \times \frac{11}{12}\right) = \$454.76 \times 0.903750 = \$410.99$

41. $\dfrac{\$3490}{1 + 0.125 \times \frac{91}{365}} = \dfrac{\$3490}{1.031164} = \$3384.52$

43. $\$650\left(1 + \frac{0.105}{2}\right)^2 = \$650(1.0525)^2 = \$720.04$

45. $\dfrac{\$15,400}{\left(1 + \frac{0.13}{12}\right)^6} = \dfrac{\$15,400}{1.0108333^6} = \$14,435.88$

47. $\dfrac{\$6600\left(1 + 0.085 \times \frac{153}{365}\right)}{1 + 0.125 \times \frac{82}{365}} = \dfrac{\$6600(1.035630)}{1.028082} = \$6648.46$

49. $\$1000\left[\dfrac{\left(1 + \frac{0.09}{12}\right)^7 - 1}{\frac{0.09}{12}}\right] = \$1000\left(\dfrac{0.05369613}{0.0075}\right) = \$7159.48$

51. $\dfrac{\$9500}{\dfrac{\left(1 + \frac{0.075}{4}\right)^5 - 1}{\frac{0.075}{4}}} = \dfrac{\$9500}{\dfrac{0.09733216}{0.01875}} = \$1830.07$

Concept Questions (Section 1.3)

1. If a quantity equals the base, it is 100% of the base.
   If a quantity is twice the base, it is 200% of the base, and so on.
   If a quantity is four times the base, it is 400% of the base.

3. By the same line of reasoning as in question 1, the *Portion* is 10 times the *Base*.

Exercise 1.3

1. $Portion = Rate \times Base = 0.0175 \times \$350 = \underline{\$6.13}$

3. $Rate = \dfrac{Portion}{Base} = \dfrac{\$1.50}{\$11.50} = 0.130 = \underline{13.0\%}$

5. $Base = \dfrac{Portion}{Rate} = \dfrac{\$45}{0.60} = \underline{\$75.00}$

7. $Portion = Rate \times Base = 2.333 \times \$75 = \underline{\$174.98}$

9. $Rate = \dfrac{Portion}{Base} = \dfrac{\$134}{\$67} = 2.00 = \underline{200\%}$

11. $Portion = Rate \times Base = 1.5 \times \$60 = \underline{\$90.00}$

13. $Base = \dfrac{Portion}{Rate} = \dfrac{\$1.46}{0.075} = \underline{\$19.47}$

15. $Rate = \dfrac{Portion}{Base} = \dfrac{\$590}{\$950} = 0.621 = \underline{62.1\%}$

17. $Base = \dfrac{Portion}{Rate} = \dfrac{\$100}{0.95} = \underline{\$105.26}$

19. $Rate = \dfrac{Portion}{Base} = \dfrac{30 \text{ metres}}{3000 \text{ metres}} = 0.0100 = \underline{1.00\%}$

21. $Portion = Rate \times Base = 0.005 \times \$10.00 = \underline{\$0.05}$

23. $Base = \dfrac{Portion}{Rate} = \dfrac{\$180}{1.20} = \underline{\$150.00}$

25. $Portion = Rate \times Base = 1.305 \times \$455 = \underline{\$593.78}$

27. $Base = \dfrac{Portion}{Rate} = \dfrac{\$281.25}{2.25} = \underline{\$125.00}$

29. $Base = \dfrac{Portion}{Rate} = \dfrac{\$10}{0.005} = \underline{\$2000.00}$

31. Bonus as a percentage of sales $= \dfrac{Portion}{Base} = \dfrac{\$7980}{\$532,000} = 0.0150 = \underline{1.50\%}$

    Bonus as a percentage of salary $= \dfrac{\$7980}{\$45,000} = 0.177 = \underline{17.7\%}$

33. Shots scored from 2-point zone $= Rate \times Base = 0.545454 \times 33 = 18$
    Shots scored from 3-point distance $= 0.46667 \times 15 = 7$
    Foul shots scored $= 0.793 \times 29 = 23$
    Total points scored $= 18(2) + 7(3) + 23(1) = \underline{80}$

35. The budgeted expenses are the *Base* while the actual expenses are the *Portion*.
    Budgeted expenses $= \dfrac{Portion}{Rate} = \dfrac{\$169,400}{1.10} = \underline{\$154,000.00}$

37. Number of hours in a 31-day month $= 31(24) = 744$
    Time available for other activities $= 744 - 700 = 44$ hours
    Percentage of time available for other activities $= \dfrac{Portion}{Base} \times 100\% = \dfrac{44}{700} \times 100\% = \underline{5.91\%}$

Exercise 1.3 *(continued)*

39. Percentage of impurities = $100\% - 99\frac{44}{100}\% = \frac{56}{100}\% = 0.56\%$

    Amount of impurities in a 150-g cake = $Rate \times Base = 0.0056 \times 150 \text{ g} = 0.840 \text{ g} = \underline{840 \text{ mg}}$

41. Full-service broker's charges = $Commission\ Rate \times Base = 0.025(600 \times \$15.85) = \$237.75$
    Discount broker's charges = $\$39 + (600 \times \$0.06) = \$75.00$
    The discount broker will charge $\$237.75 - \$75.00 = \underline{\$162.75 \text{ less}}$

43. 1000 kg of the 1% solution contains $0.01 \times 1000 \text{ kg} = 10\text{kg}$ of dissolved ingredients. After concentration, this 10 kg *(Portion)* of dissolved ingredients represent 3% *(Rate)* by weight of the concentrated solution.

    Final weight of concentrated solution *(Base)* $= \dfrac{Portion}{Rate} = \dfrac{10 \text{ kg}}{0.03} = 333.3 \text{ kg}$

    Therefore, you must boil off 1000 kg – 333.3 kg = $\underline{666.7 \text{ kg}}$ of water.

45. The dividend *(Portion)* is 8% of the par value *(Base)*.

    Par value $= \dfrac{Portion}{Rate} = \dfrac{\$3.50}{0.08} = \underline{\$43.75}$

47. Portion of commission retained = $Rate \times Base = 0.60 \times 6\% = 3.6\%$
    The $75,000 income *(Portion)* is 3.6% of sales *(Base)*.

    Sales volume $= \dfrac{Portion}{Rate} = \dfrac{\$75,000}{0.036} = \underline{\$2,083,333.33}$

49. The expected number of deaths *(Portion)* among 50,000 males *(Base)* is
    $$Rate \times Base = 0.0034 \times 50,000 = \underline{170}$$
    The number of 35-year-old males in the city of 1.45 million is $0.0083 \times 1,450,000 = 12,035$.
    The expected number of deaths in this group in a year is $0.0034 \times 12,035 = \underline{41}$.

Exercise 1.4

1. Regular weekly earnings $= \dfrac{\$58,800}{52} = \$1130.77$

    Equivalent hourly rate $= \dfrac{\$1130.77}{35} = \$32.31$

    Overtime hourly rate = $1.5(\$32.31) = \$48.47$

    Gross pay for 39-hour week = $\$1130.77 + 4(\$48.47) = \underline{\$1324.65}$

3. Regular biweekly earnings $= \dfrac{\$54,600}{26} = \$2100.00$

    Equivalent hourly wage $= \dfrac{\$2100.00}{2 \times 40} = \$26.25$

    Hasad worked 3 hours of overtime in the first week and 6.5 hours in the second week.
    Gross pay = $\$2100.00 + 9.5(1.5)\$26.25 = \underline{\$2474.06}$

5. Regular hours worked = $7.5 + 7.5 + 6 + 6 + 7.5 = 34.5$
    Overtime hours worked = $4.5 + 1 + 1.5 = 7$
    Gross earnings = $34.5(\$17.70) + 7(1.5)(\$17.70) = \underline{\$796.50}$

Exercise 1.4 *(continued)*

7. Output in excess of quota = 4 + 6 + 7 + 8 +10 =35 shirts
   Total pay = 40($7.50) + 35($3.00) = $405.00

9. *a.* Earnings will be the greater of
   $600 or 0.11(Sales) = 0.11($5636) = $619.96

   b. The salesman will earn the $600 from sales if
   0.11(Sales) = $600
   That is, if

   $$\text{Sales} = \frac{\$600}{0.11} = \$5454.55 \text{ per week}$$

11. *a.* Earnings = 0.05($20,000) + 0.075($20,000) + 0.10($14,880) = $3988.00

    b. For the same earnings from a single straight commission rate,
    Commission rate × $54,880 = $3988.00

    $$\text{Commission rate} = \frac{\$3988}{\$54,880} \times 100\% = 7.2668\%$$

13. Commission earned in August = $3296.97 − $1500.00 = $1796.97
    Hence,
    Commission rate ($151,342 − $100,000) = $1796.97

    $$\text{Commission rate} = \frac{\$1796.97}{\$51,342} \times 100\% = 3.50\%$$

15. Commission earned on first $90,000 of sales was
    0.04($40,000) + 0.05($50,000) = $4100
    Commission earned on sales in excess of $90,000 was $5350 − $4100 = $1250
    That is,
    0.06(Sales exceeding $90,000) = $1250

    $$\text{Sales exceeding } \$90,000 = \frac{\$1250}{0.06} = \$20,833.33$$

    Total sales for the month = $90,000 + $20,833.33 = $110,833.33

Concept Questions (Section 1.5)

1. You should calculate a weighted average <u>when some of the values being averaged are more important or occur more frequently than other values</u>.

3. If you <u>invest the same amount of money in each investment</u>, each rate of return has the same importance. The portfolio's rate of return will then equal the simple average of the individual rates of return.

Exercise 1.5

1. Weight each number of TV sets per household by the number of homes with that number of TVs. The weighted average number of TVs per household in the survey sample is

$$\frac{(4 \times 4) + (22 \times 3) + (83 \times 2) + (140 \times 1) + (5 \times 0)}{254} = \underline{1.53}$$

Based on the survey, we estimate the average number of TVs per household to be 1.53.

3. We should weight each "goals against" figure by the number of games in which that number was scored.

$$\text{GAA} = \frac{1(0) + 2(1) + 3(2) + 4(3) + 7(4) + 2(6) + 1(10)}{20} = \underline{3.50}$$

5. The weighted average interest rate that will be charged on the new $57,500 balance is

$$\frac{\$37,500(8\%) + \$20,000(7\%)}{\$57,500} = \underline{7.65\%}$$

7. Weight each score by the number of students who obtained that score. The weighted average score is

$$\frac{2(10) + 6(9) + 9(8) + 7(7) + 3(6) + 2(5) + 1(3)}{30} = \underline{7.53}$$

9. Note that the age of receivables (rather than the dollar amount of receivables) is to be averaged. The relative importance of each of the three age classifications is determined by the dollar amount in each category. Hence, the weighting factors are the respective dollar amounts of receivables. The (weighted) average age of accounts receivable is

$$\frac{\$12,570(30) + \$6850(60) + \$1325(90)}{\$12,570 + \$6850 + \$1325} = \frac{\$907,350}{\$20,745} = \underline{43.74 \text{ days}}$$

11. a. The weighted average cost of units purchased during the year is

$$\frac{300(\$10.86) + 1000(\$10.47) + 500(\$10.97)}{1800} = \underline{\$10.67}$$

b. The weighted average cost of the beginning inventory and units purchased during the year is

$$\frac{156(\$10.55) + 1800(\$10.674)}{1956} = \underline{\$10.66}$$

c. Value of ending inventory = 239 × Weighted average cost
$$= 239(\$10.66)$$
$$= \underline{\$2547.74}$$

13. Each gross profit margin should be weighted by the fraction of revenue obtained from the respective food category. The weighted average gross profit margin is

$$\frac{0.10(67\%) + 0.50(45\%) + 0.25(50\%) + 0.15(70\%)}{0.10 + 0.50 + 0.25 + 0.15} = \underline{52.2\%}$$

Exercise 1.5 *(continued)*

15. We want the average number of people working over the course of the year. The given figures for the number of employees added or laid off at various times are used to determine the cumulative number of people employed.

Period	No. of months	Number of employees
Jan. 1 to Mar. 31	3	14
Apr. 1 to Apr. 30	1	14 + 7 = 21
May 1 to May 31	1	21 + 8 = 29
June l to Aug. 31	3	29 + 11 = 40
Sept. 1 to Sept. 30	1	40 − 6 = 34
Oct. 1 to Dec. 31	3	34 − 14 = 20

Each number in the third column must be weighted by the number of months in the second column. The average number employed was

$$\frac{3(14) + 1(21) + 1(29) + 3(40) + 1(34) + 3(20)}{12} = \underline{25.5}$$

17.

Period	No. of months	Number of shares outstanding (millions)
Jan. 1 to Feb. 28	2	5
Mar. 1 to May 31	3	5 + 1 = 6
June 1 to Oct. 31	5	6 + 0.5 = 6.5
Nov. 1 to Dec. 31	2	6.5 + 0.75 = 7.25

Each number of shares in the third column must be weighted by the number of months in the second column. The (weighted) average number of shares outstanding was

$$\frac{[2(5) + 3(6) + 5(6.5) + 2(7.25)] \times 1\,\text{million}}{12} = 6.25 \text{ million} = \underline{6,250,000}$$

Exercise 1.6

1.

Quarter	Sales − Purchases	GST Remittance (Refund)
1	$155,365	$10,875.55
2	(340,305)	(23,821.35)
3	408,648	28,605.36
4	164,818	11,537.26

3. The GST charged in each case will be
   0.07($21,900) = $1533.00
   a. With no PST in Alberta, the total price will be
      $21,900 + $1533.00 = $23,433.00
   b. PST in Ontario = 0.08($21,900) = $1752.00
      Total price = $21,900 + $1533.00 + $1752.00 = $25,185.00
   c. PST in Quebec = 0.075($21,900 + $1533) = $1757.48
      Total price = $21,900 + $1533.00 + $1757.48 = $25,190.48

Exercise 1.6 *(continued)*

5. *a.* PST (Saskatchewan) = 0.06($87,940 − $28,637) = <u>$3558.18</u>

   b. In Prince Edward Island, consumers pay PST on the post-GST price. The GST paid on the amount subject to PST was

   0.07($87,940 − $28,637) = $4151.21

   The PST that must be remitted is

   0.10($87,940 − $28,637 + $4151.21) = <u>$6345.42</u>

7. Property tax = $\dfrac{\text{Mill rate}}{1000} \times$ Assessed value = $\dfrac{16.8629}{1000} \times \$227{,}000 = \underline{\$3827.88}$

9. Total taxes = $\dfrac{15.0294}{1000} \times \$143{,}000 + \dfrac{4.6423}{1000} \times \$467{,}000$

   = $2149.204 + $2167.954

   = <u>$4317.16</u>

11. *a.* Tax increase = $\dfrac{\text{Mill rate increase}}{1000} \times$ Assessed value

   $\$2{,}430{,}000 = \dfrac{\text{Mill rate increase}}{1000} \times \$6{,}780{,}000{,}000$

   Mill rate increase = $\dfrac{\$2430}{\$6{,}780{,}000} \times 1000 = 0.3584$

   Next year's mill rate = 7.1253 + 0.3584 = <u>7.4837</u>

   b. Next year's assessment = 1.05($6.78 billion) = $7.119 billion
   Next year's budget = Current year's taxes + $2,430,000

   $= \dfrac{7.1253}{1000} \times \$6.78 \text{ billion} + \$2{,}430{,}000$

   = $50,739,500

   Next year's school mill rate applied to next year's assessment must generate enough tax revenue to meet next year's budget. That is,

   $\$50{,}739{,}500 = \dfrac{\text{New mill rate}}{1000} \times \$7.119 \text{ billion}$

   New mill rate = $\dfrac{\$50{,}739{,}500}{\$7{,}119{,}000} = \underline{7.1273}$

Review Problems

1. *a.* $\left(2^3 - 3\right)^2 - 20 \div \left(2 + 2^3\right) = (8-3)^2 - 20 \div (2+8) = 25 - 20 \div 10 = 25 - 2 = \underline{23}$

   b. $4\left(2 \times 3^2 - 2^3\right)^2 \div (10 - 4 \times 5) = 4(2 \times 9 - 8)^2 \div (10 - 20)$

   $= 4 \times 10^2 \div (-10)$

   $= \underline{-40}$

   c. $\$213.85\left(1 - 0.095 \times \dfrac{5}{12}\right) = \$213.85(1 - 0.039583) = \underline{\$205.39}$

   d. $\dfrac{\$2315}{1 + 0.0825 \times \frac{77}{365}} = \dfrac{\$2315}{1.0174041} = \underline{\$2275.40}$

Review Problems *(continued)*

1.   *e.* $\$325.75\left(1+\dfrac{0.105}{4}\right)^2 = \$325.75(1.053189) = \underline{\$343.08}$

    f. $\dfrac{\$710}{\left(1+\frac{0.0925}{2}\right)^3} = \dfrac{\$710}{1.145266} = \underline{\$619.94}$

    g. $\$885.75\left(1+0.0775\times\dfrac{231}{365}\right) - \dfrac{\$476.50}{1+0.0775\times\frac{49}{365}} = \$885.75(1.049048) - \dfrac{\$476.50}{1.010404}$

$$= \$929.194 - \$471.593$$
$$= \underline{\$457.60}$$

    h. $\$859\left(1+\dfrac{0.0825}{12}\right)^3 + \dfrac{\$682}{\left(1+\frac{0.0825}{12}\right)^{12}} = \$859(1.020767) + \dfrac{\$682}{1.013797}$

$$= \$876.839 + \$672.718$$
$$= \underline{\$1549.56}$$

3. $Base = \dfrac{Portion}{Rate} = \dfrac{100\%}{80\%}\times\$100 = \underline{\$125.00}$

5.   Two hours = 2(60) = 120 minutes

    $Rate = \dfrac{Portion}{Base} = \dfrac{15\text{ minutes}}{120\text{ minutes}}\times100\% = \underline{12.5\%}$

7.   *Portion = Rate* x *Base*
    Hence, price increase + 0.35 x \$2.20 = \$0.77
    Selling price = \$2.20 + \$0.77 = $\underline{\$2.97}$ per share

9.   *a.*   Gross biweekly earnings = $\dfrac{\$56,600}{26} = \$2176.92$

        Equivalent hourly wage = $\dfrac{\$2176.92}{2\times37.5} = \underline{\$29.03}$

    b.   Total remuneration = \$2176.92 + 4.5(1.5) \$29.03 = $\underline{\$2372.87}$

11. Commission earnings = Commission rate (Sales − \$40,000)
     \$3188.35 − \$1000 = Commission rate (\$88,630 − \$40,000)

        Commission rate = $\dfrac{\$2188.35}{\$48,630}\times100\% = \underline{4.50\%}$

Review Problems (continued)

13.

Period	No. of months	Number of employees
July1 to Aug. 31	2	7
Sept. I to Oct. 31	2	7 + 6 = 13
Nov. 1 to Nov. 30	1	13 + 18 = 31
Dec. 1 to Feb. 28	3	31 + 23 = 54
Mar. 1 to Mar. 31	1	54 – 11 = 43
Apr. 1 to Apr. 30	1	43 – 20 = 23
May 1 to June 30	2	23 – 16 = 7

The (weighted) average number of employees was

$$\frac{4(7) + 2(13) + 1(31) + 3(54) + 1(43) + 1(23)}{12} = \underline{\underline{26.1}}$$

Self-Test Exercise

1. a. $96 - (6 - 4^2) \times 7 - 2 = 96 - (-10)7 - 2 = \underline{164}$

    b. $81 \div (5^2 - 16) - 4(2^3 - 13) = 81 \div 9 - 4(-5) = \underline{29}$

    c. $\dfrac{\$827.69}{1 + 0.125 \times \frac{273}{365}} + \$531.49\left(1 + 0.125 \times \dfrac{41}{365}\right) = \dfrac{\$827.69}{1.093493} + \$531.49(1.014041)$

    $$= \$756.923 + \$538.953$$

    $$= \underline{\$1295.88}$$

    d. $\$550.45\left(1 + 0.0875 \times \dfrac{195}{365}\right) - \dfrac{\$376.29}{1 + 0.0875 \times \frac{99}{365}} = \$550.45(1.046747) - \dfrac{\$376.29}{1.023733}$

    $$= \underline{\$208.62}$$

    e. $\$1137\left(1 + \dfrac{0.0975}{12}\right)^2 + \dfrac{\$2643}{\left(1 + \frac{0.0975}{12}\right)^3} = \$1137(1.016316) + \dfrac{\$2643}{1.024574} = \underline{\$3735.16}$

2. $Base = \dfrac{Portion}{Rate} = \dfrac{100\%}{167.5\%} \times \$100 = \underline{\$59.70}$

3. 0.15(Income exceeding \$60,000) = \$5500

    (Income exceeding \$60,000) = $\dfrac{\$5500}{0.15}$ = \$36,666.67

    Total net income = \$60,000 + \$36,666.67 = \underline{\$96,666.67}

4. Gross biweekly earnings = $\dfrac{\$61,000}{26}$ = \$2346.15

    Equivalent hourly rate = $\dfrac{\$2346.15}{75}$ = \$31.28

    Gross pay = \$2346.15 + 33(1.5)\$31.28 = \underline{\$3894.51}

5. Gross earnings = \$1000 + 0.08(\$10,000) + 0.10(\$38,670 – \$30,000) = \underline{\$2667}

Self-Test Exercise (*continued*)

6. Rate of return on the portfolio = Weighted average rate of return

$$= \frac{\$16,800(-4.3\%) + \$25,600(-1.1\%) + \$31,000(8.2\%)}{\$16,800 + \$25,600 + \$31,000}$$

$$= \underline{2.10\%}$$

7.

Period	No. of months	Cumulative investment
Jan. 1 to Feb. 28	2	$96,400
Mar. 1 to Mar. 31	1	$96,400 − $14,200 = $82,200
Apr. 1 to July 31	4	$82,200 − $21,800 = $60,400
Aug. 1 to Oct. 31	3	$60,400 + $23,700 = $84,100
Nov. 1 to Dec. 31	2	$84,100 + $19,300 = $103,400

Average investment during the year

$$= \frac{2(\$96,400) + 1(\$82,200) + 4(\$60,400) + 3(\$84,100) + 2(\$103,400)}{12}$$

$$= \underline{\$81,308.33}$$

Appendix 1B

Arithmetic Questions

1. Net Price = $25 − 0.10($25) − $5 = $\underline{\$17.50}$

2. $10^3 = 10 \times 10 \times 10 = \underline{1000}$

3. $(1 + 0.5)^3 = 1.5^3 = \underline{3.375}$

4. Customer service reps : Managers = 15 : 6 = $\underline{5 : 2}$

5. $\dfrac{\text{Customer service reps}}{\text{Total staff}} \times 100\% = \dfrac{15}{15 + 6} \times 100\% = \underline{71\%}$

6. Percent change = $\dfrac{\$13.50 - \$13.75}{\$13.75} \times 100\% = \underline{-1.82\%}$

7. $0.36^{1/2} = \sqrt{0.36} = 0.36^{0.5} = \underline{0.6}$

8. Average = $\dfrac{\$425 + \$550 + \$475 + \$550 + \$400}{5} = \underline{\$480}$

9. $6 \times \dfrac{1}{10^1} + 7 \times \dfrac{1}{10^2} + 8 \times \dfrac{1}{10^4}$ = $(6 \times 0.1) + (7 \times 0.01) + (8 \times 0.0001)$

$$= 0.6 + 0.07 + 0.0008$$

$$= \underline{0.6708}$$

10. Weighted average rate = $\dfrac{\$100,000(8\%) + \$50,000(10\%)}{\$100,000 + \$50,000} = \underline{8.67\%}$

Appendix 1B (*continued*)

<u>Algebra Questions</u>

1. $12 + 2x = 8$

    $2x = 8 - 12 = -4$

    $x = \underline{-2}$

2. $\underline{y = \$8x + \$100}$

3. $\underline{P = 2l + 2w}$

4. $\underline{2(x + \$1.25) = \$5.50}$

5. $4x + 2400 = 2200(1 + 0.02x)$

    $4x + 2400 = 2200 + 44x$

    $4x - 44x = 2200 - 2400$

    $-40x = -200$

    $\underline{x = 5}$

<u>Time Value of Money Questions</u>

1. Original investment $= \dfrac{\$20,000}{1.08^5} = \underline{\$13,611.66}$

2. Future value $= \$15,000 \times 1.035^2 = \underline{\$16,068.38}$

3. Interest $= 0.065 \times \$100 = \underline{\$6.50}$

4. $(1+i)^{-n} = (1+0.12)^{-4} = 1.12^{-4} = \underline{0.636}$

5. $\$950(1.0333333)^{12} + \$50\left(\dfrac{1.0333333^{12} - 1}{0.0333333}\right)(1.0333333) = \$988.70 + \$613.16 = \underline{\$1601.86}$

6. $\dfrac{(1+i)^n - 1}{i} = \dfrac{1.09^4 - 1}{0.04} = \underline{4.573}$

7. Future amount $= \$1200\left(\dfrac{1.05^{20} - 1}{0.05}\right) = \underline{\$39,679}$

8. Amount that should be invested is the present value of the payments.

    Present value $= \$100\left(\dfrac{1 - 1.005^{-24}}{0.005}\right) = \underline{\$2256.29}$

    Therefore, you must invest $2256.29.

9. Interest = Principal $\times$ Interest rate $\times$ Time period

    $\$400 = \$4400 \times 0.0275 \times$ Time period

    Time period $= \dfrac{\$400}{\$4400 \times 0.0275} = \underline{3.31\ years}$

2   Review and Applications of Algebra

Exercise 2.1

1. $(-p) + (-3p) + 4p = -p - 3p + 4p = \underline{0}$

3. $4x^2y + (-3x^2y) - (-5x^2y) = 4x^2y - 3x^2y + 5x^2y = \underline{6x^2y}$

5. $(6x^2 - 3xy + 4y^2) - (8y^2 - 10xy - x^2) = 6x^2 - 3xy + 4y^2 - 8y^2 + 10xy + x^2$
$$= \underline{7x^2 + 7xy - 4y^2}$$

7. $2(7x - 3y) - 3(2x - 3y) = 14x - 6y - 6x + 9y = \underline{8x + 3y}$

9. $15x - [4 - 2(5x - 6)] = 15x - 4 + 10x - 12 = \underline{25x - 16}$

11. $\dfrac{2x + 9}{4} - 1.2(x - 1) = 0.5x + 2.25 - 1.2x + 1.2 = -\underline{0.7x + 3.45}$

13. $\dfrac{8x}{0.5} + \dfrac{5.5x}{11} + 0.5(4.6x - 17) = 16x + 0.5x + 2.3x - 8.5 = \underline{18.8x - 8.5}$

15. $\dfrac{P}{1 + 0.095 \times \frac{5}{12}} + 2P\left(1 + 0.095 \times \dfrac{171}{365}\right) = 0.96192P + 2.08901P = \underline{3.0509P}$

17. $k(1 + 0.04)^2 + \dfrac{2k}{(1 + 0.04)^2} = 1.08160k + 1.84911k = \underline{2.9307k}$

19. $4a(3ab - 5a + 6b) = \underline{12a^2b - 20a^2 + 24ab}$

21. $-5xy(2x^2 - xy - 3y^2) = \underline{-10x^3y + 5x^2y^2 + 15xy^3}$

23. $(4r - 3t)(2t + 5r) = 8rt + 20r^2 - 6t^2 - 15rt = \underline{20r^2 - 7rt - 6t^2}$

25. $3(a - 2)(4a + 1) - 5(2a + 3)(a - 7) = 3(4a^2 + a - 8a - 2) - 5(2a^2 - 14a + 3a - 21)$
$$= 12a^2 - 21a - 6 - 10a^2 + 55a + 105$$
$$= \underline{2a^2 + 34a + 99}$$

27. $\dfrac{18x^2}{3x} = \underline{6x}$

29. $\dfrac{x^2y - xy^2}{xy} = \underline{x - y}$

31. $\dfrac{12x^3 - 24x^2 + 36x}{48x} = \dfrac{\underline{x^2 - 2x + 3}}{4}$

33. $\dfrac{4a^2b^3 - 6a^3b^2}{2ab^2} = \underline{2ab - 3a^2}$

35. $3d^2 - 4d + 15 = 3(2.5)^2 - 4(2.5) + 15$
$$= 18.75 - 10 + 15$$
$$= \underline{23.75}$$

37. $7x(4y - 8) = 7(3.2)(4 \times 1.5 - 8) = 22.4(6 - 8) = \underline{-44.8}$

Exercise 2.1 *(continued)*

39. $\dfrac{I}{rt} = \dfrac{\$23.21}{0.095 \times \frac{283}{365}} = \dfrac{\$23.21}{0.073658} = \underline{\$315.11}$

41. $L(1 - d_1)(1 - d_2)(1 - d_3) = \$490(1 - 0.125)(1 - 0.15)(1 - 0.05) = \underline{\$346.22}$

43. $\dfrac{S}{1 + rt} = \dfrac{\$2500}{1 + 0.085 \times \frac{123}{365}} = \dfrac{\$2500}{1.028644} = \underline{\$2430.38}$

45. $P(1 + i)^n = \$1280(1 + 0.025)^3 = \underline{\$1378.42}$

47. $R\left[\dfrac{(1 + i)^n - 1}{i}\right] = \$550\left(\dfrac{1.085^3 - 1}{0.085}\right) = \$550\left(\dfrac{0.2772891}{0.085}\right) = \underline{\$1794.22}$

49. $\dfrac{R}{i}\left[1 - \dfrac{1}{(1 + i)^n}\right] = \dfrac{\$630}{0.115}\left(1 - \dfrac{1}{1.115^2}\right) = \underline{\$1071.77}$

Exercise 2.2

1. $a^2 \times a^3 = \underline{a^5}$

3. $b^{10} \div b^6 = b^{10-6} = \underline{b^4}$

5. $(1 + i)^4 \times (1 + i)^9 = \underline{(1 + i)^{13}}$

7. $(x^4)^7 = x^{4 \times 7} = \underline{\underline{x^{28}}}$

9. $\left(t^6\right)^{\frac{1}{3}} = \underline{t^2}$

11. $\dfrac{\left(x^5\right)\left(x^6\right)}{x^9} = x^{5+6-9} = \underline{\underline{x^2}}$

13. $\left[2(1 + i)\right]^2 = \underline{4(1 + i)^2}$

15. $\dfrac{4r^5 t^6}{\left(2r^2 t\right)^3} = \dfrac{4r^5 t^6}{8r^6 t^3} = \dfrac{r^{5-6} t^{6-3}}{2} = \underline{\underline{\dfrac{t^3}{2r}}}$

17. $\left(\dfrac{3a^3 b^2}{a - b}\right)^4 = \underline{\dfrac{81a^{12} b^8}{(a - b)^4}}$

19. $\dfrac{(-2y)^3 \left(x^4\right)^{-2}}{\left(x^{-2}\right)^2 (4y)^2} = \dfrac{-8y^3 \left(x^{-8}\right)}{x^{-4} \left(16y^2\right)} = -\dfrac{yx^{-8-(-4)}}{2} = \underline{-\dfrac{y}{2x^4}}$

21. $8^{\frac{4}{3}} = \left(8^{\frac{1}{3}}\right)^4 = 2^4 = \underline{\underline{16}}$

23. $7^{\frac{3}{2}} = 7^{1.5} = \underline{18.5203}$

25. $(0.001)^{-2} = \underline{1,000,000}$

Exercise 2.2 *(continued)*

27. $(1.0085)^5 (1.0085)^3 = 1.0085^8 = \underline{1.07006}$

29. $\sqrt[3]{1.03} = 1.03^{0.\overline{3}} = \underline{1.00990}$

31. $\left(4^4\right)\left(3^{-3}\right)\left(-\dfrac{3}{4}\right)^3 = \dfrac{4^4}{3^3}\left(-\dfrac{3^3}{4^3}\right) = \underline{\underline{-4}}$

33. $\left(\dfrac{2}{3}\right)^3 \left(-\dfrac{3}{2}\right)^2 \left(-\dfrac{3}{2}\right)^{-3} = \left(\dfrac{2}{3}\right)^3 \left(\dfrac{3}{2}\right)^2 \left(-\dfrac{2}{3}\right)^3 = \dfrac{2}{3}\left(-\dfrac{2}{3}\right)^3 = -\dfrac{16}{81} = \underline{\underline{-0.197531}}$

35. $\dfrac{1.03^{16} - 1}{0.03} = \underline{\underline{20.1569}}$

37. $\dfrac{1 - 1.0225^{-20}}{0.0225} = \dfrac{0.3591835}{0.0225} = \underline{\underline{15.9637}}$

39. $(1 + 0.0275)^{1/3} = \underline{1.00908}$

Exercise 2.3

1. $10a + 10 = 12 + 9a$
    $10a - 9a = 12 - 10$
    $\qquad a = \underline{2}$

3. $0.5\,(x - 3) = 20$
    $\qquad x - 3 = 40$
    $\qquad\quad x = \underline{43}$

5. $\qquad\quad y = 192 + 0.04y$
    $y - 0.04y = 192$
    $\qquad\quad y = \dfrac{192}{0.96} = \underline{\underline{200}}$

7. $12x - 4(2x - 1) = 6(x + 1) - 3$
    $12x - 8x + 4 = 6x + 6 - 3$
    $\qquad\quad -2x = -1$
    $\qquad\quad\ \ x = \underline{0.5}$

9. $8 - 0.5(x + 3) = 0.25(x - 1)$
    $8 - 0.5x - 1.5 = 0.25x - 0.25$
    $\qquad\quad -0.75x = -6.75$
    $\qquad\qquad\ \ x = \underline{9}$

11. $3.1t + 145 = 10 + 7.6t$
    $\qquad -4.5t = -135$
    $\qquad\quad\ \ t = \underline{30}$

13. $\dfrac{x}{1.1^2} + 2x(1.1)^3 = \$1000$
    $0.8264463x + 2.622x = \$1000$
    $\qquad\quad 3.488446x = \$1000$
    $\qquad\qquad\qquad x = \underline{\$286.66}$

15. $$\frac{2x}{1.03^7} + x + x\left(1.03^{10}\right) = \$1000 + \frac{\$2000}{1.03^4}$$

$$1.626183x + x + 1.343916x = \$1000 + \$1776.974$$
$$3.970099x = \$2776.974$$
$$x = \underline{\$699.47}$$

17. $$x\left(1 + 0.095 \times \frac{84}{365}\right) + \frac{2x}{1 + 0.095 \times \frac{108}{365}} = \$1160.20$$

$$1.021863x + 1.945318x = \$1160.20$$
$$2.967181x = \$1160.20$$
$$x = \underline{\$391.01}$$

19.
$$x - y = 2 \qquad ①$$
$$3x + 4y = 20 \qquad ②$$

$① \times 3$: $\underline{3x - 3y = 6}$
Subtract: $ 7y = 14$
$ y = 2$

Substitute into equation ①:
$$x - 2 = 2$$
$$x = 4$$
$$(x, y) = \underline{(4, 2)}$$

Check: LHS of ② = 3(4) + 4(2) = 20 = RHS of ②

21.
$$4a - 3b = {-3} \qquad ①$$
$$5a - b = 10 \qquad ②$$

$① \times 1$: $4a - 3b = {-3}$
$② \times 3$: $\underline{15a - 3b = 30}$
Subtract: $-11a = -33$
$ a = 3$

Substitute into equation ②:
$$5(3) - b = 10$$
$$b = 5$$
$$(a, b) = \underline{(3, 5)}$$

Check: LHS of ① = 4(3) − 3(5) = −3 = RHS of ①

23.
$$y = 2x \qquad\qquad ①$$
$$\underline{7x - y = 35} \qquad ②$$
Add: $7x = 2x + 35$
$ 5x = 35$
$ x = 7$

Substitute into ①:
$$y = 2(7) = 14$$
$$(x, y) = \underline{(7, 14)}$$

Check: LHS of ② = 7(7) − 14 = 49 − 14 = 35 = RHS of ②

Exercise 2.3 *(continued)*

25.
$$d = 3c - 500 \qquad ①$$
$$0.7c + 0.2d = 550 \qquad ②$$

To eliminate d,

$$① \times 0.2: \qquad -0.6c + 0.2d = -100$$
$$②: \qquad \underline{0.7c + 0.2d = \;\; 550}$$
Subtract: $\qquad -1.3c + 0 \; = -650$
$$c = \;\; 500$$

Substitute into ①: $\qquad d = 3(500) - 500 = 1000$
$$(c, d) = \underline{(500,\ 1000)}$$

Check: $\qquad$ LHS of ② = 0.7(500) + 0.2(1000) = 550 = RHS of ②

27.
$$2v + 6w = 1 \qquad ①$$
$$10v - 9w = 18 \qquad ②$$

To eliminate v,

$$① \times 10: \qquad 20v + 60w = \;\; 10$$
$$② \times \underline{2:} \qquad \underline{20v - 18w = \;\; 36}$$
Subtract: $\qquad 0 + 78w = -26$
$$w = -\tfrac{1}{3}$$

Substitute into ①:
$$2v + 6\left(-\tfrac{1}{3}\right) = 1$$
$$2v = 1 + 2$$
$$v = \tfrac{3}{2}$$
$$(v, w) = \left(\tfrac{3}{2}, -\tfrac{1}{3}\right)$$

Check: $\qquad$ LHS of ② = $10\left(\tfrac{3}{2}\right) - 9\left(-\tfrac{1}{3}\right)$ = 18 = RHS of ②

29.
$$37x - 63y = 235 \qquad ①$$
$$18x + 26y = 468 \qquad ②$$

To eliminate x,

$$① \times 18: \qquad 666x - 1134y = \;\; 4230$$
$$② \times 37: \qquad \underline{666x + \;\; 962y = \;\; 17{,}316}$$
Subtract: $\qquad 0 - 2096y = -13{,}086$
$$y = 6.243$$

Substitute into ①:
$$37x - 63(6.243) = 235$$
$$37x = 628.3$$
$$x = 16.98$$
$$(x, y) = \underline{(17.0,\ 6.24)}$$

Check: $\qquad$ LHS of ② = 18(16.98) + 26(6.243) = 468.0 = RHS of ②

Exercise 2.3 *(continued)*

31.
$$0.33e + 1.67f = 292 \quad ①$$
$$1.2\,e + 0.61f = 377 \quad ②$$

To eliminate e,

① ÷ 0.33:	$e + 5.061f = 884.8$
② ÷ 1.2:	$e + 0.508f = 314.2$
Subtract:	$0 + 4.552f = 570.6$
	$f = 125.4$

Substitute into ①:

$$0.33e + 1.67(125.4) = 292$$
$$0.33e = 82.58$$
$$e = 250.2$$
$$(e, f) = \underline{(250, 125)}$$

Check: LHS of ② = $1.2(250.2) + 0.61(125.4) = 376.7$ = RHS of ②

Exercise 2.4

1. Step 2: Hits last month = 2655 after the $\frac{2}{7}$ increase.

   Let the number of hits 1 year ago be n.

   Step 3: Hits last month = Hits 1 year ago + $\frac{2}{7}$(Hits 1 year ago)

   Step 4: $2655 = n + \frac{2}{7}n$

   Step 5: $2655 = \frac{9}{7}n$

   Multiply both sides by $\frac{7}{9}$.

   $n = 2655 \times \frac{7}{9} = 2065$

   The Web site had <u>2065 hits</u> in the same month 1 year ago.

3. Step 2: Tag price = $39.95 (including 7% GST). Let the plant's pretax price be P.
   Step 3: Tag price = Pretax price + GST

   Step 4: $39.95 = P + 0.07P

   Step 5: $39.95 = 1.07P

   $P = \dfrac{\$39.95}{1.07} = \$37.34$

   The amount of GST is $39.95 − $37.34 = <u>$2.61</u>

5. Step 2: Let the basic price be P. First 20 meals at P.
      Next 20 meals at P − $2. Additional meals at P − $3.

   Step 3: Total price for 73 meals = $810

   Step 4: $20P + 20(P − \$2) + (73 − 40)(P − 3) = \$810$

   Step 5: $20P + 20P − \$40 + 33P − \$99 = \$810$
      $73P = \$810 + \$99 + \$40$

   $P = \dfrac{\$949}{73} = \underline{\$13.00}$

   The basic price per meal is $13.00.

7. Step 2: Tax rate = 38%; Overtime hourly rate = 1.5($23.50) = $35.25
Cost of canoe = $2750
Let h represent the hours of overtime Alicia must work.

Step 3: Gross overtime earnings − Income tax = Cost of the canoe

Step 4: $35.25h − 0.38($35.25h) = $2750

Step 5: $21.855h = $2750
$$h = 125.83 \text{ hours}$$

Alicia must work 125¾ hours of overtime to earn enough money to buy the canoe.

9. Step 2: Cost of radio advertising = 0.5(Cost of newspaper advertising)
Cost of TV advertising = 0.6(Cost of radio advertising)
Total advertising budget = $160,000
Let r represent the amount allocated to radio advertising

Step 3: Radio advertising + TV advertising + Newspaper advertising = $160,000

Step 4: $r + 0.6r + \dfrac{r}{0.5} = \$160,000$

Step 5: $3.6r = \$160,000$
$$r = \$44,444.44$$

The advertising budget allocations should be:
$44,444 to radio advertising,
0.6($44,444.44) = $26,667 to TV advertising, and
2($44,444.44) = $88,889 to newspaper advertising.

11. Step 2: Overall portfolio's rate return = 1.1%, equity fund's rate of return = −3.3%,
bond fund's rate of return = 7.7%.
Let e represent the fraction of the portfolio initially invested in the equity fund.

Step 3: Overall rate of return = Weighted average rate of return
= (Equity fraction)(Equity return) + (Bond fraction)(Bond return)

Step 4: $1.1\% = e(-3.3\%) + (1 - e)(7.7\%)$

Step 5: $1.1 = -3.3e + 7.7 - 7.7e$
$-6.6 = -11.0e$
$$e = 0.600$$

Therefore, 60.0% of Erin's original portfolio was invested in the equity fund.

13. Step 2: Total options = 100,000
\# of options to an executive = 2000 + \# of options to a scientist or engineer
\# of options to a scientist or engineer = 1.5(\# of options to a technician)
There are 3 executives, 8 scientists and engineers, and 14 technicians.
Let t represent the number of options to each technician.

Step 3: Total options = Total options to scientists and engineers
+ Total options to technicians + Total options to executives

Step 4: $100{,}000 = 8(1.5t) + 14t + 3(2000 + 1.5t)$

Step 5: $= 12t + 14t + 6000 + 4.5t$
$94{,}000 = 30.5t$
$$t = 3082 \text{ options}$$

Each technician will receive 3082 options,
each scientist and engineer will receive 1.5(3082) = 4623 options,
and each executive will receive 2000 + 4623 = 6623 options.

15. Step 2: Raisins cost $3.75 per kg; peanuts cost $2.89 per kg.
     Cost per kg of ingredients in 50 kg of "trail mix" is to be $3.20.
     Let p represent the weight of peanuts in the mixture.

   Step 3: Cost of 50 kg of trail mix = Cost of p kg peanuts + Cost of $(50 - p)$ kg of raisins

   Step 4: $50(\$3.20) = p(\$2.89) + (50 - p)(\$3.75)$

   Step 5: $\$160.00 = \$2.89p + \$187.50 - \$3.75p$
     $-\$27.50 = -\$0.86p$
     $p = 31.98$ kg
   <u>32.0 kg of peanuts</u> should be mixed with <u>18.0 kg of raisins</u>.

17. Step 2: Total investment = $32,760
     Sue's investment = 1.2(Joan's investment)
     Joan's investment = 1.2(Stella's investment)
     Let L represent Stella's investment.

   Step 3: Sue's investment + Joan's investment + Stella's investment = Total investment

   Step 4: Joan's investment = 1.2L
     Sue's investment = 1.2L(1.2L) = 1.44L
     1.44L + 1.2L + L = $32,760

   Step 5: $3.64L = \$32,760$
     $L = \dfrac{\$32,760}{3.64} = \$9000$

     Stella will contribute <u>$9000</u>, Joan will contribute 1.2($9000) = <u>$10,800</u>, and
     Sue will contribute 1.2($10,800) = <u>$12,960</u>

19. Step 2: Time to make X is 20 minutes.
     Time to make Y is 30 minutes.
     Total time is 47 hours. Total units = 120. Let Y represent the number of units of Y.

   Step 3: Total time = (Number of X) × (Time for X) + (Number of Y) × (Time for Y)

   Step 4: $47 \times 60 = (120 - Y)20 + Y(30)$

   Step 5: $2820 = 2400 - 20Y + 30Y$
     $420 = 10Y$
     $Y = \underline{42}$
   Forty-two units of product Y were manufactured.

21. Step 2: $\frac{3}{5}$ of a $\frac{3}{7}$ interest was sold for $27,000.

     Let the V represent the implied value of the entire partnership.

   Step 3: $\frac{3}{5}$ of a $\frac{3}{7}$ interest is worth $27,000.

   Step 4: $\dfrac{3}{5} \times \dfrac{3}{7} V = \$27,000$

   Step 5: $V = \dfrac{5 \times 7}{3 \times 3} \times \$27,000 = \underline{\$105,000}$

   b. The implied value of the entire partnership is $105,000.
   a. The implied value of Shirley's remaining interest is
     $$\dfrac{2}{5} \times \dfrac{3}{7} V = \dfrac{6}{35} \times \$105,000 = \underline{\$18,000}$$

23.   Step 2: $\frac{5}{7}$ of entrants complete Level 1. $\frac{2}{9}$ of Level 1 completers fail Level 2.

   587 students completed Level 2 last year.
   Let the N represent the original number who began Level 1.

   Step 3: $\frac{7}{9}$ of $\frac{5}{7}$ of entrants will complete Level 2.

   Step 4: $\frac{7}{9} \times \frac{5}{7}$N = 587

   Step 5: N = $\frac{9 \times 7}{7 \times 5}$ x 587 = 1056.6

   <u>1057</u> students began Level 1.

25.   Let r represent the number of regular members and s the number of student members.
   Then r + s = 583   ①
   Total revenue: $\$1070r + \$428s = \$471,014$ ②
   ① × \$428: $\underline{\$428r + \$428s = \$249,524}$
   Subtract: $\$642r +$ 0 $= \$221,490$
                                                                $r = 345$
   Substitute into ①: $345 + s = 583$
                                                                $s = 238$
   The club had <u>238 student members</u> and <u>345 regular members</u>.

27.   Let s represent the distance travelled at the lower speed (50 km/h).
   Let h represent the distance travelled at the higher speed (100 km/h).
   Since the total distance = 1000 km,
   then s + h = 1000   ①

   Since travelling time = $\dfrac{\text{Distance}}{\text{Speed}}$,

   then   Time at slower speed = $\dfrac{s}{50}$ and   Time at higher speed = $\dfrac{h}{100}$

   Since the total time = 12.3 hours,

   then $\dfrac{s}{50}$ + $\dfrac{h}{100}$ = 12.3   ②

   ② × 100: $2s$ + h = 1230
   Repeat ①: $\underline{s\quad +\quad h\ =\ 1000}$ ①
   Subtract: s +   0   =   230
   Hence, Tina drive <u>230 km at 50 km/h</u> and 1000 – 230 = <u>770 km at 100 km/h</u>.

29.   Let h represent the rate per hour and k represent the rate per km.
   Robert's cost: $2h + 47k = \$39.81$ ①
   Bryn's cost: $5h + 93k = \$93.89$ ②

   To eliminate x,
      ① × 5: $10h + 235k = \$199.05$ ①
      ② × 2: $\underline{10h + 186k = \$187.78}$ ②
   Subtract: $0 + 49k = \$\ 11.27$
                                  $k = \$0.23$ per km

   Substitute into ①:
            $2h + 47(\$0.23) = \$39.81$
                          $2h = \$39.81 - \$10.81$
                            $h = \$14.50$ per hour
   Budget Truck Rentals charged <u>\$14.50 per hour</u> plus <u>\$0.23 per km</u>.

Exercise 2.4 *(continued)*

31. Let C represent the interest rate on Canada Savings Bonds.
    Let O represent the interest rate on Ontario Savings Bonds.

Year 1 interest:	$4(\$1000)C + 6(\$1000)O = \$438$	①
Year 2 interest:	$3(\$1000)C + 4(\$1000)O = \$306$	②
① × 3:	$\$12{,}000C + \$18{,}000O = \$1314$	①
② × 4:	$\$12{,}000C + \$16{,}000O = \$1224$	②
Subtract:	$0 \quad + \quad \$2000O = \$\ \ 90$	

    $$O = \frac{\$90}{\$2000} = 0.045 = 4.5\%$$

    Substitute into ②: $\$3000C + \$4000(0.045) = \ \$306$

    $$C = \frac{\$306 - \$180}{\$3000} = 0.042 = 4.2\%$$

    The <u>Canada Savings Bonds earn 4.2% per annum</u> and
    the <u>Ontario Savings Bonds earn 4.5% per annum</u>.

33. Let x represent the number of units of product X and
    y represent the number of units of product Y. Then

	$x + \quad y = 93$	①
	$0.5x + 0.75y = 60.5$	②
① × 0.5:	$0.5x + \ \ 0.5y = \underline{46.5}$	
Subtract:	$0 + 0.25y = 14$	
	$y = 56$	
Substitute into ①:	$x + 56 = 93$	
	$x = 37$	

    Therefore, <u>37 units of X</u> and <u>56 units of Y</u> were produced last week.

35. Let M be the number of litres of milk and J be the number of cans of orange juice per
    week.

$\$1.10M + \$0.98J = \$42.20$	①
$\$1.15M + \$1.14J = \$45.85$	②

    To eliminate M,

① × 1.15:	$\$1.265M + \$1.127J = \$48.53$	
② × 1.1:	$\$1.265M + \$1.254J = \underline{\$50.435}$	
Subtract:	$0 \ - \ 0.127J = -\$1.905$	
	$J = 15$	

    Substitution of J = 15 into either equation will give M = 25. Hence <u>25 litres of milk</u>
    and <u>15 cans of orange</u> juice are purchased each week.

37. Let S represent the number of people who bought single tickets and T represent
    the number of people who bought at three-for-$5. Then

	$S + \ \ 3T = 3884$	①
	$\$2S + \$5T = \$6925$	②

    To eliminate S,

① × $2:	$\$2S + \$6T = \$7768$	
②:	$\$2S + \$5T = \underline{\$6925}$	
Subtract:	$0 + \$1T = \ \ \$843$	
	$T = 843$	

    Hence, <u>843</u> people bought tickets at the three-for-$5 discount.

Exercise 2.4 *(continued)*

39. Let P represent the annual salary of a partner and T represent the annual salary of a technician. Then

$$7P + \quad 12T = \$1,086,000 \quad ①$$
$$1.05(7P) + 1.08(12T) = \$1,156,500 \quad ②$$

$① \times 1.05$:
$$\underline{1.05(7P) + 1.05(12T) = \$1,140,300}$$

Subtract:
$$0 \quad + 0.03(12T) = \$16,200$$
$$T = \$45,000$$

Substitute into ①:
$$7P + 12(\$45,000) = \$1,086,000$$
$$P = \$78,000$$

The current annual salary of a partner is $\underline{\$78,000}$ and of a technician is $\underline{\$45,000}$.

41. Step 2: Each of 4 children receive 0.5(Wife's share).

Each of 13 grandchildren receive $0.\overline{3}$ (Child's share).
Total distribution = $759,000. Let w represent the wife's share.

Step 3: Total amount = Wife's share + 4(Child's share) + 13(Grandchild's share)

Step 4: $\$759,000 = w + 4(0.5w) + 13\left(0.\overline{3}\right)(0.5w)$

Step 5: $\$759,000 = w + 2w + 2.1\overline{6}w$

$$= 5.1\overline{6}w$$
$$w = \$146,903.23$$

Each child will receive $0.5(\$146,903.23) = \underline{\$73,451.62}$
and each grandchild will receive $0.\overline{3}(\$73,451.62) = \underline{\$24,483.87}$.

43. Step 2: Hillside charge = 2(Barnett charge) − $1000
Westside charge = Hillside charge + $2000
Total charges = $27,600. Let B represent the Barnett charge.

Step 3: Total charges = Barnett charge + Hillside charge + Westside charge

Step 4: $\$27,600 = B + 2B - \$1000 + 2B - \$1000 + \$2000$

Step 5: $\$27,600 = 5B$
$$B = \$5520$$
Hence, the Westside charge is $2(\$5520) - \$1000 + \$2000 = \underline{\$12,040}$

45. Step 2: Assembly time = 0.5(Cutting time) + 2 minutes
Painting time = 0.5(Assembly time) + 0.5 minutes
Total units = 72. Total time = 42 hours. Let C represent the cutting time.

Step 3: Time to produce one toy = Cutting time + Assembly time + Painting time

Step 4: $\dfrac{42 \times 60}{72} = C + 0.5C + 2 + 0.5(0.5C + 2) + 0.5$

Step 5: $35 = 1.75C + 3.5$
$$C = 18 \text{ minutes}$$
$\underline{\text{Cutting requires 18 minutes}}$ (per unit), $\underline{\text{assembly requires}}$ $0.5(18)+2 = \underline{11 \text{ minutes}}$, and $\underline{\text{painting requires}}$ $0.5(11) + 0.5 = \underline{6 \text{ minutes}}$.

Exercise 2.5

1. $c = \dfrac{V_f - V_i}{V_i} \times 100\% = \dfrac{\$100 - \$95}{\$95} \times 100\% = \underline{\underline{5.26\%}}$

3. $c = \dfrac{V_f - V_i}{V_i} \times 100\% = \dfrac{135kg - 35kg}{35kg} \times 100\% = \underline{\underline{285.71\%}}$

5. $c = \dfrac{V_f - V_i}{V_i} \times 100\% = \dfrac{0.13 - 0.11}{0.11} \times 100\% = \underline{\underline{18.18\%}}$

7. $V_f = V_i(1+c)_f = \$134.39[1+(-0.12)] = \$134.39(0.88) = \underline{\underline{\$118.26}}$

9. $V_f = V_i(1+c)_f = (26.3\text{ cm})(1+3.00) = \underline{105.2\text{ cm}}$

11. $V_i = \dfrac{V_f}{1+c} = \dfrac{\$75}{1+2.00} = \underline{\underline{\$25.00}}$

13. Given: $V_i = \$90$, $V_f = \$100$

$c = \dfrac{\$100 - \$90}{\$90} \times 100\% = \underline{\underline{11.11\%}}$

$100 is 11.11% more than $90.

15. Given: $c = 25\%$, $V_f = \$100$

$V_i = \dfrac{V_f}{1+c} = \dfrac{\$100}{1+0.25} = \underline{\underline{\$80.00}}$

$80.00 increased by 25% equals $100.00.

17. Given: $V_f = \$75$, $c = 75\%$

$V_i = \dfrac{V_f}{1+c} = \dfrac{\$75}{1+0.75} = \underline{\underline{\$42.86}}$

$75 is 75% more than $42.86.

19. Given: $V_i = \$759.00$, $V_f = \$754.30$

$c = \dfrac{V_f - V_i}{V_i} \times 100\% = \dfrac{\$754.30 - \$759.00}{\$759.00} \times 100\% = \underline{\underline{-0.62\%}}$

$754.30 is 0.62% less than $759.00.

21. Given: $V_i = \$75$, $c = 75\%$

$V_f = V_i(1 + c) = \$75(1 + 0.75) = \underline{\$131.25}$

$75.00 becomes $131.25 after an increase of 75%.

23. Given: $V_f = \$100$, $c = -20\%$

$V_i = \dfrac{V_f}{1+c} = \dfrac{\$100}{1+(-0.20)} = \underline{\underline{\$125.00}}$

$125 after a reduction of 20% equals $100.

25. Given: $V_f = \$549$, $c = -16.\overline{6}\%$

$V_i = \dfrac{V_f}{1+c} = \dfrac{\$549}{1+(-0.1\overline{6})} = \underline{\underline{\$658.80}}$

$658.80 after a reduction of 16.$\overline{6}$% equals $549.

Exercise 2.5 (continued)

27. Given: $V_i = \$102$, $c = -2\%$

$V_f = V_i(1 + c) = \$102(1 - 0.02) = \underline{\$99.96}$

$\$102$ after a decrease of 2% is $99.96.

29. Given: $V_i = \$250$, $V_f = \$750$

$c = \dfrac{V_f - V_i}{V_i} \times 100\% = \dfrac{\$750 - \$250}{\$250} \times 100\% = \underline{200.00\%}$

$\$750$ is 200.00% more than $250.

31. Given: $c = 0.75\%$, $V_i = \$10,000$

$V_f = V_i(1 + c) = \$10,000(1 + 0.0075) = \underline{\$10,075.00}$

$\$10,000$ after an increase of $\frac{3}{4}\%$ is $10,075.00.

33. Given: $c = 150\%$, $V_f = \$575$

$V_i = \dfrac{V_f}{1 + c} = \dfrac{\$575}{1 + 1.5} = \underline{\$230.00}$

$\$230.00$ when increased by 150% equals $575.

35. Given: $V_i = \$150$, $c = 150\%$

$V_f = V_i(1 + c) = \$150(1 + 1.5) = \underline{\$375.00}$

$\$150$ after an increase of 150% is $375.00.

37. Given: $V_f = \$148.35$, $c = 15\%$

$V_i = \dfrac{V_f}{1 + c} = \dfrac{\$148.35}{1.15} = \underline{\$129.00}$

The coat's sticker price was $129.00.

39. a. . Given: $V_i = 32,400$, $V_f = 27,450$

$c = \dfrac{V_f - V_i}{V_i} \times 100\% = \dfrac{27,450 - 32,400}{32,400} \times 100\% = \underline{-15.28\%}$

The number of hammers sold declined by 15.28%.

   b. Given: $V_i = \$15.10$, $V_f = \$15.50$

$c = \dfrac{V_f - V_i}{V_i} \times 100\% = \dfrac{\$15.50 - \$15.10}{\$15.10} \times 100\% = \underline{2.65\%}$

The average selling price increased by 2.65%.

   c. Year 1 revenue = $32,400(\$15.10) = \$489,240$
   Year 2 revenue = $27,450(\$15.50) = \$425,475$

$c = \dfrac{V_f - V_i}{V_i} \times 100\% = \dfrac{\$425,475 - \$489,240}{\$489,240} \times 100\% = \underline{-13.03\%}$

The revenue decreased by 13.03%.

41. Pick an arbitrary price, say $1.00, for a bar of the soap.

 The former unit price was $V_i = \dfrac{\$1.00}{100 \text{ g}} = \$0.01$ per gram.

 The new unit price is $V_f = \dfrac{\$1.00}{90 \text{ g}} = \$0.011111$ per gram.

 The percent increase in unit price is
$$c = \frac{V_f - V_i}{V_i} \times 100\% = \frac{\$0.011111 - \$0.01}{\$0.01} \times 100\% = \underline{11.11\%}$$

43. Initial unit price $= \dfrac{\$7.98}{3.6 \text{ kg}} = \$2.2167$ per kg

 Final unit price $= \dfrac{\$6.98}{3 \text{ kg}} = \$2.3267$ per kg

 The percent increase in unit price is
$$c = \frac{V_f - V_i}{V_i} \times 100\% = \frac{\$2.3267 - \$2.2167}{\$2.2167} \times 100\% = \underline{4.96\%}$$

45. Current unit price $= \dfrac{449 \text{ cents}}{500 \text{ ml}} = 0.8980$ cents per ml

 New unit price = 1.10(0.8980 cents per ml) = 0.9878 cents per ml
 Price of a 425-ml container = (425 ml) × (0.9878 cents per ml) = 419.8 cents = $\underline{\$4.20}$

47. Given: $V_f = 599$, $c = 6\%$
$$V_i = \frac{V_f}{1+c} = \frac{599}{1.06} = \underline{565}$$
 565 units were sold in the previous quarter.

49. Given: For 2000, $V_f - V_i = -\$1.00$, $V_f = \$4.00$
 For 2001, $V_f - V_i = -\$1.00$, $V_i = \$4.00$
$$c(2000) = \frac{V_f - V_i}{V_i} \times 100\% = \frac{-\$1.00}{\$5.00} \times 100\% = \underline{\underline{-20.00\%}}$$
$$c(2001) = \frac{V_f - V_i}{V_i} \times 100\% = \frac{-\$1.00}{\$4.00} \times 100\% = \underline{\underline{-25.00\%}}$$
 The share price fell by 20.00% in 2000 and 25.00% in 2001.

51. Given: $V_f = \$4.360$ million, $c = 18\%$
$$V_i = \frac{V_f}{1+c} = \frac{\$4.360 \text{ million}}{1 + 0.18} = \underline{\underline{\$3.695 \text{ million}}}$$
 The dollar amount of the revenue increase is
$$V_f - V_i = (\$4.360 - \$3.695) \text{ million} = \underline{\$665,000}$$
 [Since the given revenue is rounded at the $0.001 million (nearest $1000),
 we also round the calculated result to this precision.]

53. Given: $V_i = 10.5\%$. $V_f = 9.75\%$

$$c = \frac{V_f - V_i}{V_i} \times 100\% = \frac{9.75 - 10.5}{10.5} \times 100\% = \underline{\underline{7.14\%}}$$

The amount of interest is reduced by 7.14%.

55. Given: $V_f = \$0.45$, $c = 76\%$

$$V_i = \frac{V_f}{1 + c} = \frac{\$0.45}{1 + (-0.76)} = \$1.88$$

Price decline $= V_i - V_f = \$1.88 - \$0.45 = \underline{\$1.43}$

The share price dropped by \$1.43.

57. Given: For the appreciation, V_i = Purchase price, $c = 140\%$, V_f = List price

For the price reduction, V_i = List price, $c = -10\%$, $V_f = \$172,800$

$$\text{List price} = \frac{V_f}{1 + c} = \frac{\$172,800}{1 + (-0.1)} = \$192,000$$

$$\text{Original purchase price} = \frac{V_f}{1 + c} = \frac{\$192,000}{1 + 1.4} = \underline{\underline{\$80,000}}$$

The owner originally paid \$80,000 for the property.

59. If General Paint's prices are marked down by 30%, then

General Paint's prices $= 0.70$(Cloverdale Paint's prices)

Hence, Cloverdale's prices $= \dfrac{\text{General Paint's prices}}{0.70} = 1.4286$(General Paint's prices)

Therefore, you will pay <u>42.86% more</u> at Cloverdale Paint.

61. Canada's exports to US exceeded imports from the US by 23%.

That is,   Exports $= 1.23$(Imports)

Therefore,   Imports $= \dfrac{\text{Exports}}{1.23} = 0.8130$(Exports)

That is, Canada's imports from US (= US exports to Canada) were

$$1 - 0.8130 = 0.1870 = \underline{18.70\%}$$

less than Canada's exports to US (= US imports from Canada.)

63. Suppose the initial ratio is $\dfrac{x}{y}$.

If the denominator is reduced by 20%, then

$$\text{Final ratio} = \frac{x}{y - 0.20y} = \frac{x}{0.8y} = 1.25\frac{x}{y}$$

That is, the value of the ratio <u>increases by 25%.</u>

65. Given: Operating expenses $= 0.40$(Revenue)

Then   Revenue $= \dfrac{\text{Operating expenses}}{0.40} = 2.5$(Operating expenses)

That is, Revenue is 250% of Operating expenses, or

Revenue exceeds Operating expenses by $250\% - 100\% = \underline{150\%}$.

Exercise 2.5 *(continued)*

67. Use ppm as the abbreviation for "pages per minute".
    Given: Lightning printer prints 30% more ppm than the Reliable printer.
    That is, the Lightning's printing speed is 1.30 times the Reliable's printing speed.
    Therefore, the Reliable's printing speed is

    $$\frac{1}{1.3} = 0.7692 = 76.92\% \text{ of the Lightning's printing speed}$$

    Therefore, the Reliable's printing speed is
    $$100\% - 76.92\% = 23.08\% \text{ less than the Lighting's speed.}$$
    The Lightning printer will require <u>23.08% less time</u> than the Reliable for a long printing job.

69. Let us use OT as an abbreviation for "overtime".
    The number of OT hours permitted by this year's budget is

    $$\text{OT hours (this year)} = \frac{\text{OT budget (this year)}}{\text{OT hourly rate (this year)}}$$

    The number of overtime hours permitted by next year's budget is

    $$\text{OT hours (next year)} = \frac{\text{OT budget (next year)}}{\text{OT hourly rate (next year)}} = \frac{1.03\left[\text{OT budget (this year)}\right]}{1.11\left[\text{OT hourly rate (this year)}\right]}$$

    $$= 0.9279\frac{\text{OT budget (this year)}}{\text{OT hourly rate (this year)}}$$

    $$= 92.79\% \text{ of this year's OT hours}$$

    The number of OT hours must be reduced by $100\% - 92.79\% = \underline{7.21\%}$.

Concept Questions (Section 2.6)

1. A "capital loss" is the reduction in the market value of an investment during the holding period.

3. Yes. If the expenses associated with an investment exceed the income from the investment, then the net income and the income yield will be negative. For example, if you hold a piece of raw land as an investment, you will have no income from the property but you must pay property taxes each year. The net income and income yield are then negative.

5. Yes. Suppose, for example, you bought a $160,000 condominium as an investment property using $40,000 of your own money and $120,000 borrowed on a mortgage loan. Subsequently, the condo's market value fell to $100,000 because "leaky condo" problems were discovered in the building. At that point, you have lost more than 100% of your initial $40,000 investment because the condo's market value is less than the amount owed on the mortgage loan. You must still repay the balance on the loan after the proceeds of the sale are applied to the loan.

Exercise 2.6

Problem	Income yield $\left(\dfrac{Income}{V_i} \times 100\%\right)$	Capital gain yield $\left(\dfrac{V_f - V_i}{V_i} \times 100\%\right)$	Rate of total return (Income yield + Capital gain yield)
1.	$\dfrac{\$10}{\$100} \times 100\% = \underline{10.00\%}$	$\dfrac{\$110 - \$100}{\$100} \times 100\% = \underline{10.00\%}$	$10\% + 10\% = \underline{20.00\%}$
3.	$\dfrac{\$10}{\$90} \times 100\% = \underline{11.11\%}$	$\dfrac{\$86 - \$90}{\$90} \times 100\% = \underline{-4.44\%}$	$\underline{6.67\%}$
5.	$\dfrac{\$141}{\$1367} \times 100\% = \underline{10.31\%}$	$\dfrac{\$1141 - \$1367}{\$1367} \times 100\% = \underline{-16.53\%}$	$\underline{-6.22\%}$
7.	$\dfrac{\$200}{\$2500} \times 100\% = \underline{8.00\%}$	$\dfrac{\$0 - \$2500}{\$2500} \times 100\% = \underline{-100.00\%}$	$\underline{-92.00\%}$

9. Given: $V_i = \$2000$, $V_f = \$2200$, Income yield = 5%

Since   Income yield = $\dfrac{Income}{V_i} \times 100\%$

Then   5% = $\dfrac{Income}{\$2000} \times 100\%$

Income = 0.05 x $2000 = \underline{\$100.00}$

Capital gain yield = $\dfrac{V_f - V_i}{V_i} \times 100\% = \dfrac{\$2200 - \$2000}{\$2000} \times 100\% = \underline{10.00\%}$

Rate of total return = Income yield + Capital gain yield = 5% + 10.00% = $\underline{15.00\%}$

11. Given: $V_i = \$3730$, Income = $250, Rate of total return = 5%

Income yield = $\dfrac{Income}{V_i} \times 100\% = \dfrac{\$250}{\$3730} \times 100\% = 6.7024\% = \underline{6.70\%}$

Since   Rate of total return = Capital gain yield + Income yield
Then   Capital gain yield = Rate of total return − Income yield
$$= 5.00\% - 6.7024\%$$
$$= \underline{-1.70\%}$$

Since   Capital gain yield = $\dfrac{V_f - V_i}{V_i} \times 100\%$

Then $-1.7024\% = \dfrac{V_f - \$3730}{\$3730} \times 100\%$

$-0.017024 \times \$3730 = V_f - \$3730$

$V_f = -\$63.50 + \$3730 = \underline{\$3666.50}$

13. Given: V_f = \$1800, Capital gain yield = – 40%, Rate of total return = – 30%

Capital gain yield = $\dfrac{V_f - V_i}{V_i} \times 100\%$

$-40\% = \dfrac{\$1800 - V_i}{V_i} \times 100\%$

$-0.40 V_i = \$1800 - V_i$

$V_i - 0.40 V_i = \$1800$

$V_i = \dfrac{\$1800}{0.6} = \underline{\$3000.00}$

Income yield = Rate of total return – Capital gain yield = – 30% – (– 40%) = <u>10.00%</u>

Income = Income yield × V_i = 0.10 × \$3000 = <u>\$300.00</u>

15. Given: V_i = \$1600, Income yield = 8%, Rate of total return = 0%

Income = Income yield × V_i = 0.08 × \$1600 = <u>\$128.00</u>

Since Rate of total return = 0%,

Then   Capital gain yield = – Income yield = <u>– 8.00%</u>

$V_f = V_i$ + Capital gain = \$1600 – \$128.00 = <u>\$1472.00</u>

17.

Security	Income yield $\dfrac{Income}{V_i} \times 100\%$	Capital gain yield $\dfrac{V_f - V_i}{V_i} \times 100\%$	Rate of total return Income yield + Capital gain yield
Nortel shares (2002)	<u>0.00%</u>	$\dfrac{\$2.52 - \$11.90}{\$11.90} \times 100\% = \underline{\underline{-78.82\%}}$	0.00% – 78.82% = <u>–78.82%</u>
Nortel shares (2003)	<u>0.00%</u>	$\dfrac{\$5.49 - \$2.52}{\$2.52} \times 100\% = \underline{117.86\%}$	0.00% + 117.86% = <u>117.86%</u>
Ontario bonds (2002)	$\dfrac{\$76.00}{\$1177.30} \times 100\%$ = <u><u>6.46%</u></u>	$\dfrac{\$1241.00 - \$1177.30}{\$1177.30} \times 100\%$ = <u>5.41%</u>	6.46% + 5.41% = <u>11.87%</u>
Ontario bonds (2003)	$\dfrac{\$76.00}{\$1241.00} \times 100\%$ = <u><u>6.12%</u></u>	$\dfrac{\$1264.40 - \$1241.00}{\$1241.00} \times 100\%$ = <u><u>1.89%</u></u>	6.12% + 1.89% = <u>8.01%</u>
Templeton Grth (2002)	<u>0.00%</u>	$\dfrac{\$8.26 - \$10.48}{\$10.48} \times 100\% = \underline{\underline{-21.18\%}}$	0.00% – 21.18% = <u>–21.18%</u>
Templeton Grth (2003)	<u>0.00%</u>	$\dfrac{\$9.47 - \$8.26}{\$8.26} \times 100\% = \underline{14.65\%}$	0.00% + 14.65% = <u>14.65%</u>

Exercise 2.6 *(continued)*

19. Security	Income yield $\dfrac{Income}{V_i} \times 100\%$	Capital gain yield $\dfrac{V_f - V_i}{V_i} \times 100\%$	Rate of total return Income yield + Capital gain yield
Talisman shares (2002)	$\dfrac{\$0.60}{\$60.50} \times 100\%$ $= 0.99\%$	$\dfrac{\$56.85 - \$60.50}{\$60.50} \times 100\%$ $= -6.03\%$	$= 0.99\% - 6.03\%$ $= \underline{-5.04\%}$
Talisman shares (2003)	$\dfrac{\$0.80}{\$56.85} \times 100\%$ $= 1.41\%$	$\dfrac{\$73.52 - \$56.85}{\$56.85} \times 100\%$ $= 29.32\%$	$1.41\% + 29.32\%$ $= \underline{30.73\%}$
HydroOne bonds (2002)	$\dfrac{\$71.50}{\$1081.90} \times 100\%$ $= 6.61\%$	$\dfrac{\$1110.40 - \$1081.90}{\$1081.90} \times 100\%$ $= 2.63\%$	$6.61\% + 2.63\%$ $= \underline{9.24\%}$
HydroOne bonds (2003)	$\dfrac{\$71.50}{\$1110.40} \times 100\%$ $= 6.44\%$	$\dfrac{\$1134.00 - \$1110.40}{\$1110.40} \times 100\%$ $= 2.13\%$	$6.44\% + 2.13\%$ $= \underline{8.56\%}$
RBC US Index Fd. (2002)	$\dfrac{\$0.10}{\$11.40} \times 100\%$ $= 0.88\%$	$\dfrac{\$8.73 - \$11.40}{\$11.40} \times 100\%$ $= -23.42\%$	$0.88\% - 23.42\%$ $= \underline{-22.54\%}$
RBC US Index Fd. (2003)	$\dfrac{\$0.06}{\$8.73} \times 100\%$ $= 0.69\%$	$\dfrac{\$9.04 - \$8.73}{\$8.73} \times 100\%$ $= 3.55\%$	$0.69\% + 3.55\%$ $= \underline{4.24\%}$

21. The income yield will be $\dfrac{Income}{V_i} \times 100\% = \dfrac{\$1.35}{\$43.29} \times 100\% = 3.119\%$

For a rate of total return = 10%,
   Capital gain yield = Rate of total return – Income yield = 10% – 3.119% = 6.881%
The end-of-2004 TD Bank share price must be
   $V_i(1 + c) = \$43.29(1 + 0.06881) = \underline{\$46.27}$

23. Given: $V_i = \$37, V_f = \$40$, Income = $0.60

Income yield $= \dfrac{Income}{V_i} \times 100\% = \dfrac{\$0.60}{\$37} \times 100\% = \underline{1.62\%}$

Capital gain yield $= \dfrac{V_f - V_i}{V_i} \times 100\% = \dfrac{\$40 - \$37}{\$37} \times 100\% = \underline{8.11\%}$

Rate of total return = Income yield + Capital gain yield = 1.62% + 8.11% = $\underline{9.73\%}$

25. Given: $V_i = \$1053.25, V_f = \$1021.75$, Income = 2($35) = $70

Income yield $= \dfrac{Income}{V_i} \times 100\% = \dfrac{\$70}{\$1053.25} \times 100\% = \underline{6.65\%}$

Capital gain yield $= \dfrac{V_f - V_i}{V_i} \times 100\% = \dfrac{\$1021.75 - \$1053.25}{\$1053.25} \times 100\% = \underline{-2.99\%}$

Rate of total return = Income yield + Capital gain yield = 6.65% + (– 2.99%) = $\underline{3.66\%}$

Exercise 2.6 *(continued)*

27. Given: V_i = $1000, Income = 2 × $47.50 = $95.00, V_f = $1034

    a. Income yield = $\dfrac{Income}{V_i} \times 100\%$ = $\dfrac{\$95.00}{\$1000} \times 100\%$ = <u>9.50%</u>

    b. Capital gain yield = $\dfrac{V_f - V_i}{V_i} \times 100\%$ = $\dfrac{\$1034 - \$1000}{\$1000} \times 100\%$ = <u>3.40%</u>

    c. Total return = Income + Capital gain = 10($95 + $34) = <u>$1290.00</u>

    d. Rate of total return = Income yield + Capital gain yield = 9.50% + 3.40% = <u>12.90%</u>

29. Given: V_i = $13.50, V_f = $15.25, Income = 3($0.50) = $1.50

    Capital gain = $15.25 − $13.50 = $1.75 per share

    Rate of total return = $\dfrac{Income + Capital\ gain}{V_i} \times 100\%$ = $\dfrac{\$1.75 + \$1.50}{\$13.50} \times 100\%$ = <u>24.07%</u>

31. Given: V_i = $150,000 + $30,000 = $180,000

    Income = 10($1200) − $2900 = $9100 for the year.

    a. If V_f = $220,000, then capital gain = $220,000 − $180,000 = $40,000 and

    $$Rate\ of\ total\ return = \frac{Income + Capital\ gain}{V_i} \times 100\%$$

    $$= \frac{\$9100 + \$40,000}{\$180,000} \times 100\%$$

    $$= \underline{27.28\%}$$

    b. The selling commission is 0.06 x $220,000 = $13,200.

    Net of the commission, Capital gain = $40,000 − $13,200 = $26,800

    $$Rate\ of\ total\ return = \frac{\$9100 + \$26,800}{\$180,000} \times 100\% = \underline{19.94\%}$$

33. Given: Purchase price = $145,000; Rent = $850 per month;
    Down payment = 0.3($145,000); Amount borrowed = 0.7($145,000);
    Property taxes = $1800 per year; Strata (maintenance) fee = $130 per month;
    Mortgage interest = $6160 in the first year

    Luongo's personal investment, V_i = 0.30($145,000) = $43,500

    Net income for the year = 12($850) − $1800 − 12($130) − $6160 = $680

    a. If capital gain yield = −2.0%,

    Capital loss = 0.02($145,000) = $2900

    $$Rate\ of\ total\ return = \frac{Income + Capital\ gain}{V_i} \times 100\%$$

    $$= \frac{\$680 - \$2900}{\$43,500} \times 100\%$$

    $$= \underline{-5.10\%}$$

    b. If capital gain yield = 2.0%,

    Capital gain = 0.02($145,000) = $2900

    $$Rate\ of\ total\ return = \frac{\$680 + \$2900}{\$43,500} \times 100\% = \underline{8.23\%}$$

33. c. If capital gain yield = 4.0%,

Capital gain = 0.04($145,000) = $5800

$$\text{Rate of total return} = \frac{\$680 + \$5800}{\$43,500} \times 100\% = \underline{14.90\%}$$

35. Given: V_i = $5000 ÷ 400 = $12.50 per unit, Rate of total return = 22%, V_f = $13.75

Income + Capital gain = $\dfrac{\text{Rate of total return}}{100\%} \times V_i$ = 0.22 × $12.50 = $2.75

Since   Capital gain = $V_f - V_i$ = $13.75 − $12.50 = $1.25

Then   Income = $2.75 − $1.25 = $\underline{\$1.50}$

The fund distributed $1.50 per unit during the year.

37. Given: Capital gain yield = −8%, Rate of total return = 1%, Income = 2($52.50) = $105.00

Income yield = Rate of total return − Capital gain yield = 1% − (−8%) = 9%

$$V_i = \frac{100\%}{\text{Income yield}} \times \text{Income} = \frac{100\%}{9\%} \times \$105 = \$1166.67$$

Capital gain = Capital gain yield × V_i = −0.08 × $1167.67 = − $93.33

Current price, $V_f = V_i +$ Capital gain = $1166.67 − $93.33 = $\underline{\$1073.34}$

39. Given: Capital gain = 0.06 × $230,000 = $13,800

Income = 12(Monthly rental) − $12,400 − 12($300) − $2400

Required rate of total return = 15%

Ed's investment, V_i = 40% of $230,000 = $92,000

Capital gain yield = $\dfrac{Capital\ gain}{V_i} \times 100\%$ = $\dfrac{\$13,800}{\$92,000} \times 100\%$ = 15%

Required income yield = Required rate of total return − Capital gain yield

           = 15% − 15%

           = 0%

Hence, Income = 0 and

         Income = 0 = 12(Monthly rental) − $12,400 − 12($300) − $2400

                = 12(Monthly rental) − $18,400

Monthly rental = $\dfrac{\$18,400}{12}$ = $\underline{\$1533.33}$

The monthly rental income would have to be $1533.33 for Ed's rate of return on equity to be 15%.

Concept Questions (Section 2.7)

1. No. If you think of the relevant formula, $V_f = V_i(1 + c_1)(1 + c_2)$, the order of the percent changes affects the order of multiplication. However, it is a basic axiom of mathematics that the order of multiplication does not affect the product.

3. The overall percent change is larger because each successive change acts on previous increases as well as the original amount.

Exercise 2.7

1. Given: $c_1 = 0.05$, $c_2 = 0.03$, $c_3 = 0.01$, $V_i = \$15.00$
   The hourly wage after the three increases will be
   $$V_f = V_i(1 + c_1)(1 + c_2)(1 + c_3) = \$15.00(1.05)(1.03)(1.01) = \underline{\$16.38/hour}$$

3. Given: $c_1, \ldots, c_5 = 0.102, 0.124, 0.109, 0.057, 0.044$
   Let V_i represent the beginning price level. The price level at the end of the 5 years was
   $$V_f = V_i(1 + c_1)(1 + c_2)\cdots(1 + c_5) = V_i(1.102)(1.124)(1.109)(1.057)(1.044) = 1.5158V_i$$
   The percent increase in the price level during the five years was $\underline{51.58\%}$.

5. No. In making the claim, the CEO appears to have made the mistake of adding −50% and 60% to arrive at their combined effect. Suppose we let E_i represent the earnings in the year before the 50% decline. After the 50% decline and the subsequent 60% rise,
   $$E_f = E_i(1 + c_1)(1 + c_2) = E_i(1 - 0.50)(1 + 0.60) = 0.80\,E_i$$
   That is, after the 60% increase in earnings, <u>earnings were still at only 80% of their level before the 50% decline</u>.

7. Given: $c_1 = c_2 = 0.25$
   $$V_f = V_i(1 + c_1)(1 + c_2) = V_i(1.25)^2 = 1.5625V_i$$
   The percent increase over the entire two years was $\underline{56.25\%}$.

9. Given: $c_1 = 0.50$, $V_f = V_i$
   Substitute in $V_f = V_i(1 + c_1)(1 + c_2)$
   $$V_i = V_i(1.50)(1 + c_2)$$
   $$1 = 1.50(1 + c_2)$$
   $$c_2 = \tfrac{1}{1.5} - 1 = -0.3\overline{3} = \underline{-33.33\%}$$
   A 33.33% decline in the second year will wipe out a 50% gain in the first year.

11. Given: $c_1 = -0.50$, $V_f = V_i$
    Substitute in $V_f = V_i(1 + c_1)(1 + c_2)$
    $$V_i = (1 - 0.5)(1 + c_2)$$
    $$c_2 = \tfrac{1}{0.5} - 1 = 1.0000$$
    A $\underline{100.00\%}$ return in the second year is required to break even.

13. Given: $c_1 = c_2 = 0.10$, $V_f = 1.30V_i$
    Substitute in $V_f = V_i(1 + c_1)(1 + c_2)(1 + c_3)$
    $$1.30V_i = V_i(1.10)(1.10)(1 + c_3)$$
    $$1.30 = 1.21(1 + c_3)$$
    $$c_3 = \tfrac{1.30}{1.21} - 1 = 0.0744$$
    A return of $\underline{7.44\%}$ in the third year will produce a cumulative gain of 30%.

15. Given: $c_1 = 0.35$, $c_2 = 0.40$, $c_3 = 0.30$, $c_4 = 0.25$
    Then $V_f = V_i(1 + c_1)(1 + c_2)\cdots(1 + c_4) = V_i(1.35)(1.40)(1.30)(1.25) = 3.07125V_i$
    $$c = \frac{V_f - V_i}{V_i} \times 100\% = \frac{3.07125V_i - V_i}{V_i} \times 100\% = \underline{207.13\%}$$
    The cumulative percent increase was 207.13%.

17. Given: $c_1 = -0.20$, $c_2 = -0.40$, $c_3 = -0.60$, V_i = $1 billion
    a. Substitute in $V_f = V_i(1 + c_1)(1 + c_2)(1 + c_3)$
    $$= \$1000 \text{ million}(1 - 0.20)(1 - 0.40)(1 - 0.60)$$
    $$= \underline{\$192 \text{ million}}$$
    The deficit will be $192 million after the third year.

    b. V_f = $1000 million$(1 - 0.20)(1 - 0.40)$ = $480 million
    The projected decrease in the third year is $480 million – $192 million = $\underline{\$288 \text{ million}}$

19. After 10 years of 10% annual increases, $V_f = V_i(1.10)^{10} = 2.5937V_i$
    After 5 years of 20% increases and 5 years of 0% increases, $V_f = V_i(1.20)^5 = 2.4883V_i$
    The cumulative percent increase is $\underline{159.37\%}$ in the first case and $\underline{148.83\%}$ in the second.
    The constant 10% increases produce a 10.54% higher cumulative increase.

21. Given: $c_1 = -0.09$, $c_2 = -0.07$, $c_3 = -0.05$, V_i = 18,750
    a. Substitute in $V_f = V_i(1 + c_1)(1 + c_2)(1 + c_3) = 18,750(0.91)(0.93)(0.95) = \underline{15,075}$
    The company will have 15,075 employees after the third year.

    b. The number of employees cut in the second year will be 7% of the employees remaining after the first year.
    Number cut = $0.07V_f$ (after 1 year) = $0.07(V_i)(1 + c_1) = 0.07(18,750)(0.91) = \underline{1194}$.

23. Given: $c_1 = -0.053$, $c_2 = -0.104$, 3-year change = –0.22
    $$V_f = V_i(1 - 0.22)$$
    $$= V_i(1 - 0.53)(1 - 0.104)(1 + c_3)$$
    Hence, $0.78V_i = V_i(0.947)(0.896)(1 + c_3)$
    $$1 + c_3 = \frac{0.78}{(0.947)(0.896)}$$
    $$c_3 = 0.9193 - 1 = -0.0807$$
    The decrease in 2002 was $\underline{8.07\%}$.

25. Given: $c_1 = -0.35$, $c_2 = -0.55$, $c_3 = -0.80$, V_f = $0.75
    a. The share price at the beginning of the 3 years was
    $$V_i = \frac{V_f}{(1 + c_1)(1 + c_2)(1 + c_3)} = \frac{V_f}{(1 - 0.35)(1 - 0.55)(1 - 0.80)} = \underline{\$12.82}$$

    b. The drop in the share price in the third year was 80% of the price at the end of the second year. Hence,
    Price drop = $0.80V_f$(after 2 years) = $0.80(\$12.82)(1 - 0.35)(1 - 0.55) = \underline{\$3.00}$

27. The value at the end of 2003 of an initial investment V_i in the AGF Canadian Stock fund was
    $$V_f = V_i(1 + 0.326)(1 + 0.202)(1 - 0.043)(1 - 0.14)(1 + 0.222) = 1.60299V_i$$
    Therefore, the percent increase in the value of the fund was $\underline{60.30\%}$.

    Over the same period the S&P/TSX Total Return Index increased from V_i to
    $$V_f = (1 + 0.317)(1 + 0.074)(1 - 0.126)(1 - 0.124)(1 + 0.259) = 1.36343V_i$$
    Therefore, the percent increase in S&P/TSX Total Return Index was 36.343%.
    The AGF Canadian Stock fund <u>outperformed</u> the S&P/TSX Total Return Index <u>by</u>
    $$60.299\% - 36.343\% = \underline{23.96\%}$$

29. The value at the end of 2003 of an initial investment of V_i in the RBC Canadian Equity fund was

$$V_f = V_i(1 + 0.240)(1 + 0.103)(1 - 0.057)(1 - 0.070)(1 + 0.211) = 1.45257V_i$$

Therefore, the percent increase in the value of the fund was <u>45.26%</u>.

Over the same period the S&P/TSX Total Return Index increased from V_i to
$$V_f = (1 + 0.317)(1 + 0.074)(1 - 0.126)(1 - 0.124)(1 + 0.259) = 1.36343V_i$$
Therefore, the percent increase in S&P/TSX Total Return Index was 36.343%.
The RBC Canadian Equity fund <u>outperformed</u> the S&P/TSX Total Return Index <u>by</u>
45.257% − 36.343% = <u>8.91%</u>

Review Problems

1. a. $\dfrac{9y - 7}{3} - 2.3(y - 2) = 3y - 2.\overline{3} - 2.3y + 4.6 = \underline{\underline{0.7y + 2.2\overline{6}}}$

    b. $P\left(1 + 0.095 \times \dfrac{135}{365}\right) + \dfrac{2P}{1 + 0.095 \times \frac{75}{365}} = 1.035137P + 1.961706P = \underline{\underline{2.996843P}}$

3. a. $L(1 - d_1)(1 - d_2)(1 - d_3) = \$340(1 - 0.15)(1 - 0.08)(1 - 0.05) = \underline{\underline{\$252.59}}$

    b. $\dfrac{R}{i}\left[1 - \dfrac{1}{(1+i)^n}\right] = \dfrac{\$575}{0.085}\left[1 - \dfrac{1}{(1+0.085)^3}\right] = \$6764.706(1 - 0.7829081) = \underline{\underline{\$1468.56}}$

5. a. $\dfrac{(1.00\overline{6})^{240} - 1}{0.00\overline{6}} = \dfrac{4.926802 - 1}{0.00\overline{6}} = \underline{\underline{589.020}}$

    b. $(1 + 0.025)^{1/3} - 1 = \underline{\underline{0.00826484}}$

7. a. Given: $c = 17.5\%$, $V_i = \$29.43$
    $V_f = V_i(1 + c) = \$29.43(1.175) = \underline{\underline{\$34.58}}$
    \$34.58 is 17.5% more than \$29.43.

    b. Given: $V_f = \$100$, $c = -80\%$
    $V_i = \dfrac{V_f}{1+c} = \dfrac{\$100}{1 - 0.80} = \underline{\underline{\$500.00}}$
    80% off \$500 leaves \$100.

    c. Given: $V_f = \$100$, $c = -15\%$
    $V_i = \dfrac{V_f}{1+c} = \dfrac{\$100}{1 - 0.15} = \underline{\underline{\$117.65}}$
    \$117.65 reduced by 15% equals \$100.

    d. Given: $V_i = \$47.50$, $c = 320\%$
    $V_f = V_i(1 + c) = \$47.50(1 + 3.2) = \underline{\underline{\$199.50}}$
    \$47.50 after an increase of 320% is \$199.50.

    e. Given: $c = -62\%$, $V_f = \$213.56$
    $V_i = \dfrac{V_f}{1+c} = \dfrac{\$213.56}{1 - 0.62} = \underline{\underline{\$562.00}}$
    \$562 decreased by 62% equals \$213.56.

7. f. Given: $c = 125\%$, $V_f = \$787.50$

$$V_i = \frac{V_f}{1+c} = \frac{\$787.50}{1+1.25} = \$350.00$$

$350 increased by 125% equals $787.50.

g. Given: $c = -30\%$, $V_i = \$300$

$$V_f = V_i(1+c) = \$300(1-0.30) = \$210.00$$

$210 is 30% less than $300.

9. Given: For the first year, $V_i = \$3.40$, $V_f = \$11.50$.
    For the second year, $V_i = \$11.50$, $c = -35\%$.

a. $$c = \frac{V_f - V_i}{V_i} \times 100\% = \frac{\$11.50 - \$3.40}{\$3.40} \times 100\% = 238.24\%$$

The share price increased by 238.24% in the first year.

b. Current share price, $V_f = V_i(1+c) = \$11.50(1-0.35) = \underline{\$7.48}$.

11. Given: For each bond, $V_i = \$1000$, $V_f = \$980$, annual income = 2($40) = $80

a. Income yield $= \dfrac{\text{Income}}{V_i} \times 100\% = \dfrac{\$80}{\$1000} \times 100\% = \underline{8.00\%}$

The interest yield was 8.00%.

b. Capital gain yield $= \dfrac{V_f - V_i}{V_i} \times 100\% = \dfrac{\$980 - \$1000}{\$1000} \times 100\% = \underline{-2.00\%}$

c. Total return = Income + Capital gain = 15($80) + 15($980 – $1000) = $\underline{\$900.00}$

d. Rate of total return = Income yield + Capital gain yield = 8.00% – 2.00% = $\underline{6.00\%}$

13. Given: $c_1 = 0.23$, $c_2 = 0.10$, $c_3 = -0.15$, $c_4 = 0.05$, $V_f = \$30.50$

a. Substitute in $V_f = V_i(1 + c_1)\ (1 + c_4)$ and solve for V_i

$$\$30.50 = V_i(1.23)(1.10)(0.85)(1.05)$$

$$V_i = \frac{\$30.50}{1.20755} = \$25.26$$

A share's initial price was $25.26.

b. The decline in the third year was 15% of the price at the end of the second year. That is,

Price decline = $0.15V_f$(after 2 years) = 0.15($25.26)(1.23)(1.10) = $\underline{\$5.13}$

The share price declined by $5.13 in the third year.

15. Given: Total initial investment = $7800; Value 1 year later = $9310
    Percent change in ABC portion = 15%
    Percent change in XYZ portion = 25%

Let X represent the amount invested in XYZ Inc.
The solution "idea" is:

(Amount invested in ABC)1.15 + (Amount invested in XYZ)1.25 = $9310

Hence,

$$(\$7800 - X)1.15 + (X)1.25 = \$9310$$
$$\$8970 - 1.15X + 1.25X = \$9310$$
$$0.10X = \$9310 - \$8970$$
$$X = \$3400$$

Rory invested $\underline{\$3400 \text{ in XYZ}}$ Inc. and $7800 – $3400 = $\underline{\$4400 \text{ in ABC}}$ Ltd.

Review Problems *(continued)*

17. 60% of a $\frac{3}{8}$ interest was purchased for $25,000.

Let the V represent the implied value of the entire partnership.

Then $\quad 0.60 \times \dfrac{3}{8}$ V = $25,000

$$V = \frac{8 \times \$25{,}000}{0.60 \times 3} = \underline{\$111{,}111}$$

The implied value of the chalet was $111,111.

19. Let b represent the base salary and r represent the commission rate. Then

$\qquad$ r($27,000) + b = $2815.00 $\quad$ ①
$\qquad$ r($35,500) + b = $3197.50 $\quad$ ②

Subtract: $\qquad$ −$8500r $\quad$ = $\quad$ $382.50

$\qquad\qquad\qquad$ r = 0.045

Substitute into ①: 0.045($27,000) + b = $2815

$\qquad\qquad\qquad\qquad$ b = $1600

Deanna's base salary is $\underline{\text{\$1600 per month}}$ and her commission rate is $\underline{4.5\%}$.

Self-Test Exercise

1. a. $6(4y - 3)(2 - 3y) - 3(5 - y)(1 + 4y) = 6(8y - 12y^2 - 6 + 9y) - 3(5 + 20y - y - 4y^2)$
   $$= \underline{-60y^2 + 45y - 51}$$

   b. $\dfrac{5b - 4}{4} - \dfrac{25 - b}{1.25} + \dfrac{7}{8}b = 1.25b - 1 - 20 + 0.8b + 0.875b = \underline{2.925b - 21}$

   c. $\dfrac{x}{1 + 0.085 \times \frac{63}{365}} + 2x\left(1 + 0.085 \times \dfrac{151}{365}\right) = 0.985541x + 2.070329x = \underline{3.05587x}$

   d. $\dfrac{96nm^2 - 72n^2m^2}{48n^2m} = \dfrac{4m - 3nm}{2n} = \dfrac{4m}{2n} - \dfrac{3nm}{2n} = 2\dfrac{m}{n} - 1.5m$

2. $P(1 + i)^n + \dfrac{S}{1 + rt} = \$2500(1.1025)^2 + \dfrac{\$1500}{1 + 0.09 \times \frac{93}{365}} = \$3038.766 + \$1466.374 = \underline{\$4505.14}$

3. a. $\dfrac{\left(-3x^2\right)^3\left(2x^{-2}\right)}{6x^5} = \dfrac{\left(-27x^6\right)\left(2x^{-2}\right)}{6x^5} = \underline{-\dfrac{9}{x}}$

   b. $\dfrac{\left(-2a^3\right)^{-2}\left(4b^4\right)^{3/2}}{\left(-2b^3\right)\left(0.5a\right)^3} = \dfrac{\left(\frac{1}{4a^6}\right)\left(8b^6\right)}{\left(-2b^3\right)\left(0.125a^3\right)} = \underline{-\dfrac{8b^3}{a^9}}$

4. a. $1.0075^{24} = \underline{1.19641}$

   b. $(1.05)^{1/6} - 1 = \underline{0.00816485}$

   c. $\dfrac{(1 + 0.0075)^{36} - 1}{0.0075} = \underline{41.1527}$

   d. $\dfrac{1 - (1 + 0.045)^{-12}}{0.045} = \underline{9.11858}$

5. a. $$\frac{2x}{1+0.13\times\frac{92}{365}} + x\left(1+0.13\times\frac{59}{365}\right) = \$831$$

$$1.936545x + 1.021014x = \$831$$
$$2.957559x = \$831$$
$$x = \underline{\$280.97}$$

b. $$3x(1.03^5) + \frac{x}{1.03^3} + x = \frac{\$2500}{1.03^2}$$

$$3.47782x + 0.91514x + x = \$2356.49$$
$$x = \underline{\$436.96}$$

6. Given: Last year's revenue = \$2,347,000
      Last year's expenses = \$2,189,000

 a. Given: Percent change in revenue = 10%; Percent change in expenses = 5%
     Anticipated revenues, $V_f = V_i(1 + c) = \$2,347,000(1.1) = \$2,581,700$
     Anticipated expenses = $\$2,189,000(1.05) = \underline{\$2,298,450}$
     Anticipated profit   =   \$283,250
     Last year's profit   =   \$2,347,000 − \$2,189,000 = \$158,000

     Percent increase in profit = $\dfrac{\$283,250 - \$158,000}{\$158,000} \times 100\% = \underline{\underline{79.27\%}}$

 b. Given: c(revenue) = −10%; c(expenses) = − 5%
     Anticipated revenues = \$2,347,000(1 − 0.10) = \$2,112,300
     Anticipated expenses = \$2,189,000(1 − 0.05) = $\underline{\$2,079,550}$
     Anticipated profit   \$32,750

     Percent change in profit = $\dfrac{\$32,750 - \$158,000}{\$158,000} \times 100\% = \underline{\underline{-79.27\%}}$

     The operating profit will decline by 79.27%.

7. Given: Purchase price = \$95,000; Amount invested = \$45,000
      First year's rental income = 12(\$500) = \$6000
      Second year's rental income = 10(\$525) = \$5250
      Property taxes = \$1456 and \$1515 in years 1 and 2
      Interest expense = \$5453 and \$5387 in years 1 and 2
      Selling price = \$112,000 less 5.5% commission
    Net rental income = \$6000 + \$5250 − \$1456 − \$1515 − \$5453 − \$5387 = − \$2561
    Capital gain = \$112,000(1 − 0.055) − \$95,000 = \$10,840

    Rate of total return = $\dfrac{\text{Net rental income} + \text{Capital gain}}{\text{Initial investment}} \times 100\%$

    $$= \frac{-\$2561 + \$10,840}{\$45,000} \times 100\%$$

    $$= \underline{18.40\%}$$

    For the 2-year holding period, the rate of total return on investment was 18.40%.

8. Given: $V_f = 3V_i$, $c_1 = 0.25$, $c_2 = 0.30$, $c_3 = 0.35$
       $V_f = V_i(1+ 0.25)(1 + 0.30)(1 + 0.35)(1 + c_4) = 3V_i$
    Hence, $2.19375(1 + c_4) = 3$

    $$c_4 = \frac{3}{2.19375} - 1 = 0.3675$$

    To reach the targeted level, R & D spending in the fourth year must increase by $\underline{36.75\%}$.

9. Given: $V_i = \$6.50$, $c_1 = 1.10$, $c_2 = -0.55$, $c_3 = -0.55$
    a. The price at the end of the third year was
        $V_f = \$6.50(1 + 1.10)(1 - 0.55)(1 - 0.55) = \$2.76$
        The overall percent change is
        $$c = \frac{V_f - V_i}{V_i} \times 100\% = \frac{\$2.76 - \$6.50}{\$6.50} \times 100\% = \underline{\underline{-57.54\%}}$$
        The share price declined by 57.54% during the 3-year period.

    b. In the second year, the share price dropped by 55% of the price at the end of the first year. That is,
        Price drop $= 0.55V_f$ (after 1 year) $= 0.55(\$6.50)(1 + 1.1) = \underline{\$7.51}$
        The share price dropped by $7.51 in the second year.

10. Given: Ken's share = 0.80(Hugh's share) + $15,000; Total distribution = $98,430
    Let H represent Hugh's share. Then
    $\qquad$ Hugh's share + Ken's share = Total distribution
    $\qquad\qquad$ H + 0.8H + $15,000 = $98,430
    $\qquad\qquad\qquad\qquad$ 1.8H = $83,430
    $\qquad\qquad\qquad\qquad\quad$ H = $46,350
    <u>Hugh should receive $46,350</u> and <u>Ken should receive</u> $98,430 − $46,350 = <u>$52,080</u>.

11. The income yield will be $\dfrac{Income}{V_i} \times 100\% = \dfrac{\$71.50}{\$1134.00} \times 100\% = 6.305\%$

    For the rate of total return to be 6%,
    $\qquad$ Capital gain yield = 6% − Income yield
    $\qquad\qquad\qquad\qquad = 6\% - 6.305\%$
    $\qquad\qquad\qquad\qquad = -0.305\%$
    and the end-of-2004 price $= V_i(1 + c)$
    $\qquad\qquad\qquad\qquad = \$1134.00(1 - 0.00305)$
    $\qquad\qquad\qquad\qquad = \underline{\$1130.54}$

12. $\qquad\qquad$ $3x + 5y = 11$ $\qquad$ ①
    $\qquad\qquad$ $2x - y = 16$ $\qquad$ ②
    To eliminate y,
    $\qquad\qquad$ ①: $\qquad$ $3x + 5y = 11$
    $\qquad\qquad$ ② × 5: $\underline{10x - 5y = 80}$
    Add: $\qquad\qquad$ $13x + 0 = 91$
    $\qquad\qquad\qquad\qquad$ $x = 7$
    Substitute into equation ②: $2(7) - y = 16$
    $\qquad\qquad\qquad\qquad\qquad\qquad$ $y = -2$
    Hence, $\qquad\qquad$ <u>(x, y) = (7, −2)</u>

13. Let S represent the number of cucumbers sold individually and
    let F represent the number of four-cucumber packages sold in the promotion. Then

$$S + 4F = 541 \quad ①$$
$$\$0.98S + \$2.94F = \$418.46 \quad ②$$

To eliminate S,

$$① \times \$0.98: \quad \$0.98S + \$3.92F = \$530.18$$
$$②: \quad \underline{\$0.98S + \$2.94F = \$418.46}$$

Subtract: $\quad\quad\quad 0 + \$0.98F = \$111.72$
$$F = 114$$

Hence, a total of $4 \times 114 = \underline{456 \text{ cucumbers}}$ were sold
on the four-for-the-price-of-three promotion.

14. Let the regular season ticket prices be R for the red section and B for the
    blue section. Then

$$2500R + 4500B = \$50,250 \quad ①$$
$$2500(1.3R) + 4500(1.2B) = \$62,400 \quad ②$$

$$① \times 1.2: \quad \underline{2500(1.2R) + 4500(1.2B) = \$60,300}$$

Subtract: $\quad 2500(0.1R) + \quad\quad 0 = \$2100$
$$R = \$8.40$$

Substitute into ①: $\quad 2500(\$8.40) + 4500B = \$50,250$
$$B = \$6.50$$

The ticket prices for the playoffs cost

$$1.3 \times \$8.40 = \underline{\$10.92} \text{ in the "reds"}$$
$$\text{and } 1.2 \times \$6.50 = \underline{\$7.80} \text{ in the "blues"}.$$

3   Ratios and Proportions

Exercise 3.1

1. $12:64 = \underline{3:16}$ (each term divided by 4)

3. $45:15:30 = 9:3:6$ (each term divided by 5)
           $= \underline{3:1:2}$ (each term divided by 3)

5. $0.08 : 0.12 = 8:12$ (each term multiplied by 100)
           $= \underline{2:3}$ (each term divided by 4)

7. $0.84 : 1.4 : 1.96 = 84:140:196$ (each term multiplied by 100)
           $= 21:35:49$ (each term divided by 4)
           $= \underline{3:5:7}$ (each term divided by 7)

9. $0.24 : 0.39 : 0.15 = 24:39:15$
               $= \underline{8:13:5}$ (each term divided by 3)

11. $\dfrac{1}{8}:\dfrac{3}{4} = \left(\dfrac{1}{8}\times 8\right):\left(\dfrac{3}{4}\times 8\right) = \underline{1:6}$

13. $\dfrac{3}{5}:\dfrac{6}{7} = \left(\dfrac{3}{5}\times 5\times 7\right):\left(\dfrac{6}{7}\times 5\times 7\right) = 21:30 = \underline{7:10}$

15. $1\dfrac{1}{4}:1\dfrac{2}{3} = \dfrac{5}{4}:\dfrac{5}{3} = \left(\dfrac{5}{4}\times 4\times 3\right):\left(\dfrac{5}{3}\times 4\times 3\right) = 15:20 = \underline{3:4}$

17. $4\dfrac{1}{8}:2\dfrac{1}{5} = \dfrac{33}{8}:\dfrac{11}{5} = \left(\dfrac{33}{8}\times\dfrac{8\times 5}{11}\right):\left(\dfrac{11}{5}\times\dfrac{8\times 5}{11}\right) = \underline{15:8}$

19. $\dfrac{1}{15}:\dfrac{1}{5}:\dfrac{1}{10} = 1:3:\dfrac{3}{2}$ (each term multiplied by 15)
                 $= \underline{2:6:3}$ (each term multiplied by 2)

21. $7.6 : 3 = \underline{2.53 :1}$ (each term divided by 3)

23. $0.177 : 0.81 = \underline{1 : 4.58}$ (each term divided by 0.177)

25. $\dfrac{3}{7}:\dfrac{19}{17} = \left(\dfrac{3}{7}\times\dfrac{7}{3}\right):\left(\dfrac{19}{17}\times\dfrac{7}{3}\right) = \underline{1:2.61}$

27. $77:23:41 = \underline{3.35 : 1 : 1.78}$ (each term divided by 23)

29. $3.5 : 5.4 : 8 = \underline{1 : 1.54 : 2.29}$ (each term divided by 3.5)

31. $\dfrac{5}{8}:\dfrac{17}{11}:\dfrac{6}{7} = \left(\dfrac{5}{8}\times\dfrac{8}{5}\right):\left(\dfrac{17}{11}\times\dfrac{8}{5}\right):\left(\dfrac{6}{7}\times\dfrac{8}{5}\right) = \underline{1: 2.47 : 1.37}$

33. Sales in A : Sales in B : Sales in C = $25\%:35\%:40\% = \underline{5:7:8}$

35. Debt : Preferred equity : Common equity
     $= (\$3.6 - \$0.55 - \$1.2) : \$0.55 : \$1.2$
     $= 1.85 : 0.55 : 1.2$
     $= \underline{3.36 : 1 : 2.18}$ (each term divided by 0.55)

Exercise 3.1 (continued)

37. Education : Health services : Social services
    = \$1560 : \$1365 : \$975
    = 312 : 273 : 195 (each term divided by \$5)
    = 104 : 91 : 65   (each term divided by 3)
    = <u>8 : 7 : 5</u>   (each term divided by 13)

39. Add 250 ml of oil to 5 l (= 5000 ml) of gasoline.
    Gasoline : Oil = 5000 : 250
    = 500: 25   (each term divided by 10)
    = <u>20 : 1</u>   (each term divided by 25)

Exercise 3.2

1. $9:7 = 54:b$

    $$\frac{9}{7} = \frac{54}{b}$$

    $9b = 7(54)$

    $b = \underline{42.0}$

3. $88:17 = a:45$

    $$\frac{88}{17} = \frac{a}{45}$$

    $88(45) = 17a$

    $a = \underline{233}$

5. $1.89:0.31 = 175:k$

    $$\frac{1.89}{0.31} = \frac{175}{k}$$

    $$k = \frac{0.31(175)}{1.89} = \underline{28.7}$$

7. $0.043:y = 550:198$

    $$\frac{0.043}{y} = \frac{550}{198}$$

    $$y = \frac{0.043 \times 198}{550} = \underline{0.0155}$$

9. $m : \frac{3}{4} = \frac{1}{2} : \frac{9}{8}$

    $$\frac{m}{\frac{3}{4}} = \frac{\frac{1}{2}}{\frac{9}{8}}$$

    $$m = \frac{3}{4} \times \frac{1}{2} \times \frac{8}{9} = \underline{\frac{1}{3}}$$

11. $6:7:5 = n:105:m$

    $$\frac{6}{7} = \frac{n}{105} \qquad \text{and} \qquad \frac{7}{5} = \frac{105}{m}$$

    $$n = \frac{6(105)}{7} = \underline{90.0} \qquad\qquad m = \frac{5 \times 105}{7} = \underline{75.0}$$

Exercise 3.2 (continued)

13. $625:f:500 = g:3:4$

$$\frac{625}{500} = \frac{g}{4} \qquad \text{and} \qquad \frac{f}{500} = \frac{3}{4}$$

$$g = \frac{4(625)}{500} = \underline{5.00} \qquad\qquad f = \frac{3(500)}{4} = \underline{375}$$

15. $0.69:1.17:0.4 = r:s:6.5$

$$\frac{0.69}{0.4} = \frac{r}{6.5} \qquad \text{and} \qquad \frac{1.17}{0.4} = \frac{s}{6.5}$$

$$r = \frac{6.5(0.69)}{0.4} = \underline{11.2} \qquad\qquad s = \frac{6.5(1.17)}{0.4} = \underline{19.0}$$

17. Let the neighbour's taxes be T.

$$\frac{T}{\$2376} = \frac{\$235,000}{\$210,000}$$

$$T = \frac{235}{210} \times \$2376 = \underline{\$2658.86}$$

The neighbour's taxes are $2658.86.

19. Let the hours of operation be h.

$$\frac{1\frac{1}{2}}{h} = \frac{4}{29.5}$$

$$h = \frac{29.5(1.5)}{4} = \underline{11.06 \text{ hours}}$$

The generator has been operated for 11.06 hours since it was last refuelled.

21. Let the expected hours of direct labour be H.

$$\frac{2.3}{H} = \frac{\$87}{\$39,150}$$

$$H = \frac{2.3(\$39,150)}{\$87} = 1035$$

Total budget for direct labour = 1035($18.25) = $\underline{\$18,888.75}$.

23. Let the first-half sales of Ford be S_F and of Chrysler be S_C. Then

$$\frac{S_F}{\$10.8B} = \frac{92}{121} \qquad \text{and} \qquad \frac{\$10.8B}{S_C} = \frac{121}{35}$$

$$S_F = \frac{92}{121} \times \$10.8B \qquad\qquad S_C = \frac{35}{121} \times \$10.8B$$

$$= \underline{\$8.21 \text{ billion}} \qquad\qquad\qquad = \underline{\$3.12 \text{ billion}}$$

The first-half sales of Ford will be $8.21 billion and of Chrysler will be $3.12 billion.

Exercise 3.2 (continued)

25. Let S, W, and O represent sales, wholesale costs, and overhead expenses, respectively.
    Then   S:W:O = 3.66 : 2.15 : 1.13
    If S = $5.03 million, then

    $$\frac{\$5.03 \text{ million}}{W} = \frac{3.66}{2.15} \quad \text{and} \quad \frac{\$5.03 \text{ million}}{O} = \frac{3.66}{1.13}$$

    $$W = \frac{2.15}{3.66} \times \$5.03 \text{ million} = \underline{\$2.95 \text{ million}}$$

    $$O = \frac{1.13}{3.66} \times \$5.03 \text{ million} = \underline{\$1.55 \text{ million}}$$

    Economart's wholesale costs would have been $2.955 million and
    its overhead expenses $1.553 million.

27. Let S, B, and T represent the number of students, the annual budget,
    and the number of teachers. Then
                    S:B:T = 13,450 : $66.3 million : 635
    If MSD had the same ratios in relation to its enrolment of 10,320,

    $$\frac{10,320}{B} = \frac{13,450}{\$66.3 \text{ million}} \quad \text{and} \quad \frac{10,320}{T} = \frac{13,450}{635}$$

    $$B = \frac{10,320}{13,450} \times \$66.3 \text{ million} = \$50.87 \text{ million}$$

    $$T = \frac{10,320}{13,450} \times 635 = 487$$

    To bring its budget and staffing in line with the average proportion,
    MSD would have to <u>reduce</u> its budget by

    $$\$52.1 \text{ million} - \$50.87 \text{ million} = \underline{\$1.23 \text{ million}}$$

    and <u>reduce</u> its staff by 498 − 487 = <u>11 teachers</u>

Exercise 3.3

1. Refund : Subscription price = Remaining issues : Total issues

   $$\frac{\text{Refund}}{\$136} = \frac{2 \times 52 - 17}{3 \times 52}$$

   $$\text{Refund} = \frac{87}{156} \times \$136 = \underline{\$75.85}$$

3. Refund : Two-year fee = Remaining days : Total days

   $$\frac{\text{Refund}}{\$495} = \frac{(2 \times 365) - (29 + 30 + 31 + 31 + 9)}{2 \times 365} = \frac{730 - 130}{730}$$

   $$\text{Refund} = \$495 \times \frac{600}{730} = \underline{\$406.85}$$

5. *a.*   Deductible expenses : Total expenses = Rooms used for business : Total rooms

$$\frac{\text{Deductible expenses}}{\$8756} = \frac{2}{11}$$

$$\text{Deductible expenses} = \frac{2}{11} \times \$8756 = \underline{\$1592.00}$$

b.
$$\frac{\text{Deductible expenses}}{\$8756} = \frac{360}{1470 + 360}$$

$$\text{Deductible expenses} = \frac{360}{1830} \times \$8756 = \underline{\$1722.49}$$

7.   A's share : B's share : C's share : Total = 3 : 8 : 5 : 16

   a.   A's premium $= \frac{3}{16} \times \$900,000 = \underline{\$168,750}$

        B's premium $= \frac{8}{16} \times \$900,000 = \underline{\$450,000}$

        C's premium $= \frac{5}{16} \times \$900,000 = \underline{\$281,250}$

   b.   A's exposure $= \frac{3}{16} \times \$38,600,000 = \underline{\$7,237,500}$

        B's exposure $= \frac{8}{16} \times \$38,600,000 = \underline{\$19,300,000}$

        C's exposure $= \frac{5}{16} \times \$38,600,000 = \underline{\$12,062,500}$

9.   Let L, C, and M be the investments of Larry, Curley, and Moe, respectively.
    Let T represent the total investment.
    We are given: L : C : M : T = 1 : 1.35 : 0.85 : 3.2

   a.   If T = $102,400, then

$$\frac{L}{\$102,400} = \frac{1}{3.2}, \quad \frac{C}{\$102,400} = \frac{1.35}{3.2}, \quad \frac{M}{\$102,400} = \frac{0.85}{3.2}$$

      Therefore,

$$L = \frac{\$102,400}{3.2} = \underline{\$32,000}$$

$$C = \frac{\$102,400 \times 1.35}{3.2} = \underline{\$43,200}$$

$$M = \frac{\$102,400 \times 0.85}{3.2} = \underline{\$27,200}$$

      Larry contributed $32,000, Curley contributed $43,200, and Moe contributed $27,200.

   b.   Since C : M = 1.35 : 0.85,

      Then $\frac{C}{\$6528} = \frac{1.35}{0.85}$ and $C = \frac{1.35}{0.85} \times \$6528 = \underline{\$10,368}$

      Curley's investment was $10,368.

Exercise 3.3 (continued)

11. Total investment = $25,300,000 + $17,250,000 + $11,900,000 = $54,450,000
    Total sales = $21,200,000 + $8,350,000 + $7,450,000 = $37,000,000

    a. Industrial Products cost : Total costs = $25,300,000 : $54,450,000

    Industrial Products cost = $\dfrac{25,300}{54,450} \times \$839,000$ = $\underline{\$389,838.38}$

    Similarly,

    Fine Paper cost = $\dfrac{17,250}{54,450} \times \$839,000$ = $\underline{\$265,798.90}$

    Containers & Packaging cost = $\dfrac{11,900}{54,450} \times \$839,000$ = $\underline{\$183,362.72}$

    b. Industrial Products cost = $\dfrac{21,200}{37,000} \times \$839,000$ = $\underline{\$480,724.32}$

    Fine Paper cost = $\dfrac{8350}{37,000} \times \$839,000$ = $\underline{\$189,341.89}$

    Containers & Packaging cost = $\dfrac{7450}{37,000} \times \$839,000$ = $\underline{\$168,933.78}$

13. Total number of outstanding shares = 1550

    a. Value of X's shares : Value of company = Shares owned by X : Total number of shares

    $\dfrac{\$175,000}{\text{Value of company}} = \dfrac{500}{1550}$

    Value of company = $\dfrac{1550}{500} \times \$175,000 = \underline{\$542,500}$

    b. Number of shares already owned by W, Y, and Z is 1050.
       From the 500 shares owned by X,

    W's allocation : 500 = W's current shares : Total of W, Y, and Z

    W's allocation = $\dfrac{300}{1050} \times 500$ = 142.9 shares

    Similarly,

    Y's allocation = $\dfrac{350}{1050} \times 500$ = 166.7 shares

    Z's allocation = $\dfrac{400}{1050} \times 500$ = 190.47 shares

    After the buy-out,
       W will own 300 + 143 = <u>443 shares</u>
       Y will own 350 + 167 = <u>517 shares</u>, and
       Z will own 400 + 190 = <u>590 shares</u>

    c. W's contribution : $175,000 = W's allocation : 500

    W's contribution = $\dfrac{143}{500} \times \$175,000 = \underline{\$50,050}$

    Similarly,

    Y's contribution = $\dfrac{167}{500} \times \$175,000 = \underline{\$58,450}$

    Z's contribution = $\dfrac{190}{500} \times \$175,000 = \underline{\$66,500}$

Exercise 3.4

1. $$\frac{C\$c}{US\$1856} = \frac{C\$1.2885}{US\$1.00}$$

   $$C\$c = \frac{C\$1.2885}{US\$1.00} \times US\$1856 = \underline{C\$2391.46}$$

3. $$\frac{¥y}{C\$14,500} = \frac{¥83.01}{C\$1.00}$$

   $$¥y = \frac{¥83.01}{C\$1.00} \times C\$14,500 = \underline{¥1,203,645}$$

5. $$\frac{C\$c}{€3251} = \frac{C\$1.6224}{€1.00}$$

   $$C\$c = \frac{C\$1.6224}{€1.00} \times €3251 = \underline{C\$5274.42}$$

7. $$\frac{C\$c}{¥756,000} = \frac{C\$0.01205}{¥1.00}$$

   $$C\$c = \frac{C\$0.01205}{¥1.00} \times ¥756,000 = \underline{C\$9109.80}$$

9. $$\frac{£b}{C\$94,350} = \frac{£0.4330}{C\$1.00}$$

   $$£b = \frac{£0.4330}{C\$1.00} \times C\$94,350 = \underline{£40,853.55}$$

11. $$\frac{€x}{C\$49,900} = \frac{€0.6164}{C\$1.00}$$

    $$€x = \frac{€0.6164}{C\$1.00} \times C\$49,900 = \underline{€30,758.36}$$

13. a. $$\frac{\text{Sw kr } x}{C\$1.00} = \frac{\text{Sw kr } 1.00}{C\$0.1795}$$

    $$\text{Sw kr } x = \frac{\text{Sw kr } 1.00}{C\$0.1795} \times C\$1.00 = \underline{\text{Sw kr } 5.571}$$

    b. $$\frac{US\$x}{S\$1.00} = \frac{US\$1.00}{S\$1.7021}$$

    $$US\$x = \frac{US\$1.00}{S\$1.7021} \times S\$1.00 = \underline{US\$0.58751}$$

    c. $$\frac{\text{Mex peso } x}{¥1.00} = \frac{\text{Mex peso } 1.00}{¥9.649}$$

    $$\text{Mex peso } x = \frac{\text{Mex peso } 1.00}{¥9.649} \times ¥1.00 = \underline{\text{Mex peso } 0.10364}$$

    d. $$\frac{C\$x}{\text{Rupee } 1.00} = \frac{C\$1.00}{\text{Rupee } 35.34}$$

    $$C\$x = \frac{C\$1.00}{\text{Rupee } 35.34} \times \text{Rupee } 1.00 = \underline{C\$0.02830}$$

Exercise 3.4 (*continued*)

15. $\dfrac{C\$c}{US\$48} = \dfrac{C\$1.2885}{US\$1.00}$

$C\$c = \dfrac{C\$1.2885}{US\$1.00} \times US\$48 = C\$61.85$

After deduction of the 1.5% commission, Simon will receive
$$V_f = V_i(1+c) = C\$61.85(1 - 0.015) = \underline{C\$60.92}$$

17. $\dfrac{C\$c}{\pounds350} = \dfrac{C\$2.3097}{\pounds1.00}$

$C\$c = \dfrac{C\$2.3097}{\pounds1.00} \times \pounds350 = C\$808.40$

After deducting the 0.75% exchange fee, Lois will receive
$$V_f = V_i(1+c) = C\$808.40(1 - 0.0075) = \underline{C\$802.33}$$

19. Convert the American price to C\$.

$\dfrac{C\$c}{US\$5.80} = \dfrac{C\$1.2885}{US\$1.00}$

$C\$c = \dfrac{C\$1.2885}{US\$1.00} \times US\$5.80 = C\$7.47$

Cheese is C\$7.50 − C\$7.47 = $\underline{\text{C\$0.03 per pound less expensive in the U.S.}}$

21. The Royal Bank will sell £ at C\$2.3707 per £. For C\$2000, you will receive
$$C\$2000 \times \dfrac{\pounds1}{C\$2.3707} = \pounds843.63$$

ICE will sell £ at C\$2.3707 per £. For C\$2000, you will receive
$$(C\$2000 - C\$3.50) \times \dfrac{\pounds1}{C\$2.48} = \pounds805.04$$

You will obtain £843.63 − £805.04 = $\underline{\pounds38.59\ \text{more}}$ from the Royal Bank.

23. ICE will buy US\$ at C\$1.266 per US\$. For US\$165, you will receive
$$\left(US\$165 \times \dfrac{C\$1.266}{US\$1}\right) - C\$3.50 = C\$205.39$$

The Royal Bank will buy US\$ at C\$1.3055 per US\$. For US\$165, you will receive
$$US\$165 \times \dfrac{C\$1.3055}{US\$1} = C\$215.41$$

You will receive C\$215.41 − C\$205.39 = $\underline{\text{C\$10.02 less}}$ from ICE.

25. *a.* At the mid-rate, £250 would cost $\pounds250 \times \dfrac{C\$2.309}{\pounds1} = C\$577.25$

At the Royal Bank's sell rate, you would pay $\pounds250 \times \dfrac{C\$2.3707}{\pounds1} = C\$592.68$

The % transaction cost is $\dfrac{\$592.68 - \$577.25}{\$577.25} \times 100\% = \underline{2.67\%\ \text{at the Royal Bank}}$

At ICE's sell rate, you would pay $\pounds250 \times \dfrac{C\$2.48}{\pounds1} + C\$3.50 = C\$623.50$

The % transaction cost is $\dfrac{\$623.50 - \$577.25}{\$577.25} \times 100\% = \underline{8.01\%\ \text{at ICE}}$.

25. *b.* At the mid-rate, £16 would sell for $£16 \times \dfrac{C\$2.309}{£1} = C\$36.94$

At the Royal Bank's buy rate, you would receive $£16 \times \dfrac{C\$2.2627}{£1} = C\$36.20$

The % transaction cost is $\dfrac{\$36.94 - \$36.20}{\$36.94} \times 100\% = \underline{2.00\% \text{ at the Royal Bank}}$

At ICE's buy rate, you would receive $£16 \times \dfrac{C\$2.15}{£1} - C\$3.50 = C\$30.90$

The % transaction cost is $\dfrac{\$36.94 - \$30.90}{\$36.94} \times 100\% = \underline{16.35\% \text{ at ICE}}$.

27. Let €*x* represent the number of Euros.
Converting C\$1150 directly to €,

$$\frac{€x}{C\$1150} = \frac{€0.6164}{C\$1.00}$$

$$€x = \frac{€0.6164}{C\$1.00} \times C\$1150 = \underline{€708.86}$$

Converting C\$1150 first to £,

$$\frac{£b}{C\$1150} = \frac{£0.4330}{C\$1.00}$$

$$£b = \frac{£0.4330}{C\$1.00} \times C\$1150 = £497.95$$

Converting £497.95 to €,

$$\frac{€x}{£497.95} = \frac{€1.4237}{£1.00}$$

$$€x = \frac{€1.4237}{£1.00} \times £497.95 = \underline{€708.93}$$

To the four-figure precision of the given exchange rates, the two outcomes are the same.

29. Given: US\$3.39 buys 1US gallon or 3.785 litres.
The price per litre in the United States is $\dfrac{US\$3.39}{3.785} = US\$0.89564$.

Converting this US\$ price of 1 litre to C\$,

$$\frac{C\$c}{US\$0.89564} = \frac{C\$1.2885}{US\$1.00}$$

$$C\$c = \frac{C\$1.2885}{US\$1.00} \times US\$0.89564 = C\$1.154 \text{ per litre}$$

In Canada, milk costs $\dfrac{C\$4.59}{4} = C\$1.1475$ per litre

Therefore, milk costs $C\$1.154 - \frac{C\$3.79}{4} = C\$0.2705$ per litre less in Canada.

That is, milk is $\dfrac{C\$1.154 - C\$1.1475}{C\$1.1475} \times 100\% = \underline{0.57\% \text{ less expensive in Canada}}$.

Exercise 3.4 (*continued*)

31. The cost of the holiday under the first option is

$$2(\text{US}\$656) + £87 + 2(£1150) = \text{US}\$1312 + £2387$$

The cost of this option in C$ is

$$\text{US}\$1312 \times \frac{\text{C}\$1.2885}{\text{US}\$1.00} \ + \ £2387 \times \frac{\text{C}\$2.3097}{£1.00} = \text{C}\$1690.51 \ + \ \text{C}\$5513.25$$

$$= \text{C}\$7203.76$$

The cost of the alternative all-inclusive package is 2(C$3595) = C$7190

Therefore, the <u>all-inclusive package</u> is C$7203.76 – C$7190.00 = <u>C$13.76 cheaper</u>.

33. The Ontario price is $\dfrac{\text{C}\$22.95}{750 \text{ ml}} = \dfrac{\text{C}\$22.95}{0.750 \text{ litre}} = \text{C}\$30.60$ per litre

The C$ equivalent of US$16.95 (per 40 ounces) is

$$\text{US}\$16.95 \times \frac{\text{C}\$1.2885}{\text{US}\$1} = \text{C}\$21.84$$

which buys $\quad 40 \text{ ounces} \times \dfrac{1 \text{ litre}}{35.2 \text{ ounces}} = 1.1364 \text{ litres}$

Therefore, the cost of duty-free rum works out to

$$\frac{\text{C}\$21.84}{1.1364 \text{ litres}} = \text{C}\$19.22 \text{ per litre}$$

The percent saving (based on the Ontario price) is

$$\frac{\text{C}\$30.60 - \text{C}\$19.22}{\text{C}\$30.60} \times 100\% = \underline{37.2\%}$$

Concept Questions (Section 3.5)

1. If the number of units of currency N per unit of currency M decreases, it then requires *less* of currency N to purchase 1 unit of M. Therefore, currency N has strengthened.

3. If currency G weakens relative to currency H, it will require more of currency G to purchase 1 unit of H. Therefore, the exchange rate expressed as units of G per unit of H will increase.

Exercise 3.5

1. Initially, $\qquad$ C$1.00 = £0.4330

   Finally, $\qquad$ C$1.00 = £0.4330 + £0.054 = £0.4870

   C$1.00 buys more £ after the change. Therefore, the C$ has appreciated and the <u>£ has depreciated</u> from

   $$\frac{\text{C}\$1.00}{£0.4330} \quad \text{to} \quad \frac{\text{C}\$1.00}{£0.4870}$$

   That is, from C$2.3095 to C$2.0534

   The percent change is $\dfrac{2.0534 - 2.3095}{2.3095} \times 100\% = \underline{-11.09\%}$

Exercise 3.5 (*continued*)

3. Initially, C\$1.00 buys €0.6164
   If the C\$ weakens by 0.5%, it will buy only
   $$V_f = V_i(1+c) = €0.6164(1 - 0.005) = €0.6133$$

   The new exchange rates are

   €0.6133 per C\$1.00 and $\dfrac{C\$1.00}{€0.6133}$ = C\$1.6305 per €1.00

5. Initially, C\$2.3097 buys £1.00.
   Finally, C\$2.3097 − C\$0.0017 = C\$2.3080 buys £1.00.

   C\$1.00 will then buy £$\dfrac{1}{2.3080}$ = £0.4333

7. Initially, C\$1.00 buys £0.4330.
   Finally, C\$1.00 buys £0.4330 + £0.0021 = £0.4351.

   £1.00 will then buy C\$$\dfrac{1}{0.4351}$ = C\$2.2983

9. If the C\$ per US\$ exchange rate decreases from
   $\qquad$ C\$1.2885 $\qquad$ to $\qquad$ C\$1.2885 − C\$0.005 = C\$1.2835
   then the US\$ per C\$ exchange rate increases from

   $\qquad$ US\$$\dfrac{1}{1.2885}$ $\qquad$ to $\qquad$ US\$$\dfrac{1}{1.2835}$
   That is, from US\$0.7761 toUS\$0.7791, an increase of US\$0.0030.

11. If the ¥ per A\$ exchange rate increases from ¥81.16 to ¥82.16,
    then the A\$ per ¥ exchange rate decreases from

    $\qquad$ A\$$\dfrac{1}{81.16}$ $\qquad$ to $\qquad$ A\$$\dfrac{1}{82.16}$
    That is, from A\$0.01232 to A\$0.01217, a decrease of A\$0.00015.

13. Initially, $\qquad$ US\$0.7623 = C\$1.00
    Finally, $\qquad$ US\$0.7766 = C\$1.00

    Initially, $\dfrac{C\$price}{US\$1500} = \dfrac{C\$1.00}{US\$0.7623}$

    That is, C\$ price = $\dfrac{C\$1.00}{US\$0.7623} \times US\$1500 = C\$1967.73$

    Finally, C\$ price = $\dfrac{C\$1.00}{US\$0.7766} \times US\$1500 = C\$1931.50$

    Price change = C\$1931.50 − C\$1967.73 = −C\$36.23
    That is, a C\$36.23 decrease.

15. Initially, $\qquad$ £0.4218 = C\$1.00
    Finally, $\qquad$ £0.4335 = C\$1.00

    Initially, $\dfrac{C\$revenue}{£23,000} = \dfrac{C\$1.00}{£0.4218}$

    That is, C\$ revenue = $\dfrac{C\$1.00}{£0.4218} \times £23,000 = C\$54,528.21$

    Finally, C\$ revenue = $\dfrac{C\$1.00}{£0.4335} \times £23,000 = C\$53,056.52$

    Revenue change = C\$53,056.52 − C\$54,528.21 = − C\$1471.69
    That is, a C\$1471.69 decrease.

Exercise 3.6

1. Index number $= \dfrac{\text{Price or value on the selected date}}{\text{Price or value on the base date}} \times \text{Base value} = \dfrac{\$4961}{\$3278} \times 100 = \underline{151.3}$

3. $\dfrac{\text{Current value}}{\text{Value on base date}} = \dfrac{\text{Current index number}}{\text{Base value}}$

    $\dfrac{\text{Current value}}{\$7532} = \dfrac{119.5}{100}$

    Current value $= \dfrac{119.5}{100} \times \$7532 = \underline{\$9001}$

5. Index number $= \dfrac{\text{Price or value on the selected date}}{\text{Price or value on the base date}} \times \text{Base value} = \dfrac{\$689}{\$735} \times 10 = \underline{9.374}$

7. $\dfrac{\text{Current value}}{\text{Value on base date}} = \dfrac{\text{Current index number}}{\text{Base value}}$

    $\dfrac{\$7729}{\text{Value on base date}} = \dfrac{2120}{1000}$

    Value on base date $= \dfrac{1000}{2120} \times \$7729 = \underline{\$3646}$

9. Ending CPI $= \dfrac{\text{Price of "CPI basket" on the selected date}}{\text{Price of "CPI basket" on the base date}} \times 100 = \dfrac{\$26,090}{\$21,350} \times 100 = \underline{122.20}$

11. In order to have the same purchasing power, the amount of money must increase in proportion to the CPI. Therefore,

    $\dfrac{\text{Amount at the end of the year}}{\text{Amount at the beginning of the year}} = \dfrac{\text{CPI at the end of the year}}{\text{CPI at the beginning of the year}}$

    $\dfrac{\text{Amount at the end}}{\$1000} = \dfrac{108.9}{106.3}$

    Amount at the end $= \dfrac{108.9}{106.3} \times \$1000 = \underline{\$1024.46}$

13. Costs have increased in proportion to the respective index.

    a. Goods cost $\dfrac{112.0}{96.8} \times \$1000 = \underline{\$1157.02}$ at the end of the 10-year period.

    b. Services cost $\dfrac{115.1}{95.2} \times \$1000 = \underline{\$1209.03}$ at the end of the 10-year period.

    c. Services cost 20.90% more. Goods cost 15.70% more.
        The cost of <u>services rose</u> 20.90% – 15.70% = <u>5.20% more than</u> the cost of <u>goods</u>.

15. Consumer prices rose by $\dfrac{115.1 - 95.3}{95.3} \times 100\% = \underline{20.78\%}$

    Portfolio rose by $\dfrac{8934 - 3257}{3257} \times 100\% = \underline{174.30\%}$

Exercise 3.6 (*continued*)

17. *a.* To maintain purchasing power, the amount of money must increase in proportion to the CPI.

$$\frac{\text{Amount (1983)}}{\text{Amount (1978)}} = \frac{\text{CPI (1983)}}{\text{CPI (1978)}}$$

Amount (1983) = $\frac{114.1}{70.8} \times \$100 = \underline{\$161.16}$

b. Inflation rate = Percent change in the CPI

Inflation rate (1978) = $\frac{\text{CPI (beginning 1979)} - \text{CPI (beginning 1978)}}{\text{CPI (beginning 1978)}} \times 100\%$

$$= \frac{77.1 - 70.8}{70.8} \times 100\%$$

$$= \underline{8.90\%}$$

Inflation rate (1979) = $\frac{84.5 - 77.1}{77.1} \times 100\% = \underline{9.60\%}$

Inflation rate (1980) = $\frac{94.6 - 84.5}{84.5} \times 100\% = \underline{11.95\%}$

Inflation rate (1981) = $\frac{105.4 - 94.6}{94.6} \times 100\% = \underline{11.42\%}$

Inflation rate (1982) = $\frac{114.1 - 105.4}{105.4} \times 100\% = \underline{8.25\%}$

Review Problems

1. *a.* 0.18 : 0.60 : 0.45 = 18:60:45 = 6:20:15

   b. $\frac{9}{8} : \frac{3}{4} : \frac{3}{2} = 9:6:12$ (each term multiplied by 8)

        $= \underline{3:2:4}$ (each term divided by 3)

   c. $\frac{1}{6} : \frac{1}{3} : \frac{1}{9} = 1:2:\frac{2}{3}$ (each term multiplied by 6)

        $= \underline{3:6:2}$ (each term multiplied by 3)

   d. $6\frac{1}{4} : 5 : 8\frac{3}{4} = \frac{25}{4} : 5 : \frac{35}{4} = 25:20:35$ (each term multiplied by 4)

        $= \underline{5:4:7}$ (each term divided by 5)

3. Mark's holding : Ben's holding : Tanya's holding = 4250 : 2550 : 5950

        = 85:51:119   (each term divided by 50)

        = $\underline{5:3:7}$ (each term divided by 17)

5. Sales of D : Sales of E : Sales of F = 13:17:21

   If sales of E = \$478,000,

   $\frac{\text{D sales}}{\$478,000} = \frac{13}{17}$ and $\frac{\$478,000}{\text{F sales}} = \frac{17}{21}$

   D sales = $\frac{13}{17} \times \$478,000 = \$365,529$

   and   F sales = $\frac{21}{17} \times \$478,000 = \$590,471$

   The expected sales of department D are $\underline{\$365,529}$ and of department F are $\underline{\$590,471}$.

Chapter 3: Ratios and Proportions

7. Given: A:B:C:D:Total costs = 1260 : 3800 : 1550 : 2930 : Total area
   where Total costs = $28,575 and Total area = 9540 square feet.

   Then $\dfrac{A}{\$28,575} = \dfrac{1260}{9540}$

   A's share = $\dfrac{1260}{9540} \times \$28,575 = \underline{\$3774.06}$

   Similar calculations for B's, C's, and D's allocations give $\underline{\$11,382.08}$, $\underline{\$4642.69}$, and $\underline{\$8776.18}$, respectively.

9. 0.5($84,780) = $42,390 should be allocated in proportion to each partner's investment and $42,390 should be allocated in proportion to hours worked. Let H, D, and L represent Huey's, Dewey's, and Louie's shares, respectively. For the allocation in respect of investments,

   H:D:L:$42,390 = $70,000 : $30,000 : $45,000 : $145,000 = 14:6:9:29

   Then $\dfrac{H}{\$42,390} = \dfrac{14}{29}$

   and $H = \dfrac{14}{29} \times \$42,390 = \$20,464.138$

   Similarly, D = $8770.345 and L = $13,155.517
   For the allocation in respect of hours worked,

   H: D: L: $42,390 = 425 : 1680 : 1440 : 3545

   Then $\dfrac{H}{\$42,390} = \dfrac{425}{3545}$

   and $H = \dfrac{425}{3545} \times \$42,390 = \$5082.017$

   Similarly, Dewey's share is $20,088.914 and Louie's share is $17,219.069.
   The combined allocations are:

   $20,464.138 + $5082.017 = $\underline{\$25,546.16 \text{ to Huey}}$
   $8770.345 + $20,088.914 = $\underline{\$28,859.26 \text{ to Dewey}}$
   $13,155.517 + $17,219.069 = $\underline{\$30,374.59 \text{ to Louie}}$

11. Initially, X1.00 purchases Y0.05614.
    After weakening 1.5%, X1.00 will purchase only
    Y0.05614 − 0.015(Y0.05614) = Y0.055298
    The exchange rates are then

    $\underline{\text{Y0.055298 per X1.00}}$ and $X\dfrac{1}{0.055298} = \underline{\text{X18.084 per Y1.00}}$

13. a. Inflation rate = Percent change in CPI

    (i) Inflation rate (4th year) = $\dfrac{105.7 - 103.3}{103.3} \times 100\% = \underline{2.3\%}$

    (ii) Inflation rate (5th year) = $\dfrac{108.9 - 105.7}{105.7} \times 100\% = \underline{3.0\%}$

    b. To maintain purchasing power, the amount of money must increase in proportion to the CPI.

    $\dfrac{\text{Amount (end)}}{\text{Amount (beginning)}} = \dfrac{\text{CPI (end)}}{\text{CPI (beginning)}}$

    Amount (end) = $\dfrac{108.9}{96.4} \times \$100 = \underline{\$112.97}$

Self-Test Exercise

1. *a.* $65:43 = 27.3 : x$

$$\frac{65}{43} = \frac{27.3}{x}$$

$$65x = 43(27.3)$$

$$x = \underline{18.06}$$

 b. $1410 : 2330 : 870 = a:550:b$

$$\frac{1410}{2330} = \frac{a}{550} \qquad \text{and} \qquad \frac{2330}{870} = \frac{550}{b}$$

$$a = \frac{1410}{2330} \times 550 = \underline{332.8} \qquad\qquad b = \frac{870}{2330} \times 550 = \underline{205.4}$$

2. Initially, Milan : Stephen : Fred : $135,000 = 3:4:2:9$

$$\frac{\text{Milan's investment}}{\$135,000} = \frac{3}{9}$$

Milan's investment $= \frac{3}{9} \times \$135,000 = \$45,000$

We similarly obtain

Stephen's investment = \$60,000 and Fred's investment = \$20,000.
After each partner contributes an additional \$10,000,
Milan : Stephen : Fred = \$55,000 : \$70,000 : \$30,000 = $\underline{11{:}14{:}6}$

3. Assuming $$\frac{\text{Test market sales}}{\text{Test market population}} = \frac{\text{Forecast 3-month sales}}{\text{Total population}}$$

 Then $$\frac{543}{120,000} = \frac{\text{Forecast 3-month sales}}{21,000,000}$$

 and Forecast 3-month sales $= \dfrac{543}{120,000} \times 21,000,000 = \underline{95,025 \text{ units}}$

4. Education : Health care : Social services $= 29:31:21$
\$13.7 billion : Health care : Social services $= 29:31:21$

$$\frac{\$13.7 \text{ billion}}{\text{Health care}} = \frac{29}{31} \qquad \text{and} \qquad \frac{\$13.7 \text{ billion}}{\text{Social services}} = \frac{29}{21}$$

Health care allocation $= \frac{31}{29} \times \$13.7$ billion $= \underline{\$14.64 \text{ billion}}$

Social services allocation $= \frac{21}{29} \times \$13.7$ billion $= \underline{\$9.92 \text{ billion}}$

5. We are given $L:M:N:P = 1.5 : 1.0 : 0.75 : 0.5$
If N = \$2000, then L:\$2000 = 1.5 : 0.75 and

$$\frac{L}{\$2000} = \frac{1.5}{0.75} = 2$$

$$L = 2(\$2000) = \$4000$$

Similarly, M = \$2666.67 and P = \$1333.33.
<u>Ms. L received \$4000</u>, <u>Mr. M received \$2666.67</u>, and <u>Mr. P received \$1333.33</u>.

6. Let W, S, and SS represent the wife's, son's, and stepson's shares, respectively. Then,

$$W:S:SS = \frac{7}{5}:1:\frac{5}{7} = 49:35:25 \quad \text{(after multiplying by 35)}$$

For a total distribution of $331,000,

W:S:SS:$331,000 = 49:35:25:(49 + 35 + 25)

Therefore,

$$\frac{W}{\$331,000} = \frac{49}{109} \quad \text{and}$$

$$W = \frac{49}{109} \times \$331,000 = \$148,798.17$$

Similarly, S = $106,284.40 and SS = $75,917.43.

Rounded to the nearest dollar, Mrs. Nolan will receive $148,798.17, the son will receive $106,284.40, and the stepson will receive $75,917.43.

7. $$\frac{\text{rupiah } x}{\text{C}\$1500} = \frac{\text{rupiah } 1.00}{\text{C}\$0.0001561}$$

$$\text{rupiah } x = \frac{\text{lira } 1.00}{\text{C}\$0.0001561} \times \text{C}\$1500 = \underline{\text{rupiah } 9,609,225}$$

8. To maintain purchasing power,

$$\frac{\text{New hourly rate}}{\text{Old hourly rate}} = \frac{\text{Current CPI}}{\text{Old CPI}}$$

$$\text{New rate} = \frac{108.4}{102.6} \times \$22.25 = \underline{\$23.51 \text{ per hour}}$$

9. Initially, ¥78.11 = C$1.00; Finally, ¥80.89 = C$1.00

Initially, $$\frac{\text{C}\$\text{price}}{¥2,965,000} = \frac{\text{C}\$1.00}{¥78.11}$$

That is, C$ price = $\frac{\text{C}\$1.00}{¥78.11} \times ¥2,965,000 = \text{C}\$37,959.29$

Finally, C$ price = $\frac{\text{C}\$1.00}{¥80.89} \times ¥2,965,000 = \text{C}\$36,6554.72$

Price change = C$37,959.29 − C$36,654.72 = C$1304.57 decrease.

10. Price of West Virginia coal = $\frac{\text{US}\$51}{1\,\text{ton}} = \frac{\text{US}\$51}{2000\,\text{lb}} \times \frac{2205\,\text{lb}}{1\,\text{metric ton}} = \frac{\text{US}\$56.2275}{1\,\text{metric ton}}$

Price of West Virginia coal in C$ = $\frac{\text{US}\$56.2275}{1\,\text{metric ton}} \times \frac{\text{C}\$1.00}{\text{US}\$0.75} = \text{C}\$74.97 \text{ per metric ton}$

It is C$74.97 − C$73.00 = C$1.97 per metric tonne cheaper to purchase Alberta coal.

4   Mathematics of Merchandising

Exercise 4.1

1. Amount of discount = $dL = 0.3\overline{3}(\$249) = \underline{\$83.00}$
   Net price = L − discount = \$249.00 − \$83.00 = $\underline{\$166.00}$

3. Amount of discount = L − N = \$127.98 − \$106.65 = $\underline{\$21.33}$
   Discount rate, $d = \dfrac{\text{Amount of discount}}{L} \times 100\% = \dfrac{\$21.33}{\$127.98} \times 100\% = \underline{16\tfrac{2}{3}\%}$

5. List price = $\dfrac{\text{Discount}}{d} = \dfrac{\$612.50}{0.35} = \underline{\$1750.00}$
   Net price = List price − Discount = \$1750.00 − \$612.50 = $\underline{\$1137.50}$

7. List price = N + Discount = \$15.07 + \$12.33 = $\underline{\$27.40}$
   Discount rate = $\dfrac{\text{Discount}}{L} \times 100\% = \dfrac{\$12.33}{\$27.40} \times 100\% = \underline{45.0\%}$

9. List price, $L = \dfrac{N}{1-d} = \dfrac{\$2849.00}{1-0.125} = \underline{\$3256.00}$
   Discount = L − N = \$3256.00 − \$2849.00 = $\underline{\$407.00}$

11. Net price, $N = L(1 - d_1)(1 - d_2) = \$99.00(1 - 0.30)(1 - 0.16667) = \underline{\$57.75}$
    Discount = L − N = \$99.00 − \$57.75 = $\underline{\$41.25}$

13. List price, $L = \dfrac{N}{(1-d_1)(1-d_2)(1-d_3)} = \dfrac{\$93.03}{(1-0.25)(1-0.1)(1-0.075)} = \underline{\$149.00}$
    Discount = L − N = \$149.00 − \$93.03 = $\underline{\$55.97}$

15. Net price, $N = L(1 - d) = \$135.00\,(1 - 0.38) = \underline{\$83.70}$

17. List price = $\dfrac{\text{Discount}}{d} = \dfrac{\$223.14}{0.375} = \$595.04$
    Net price = L − Discount = \$595.04 − \$223.14 = $\underline{\$371.90}$

19. Discount amount = L − N = \$369.00 − \$287.82 = \$81.18
    Discount rate = $\dfrac{\text{Discount}}{L} \times 100\% = \dfrac{\$81.18}{\$369.00} \times 100\% = \underline{22.0\%}$

21. Net price (Niagara) $= L(1 - d)$
                                $= \$72.00\,(1 - 0.24)$
                                $= \$54.72$
    Net price (Silverwood) $= L(1 - d)$
                  $\$54.72 = \$74.50(1 - d)$
           $1 - d = \dfrac{\$54.72}{\$74.50} = 0.7345$
    d(Silverwood) = 1 − 0.7345 = 0.2655 = $\underline{26.55\%}$

23. Selling price, $L = \dfrac{N}{1-d} = \dfrac{\$160{,}555.50}{1-0.055} = \underline{\$169{,}900.00}$

Exercise 4.1 *(continued)*

25. a. Net investment, $N = L(1 - d) = \$5500(1 - 0.055) = \underline{\$5197.50}$

    b. Total amount placed, $L = \dfrac{N}{1-d} = \dfrac{\$6426}{1-0.055} = \$6800$

    Commission paid $= L - N = \$6800 - \$6426 = \underline{\$374.00}$

27. Beginning value, $L = \dfrac{N}{1-d} = \dfrac{9561}{1-0.013} = 9686.9$

    Index decline $= L - N = 9686.9 - 9561 = \underline{125.9 \text{ points}}$

29. a. Amount in prior year's budget, $L = \dfrac{\text{Amount cut}}{d} = \dfrac{\$264 \text{ million}}{0.054} = \$4888.9 \text{ million}$

    New budget $= L - \text{Amount cut} = \$4888.9 \text{ million} - \$264 \text{ million} = \underline{\$4624.9 \text{ million}}$

    b. Current manpower, $L = \dfrac{N}{1-d} = \dfrac{58,600}{1-0.021} = 59,857$

    Proposed cut $= L - N = 59,857 - 58,600 = \underline{1257 \text{ people}}$

31. a. $N = L(1 - d_1)(1 - d_2)(1 - d_3)$

    $= \$11,500(1 - 0.25)(1 - 0.075)(1 - 0.05)$

    $= \underline{\$7579.22}$

    b. Quantity discount $= d_2 L(1 - d_1)$

    $= 0.075(\$11,500)(1 - 0.25)$

    $= \underline{\$646.88}$

    c. Joint promotion discount $= d_3 L(1 - d_1)(1 - d_2)$

    $= 0.05(\$11,500)(0.75)(0.925)$

    $= \underline{\$398.91}$

33. $N = L(1 - d_1)(1 - d_2)$

    $1 - d_2 = \dfrac{N}{L(1-d_1)} = \dfrac{\$36.66}{\$48.75(1-0.20)} = 0.9400$

    $d_2 = 1 - 0.9400 = 0.0600 = \underline{6.00\%}$

35. a. Service discount $= d_2 L(1 - d_1)$

    $= 0.125(\$3000)(1 - 0.20)$

    $= \underline{\$300.00}$

    b. Advertising and promotion discount $= d_3 L(1 - d_1)(1 - d_2)$

    $= 0.05(\$3000)(1 - 0.20)(1 - 0.125)$

    $= \underline{\$105.00}$

Exercise 4.2

1. $N = L(1 - d) = \$2365(1 - 0.02) = \underline{\$2317.70}$

3. $N = L(1 - d) = \$815.49(1 - 0.02) = \underline{\$799.18}$

5. Payment $= (\text{Amount credited})(1 - d) = \$1365.00(1 - 0.02) = \underline{\$1337.70}$

    Balance $= \text{Invoice amount} - \text{Amount credited} = \$2365.00 - \$1365.00 = \underline{\$1000.00}$

7. Amount credited = Invoice amount − Balance = $3765.25 − $2042.28 = <u>$1722.97</u>
   Payment = L(1 − d) = $1722.97(1 − 0.0133333) = <u>$1700.00</u>

9. The 2% discount period ends on June 1.
   The 1% discount period ends on June 11.
   a. The payment qualifies for a 2% discount.
      Payment = (Invoice amount)(1 − d) = $5076.64(1 − 0.02) = <u>$4975.11</u>
   b. The payment qualifies for a 1% discount.
      Payment = $5076.64(1 − 0.01) = <u>$5025.87</u>
   c. Same answer as in part *b*.

11. Amount credited = $\dfrac{\text{Payment}}{1-d} = \dfrac{\$2000}{1-0.02} = \$2040.82$
    Balance owed = $5076.64 − $2040.82 = <u>$3035.82</u>

13. a. The May 26 payment qualifies for a 2% discount.
       The June 4 payment qualifies for a 1% discount.
       Amount credited = $\dfrac{\$1000}{1-0.02} + \dfrac{\$1000}{1-0.01} = \$1020.41 + \$1010.10 = \$2030.51$
       Balance owed = $5076.64 − $2030.51 = <u>$3046.13</u>
    b. The credit period ends on May 22 + 30 days = <u>June 21</u>

15. The June 20 invoice does not qualify for a cash discount on July 4.
    Payment = $485 + $367(1 − 0.015) + $722(1 − 0.015) = <u>$1557.67</u>

17. Total amount credited = $\dfrac{\$900}{1-0.025} + \dfrac{\$850}{1-0.01} + \$700$
    $= \$923.08 + \$858.59 + \$700$
    $= \$2481.67$
    Balance owed = $2856.57 − $2481.67 = <u>$374.90</u>

19. Amount required to settle invoice #535 = $3228.56
    Amount required to settle invoice #598 = $2945.31(1 − 0.02) = $2886.40
    Amount to be applied to invoice #678 = $10,000.00 − $3228.56 − $2886.40 = $3885.04
    Amount credited to invoice #678 = $\dfrac{\$3885.04}{1-0.04} = \$4046.91$
    Balance owed on invoice #678 = $6217.69 − $4046.91 = $2170.78
    Payment on August 15 to settle invoice #678 = $2170.78(1 − 0.02) = <u>$2127.36</u>

21. Let the amount of each payment be represented by x. The total amount credited will be
    $$\frac{x}{1-0.02} + \frac{x}{1-0.01} + x = \$2956.60$$
    $$3.030509x = \$2956.60$$
    $$x = \underline{\$975.61}$$
    Each of the three payments should be $975.61.

Concept Questions (Section 4.3)

1. Both quantities have the same numerator, but the rate of markup has the smaller denominator (since $C<S$). Therefore, the rate of markup is larger than the gross profit margin.

3. Yes. If an item is marked up (M) by more than the unit cost (C), then

$$\text{Rate of markup} = \frac{M}{C} \times 100\% > 100\%$$

5. No. At the break-even point, there is no profit. The selling price at the break-even point still covers E as well as C. If an item is sold at cost, the merchant will *lose* E per unit sold.

Exercise 4.3

1. Enter the given data on a markup diagram.

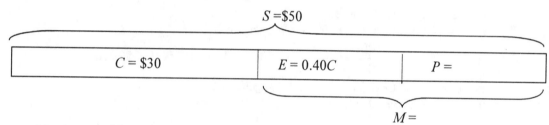

$S = \$50$

| C = \$30 | E = 0.40C | P = |

$M =$

    a. $M = S - C = \$50 - \$30 = \underline{\$20.00}$ (enter on the diagram)
    b. $E = 0.4C = 0.4(\$30) = \underline{\$12.00}$ (enter on the diagram)
    c. $P = M - E = \$20 - \$12 = \underline{\$8.00}$

    d. Rate of markup $= \dfrac{M}{C} \times 100\% = \dfrac{\$20}{\$30} \times 100\% = \underline{66.67\%}$

    e. Gross profit margin $= \dfrac{M}{S} \times 100\% = \dfrac{\$20}{\$50} \times 100\% = \underline{40.00\%}$

3. Enter the given data on a markup diagram.

$S = \$79.50$

| C = \$55.65 | E = 0.30S = | P = |

$M =$

    a. $M = S - C = \$79.50 - \$55.65 = \underline{\$23.85}$ (enter on diagram)
    b. $E = 0.3S = 0.3(\$79.50) = \underline{\$23.85}$ (enter on diagram)
    c. $P = M - E = \$23.85 - \$23.85 = \underline{\$0}$

    d. Rate of markup $= \dfrac{M}{C} \times 100\% = \dfrac{\$23.85}{\$55.65} \times 100\% = \underline{42.86\%}$

    e. Gross profit margin $= \dfrac{M}{S} \times 100\% = \dfrac{\$23.85}{\$79.50} \times 100\% = \underline{30.00\%}$

5. a. $M = S - C = \$77.00 - \$53.90 = \underline{\$23.10}$
    b. $E = 0.35S = 0.35(\$77.00) = \underline{\$26.95}$
    c. $P = M - E = \$23.10 - \$26.95 = \underline{- \$3.85}$ (loss)

    d. Rate of markup $= \dfrac{M}{C} \times 100\% = \dfrac{\$23.10}{\$53.10} \times 100\% = \underline{42.86\%}$

    e. Gross profit margin $= \dfrac{M}{S} \times 100\% = \dfrac{\$23.10}{\$77.00} \times 100\% = \underline{30.00\%}$

7. $S = C + M = \$152.50 + \$47.45 = \underline{\$199.95}$

    Rate of markup $= \dfrac{M}{C} \times 100\% = \dfrac{\$47.75}{\$152.50} \times 100\% = \underline{31.11\%}$

    Gross profit margin $= \dfrac{M}{S} \times 100\% = \dfrac{\$47.75}{\$199.95} \times 100\% = \underline{23.73\%}$

9. $C = S - M = \$1990 - \$435 = \underline{\$1555}$

    Rate of markup $= \dfrac{M}{C} \times 100\% = \dfrac{\$435}{\$1555} \times 100\% = \underline{27.97\%}$

    Gross profit margin $= \dfrac{M}{S} \times 100\% = \dfrac{\$435}{\$1990} \times 100\% = \underline{21.86\%}$

11. Since $\dfrac{M}{C} \times 100\% = \dfrac{M}{\$8.89} \times 100\% = 90\%$,

    then $M = 0.9 \times \$8.89 = \underline{\$8.00}$
    $S = C + M = \$8.89 + \$8.00 = \underline{\$16.89}$

    Gross profit margin $= \dfrac{M}{S} \times 100\% = \dfrac{\$8.00}{\$16.89} \times 100\% = \underline{47.37\%}$

13. Given: $C = \$10.95$; $S = \$24.95$
    Therefore, $M = S - C = \$24.95 - \$10.95 = \$14.00$

    Rate of markup $= \dfrac{M}{C} \times 100\% = \dfrac{\$14.00}{\$10.95} \times 100\% = \underline{127.85\%}$

    Gross profit margin $= \dfrac{M}{S} \times 100\% = \dfrac{\$14.00}{\$24.95} \times 100\% = \underline{56.11\%}$

15. Given: $C = \$19$ per cake; $S = 12(\$4.50) = \$54$ per cake
    Then $M = S - C = \$54 - \$19 = \$35$ per cake

    Rate of markup $= \dfrac{M}{C} \times 100\% = \dfrac{\$35}{\$19} \times 100\% = \underline{184.21\%}$

    Gross profit margin $= \dfrac{M}{S} \times 100\% = \dfrac{\$35}{\$54} \times 100\% = \underline{64.81\%}$

Exercise 4.3 (continued)

17. $C = N = L(1 - d_1)(1 - d_2) = \$380(1 - 0.20)(1 - 0.10) = \$273.60$

    a. Enter the given information on a markup diagram.

    $S = C + E + P = \$273.60 + 57.00 + \$33.00 + = \underline{\$363.60}$

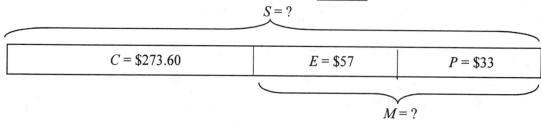

    b. $M = E + P = \$57.00 + \$33.00 = \$90.00$

    Rate of markup $= \dfrac{M}{C} \times 100\% = \dfrac{\$90.00}{\$273.60} \times 100\% = \underline{32.89\%}$

    c. Gross profit margin $= \dfrac{M}{S} \times 100\% = \dfrac{\$90.00}{\$363.60} \times 100\% = \underline{24.75\%}$

    d. $S(\text{break-even}) = C + E = \$273.60 + \$57.00 = \underline{\$330.60}$

19. Given: $S = \$54.95$; $M = 0.45C$

    a. Substitute into $S = C + M$

    $\$54.95 = 0.45C + C$

    $C = \dfrac{\$54.95}{1.45} = \underline{\$37.90}$

    b. $M = S - C = \$54.95 - \$37.90 = \$17.05$

    Gross profit margin $= \dfrac{M}{S} \times 100\% = \dfrac{\$17.05}{\$54.95} \times 100\% = \underline{31.03\%}$

21. Given: $M = 0.60S$

    Choose any value of S, say $S = \$1.00$ per head of lettuce.

    Then $M = \$0.60$ and $C = \$0.40$

    Rate of markup $= \dfrac{M}{C} \times 100\% = \dfrac{\$0.60}{\$0.40} \times 100\% = \underline{150\%}$

23. Given: $C = \$15$, $M = 0.90C$, $E = 0.20S$

    $S(\text{break-even}) = C + M = \$15 + 0.90(\$15) = \underline{\$28.50}$

    $E = 0.20S = 0.20(\$28.50) = \$5.70$

    Therefore,

    $P = S - C - E = \$28.50 - \$15 - \$5.70 = \underline{\$7.80}$

25. Given: $C = N = L(1 - d_1)(1 - d_2) = \$36(1 - 0.30)(1 - 0.05) = \$23.94$

    $E = 0.20S$ and $P = 0.12S$

    Substitute these values into $S = E + P + C$ and solve for S.

    $S = 0.20S + 0.12S + \$23.94$

    $0.68S = \$23.94$

    $S = \dfrac{\$23.94}{0.68} = \underline{\underline{\$35.21}}$

27. Given: $M = 0.40S$, $E = 0.30C$, $S = \$495$

    Therefore, $M = 0.40(\$495) = \$198$

    $C = S - M = \$495 - \$198 = \$297$

    $P = M - E = \$198 - 0.30(\$297) = \underline{\$108.90}$

Concept Questions (Section 4.4)

1. No. The base for the rate of markup is the unit cost C. The base for the markdown is the selling price S. Since $C < S$, a 40% markup represents a smaller dollar amount than a 40% markdown on the same item. A 40% markup followed by a 40% markdown will give a reduced selling price that is *less* than C.

Exercise 4.4

1. Given: $C = \$185$, $M = 0.50C$, $D = \$60$
   Enter these values on a markup/markdown diagram.

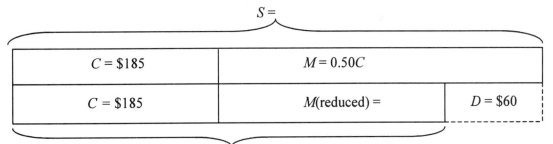

$$S =$$

C = \$185	M = 0.50C	
C = \$185	M(reduced) =	D = \$60

$$S(\text{reduced}) =$$

$M = 0.5C = 0.5(\$185) = \$92.50$

$S = C + M = \$185 + \$92.50 = \underline{\$277.50}$

Gross profit margin $= \dfrac{M}{S} \times 100\% = \dfrac{\$92.50}{\$277.50} \times 100\% = \underline{33.33\%}$

Rate of markdown $= \dfrac{D}{S} \times 100\% = \dfrac{\$60}{\$277.50} \times 100\% = \underline{21.62\%}$

$S(\text{reduced}) = S - D = \$277.50 - \$60 = \underline{\$217.50}$

3. Given: $C = \$24.99$; $S = \$49.98$; $S(\text{reduced}) = \$24.99$
   Enter these values on a markup/markdown diagram.

$$S = \$49.98$$

C = \$24.99	M =	
C = \$24.99	M(reduced) =	D =

$$S(\text{reduced}) = \$24.99$$

From the upper part of the diagram, $M = S - C = \$49.98 - \$24.99 = \$24.99$

From the lower part, $D = S - S(\text{reduced}) = \$49.98 - \$24.99 = \underline{\$24.99}$

Rate of markup $= \dfrac{M}{C} \times 100\% = \dfrac{\$24.99}{\$24.99} \times 100\% = \underline{100.0\%}$

Gross profit margin $= \dfrac{M}{S} \times 100\% = \dfrac{\$24.99}{\$49.98} \times 100\% = \underline{50\%}$

Rate of markdown $= \dfrac{D}{S} \times 100\% = \dfrac{\$24.99}{\$49.98} \times 100\% = \underline{50\%}$

Exercise 4.4 *(continued)*

5. Given: $C = \$19.25$; $M = 0.35S$, $D = 0.25S$
   Enter these values on a markup/markdown diagram.

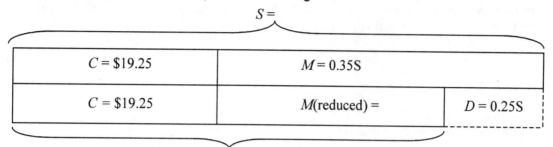

$S =$

| $C = \$19.25$ | $M = 0.35S$ | |
| $C = \$19.25$ | M(reduced) = | $D = 0.25S$ |

S(reduced) =

From the upper part of the diagram, $S = C + M = \$19.25 + 0.35S$
That is, $\qquad S - 0.35S = \$19.25$
$\qquad\qquad S = \$19.25/0.65 = \$29.62$
$M = S - C = \$29.62 - \$19.25 = \$10.37$
Rate of markup = $\dfrac{M}{C} \times 100\% = \dfrac{\$10.37}{\$19.25} \times 100\% = \underline{53.87\%}$
$D = 0.25S = 0.25(\$29.62) = \underline{\$7.41}$
S(reduced) $= S - D = \$29.62 - \$7.41 = \underline{\$22.21}$

7. a. $M = S - C = \$59.98 - \$37.50 = \$22.48$
   $\qquad$ Rate of markup = $\dfrac{M}{C} \times 100\% = \dfrac{\$22.48}{\$37.50} \times 100\% = \underline{59.95\%}$
   b. Gross profit margin = $\dfrac{M}{S} \times 100\% = \dfrac{\$22.48}{\$59.98} \times 100\% = \underline{37.48\%}$
   c. $D = S - S$(reduced) $= \$59.98 - \$37.50 = \$22.48$
   $\qquad$ Rate of markdown = $\dfrac{D}{S} \times 100\% = \dfrac{\$22.48}{\$59.98} \times 100\% = \underline{37.48\%}$

9. Given: $C = \$193.60$; $M = 0.45S$; $D = 0.35S$
   Enter these values on a markup/markdown diagram.

$S =$

| $C = \$193.60$ | $M = 0.45S$ | |
| $C = \$193.60$ | M(reduced) = | $D = 0.35S$ |

S(reduced) =

From the upper part of the diagram, $S = C + M = \$193.60 + 0.45S$
That is, $\qquad S - 0.45S = \$193.60$
$\qquad\qquad S = \dfrac{\$193.60}{0.55} = \$352.00$
$D = 0.35S = 0.35(\$352.00) = \$123.20$
S(reduced) $= S - D = \$352.00 - \$123.20 = \underline{\$228.80}$

Exercise 4.4 (continued)

11. Given: $S_C = \$69.95$; $S_D = \$64.95$

    a. $S_D(\text{reduced}) = \$64.95(1 - 0.20) = \$51.96$

       C's discount = $\$69.95 - \$51.96 = \$17.99$

       To match D's price, C must give a discount rate of $\dfrac{\$17.99}{\$69.95} \times 100\% = \underline{25.72\%}$

    b. $S_C(\text{reduced}) = \$69.95(1 - 0.20) = \$55.96$

       C's discount = $\$64.95 - \$55.96 = \$8.99$

       To match C's price, D must give a discount rate of $\dfrac{\$8.99}{\$64.95} \times 100\% = \underline{13.84\%}$

Exercise 4.5

1. Given: $C = \$37.25$; $E = 0.20C = 0.20(\$37.25) = \$7.45$;
   $M = 0.60C = 0.60(\$37.25) = \$22.35$; and $S(\text{reduced}) = \$41.72$

   Then $S = C + M = \$37.25 + \$22.35 = \underline{\$59.60}$

   $D = S - S(\text{reduced}) = \$59.60 - \$41.72 = \$17.88$

   Rate of markdown = $\dfrac{D}{S} \times 100\% = \dfrac{\$17.88}{\$59.60} \times 100\% = \underline{30.00\%}$

   $P(\text{reduced}) = S(\text{reduced}) - C - E = \$41.72 - \$37.25 - \$7.45 = -\$2.98$

   That is, the reduced profit is a $\underline{\$2.98 \text{ loss}}$.

3. Given: $C = \$98.00$; $S = \$147.00$; $E = 0.18S = 0.18(\$147.00) = \$26.46$;
   and $D = 0.16667(S) = 0.16667(\$147.00) = \$24.50$

   Then $M = S - C = \$147.00 - \$98.00 = \$49.00$

   Rate of markup = $\dfrac{M}{C} \times 100\% = \dfrac{\$49.00}{\$147.00} \times 100\% = \underline{33.33\%}$

   $S(\text{reduced}) = S - D = \$147.00 - \$24.50 = \underline{\$122.50}$

   $P(\text{reduced}) = S(\text{reduced}) - C - E = \$122.50 - \$98.00 - \$26.46 = -\$1.96$

   That is, the reduced profit is a $\underline{\$1.96 \text{ loss}}$.

5. Given: $C = \$81$; $M = 0.40S$; Rate of markdown = 20%

   Since $\quad C = S - M = S - 0.40S = 0.60S$

   Then $\quad S = \dfrac{C}{0.6} = \dfrac{\$81}{0.6} = \$135$

   and $\quad S(\text{reduced}) = \$135(1 - 0.20) = \underline{\$108.00}$

7. Given: $M = 0.45S$; $S = \$140$; $M(\text{reduced}) = 0.20C$

   Then $\quad M = 0.45(\$140) = \$63$

   and $\quad C = S - M = \$140 - \$63 = \$77$

   Therefore, $\quad S(\text{reduced}) = C + M(\text{reduced}) = C + 0.20C = 1.2(\$77) = \$92.40$

   and $\quad$ Rate of markdown = $\dfrac{D}{S} \times 100\% = \dfrac{\$140 - \$92.40}{\$140} \times 100\% = \underline{34.00\%}$

Exercise 4.5 *(continued)*

9. $C = N = L(1 - d_1)(1 - d_2) = \$480(1 - 0.40)(1 - 0.25) = \$216.00$

   a. $M = 1.2C = 1.2(\$216) = \$259.20$
       $S = C + M = \$216 + \$259.20 = \$475.20$
       $S(\text{reduced}) = S - D = \$475.20 - 0.40(\$475.20) = \underline{\$285.12}$

   b. $M(\text{reduced}) = S(\text{reduced}) - C = \$285.12 - \$216.00 = \$69.12$

       Rate of markup (reduced)$= \dfrac{M(\text{reduced})}{C} \times 100\% = \dfrac{\$69.12}{\$216.00} \times 100\% = \underline{32.00\%}$

   c. $P(\text{reduced}) = M(\text{reduced}) - E = \$69.12 - 0.55(\$216.00) = -\$49.68$
       That is, the reduced profit is a $\underline{\$49.68 \text{ loss}}$.

11. $C = N = L(1 - d) = \$360(1 - 0.25) = \$270$

   a. At the break-even point, $D = P = 0.15S$
       Therefore, to break even,

       Rate of markdown $= \dfrac{D}{S} \times 100\% = \dfrac{0.15S}{S} \times 100\% = \underline{15.00\%}$

   b. If $D = 0.15S$ results in break-even;
       then $D = 0.20S$ will result in a loss of $0.05S$.
       $S = C + E + P = \$270.00 + 0.16667S + 0.15S$
       Solving for S, we obtain
       $\qquad 0.68333S = \$270.00$
       $\qquad\qquad\quad S = \$395.12$
       $\underline{\text{Loss}}$ per unit $= 0.05S = 0.05(\$395.12) = \underline{\$19.76}$

13. $C = N = L(1 - d_1)(1 - d_2) = \$30(1 - 0.45)(1 - 0.10) = \$14.85$
     $S = C + E + P = C + 0.5C + 0.3C = 1.8C = 1.8(\$14.85) = \$26.73$
     If the markdown results in a loss of $0.25E$, then
     $D = P + 0.25E = 0.3C + 0.25(0.5C) = 0.425C = 0.425(\$14.85) = \$6.31$

     Rate of markdown $= \dfrac{D}{S} \times 100\% = \dfrac{\$6.31}{\$26.73} \times 100\% = \underline{23.61\%}$

15. $C = N = L(1 - d_1)(1 - d_2) = \$72(1 - 0.40)(1 - 0.15) = \$36.72$

   a. If $M = 0.40S$, then $C = 0.40S$ (since $S = C + M$)

       Therefore, $S = \dfrac{C}{0.60} = \dfrac{\$36.72}{0.60} = \$61.20$

       $D = S - S(\text{reduced}) = \$61.20 - \$45.90 = \$15.30$

       Rate of markdown $= \dfrac{D}{S} \times 100\% = \dfrac{\$15.30}{\$61.20} \times 100\% = \underline{25.00\%}$

   b. $P(\text{reduced}) = S(\text{reduced}) - C - E = \$45.90 - \$36.72 - 0.25(\$61.20) = \underline{-\$6.12}$
       That is, a $\underline{\text{loss of \$6.12}}$ per sweater.

   c. $M(\text{reduced}) = S(\text{reduced}) - C = \$45.90 - \$36.72 = \$9.18$

       Rate of markup (reduced) $= \dfrac{M(\text{reduced})}{C} \times 100\% = \dfrac{\$9.18}{\$36.72} \times 100\% = \underline{25.00\%}$

17. Given: C = $665; $D = 0.20S$; and M(reduced) = 0.30S(reduced)
    Enter the given amounts on a markup/markdown diagram.

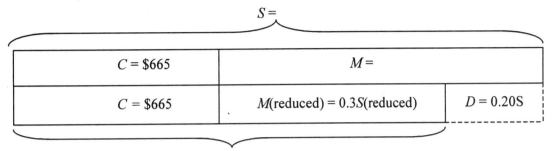

$$S =$$

| $C = \$665$ | $M =$ | |
| $C = \$665$ | M(reduced) = 0.3S(reduced) | $D = 0.20S$ |

$$S(\text{reduced}) =$$

  a. From the lower part of the diagram,
$$S(\text{reduced}) = C + M(\text{reduced}) = \$665 + 0.3S(\text{reduced})$$
$$S(\text{reduced}) = \frac{\$665}{0.7} = \underline{\$950.00}$$

  b. Also, $S = S(\text{reduced}) + D = \$950.00 + 0.20S$
Solving for S,
$$S = \frac{\$950.00}{0.80} = \underline{\$1187.50}$$

19. $C = N = L(1 - d_1)(1 - d_2) = \$2400(1 - 0.30)(1 - 0.15) = \$1428.00$
    Given: $E = 0.40C$ and P(reduced) $= 0.25C$ when $D = 0.20S$

  a. $S(\text{reduced}) = C + E + P(\text{reduced}) = C + 0.4C + 0.25C = 1.65C = 1.65(\$1428) = \underline{\$2356.20}$
Since $S(\text{reduced}) = S - D$
then $\$2356.20 = S - 0.20S = 0.80S$
        $S = \underline{\$2945.25}$

  b. At $D = 0.3\bar{3}S$,
$$S(\text{special}) = S - D = S - 0.3\bar{3}S = 0.6\bar{6}S = 0.6\bar{6}\,(\$2945.25) = \$1963.50$$
$$\begin{aligned} P(\text{special}) &= S(\text{special}) - C - E \\ &= \$1963.50 - C - 0.4C \\ &= \$1963.50 - 1.4C \\ &= \$1963.50 - 1.4(\$1428) \\ &= -\$35.70 \end{aligned}$$
That is, there was a <u>loss of $35.70</u> at the special price.

Review Problems

1. Discount, dL = $136.92

    $$0.28L = \$136.92$$

    $$L = \$489.00$$

    N = $489.00 − $136.92 = <u>$352.08</u>

3. N = L(1 − d) = $43.00(1 − 0.25) = $32.25

    Discount = $44.50 − $32.25 = $12.25

    Discount rate = $\dfrac{\$12.25}{\$44.50} \times 100\% = \underline{27.53\%}$

5. *a.* Fee = 0.029($28,476) = <u>$825.80</u>

   b. dL = $981.71

    $L = \dfrac{\$981.71}{0.029} = \underline{\$33,852.07}$

7. Beginning price, $L = \dfrac{N}{1-d} = \dfrac{\$1.10}{1-0.78} = \underline{\$5.00}$

9. *a.* 1985 population, $L = \dfrac{N}{(1-d_1)(1-d_2)(1-d_3)} = \dfrac{9320}{(1-0.032)(1-0.052)(1-0.047)} = \underline{10,657}$

   b. 1985 − 1989 decline = d_1L = 0.032(10,657) = <u>341</u>

    1990 − 1994 decline = d_2(10,657 − 341) = 0.052(10,316) = <u>536</u>

    1995 − 1999 decline = d_3(10,316 − 536) = 0.047(9780) = <u>460</u>

11. Total amount credited = $\dfrac{\$1100}{1-0.02} + \dfrac{\$900}{1-0.01} + \$800 = \$2831.54$

    Balance owed = $3691.00 − $2831.54 = <u>$859.46</u>

13. Given: M = 0.55S

    Choose any value of S, say S = $3.00 per pound.

    Then M = 0.55($3.00) = $1.65 and $C = S − M$ = $3.00 − $1.65 = $1.35

    Rate of markup = $\dfrac{M}{C} \times 100\% = \dfrac{\$1.65}{\$1.35} \times 100\% = \underline{122.22\%}$

15. Given: C = $492; D = 0.30S; and M = 0.40S

    $S = C + M$ = $492 + 0.40$S$

    $$0.60S = \$492$$

    $S = \dfrac{\$492}{0.6} = \$820$

    S(reduced) = $S − D$ = $820 − 0.30($820) = <u>$574.00</u>

Review Problems (continued)

17. Given: $S = \$489$, $E = 0.20C$, and $P = 0.1\overline{6}C$

    a.   Substitute into $S = C + E + P$

$$\$489 = C + 0.20C + 0.1\overline{6}C = 1.3\overline{6}C$$

$$C = \frac{\$489}{1.3\overline{6}} = \$357.80$$

           To break even, $D = P = 0.1\overline{6}C = 0.1\overline{6}(\$357.80) = \underline{\$59.63}$

    b.   If $S(\text{reduced}) = C = \$357.80$

           then $D = S - S(\text{reduced}) = \$489 - \$357.80 = \$131.20$

           and Rate of markdown $= \dfrac{D}{S} \times 100\% = \dfrac{\$131.20}{\$489} \times 100\% = \underline{26.83\%}$

Self-Test Exercise

1. $N_A = L(1 - d) = \$196.00(1 - 0.20) = \$156.80$

     $N_B = L(1 - d) = \$186.60(1 - 0.1\overline{6}) = \$155.50$

     <u>Source B is $1.30 cheaper</u>.

2.   Discount = dL

     $\$337.05 = 0.225L$

          $L = \$1498.00$

     $N = L - dL = \$1498.00 - \$337.05 = \underline{\$1160.95}$

3.   Lowest selling price, $L = \dfrac{N}{1 - d} = \dfrac{\$160,000}{1 - 0.055} = \underline{\$169,300}$

4. a. $N = L(1 - d_1)(1 - d_2)(1 - d_3) = \$1195(1 - 0.25)(1 - 0.08\overline{3})(1 - 0.05) = \underline{\$780.48}$

   b. $L = \dfrac{N}{(1 - d_1)(1 - d_2)(1 - d_3)} = \dfrac{\$470.25}{(1 - 0.25)(1 - 0.08\overline{3})(1 - 0.05)} = \underline{\$720.00}$

   c.   Using the data from part a,

        Discount $= \$1195.00 - \$780.48 = \$414.52$

        Equivalent single discount rate $= \dfrac{\text{Discount}}{L} = \dfrac{\$414.52}{\$1195.00} = 0.3469 = \underline{34.69\%}$

   d.   Amount of discount for a January order $= d_3L(1 - d_1)(1 - d_2)$

$$= 0.05(\$1000)(1 - 0.25)(1 - 0.08\overline{3})$$

$$= \underline{\$34.38}$$

5. a.   Beginning price, $L = \dfrac{\text{Ending price}, N}{(1 - d_1)(1 - d_2)(1 - d_3)}$

$$= \dfrac{\$0.50}{(1 - 0.40)(1 - 0.60)(1 - 0.70)}$$

$$= \underline{\$6.94}$$

   b.   Decline in Year 2 $= d_2L(1 - d_1)$

$$= 0.60(\$6.94)(1 - 0.40)$$

$$= \underline{\$2.50}$$

6. Amount credited on December 2 = $\dfrac{\$4000}{1-0.03}$ = $4123.71

    Balance owed after December 2 payment = $7260 − $4123.71 = $3136.29
    Payment to settle invoice on December 16 = $3136.29(1 − 0.015) = $3089.25

7. Amount credited = $887.00 − $378.09 = $509.91

    Discount rate = $\dfrac{\$8.91}{\$508.91}$ × 100% = 1.75%

8. *a.* Given: S = $87.49 and M = 0.30C
    Substitute into $S = C + M$
    $87.49 = C + 0.30C$

    $C = \dfrac{\$87.49}{1.3}$ = $67.30

   b. Given: S = $87.49 and M = 0.30S
    Substitute into $S = C + M$
    $87.49 = C + 0.30(\$87.49)$
    C = $61.24

9. $C = N = L(1 - d_1)(1 - d_2)$ = $19.50(1 − 0.4) = $11.70

    Given: E = 0.3$\overline{3}S$ and P = 0.10S

   a. Substitute into $S = C + E + P$
    S = $11.70 + 0.3$\overline{3}S$ + 0.10S
    $S - 0.4\overline{3}S$ = $11.70
    S = $20.65

   b. $M = S - C$ = $20.65 − $11.70 = $8.95

    Rate of markup = $\dfrac{M}{C}$ × 100% = $\dfrac{\$8.95}{\$11.70}$ × 100% = 76.50%

   c. Break-even price = $S - P$ = $20.65 − 0.1($20.65) = $18.59

10. Given: E = 0.3$\overline{3}C$ and P = 0.20C

   a. Substitute into $S = C + E + P$
    $S = C + 0.3\overline{3}C + 0.20C = 1.5\overline{3}C$
    That is, regular S is 153.33% of cost.

   b. For member purchases, D = 0.10C

    Rate of markdown = $\dfrac{D}{S}$ × 100% = $\dfrac{0.10C}{1.5\overline{3}C}$ × 100% = 6.52%

11. $C = N = L(1 - d_1)(1 - d_2) = \$360(1 - 0.3\overline{3})(1 - 0.10) = \$216.00$

      Given: $M = 0.40S$, $E = 0.22S$, and S(reduced) = \$270

   a. $S = C + M = \$216.00 + 0.40S$

        $0.60S = \$216$

           $S = \$360$

      $D = S - S$(reduced) = \$360 - \$270 = \$90.00

      Rate of markdown $= \dfrac{D}{S} \times 100\% = \dfrac{\$90}{\$360} \times 100\% = \underline{25.00\%}$

   b. P(reduced) = S(reduced) $- C - E = \$270 - \$216 - 0.22(\$360) = -\$25.20$

      That is, there was a <u>loss of \$25.20 per pair</u>.

   c. M(reduced) = S(reduced) $- C = \$270 - \$216 = \$54$

      Rate of markup $= \dfrac{M(\text{reduced})}{C} \times 100\% = \dfrac{\$54}{\$216} \times 100\% = \underline{25.00\%}$

Exercise 4A

1. <u>\$3765.25</u> since the payment was made within 30 days after the end of the invoicing month (December).

3. The cash discount applies to payments made within the period May 29 to June 7 inclusive. On June 8 the full amount, <u>\$1450.61</u>, must be paid.

5. Payment, N = L(1 − d) = \$1421.32(1 − 0.015) = <u>\$1400.00</u>
    Balance = \$2365 − \$1421.32 = <u>\$943.68</u>

7. Amount credited = \$1450.61 − \$943.00 = <u>\$507.61</u>
    Cash discount = \$507.61 − \$500.00 = \$7.61
    Discount rate $= \dfrac{\$7.61}{507.61} \times 100\% = \underline{1.50\%}$

9. a.   April 30 + 15 days = <u>May 15</u>

  b.   May 15 + 20 days = <u>June 4</u>

  c.   Payment = (Amount credited)(1 − d) = \$800(1 − 0.015) = <u>\$788.00</u>

  d.   Amount credited $= \dfrac{\text{Amount paid}}{1 - d} = \dfrac{\$800}{1 - 0.015} = \$812.18$

      Balance = \$2678.50 − \$800.00 − \$812.18 = <u>\$1066.32</u>

  e.   Amount credited = \$1066.32 − \$800.00 = \$266.32
          Payment = \$266.32(1 − 0.015) = <u>\$262.33</u>

11. a.   Amount credited $= \dfrac{\text{Amount paid}}{1 - d} = \dfrac{\$8000}{1 - 0.02} = \underline{\$8163.27}$

  b.   Balance = \$14,772.00 − \$8163.27 = <u>\$6608.73</u>

13. Net invoice amount = 4(\$3900)(1 − 0.20)(1 − 0.07) + 6(\$4880)(1 − 0.25)(1 − 0.05)
                     = \$11,606.40 + \$29,280.00
                     = \$32,468.40
      Amount credited = 0.5(\$32,468.40) = \$16,234.20
      Payment = \$16,234.20(1 − 0.025) = <u>\$15,828.35</u>

5   Applications of Linear Equations

Exercise 5.1

1. a. <u>Variable cost</u>   e. <u>Fixed cost</u>
   b. <u>Fixed cost</u>   f. <u>Mixed cost</u>
   c. <u>Mixed cost</u>   g. <u>Variable cost</u>
   d. <u>Variable cost</u>   h. <u>Fixed cost</u>

3. Total variable costs = $1,600,000 – $400,000 = $1,200,000
   If production increases by 20% (from 50,000 to 60,000 units), total
   variable costs will also increase by 20% from
         $1,200,000   to   1.2($1,200,000) = $1,440,000
   and total costs will increase from
         $1,600,000   to $400,000 + $1,440,000 = <u>$1,840,000</u>

Concept Questions (Exercise 5.2)

1. a. Since $CM = S - VC$, CM will <u>increase</u> if S is increased.

   b. Raw materials are part of VC. VC will decrease if the cost of raw materials decreases.
      Therefore, CM will <u>increase</u>.

   c. The property tax is part of FC. There will <u>no change in CM</u>.

   d. The salaries of executives are part of FC. There will <u>no change in CM</u>.

   e. Wages of production workers are part of VC. VC will increase and <u>CM will decrease</u>.

3. a. The <u>break-even volume will be lowered</u> since fewer units need to be sold to cover the
      reduced fixed costs.

   b. If unit variable costs (VC) increase, the contribution margin ($CM = S - VC$) decreases
      and more units must be sold to cover the unchanged fixed costs. Therefore, the <u>break-
      even point is higher</u>.

   c. <u>No change</u>—the actual sales volume does not affect the break-even point.

   d. If S decreases, the contribution margin ($CM = S - VC$) decreases and more units must
      be sold to cover the unchanged fixed costs. Therefore, the <u>break-even point is higher</u>.

   e. If the contribution rate (or ratio) CR increases, a larger portion of each unit's selling
      price is available to pay fixed costs. Therefore, the <u>break-even point is lower</u>.

Exercise 5.2

1. Given: S = $30; VC = $10; FC = $100,000 per year
   a. Each toy sold contributes
      $$CM = S - VC = \$30 - \$10 = \$20$$
      to the payment of fixed costs. To cover $100,000 of fixed costs
      (and break even), Toys-4-U needs to sell
      $$\frac{FC}{CM} = \frac{\$100,000 \text{ per year}}{\$20} = \underline{5000 \text{ toys per year}}$$
   b. Break-even revenue = 5000($30) = <u>$150,000 per year</u>

Exercise 5.2 *(continued)*

3. Given: $S = \$3.20$; $VC = \$1.20$; $FC = \$250$ per month

   a. $FC = 12(\$250) = \$3000$ per year

   Each jar sold contributes
   $$CM = S - VC = \$3.20 - \$1.20 = \$2.00$$
   to the payment of fixed costs. To cover $3000 of fixed costs
   (and break even), Ingrid must sell
   $$\frac{FC}{CM} = \frac{\$3000 \text{ per year}}{\$2.00} = \underline{1500 \text{ jars per year}}$$

   b. If Ingrid sells 3000 jars per year, this sales level is 1500 jars above break-even. Each
   of these jars contributes $CM = \$2.00$ to profit.
   Total profit = $1500(\$2.00) = \underline{\$3000}$

5. Given: $S = \$2.50$; $VC = \$1.00$; $FC = \$60,000$ per month

   a. $CM = S - VC = \$2.50 - \$1.00 = \$1.50$ per disc
   $$\text{Break-even volume} = \frac{FC}{CM} = \frac{\$60,000}{\$1.50} = \underline{40,000 \text{ discs per month}}$$

   b. For $NI = \$7500$ per month, sales must be
   $$\frac{NI}{CM} = \frac{\$7500}{\$1.50} = 5000 \text{ units above breakeven.}$$
   Total sales must be 40,000 + 5000 = $\underline{45,000 \text{ discs per month}}$

7. Given: $S = 10¢$ per copy; $FC = \$300$ per month;
   $$VC = 1.5¢ + \frac{\$5.00}{500} + \frac{\$100.00}{5000} + 0.5¢ = 5¢ \text{ per copy}$$

   a. $CM = S - VC = 10¢ - 5¢ = 5¢$ per copy
   $$\text{Break-even volume} = \frac{FC}{CM} = \frac{\$300}{\$0.05} = \underline{6000 \text{ copies per month}}$$

   b. Each additional 1000 copies per month will add profit of
   $1000CM = 1000(\$0.05) = \underline{\$50 \text{ per month}}$

9. Given: Capacity = 250 units per week

   a. $S = \$20$, $VC = \$12$, $FC = \$1200$ per week
   $$CM = S - VC = \$20 - \$12 = \$8.00$$
   $$\text{Break-even volume} = \frac{FC}{CM} = \frac{\$1200}{\$8} = \underline{150 \text{ units per week}}$$

   b. (i) At 30 units per week short of breakeven,
   there will be a loss of $X(CM) = 30(\$8) = \$240$/week.
   At 100 units per week above breakeven,
   there will be a profit of $100(\$8) = \$800$/week.

   c. For a net income of $400/week, sales must be
   $$\frac{NI}{CM} = \frac{\$400}{\$8} = 50 \text{ units above breakeven}$$
   Hence, sales must be 150 + 50 = $\underline{200 \text{ units per week}}$

Exercise 5.2 (continued)

11. a. Contribution rate, $CR = \dfrac{\text{Total revenue} - \text{Total variable costs}}{\text{Total revenue}} \times 100\%$

$\quad\quad = \dfrac{\$18,000,000 - \$6,000,000}{\$18,000,000} \times 100\%$

$\quad\quad = 66.\overline{6}\%$

Break - even revenue $= \dfrac{FC}{CR} = \dfrac{\$10,000,000}{0.6\overline{6}} = \$15,000,000$

If revenue of \$18,000,000 represents 90% of capacity, then

Revenue at full capacity $= \dfrac{100\%}{90\%} \times \$18,000,000 = \$20,000,000$

and break-even revenue represents $\dfrac{\$15,000,000}{\$20,000,000} \times 100\%$ = <u>75% of capacity</u>

b. At 70% of capacity,

$\quad\quad$ Revenue = 0.70(\$20,000,000) = \$14,000,000

and $\quad$ Total variable costs $= \dfrac{\$14,000,000}{\$18,000,000} \times \$6,000,000 = \$4,666,667$

Net income = \$14,000,000 − \$10,000,000 − \$4,666,667 = <u>−\$666,667</u>

That is, Beta would lose \$666,667.

13. Given: VC = \$43, S = \$70, FC = \$648,000/year = \$54,000/month

Production capacity = 3200 borgels per month

a. $CM = S - VC$ = \$70 − \$43 = \$27

$\quad$ Break-even volume $= \dfrac{FC}{CM} = \dfrac{\$54,000}{\$27}$ = <u>2000 borgels/month</u>

b. At 500 borgels/month in excess of break even,

$\quad\quad NI$ = 500(CM) = 500(\$27) = <u>\$13,500/month</u>

c. At 50% of capacity,

$\quad\quad X$ = 0.5(3200 borgels/month) = 1600 borgels/month

This is 400 borgels/month below breakeven.

Hence, Reflex will lose 400(\$27) = <u>\$10,800/month</u>

d. For NI = \$226,800/year = \$18,900/month,

$\quad\quad X = 2000 + \dfrac{\$18,900}{\$27}$ = 2700 units/month

which is $\dfrac{2700}{3200} \times 100\%$ = <u>84.4% of capacity</u>

e. If S is \$1 higher while VC and FC are unchanged,

then CM will increase by \$1 to \$28 and

$\quad\quad$ Break-even volume $= \dfrac{\$54,000}{\$28}$ = 1929

That is, the break-even volume <u>decreases by 71 borgels/month</u> for

a \$1increase in the selling price.

Exercise 5.2 *(continued)*

15. Given: In the first quarter (Q1), $TR = \$4,500,000$; $NI = \$900,000$; $X = 60,000$ tires.
    In the second quarter (Q2), $NI = \$700,000$; $X = 50,000$ tires.

    Since $TR = (S)X$, then $S = \dfrac{TR}{X} = \dfrac{\$4,500,000}{60,000} = \underline{\$75\ per\ tire}$

    Also, $TR = \$75 \times 50,000 = \underline{\$3,750,000\ in\ Q2}$.

    Since $NI = (CM)X - FC$

then for Q1,	$\$900,000 = (CM)60,000 - FC$	①
and for Q2,	$\underline{\$700,000 = (CM)50,000 - FC}$	②
Subtract:	$\$200,000 = (CM)10,000$	

    $$CM = \frac{\$200,000}{10,000} = \underline{\$20\ per\ tire}$$

    Substitute $CM = \$20$ into ②:

    $$\$700,000 = (\$20)50,000 - FC$$

    Therefore, $FC = \$1,000,000 - \$700,000 = \underline{\$300,000\ per\ quarter}$

    Since $CM = S - VC$
    then $VC = S - CM = \$75 - \$20 = \underline{\$55\ per\ tire}$

17. a. (Total) variable costs = Sales $- FC - NI$
       = $\$400,000 - \$100,000 - \$60,000$
       = $\underline{\$240,000}$

    $$X = \frac{FC + NI}{CM} = \frac{\$100,000 + \$60,000}{\$20} = \underline{8000\ units}$$

    b. $S = VC + CM = \dfrac{\$60,000}{4000} + \$10 = \$25$

       Sales $= (S)X = \$25(4000) = \underline{\$100,000}$

       $FC =$ Sales $-$ Variable costs $- NI = \$100,000 - \$60,000 - \$12,500 = \underline{\$27,500}$

    c. Variable costs = Sales $- FC - NI = \$360,000 - \$90,000 - \$60,000 = \underline{\$210,000}$

    $$CM = \frac{FC + NI}{X} = \frac{\$90,000 + \$60,000}{5000} = \underline{\$30.00}$$

19. Given: $S = \$135$, $VC = \$110$, $FC = \$700$ for 15 to 36 participants

    a. $CM = S - VC = \$135 - \$110 = \underline{\$25}$

       To break even, $X = \dfrac{FC}{CM} = \dfrac{\$700}{\$25} = \underline{28\ participants}$

    b. If $X = 36$ (which is 8 participants *above* breakeven),
       then $NI = 8(CM) = 8(\$25) = \underline{\$200}$

    c. A loss of $\$200$ will be incurred if there are

       $$\frac{NI}{CM} = \frac{\$200}{\$25} = 8\ fewer\ \text{participants than breakeven}$$

       Hence, the minimum number of participants is $28 - 8 = \underline{20}$.

21. Given: If $S = \$23$, $FC = \$2700$, then $VC = \$12 + 0.1(\$23) = \$14.30$
    If $S = \$28$, $FC = \$2700$, then $VC = \$12 + 0.1(\$28) = \$14.80$

$S = \$23$	$S = \$28$

    a. $CM = \$23 - \$14.30 = \$8.70$ $CM = \$28 - \$14.80 = \$13.20$

    To break even,   To break even,

    $$X = \frac{FC}{CM} = \frac{\$2700}{\$8.70} = 310.34 = \underline{311} \qquad X = \frac{FC}{CM} = \frac{\$2700}{\$13.20} = 204.55 = \underline{205}$$

    We have rounded up to get the *smallest* number of tickets
    that will make $NI = 0$ or a small profit.

    b. If 400 tickets are sold,   If 300 tickets are sold,
    $NI = \$8.70(400 - 310.34)$ $NI = \$13.20(300 - 204.55)$
         $= \underline{\$780}$ $= \underline{\$1260}$

23. Given: $S = \$37.50$, $VC = \$13.25$, $FC = \$5600$/month

    a. Last year's $CM = S - VC = \$37.50 - \$13.25 = \$24.25$

    Last year's break-even volume $= \dfrac{FC}{CM} = \dfrac{\$5600}{\$24.25} = 231$ units/month

    This year, $VC = \$15$, $FC = \$6000$/month. For the break-even
    volume to still be 231 griddles/month,

    $$CM = \frac{FC}{\text{Break - even volume}} = \frac{\$6000}{231} = \$25.97 \text{ and}$$

    $S = VC + CM = \$15 + \$25.97 = \underline{\$40.97}$

    b. Last year's $NI = (CM)X - FC = (\$24.25)300 - \$5600 = \$1675.00$. In order that
    this year's profit also be $\$1675$/month on sales of 300 griddles/month,
        $\$1675 = 300CM - \$6000$

    $$CM = \frac{\$7675}{300} = \$25.58$$

    and $S = CM + VC = \$25.58 + \$15 = \underline{\$40.58}$

25. Given: $S = \$90$/tonne, $VC = \$21 + \$12 = \$33$ per tonne,
    $FC = \$200 + \$300 + \$225 = \$725$ per hectare

    a. $CM = S - VC = \$90 - \$33 = \$57$ per tonne

    Break-even yield $= \dfrac{FC}{CM} = \dfrac{\$725 \text{ per tonne}}{\$57 \text{ per tonne}} = \underline{12.72 \text{ tonnes/hectare}}$

    b. If $S = \$95$ per tonne, then $CM = \$62$ per tonne and

    Break-even yield $= \dfrac{\$725 \text{ per hectare}}{\$62 \text{ per tonne}} = 11.69$ tonnes/hectare

    The break-even yield is lowered by
         $12.72 - 11.69 = \underline{1.03 \text{ tonnes/hectare}}$

    c. (i) If $X = 15$ tonnes/hectare (which is 2.28 tonnes/hectare *above* breakeven),
          $NI = 2.28(CM) = 2.28(\$57) = \underline{\$130 \text{ per hectare}}$

    (ii) If $X = 10$ tonnes/hectare (which is 2.72 tonnes/hectare *below* breakeven),
         the <u>loss</u> will be $2.72(\$57) = \underline{\$155 \text{ per hectare}}$.

Exercise 5.3

1. Given: $S = \$30$; $VC = \$10$; $FC = \$100,000$ per year
   a. $TR = (S)X = \$30X$
   $TC = (VC)X + FC = \$10X + \$100,000$
   To break even, $TR = TC$
   Then,　　$\$30X = \$10X + \$100,000$
   　　　　$\$20X = \$100,000$
   　　　　　$X = \underline{5000\text{ toys per year}}$

   b. Break-even revenue $= (S)X = \$30(5000) = \underline{\$150,000\text{ per year}}$

3. Given: $S = \$3.20$; $VC = \$1.20$; $FC = \$250$ per month
   a. $FC = 12(\$250) = \$3000$ per year
   $TR = (S)X = \$3.20X$
   $TC = (VC)X + FC = \$1.20X + \$3000$
   To break even, $TR = TC$
   Then,　　$\$3.20X = \$1.20X + \$3000$
   　　　　$\$2.00X = \$3000$
   　　　　　$X = \underline{1500\text{ jars per year}}$

   b. If Ingrid sells 3000 jars per year,
   $NI = (S - VC)X - FC = (\$3.20 - \$1.20)3000 - \$3000 = \underline{\$3000}$

5. Given: $S = \$2.50$; $VC = \$1.00$; $FC = \$60,000$ per month
   a. $TR = (S)X = \$2.50X$
   $TC = (VC)X + FC = \$1.00X + \$60,000$
   To break even, $TR = TC$
   Then,　　$\$2.50X = \$1.00X + \$60,000$
   　　　　$\$1.50X = \$60,000$
   　　　　　$X = \underline{40,000\text{ discs per month}}$

   b. $NI = (S - VC)X - FC$
   If $NI = \$7500$ per month, then
   　　$\$7500 = (\$2.50 - \$1.00)X - \$60,000$
   $$X = \frac{\$60,000 + 7500}{\$1.50} = \underline{45,000\text{ discs per month}}$$

7. Given: $S = 10¢$ per copy; $FC = \$300$ per month;
   $$VC = 1.5¢ + \frac{\$5.00}{500} + \frac{\$100.00}{5000} + 0.5¢ = 5¢\text{ per copy}$$
   a. $TR = (S)X = \$0.10X$
   $TC = (VC)X + FC = \$0.05X + \$300$
   To break even, $TR = TC$
   Then,　　$\$0.10X = \$0.05X + \$300$
   　　　　$\$0.05X = \$300$
   　　　　　$X = \underline{6000\text{ copies per month}}$

   b. If $X = 6000 + 1000 = 7000$ copies per month.
   $NI = (S - VC)X - FC = (\$0.10 - \$0.05)7000 - \$300 = \underline{\$50\text{ per month}}$
   The additional 1000 copies add $50 per month profit.

9. Given: Capacity = 250 units per week
    $S = \$20$, $VC = \$12$, $FC = \$1200$ per week

 a $TR = (S)X = \$20X$
    $TC = (VC)X + FC = \$12X + \$1200$
    To break even, $TR = TC$
    Therefore, $\$20X = \$12X + \$1200$
    $X = \underline{150 \text{ units/week}}$

 b $NI = TR - TC = \$20X - \$12X - \$1200 = \$8X - \$1200$
    (i)   If $X = 120$ units/week,
       then $NI = \$8(120) - \$1200 = -\$240$
       There will be a <u>loss of $240/week</u>.

    (ii)   If $X = 250$ units/week,
       then $NI = \$8(250) - \$1200 = \underline{\$800/\text{week profit}}$.

 c If $NI = \$400$/week,
    then $400 = \$8X - \$1200$
    $\$1600 = \$8X$
    $X = \underline{200 \text{ units/week}}$

11. Given: At 90% of capacity, $TR = \$18{,}000{,}000$, Total variable costs = $6,000,000,
    $FC = \$10{,}000{,}000$ per year, and $NI = \$2{,}000{,}000$

 a. Let $S = \$1$. Then at 90% of capacity, $X = 18{,}000{,}000$ units
    and $VC = \dfrac{\text{Total variable costs}}{18{,}000{,}000} = \dfrac{\$6{,}000{,}000}{18{,}000{,}000} = \$0.3\bar{3}$
    At the break-even point, $TR = TC$
    $(S)X = (VC)X + FC$
    $\$1X = \$0.3\bar{3}X + \$10{,}000{,}000$
    $\$0.6\bar{6}X = \$10{,}000{,}000$
    $X = 15{,}000{,}000$
    If $TR = \$18{,}000{,}000$ represents 90% of capacity, then
    TR at full capacity $= \dfrac{100\%}{90\%} \times \$18{,}000{,}000 = \$20{,}000{,}000$

    and break-even revenue represents $\dfrac{\$15{,}000{,}000}{\$20{,}000{,}000} \times 100\% = \underline{75\% \text{ of capacity}}$

 b. At 70% of capacity,
    Revenue = $0.70(\$20{,}000{,}000) = \$14{,}000{,}000$
    and   Total variable costs $= \dfrac{\$14{,}000{,}000}{\$18{,}000{,}000} \times \$6{,}000{,}000 = \$4{,}666{,}667$
    Net income = $\$14{,}000{,}000 - \$10{,}000{,}000 - \$4{,}666{,}667 = \underline{-\$666{,}667}$
    That is, Beta would lose $666,667.

13. Given: $VC = \$43$, $S = \$70$, $FC = \$648{,}000$/year = $54,000/month
    Production capacity = 3200 borgels per month
 a. $TR = (S)X = \$70X$
    $TC = (VC)X + FC = \$43X + \$54{,}000$
    At break even, $TR = TC$
    $\$70X = \$43X + \$54{,}000$
    $\$27X = \$54{,}000$
    $X = \underline{2000 \text{ borgels/month}}$

---

13. *b.* $NI = TR - TC = \$70X - \$43X - \$54,000 = \$27X - \$54,000$
    If $X = 2500$ borgels/month,
    $$NI = \$27(2500) - \$54,000 = \underline{\$13,500/month}$$

    c. At 50% capacity, $X = 0.5(3200$ borgels/month$) = 1600$ borgels/month and
    $$NI = \$27(1600) - \$54,000 = -\$10,800/month.$$
    Reflex will <u>lose $10,800/month</u> in the recession.

    d. For $NI = \$226,800/year = \$18,900/month$,
    $$\$18,900 = \$27X - \$54,000$$
    $$\$72,900 = \$27X$$
    $$X = 2700 \text{ borgels/month}$$
    which is $\dfrac{2700}{3200} \times 100\% = \underline{84.4\% \text{ of capacity}}$.

    e. If $TR = \$71X$ while costs do not change, then
    $$\$71X = \$43X + \$54,000 \text{ at the break-even point}$$
    $$X = \frac{\$54,000}{\$71 - \$43} = 1929 \text{ borgels/month}$$
    The break-even volume decreases 71 borgels/month
    for a \$1 increase in the selling price.

15. Given: In the first quarter (Q1), $TR = \$4,500,000$; $NI = \$900,000$; $X = 60,000$ tires.
    In the second quarter (Q2), $NI = \$700,000$; $X = 50,000$ tires.

    Since $TR = (S)X$, then $\quad S = \dfrac{TR}{X} = \dfrac{\$4,500,000}{60,000} = \underline{\$75 \text{ per tire}}$

    Also, $\quad TR = \$75 \times 50,000 = \underline{\$3,750,000 \text{ in Q2}}$.

    Since $\quad NI = (S - VC)X - FC$
    then for Q1, $\quad \$900,000 = (S - VC)60,000 - FC \qquad$ ①
    and for Q2, $\quad \underline{\$700,000 = (S - VC)50,000 - FC} \qquad$ ②
    Subtract: $\quad \$200,000 = (S - VC)10,000$
    $$CM = S - VC = \frac{\$200,000}{10,000} = \underline{\$20 \text{ per tire}}$$
    $$VC = S - \$20 = \$75 - \$20 = \underline{\$55 \text{ per tire}}$$
    Substitute $S - VC = \$20$ into ②:
    $$\$700,000 = (\$20)50,000 - FC$$
    Therefore, $\quad FC = \$1,000,000 - \$700,000 = \underline{\$300,000 \text{ per quarter}}$

19. Given: $S = \$135$, $VC = \$110$, $FC = \$700$ for 15 to 36 participants
    a. $CM = S - VC = \$135 - \$110 = \underline{\$25}$
    To break even, $X = \dfrac{FC}{CM} = \dfrac{\$700}{\$25} = \underline{28 \text{ participants}}$

    b. If $X = 36$ (which is 8 participants *above* breakeven),
    then $\quad NI = 8(CM) = 8(\$25) = \underline{\$200}$

    c. A loss of \$200 will be incurred if there are
    $$\frac{NI}{CM} = \frac{\$200}{\$25} = 8 \text{ } fewer \text{ participants than breakeven}$$
    Hence, the minimum number of participants is $28 - 8 = \underline{20}$.

21. Given: If $S = \$23$, $FC = \$2700$, then $VC = \$12 + 0.1(\$23) = \$14.30$
    If $S = \$28$, $FC = \$2700$, then $VC = \$12 + 0.1(\$28) = \$14.80$

    a. To break even,

    $$X = \frac{FC}{S - VC} = \frac{\$2700}{\$23 - \$14.30} \qquad X = \frac{\$2700}{\$28 - \$14.80}$$
    $$= \underline{310\ tickets} \qquad\qquad = \underline{205\ tickets}$$

    b. $NI = (S - VC)X - FC \qquad\qquad NI = (S - VC)X - FC$
    $\quad = (\$23 - \$14.30)400 - \$2700 \qquad = (\$28 - \$14.80)300 - \$2700$
    $\quad = \underline{\$780} \qquad\qquad\qquad\qquad\qquad = \underline{\$1260}$

23. Given: $S = \$37.50$, $VC = \$13.25$, $FC = \$5600/month$

    a. Last year's break-even volume $= \dfrac{FC}{S - VC} = \dfrac{\$5600}{\$37.50 - \$13.25} = 231$ units/month

    This year, $VC = \$15$, $FC = \$6000/month$.
    For the break-even volume to remain 231 griddles/month,

    $$S - VC = \frac{FC}{Break\text{ - }even\ volume}$$

    $$S - \$15 = \frac{\$6000}{231} = \$25.97$$
    $$S = \$15 + \$25.97 = \underline{\$40.97}$$

    b. Last year's $NI = (S - VC)X - FC = (\$37.50 - \$13.25)300 - \$5600 = \$1675.00$. In order
    that this year's profit also be $1675/month on sales of 300 griddles/month,
    $\quad \$1675 = 300(S - \$15) - \$6000$

    $$S = \frac{\$7675}{300} + \$15 = \underline{\$40.58}$$

25. Given: $S = \$90/tonne$, $VC = \$21 + \$12 = \$33$ per tonne,
    $\qquad\qquad FC = \$200 + \$300 + \$225 = \$725$ per hectare

    a. To break even,

    $$X = \frac{FC}{S - VC} = \frac{\$725}{\$90 - \$33} = \underline{12.72\ tonnes\ per\ hectare}$$

    b. If $S = \$95$ per tonne instead of $90 per tonne,

    $$X = \frac{\$725}{\$95 - \$33} = 11.69\ tonnes\ per\ hectare$$

    The break-even tonnage will be reduced by <u>1.03 tonnes per hectare</u>.

    c. (i) $NI = (S - VC)X - FC = (\$90 - \$33)15 - \$725 = \underline{\$130\ per\ hectare}$.
       (ii) $NI = (\$90 - \$33)10 - \$725 = -\$155.00$ per hectare.
       That is, <u>a loss of \$155 per hectare</u>.

Exercise 5.4

1.

x:	−3	0	6
y:	−6	0	12

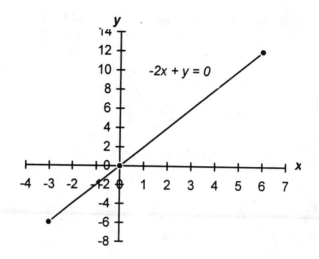

3.

x:	−3	0	6
y:	10	4	−8

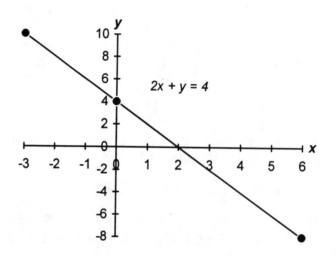

5.

x:	−8	0	12
y:	−3	3	12

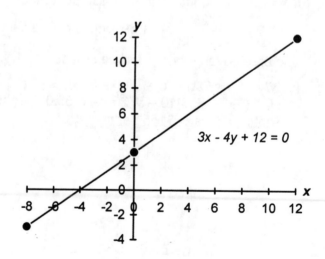

7.

x:	0	3000	6000
y:	5000	18,500	32,000

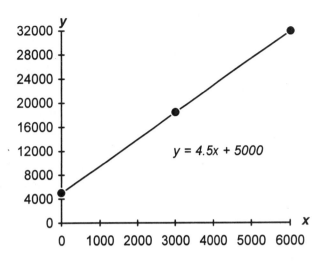

9. In each part, rearrange the equation to render it in the form $y = (\text{slope})x + (\text{intercept})$

a. $2b + 3 = 5a$
   $2b = 5a - 3$
   $b = \frac{5}{2}a - \frac{3}{2}$
   The <u>slope is</u> $\frac{5}{2}$ and the <u>b-intercept is</u> $-\frac{3}{2}$.

b. $3a - 4b = 12$
   $-4b = -3a + 12$
   $b = \frac{3}{4}a - 3$
   The <u>slope is</u> $\frac{3}{4}$ and the <u>b-intercept is</u> -3 .

c. $0 = 2400 - 4a - 5b$
   $5b = -4a + 2400$
   $b = -\frac{4}{5}a + 480$
   The <u>slope is</u> $-\frac{4}{5}$ and the <u>b-intercept is 480</u> .

d. $7a = -8b$
   $8b = -7a$
   $b = -\frac{7}{8}a$
   The <u>slope is</u> $-\frac{7}{8}$ and the <u>b-intercept is 0</u> .

11. Ehud earns $1500 per month plus 5% of sales. Then gross earnings
    $E = \$1500 + 0.05R$
    Expressing this equation in the form $y = mx + b$
    $E = 0.05R + \$1500$
    On a plot of E vs. R, <u>slope = 0.05</u> and <u>E-intercept = \$1500</u>.

Exercise 5.4 *(continued)*

13. *a.* Given: $TR = \$6X$
On a plot of *TR* vs. *X*, <u>slope = $6</u> and <u>*TR*-intercept = $0</u>.

b. $TC = \$2X + \$80,000$
On a plot of *TC* vs. *X*, <u>slope = $2</u> and <u>*TC*-intercept = $80,000</u>.

c. $NI = \$4X - \$80,000$
On a plot of *NI* vs. *X*, <u>slope = $4</u> and <u>*NI*-intercept = − $80,000</u>.

d. The steepest line is the one with the largest slope.
Therefore, the <u>*TR* line</u> is steepest.

e. The increase in *NI* per widget sold is the "change in *NI*" divided by the "change in *X*". This is just as the slope of the *NI* vs. *X* line. Therefore, *NI* increases by <u>$4</u> for each widget sold.

f. The coefficient of *X* in the *TR* equation is the unit selling price, which is unchanged. Therefore, the slope <u>remains unchanged</u>.

The coefficient of *X* in the *TC* equation is the unit cost. Therefore, the slope <u>decreases</u> (from $2 to $1.75).

The coefficient of *X* in the *TI* equation equals
(Unit selling price) − (Unit cost)
Therefore, the slope <u>increases</u> (from $4 to $4.25).

15. $x - 3y = 3$

x:	−6	3
y:	−3	0

$y = -2$

x:	−6	3
y:	−2	−2

The solution is
<u>$(x, y) = (-3, -2)$</u>.

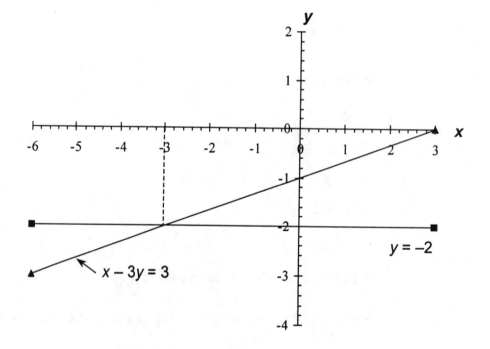

17.

$x - 3y = 0$

x:	–6	3
y:	–2	1

$x + 2y = -5$

x:	–6	3
y:	0.5	–4

The solution is
<u>$(x, y) = (-3, -1)$</u>.

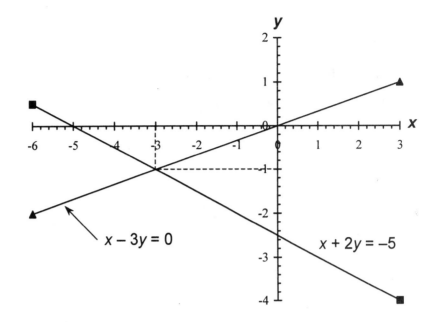

19.

$y - 3x = 11$

x:	– 4	2
y:	–1	17

$5x + 30 = 4y$

x:	– 4	2
y:	2.5	10

The solution is
<u>$(x, y) = (-2, 5)$</u>.

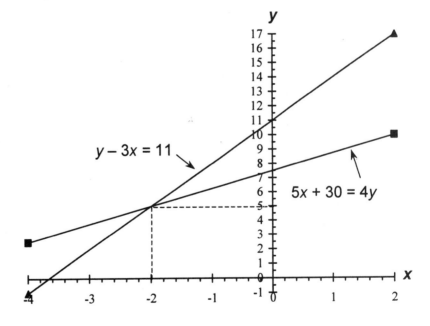

Exercise 5.4 (continued)

21.

$7p - 3q = 23$

p:	0	6
q:	−7.67	6.33

$-2p - 3q = 5$

p:	0	6
q:	−1.67	−5.67

The solution is
<u>$(p, q) = (2, -3)$</u>.

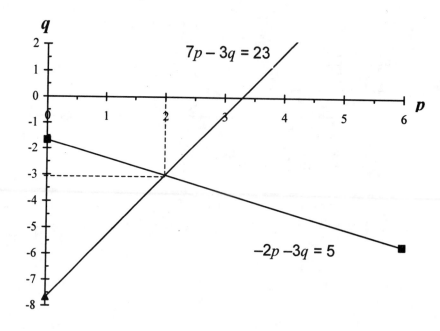

Exercise 5.5

1. Given: S = $2.50 per disc; VC = $1.00 per disc; FC = $60,000 per month.

$TR = (S)X$
$\quad = \$2.50X$
$TC = (VC)X + FC$
$\quad = \$1.00X + \$60,000$

X:	20,000	60,000
TR:	$50,000	$150,000
TC:	$80,000	$120,000

a. <u>40,000 discs/month</u>

b. <u>45,000 discs/month</u>

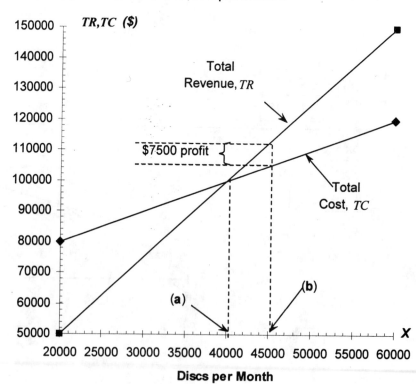

3. Given: S = \$0.10 per copy; FC = \$300 per month;

$$VC = \$0.015 + \frac{\$5.00}{500} + \frac{\$100.00}{5000} + \$0.005 = \$0.05 \text{ per copy}$$

$$TR = (S)X$$
$$= \$0.10X$$
$$TC = (VC)X + FC$$
$$= \$0.05X + \$300$$

X:	4000	8000
TR:	\$400	\$800
TC:	\$500	\$700

a. <u>6000 copies/month</u>

b. <u>\$50 per month</u>

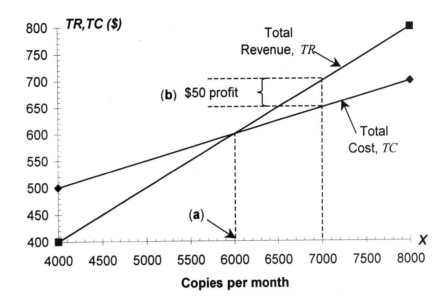

5. Given: S = \$20 per unit; VC = \$12 per unit; FC = \$1200 per week.

$$TR = (S)X$$
$$= \$20X$$
$$TC = (VC)X + FC$$
$$= \$12X + \$1200$$

X:	0	250
TR:	\$0	\$5000
TC:	\$1200	\$4200

a. <u>150 units/week</u>

b. (i) <u>\$240 loss</u>
   (ii) <u>\$800 profit</u>

c. <u>200 units/week</u>

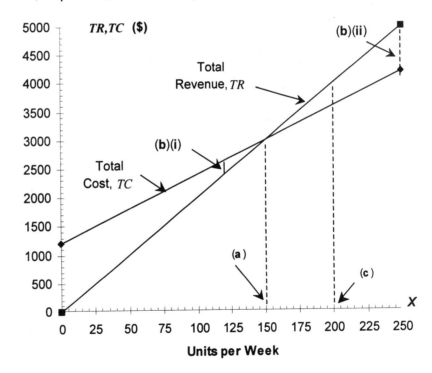

Exercise 5.5 *(continued)*

7. Given: S = \$70 per borgel; VC = \$43 per borgel;
   FC = \$648,000 per year = \$54,000 per month.

$$TR = (S)X$$
$$= \$70X$$
$$TC = (VC)X + FC$$
$$= \$43X + \$54,000$$

X:	1000	3200
TR:	\$70,000	\$224,000
TC:	\$97,000	\$191,600

a. <u>2000 borgels/month</u>

b. <u>\$13,500/month</u>

c. <u>\$10,800/month loss</u>

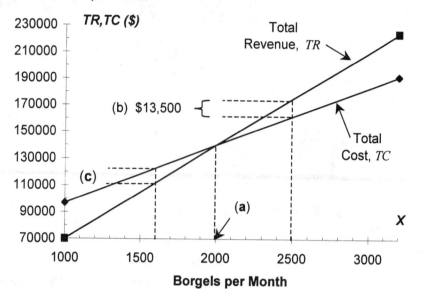

Review Problems

1. a. NI = Total contribution margin – FC = \$300,000 – \$220,000 = <u>\$80,000</u>

$$CM = \frac{\text{Total contribution margin}}{X} \quad \frac{\$300,000}{150,000} = \$2.00$$

$S = CM + VC$ = \$2.00 + \$10.00 = <u>\$12.00</u>

   b. NI = \$900,000 – \$800,000 = <u>\$100,000</u>

$$CM = \frac{\$900,000}{180,000} = \$5.00$$

$VC = S – CM$ = \$25 – \$5 = <u>\$20.00</u>

   c. $CM = S – VC$ = \$20 – \$14 = \$6.00

$$\text{Unit sales} = \frac{\text{Total } CM}{CM} = \frac{\$120,000}{\$6} = \underline{20,000}$$

NI = Total contribution margin – FC
\$12,000 = \$120,000 – FC
FC = <u>\$108,000</u>

3. Given: TR = \$10 million, FC = \$2 million,
    Total variable costs = \$6 million, X = 1 million

   a. $$CM = \frac{TR - \text{Total variable costs}}{X} = \frac{\$10\text{ million} - \$6\text{ million}}{1\text{ million}} = \underline{\$4.00}$$

   b. $$\text{Break-even point} = \frac{FC}{CM} = \frac{\$2,000,000}{\$4.00} = \underline{500,000\text{ units}}$$

   c. To have NI = \$1 million,

$$X = \text{Break-even volume} + \frac{NI}{CM} = 500,000 + \frac{\$1,000,000}{\$4.00} = \underline{750,000\text{ units}}$$

Review Problems *(continued)*

5. Given: $FC = \$45,000 + \$7000 + \$8000 = \$60,000$;
$VC = \$8.00 + 0.08(\$35) = \$10.80$; $S = \$35.00$

   a. $CM = S - VC = \$35 - \$10.80 = \$24.20$

      Break-even volume $= \dfrac{FC}{CM} = \dfrac{\$60,000}{\$24.20} = $ <u>2479 books</u>

   b. $NI = (CM)X - FC = (\$24.20)4800 - \$60,000 = $ <u>$56,160</u>

   c. If the price is reduced 10%, then $S = \$35(1 - 0.10) = \$31.50$
      and $CM = S - VC = \$31.50 - \$10.80 = \$20.70$
      If sales are 15% higher,
        $X = 4800(1 + 0.15) = 5520$ units
        $NI = (\$20.70)5520 - \$60,000 = \$54,264$
      <u>Select the \$35 price</u> because the forecast *NI* will be larger (by almost \$2000).

   d. If $FC = \$65,000$ and $VC = \$11.80$, then $CM = \$23.20$

      and break-even volume $= \dfrac{FC}{CM} = \dfrac{\$65,000}{\$23.20} = 2802$ books

      That is, the break-even volume would be increased by
        $2802 - 2479 = $ <u>323 books</u>

7. Given: $S = \$100$, $FC = \$200,000$, $VC = \$60$, Forecast $X = 8000$ units

   a. $CM = S - VC = \$100 - \$60 = \$40$

      Break-even volume $= \dfrac{FC}{CM} = \dfrac{\$200,000}{\$40} = $ <u>5000 units</u>

   b. Volume = Break-even volume $+ \dfrac{NI}{CM} = 5000 + \dfrac{\$100,000}{\$40} = $ <u>7500 units</u>

   c. If sales are $8000 - 5000 = 3000$ units above breakeven, then
      $NI = 3000(CM) = 3000(\$40) = $ <u>$120,000</u>

   d. (i) $NI = (CM)X - FC = 8000(CM) - FC$
            For each \$1 increase in *FC*, *NI* will drop \$1.
            If *FC* is 5% (or \$10,000) higher, *NI* will be <u>$10,000 lower</u>.
      (ii) If *FC* is 10% (or \$20,000) lower, *NI* will be <u>$20,000 higher</u>.

   e. (i)   If *VC* is 10% (or \$6) higher, then
              $CM = S - VC = \$100 - \$66 = \$34$, and
              $NI = 8000(CM) - FC = 8000(\$34) - \$200,000 = \$72,000$
            That is, *NI* will be $\$120,000 - \$72,000 = $ <u>$48,000 lower</u>.
      (ii) If *VC* is 5% (or \$3) lower, then
              $CM = \$100 - \$57 = \$43$ and
              $NI = 8000(\$43) - \$200,000 = \$144,000$
            That is, *NI* will be $\$144,000 - \$120,000 = $ <u>$24,000 higher</u>.
            Note the "leverage" effect here. That is, % change in $NI = -4$(% change in *VC*)

   f. (i)   If *S* is 5% (or \$5) higher, then
              $CM = \$105 - \$60 = \$45$, and
              $NI = 8000(\$45) - \$200,000 = \$160,000$
            That is, *NI* will be $\$160,000 - \$120,000 = $ <u>$40,000 higher</u>.
      (ii) If *S* is 10% (or \$10) lower, then
              $CM = \$90 - \$60 = \$30$ and
              $NI = 8000(\$30) - \$200,000 = \$40,000$
            That is, *NI* will be $\$120,000 - \$40,000 = $ <u>$80,000 lower</u>.
            Note the "leverage" effect here. That is,
              % change in $NI = 6.\overline{6} \times$(% change in *S*)
            (assuming that the sales volume does not change).

Chapter 5: Applications of Linear Equations

Review Problems *(continued)*

7. *g.* If $X = 8000$, $VC = 1.1(\$60) = \$66$. $S = \$100$, and
    $FC = 0.9(\$200,000) = \$180,000$, then
    $CM = \$100 - \$66 = \$34$ and
    $NI = 8000(\$34) - \$180,000 = \$92,000$
    That is, NI will be $\$120,000 - \$92,000 = \underline{\$28,000\ \text{lower}}$.

Self-Test Exercise

1. Given: $S = \$10$ (= Average revenue per person)).
    Plan 1: $VC = (0.1 + 0.3)S = \$4$, $FC = \$15,000$
    Plan 2: $VC = (0.1 + 0.5)S = \$6$, $FC = \$10,000$

  a.

	Plan 1	Plan 2
$CM = SP - VC$:	$\$10 - \$4 = \$6$	$\$10 - \$6 = \$4$
Break-even point $= \dfrac{FC}{CM}$:	$\dfrac{\$15,000}{\$6} = \underline{2500}$	$\dfrac{\$10,000}{\$4} = \underline{2500}$

  b. (i) At $X = 3000$, NI: $500(\$6) = \underline{\$3000}$ $500(\$4) = \underline{\$2000}$
      (ii) At $X = 2200$, NI: $-300(\$6) = -\$1800$ $-300(\$4) = -\$1200$
                                                (loss of $\$1800$)   (loss of $\$1200$)

  c. If attendance surpasses the break-even point, the 30% commission rate generates the higher profit. However, if attendance falls short of the 2500 break-even point, the 30% commission will produce the larger loss.

2. *a.* Contribution margin, $CM = S - VC = \$55 - \$12 = \$43$
    The number of room rentals per month needed to break even is
$$X = \frac{FC}{CM} = \frac{\$14,000}{\$43} = 326$$
    Full occupancy would be $30 \times 30 = 900$ rentals per month.
$$\text{Break-even occupancy rate} = \frac{326}{900} \times 100\% = \underline{36.2\%}$$

  b. (i) At 40% occupancy, $X = 0.4 \times 900 = 360$ rentals per month.
         $NI = (CM)X - FC = (\$43)360 - \$14,000 = \underline{\$1480/\text{month}}$

      (ii) At 30% occupancy, $X = 0.3 \times 900 = 270$ rentals per month.
         $NI = (\$43)270 - \$14,000 = -\$2390$
         That is, a $\underline{\text{loss of \$2390 per month}}$.

  c. In part *b* (i), we obtained a net income of $1480/month for
    a rental rate of $55 and a 40% occupancy.
    At a rental rate of $47 per unit, $CM = \$47 - \$12 = \$35$ per unit.
    At 50% occupancy, $X = 450$ units/month and
        $NI = (CM)X - FC = (\$35)450 - \$14,000 = \$1750/\text{month}$
    $\underline{\text{The owner should reduce the rental rate}}$ to $47 per unit per night since
    the net income will increase by $\$1750 - \$1480 = \$270$ per month.

www.Exercise.com

Question number		Effect of the change on the:		Break-even point
	FC line	*TC* line	*TR* line	
1.	No effect	Slope increases	No effect	At higher volume
2.	No effect	No effect	Slope increases	At lower volume
3.	Upward shift	Upward shift	No effect	At higher volume

6 Simple Interest

Exercise 6.1

1. $I = Prt = \$1500(0.095)\frac{7}{12} = \underline{\$83.13}$

3. $t = \dfrac{I}{Pr} = \dfrac{\$145.50}{\$4850(0.045)} = 0.6\overline{6}$ year = $\underline{\text{8 months}}$

5. $I = Prt = \$6800(0.077)\frac{13}{12} = \underline{\$567.23}$

7. $t = \dfrac{I}{Pr} = \dfrac{\$511.00}{\$9125(0.008)} = \underline{\text{7 months}}$

9. $I = Prt = \$5000(0.055)\frac{5}{12} = \underline{\$114.58}$

11. $P = \dfrac{I}{rt} = \dfrac{\$292.50}{(0.009)5} = \underline{\$6500.00}$

13. $r = \dfrac{I}{Pt} = \dfrac{\$103.35}{\$10,600\left(\frac{3}{12}\right)} = 0.0390 = \underline{3.90\%}$

15. $t = \dfrac{I}{Pr} = \dfrac{\$315.90}{\$2700(0.009)\text{ per month}} = \underline{\text{13 months}}$

17. Interest on the first term deposit = $Prt = \$10,000(0.039)\left(\frac{3}{12}\right) = \underline{\$97.50}$

    Principal amount of the second deposit = \$10,097.50

    Interest on the second term deposit = $\$10,097.50(0.039)\left(\frac{3}{12}\right) = \underline{\$98.45}$

    The interest earned on the second deposit is larger because both the original \$10,000 principal and the \$97.50 interest earned on the first deposit earn interest during the second 3-month term.

Exercise 6.2

1. Number of days = (October 1, 2005) − (June 17, 2005) = 274 − 168 = 106 days

    $I = Prt = \$3800(0.1075)\frac{106}{365} = \underline{\$118.63}$

3. Number of days = (May 30, 2005) − (December 1, 2004)
    $$= [(\text{May 30, 2005}) - 0] + [(\text{December 31, 2004}) - (\text{December 1, 2004})]$$
    $$= 150 + (366 - 336)$$
    $$= 180 \text{ days}$$

    $I = Prt = \$85,000(0.069)\frac{180}{365} = \underline{\$2892.33}$

5. Number of days = (April 15, 2004) − (October 16, 2003)
    $$= [(\text{April 15, 2004}) - 0] + [(\text{December 31, 2003}) - (\text{October 16, 2003})]$$
    $$= 106 + (365 - 289)$$
    $$= 182 \text{ days}$$

    $I = Prt = \$27,000(0.087)\frac{182}{365} = \underline{\$1171.28}$

7. Number of days = (July 7, 2004) − (January 15, 2004) = 189 − 15 = 174 days

    $$r = \frac{I}{Pt} = \frac{\$40.52}{\$1000\left(\frac{174}{365}\right)} \times 100\% = \underline{8.50\%}$$

9. $$t = \frac{I}{Pr} = \frac{\$50.05}{\$1000(0.0725)} = 0.690345 \text{ year} = 0.690345 \times 365 \text{ days} = 252 \text{ days}$$

    Serial number of start date = November 16, 2005− 252 days = 320 − 252 = 68
    The start date is <u>March 9, 2005</u>.

11. $$t = \frac{I}{Pr} = \frac{\$63.91}{\$1000(0.1075)} = 0.59451 \text{ year} = 0.59451 \times 365 \text{ days} = 217 \text{ days}$$

    Serial number of end date = June 26, 2004+ 217 days = 178 + 217 = 395
    That is, the end date is 395 − 366 = 29th day of 2005. Therefore,
    End date is <u>January 29, 2005</u>.

13. Number of days = (September 3) − (June 26 of same year) = 246 − 177 = 69 days

    $$I = Prt = \$2750(0.0425)\tfrac{69}{365} = \underline{\$22.09}$$

15. $$r = \frac{I}{Pt} = \frac{\$2.65}{\$2149\left(\frac{30}{365}\right)} \times 100\% = \underline{1.50\%}$$

17. $$t = \frac{I}{Pr} = \frac{\$13.36}{\$2163(0.055)} = 0.11230 \text{ year} = 0.11230 \times 365 \text{ days} = \underline{41 \text{ days}}$$

19. $$t = \frac{I}{Pr} = \frac{\$203.22}{\$6000(0.1075)} = 0.31507 \text{ year} = 0.31507 \times 365 \text{ days} = 115 \text{ days}$$

    Serial number of repayment date = November 23 + 115 days = 327 + 115 = 442
    That is, the repayment date is 442 − 365 = 77th day of the subsequent year.
    Therefore, the repayment date was <u>March 18</u> of the subsequent year.

In the following solutions to problem 21, the number of days in each interval is determined by adding the number of days for each partial month and full month in the interval. Problem 23 is solved by an alternative approach—the interval length is determined by using the serial numbers for dates (Table 6.2).

21.

Interval	Number of days	Int. rate	Interest
Mar 1 to Apr 17	31 + 16 = 47	7.5%	$57.945①
Apr 17 to June 30	14 + 31 + 29 = 74	8.0%	97.315
June 30 to Aug 1	1 + 31 = 32	7.75%	40.767
		Total:	$196.03

① $I = Prt = \$6000(0.075)\tfrac{47}{365} = \$57.945$

Interest totaling $196.03 will be owed on August 1.

23.

Interval	Number of days	Int. rate	Interest
Sept 30 to Nov 2	306 − 273 = 33	10.7%	$29.022①
Nov 2 to Jan 1	1 + 365 − 306 = 60	11.2%	55.233
Jan 1 to Feb 1	32 − 1 = 31	11.0%	28.027
		Total:	$112.28

① $I = Prt = \$3000(0.107)\tfrac{33}{365} = \$29.022$

Amount required to pay off the loan on February 1 = $P + I$ = $3000 + $112.28 = <u>$3112.28</u>

Exercise 6.3

1. $S = P(1 + rt) = \$2950\left[1 + 0.045\left(\dfrac{7}{12}\right)\right] = \$2950(1.02625) = \underline{\$3027.44}$

3. $P = \dfrac{S}{(1 + rt)} = \dfrac{\$785.16}{1 + 0.105\left(\frac{23}{365}\right)} = \dfrac{\$785.16}{1.006616} = \underline{\$780.00}$

5. $P = \dfrac{S}{(1 + rt)} = \dfrac{\$15,379.58}{1 + 0.099\left(\frac{11}{12}\right)} = \dfrac{\$15,379.58}{1.0907500} = \underline{\$14,100.00}$

7. $I = S - P = \$1828.02 - \$1750 = \$78.02$

   $r = \dfrac{I}{Pt} = \dfrac{\$78.02}{\$1750\left(\frac{5}{12}\right)} = 0.1070 = \underline{10.70\%}$

9. $I = S - P = \$798.63 - \$780.82 = \$17.81$

   $r = \dfrac{I}{Pt} = \dfrac{\$17.81}{\$780.82\left(\frac{45}{365}\right)} = 0.1850 = \underline{18.50\%}$

11. $I = S - P = \$10,000 - \$9625.63 = \$374.37$

    $t = \dfrac{I}{Pr} = \dfrac{\$374.37}{\$9625.63(0.078)} = 0.49863 \text{ year} = \underline{182 \text{ days}}$

13. $I = S - P = \$8083.33 - \$7760 = \$323.33$

    $t = \dfrac{I}{Pr} = \dfrac{\$323.33}{\$7760(0.0625)} = 0.66666 \text{ year} = \underline{8 \text{ months}}$

15. $S = P(1 + rt) = \$4500\left[1 + 0.119\left(\dfrac{15}{12}\right)\right] = \$4500(1.148750) = \underline{\$5169.38}$

17. Term = October 1 – March 26 = 274 – 85 = 189 days

    $P = \dfrac{S}{(1 + rt)} = \dfrac{\$20,000}{1 + 0.0375\left(\frac{189}{365}\right)} = \dfrac{\$20,000}{1.01941781} = \underline{\$19,619.04}$

19. In effect, there is a $20 interest charge for paying the second $1800 after 5 months instead of paying at the beginning of the year. The annual rate of simple interest is

    $r = \dfrac{I}{Pt} = \dfrac{\$120}{\$1800\left(\frac{5}{12}\right)} = 0.1600 = \underline{16.00\%}$

21. The $60 higher price for the deferred payment option may be viewed as a $60 interest charge on the cash price of $1535. The implied annual interest rate is

    $r = \dfrac{I}{Pt} = \dfrac{\$60}{\$1535\left(\frac{6}{12}\right)} = 0.0782 = \underline{7.82\%}$

    If you can earn a rate of return greater than 7.82% on a 6-month investment, you would be better off to invest the $1535 now and take A & B's deferred payment option.

23. $I = S - P = \$2100 - \$2000 = \$100$

    $t = \dfrac{I}{Pr} = \dfrac{\$100}{\$2000(0.1025)} = 0.487805 \text{ year} = 0.487805 \times 365 \text{ days} = \underline{178.05 \text{ days}}$

    The balance owed will first exceed $2100 on the 179th day after July 13. December 31 – July 13 = 365 – 194 = 171 days. Eight more days are required to surpass $2100. Therefore, the amount owed will first exceed $2100 on <u>January 8</u>.

25.

Principal	Interval	Number of days	Interest for sub-interval
$2200	June 23 to Dec 31	191	$83.46 ①
1800	Aug 5 to Dec 31	148	52.92
1300	Oct 31 to Dec 31	61	15.75
		Total:	$152.13

① $I = Prt = \$2200(0.0725)\frac{191}{365} = \$83.46$

The total amount required to pay off the loan is $5300 + $152.13 = $5452.13.

27.

Interval	Number of days	Principal	Interest rate	Maturity value
Nov 16 to Apr 1	137 ①	$7400	6.3%	$ 7574.98 ②
Dec 30 to Apr 1	93 ③	6600	5.9%	6699.22
Feb 8 to Apr 1	53 ④	9200	5.1%	9268.13
			Total:	$23,542.33

① (365 − 320) + (91 + 1) = 137 days

② $S = P(1 + rt) = \$7400\left[1+0.063\left(\frac{137}{365}\right)\right] = \$7574.98$

③ (365 − 364) + 92 = 93 days

④ 92 − 39 = 53 days

The total amount from the three term deposits on April 1 will be $23,542.33.

Concept Questions (Section 6.4)

1. "Equivalent payments" are alternative payments (on different dates) that will put the recipient in the same economic position.

3. Calculate the future value of the earlier payment at the date of the later payment. If the future value is equal to the later payment, the two payments are equivalent.

5. Calculate the equivalent values of all three payments at the same focal date. The payment with the highest equivalent value on that focal date is the one with the largest economic value.

Exercise 6.4

1. $P = \dfrac{S}{(1+rt)} = \dfrac{\$560}{1+0.1075\left(\frac{5}{12}\right)} = \$535.99$

3. $S = P(1 + rt) = \$5230\left[1+0.0925\left(\dfrac{174}{365}\right)\right] = \$5460.62$

5. $I = S - P = \$1975 - \$1936.53 = \$38.47$

$r = \dfrac{I}{Pt} = \dfrac{\$38.47}{\$1936.53\left(\frac{100}{365}\right)} = 0.0725 = 7.25\%$

7. $I = S - P = \$850.26 - \$830 = \$20.26$

$t = \dfrac{I}{Pr} = \dfrac{\$20.26}{\$830(0.099)} = 0.24656 \text{ year} = \underline{90 \text{ days later}}$

9. $I = S - P = \$4850 - \$4574.73 = \$275.27$

    $t = \dfrac{I}{Pr} = \dfrac{\$275.27}{\$4574.73(0.0875)} = 0.68768 \text{ year} = \underline{251 \text{ days earlier}}$

11. a. $S = P(1 + rt) = \$560\left[1 + 0.1075\left(\dfrac{60}{365}\right)\right] = \$569.90 < \$570$

    The <u>later payment</u> has the greater economic value.

    b. If $I = \$570 - \$560 = \$10$,

    $r = \dfrac{I}{Pt} = \dfrac{\$10}{\$560\left(\frac{60}{365}\right)} = 0.1086 = \underline{10.86\%}$

    The two payments would be equivalent if money can earn 10.86%.

13. a. $S = P(1 + rt) = \$5230 (1 + 0.006 \times 5) = \$5386.90 < \$5500$

    The <u>later payment</u> has the larger economic value.

    b. If $I = \$5500 - \$5230 = \$270$,

    $r = \dfrac{I}{Pt} = \dfrac{\$270}{\$5230(5)} = 0.0103 = \underline{1.03\% \text{ per month}}$

    The payments would be equivalent if money can earn 1.03% per month.

15. Number of days = 7 + 31 + 30 = 68

    $P = \dfrac{S}{(1+rt)} = \dfrac{\$1000}{1 + 0.05\left(\frac{68}{365}\right)} = \underline{\$990.87}$

17. Victor can expect to pay the maturity value of $450 ninety days later.

    $S = P(1 + rt) = \$450\left[1 + 0.0675\left(\frac{90}{365}\right)\right] = \underline{\$457.49}$

19. On September 10, Duncan Stereo should accept the amount that is equivalent to \$1195 on the following January 2. That is, a cash price of

    $P = \dfrac{S}{(1+rt)} = \dfrac{\$1195}{1 + 0.095\left(\frac{114}{365}\right)} = \underline{\$1160.56}$

21. Equivalent value $= \dfrac{S}{(1+rt)} = \dfrac{\$3000}{1 + 0.0675\left(\frac{6}{12}\right)} = \underline{\$2902.06 \text{ today}}$

    $= \dfrac{\$3000}{1 + 0.0675\left(\frac{4}{12}\right)} = \underline{\$2933.99 \text{ in 2 months}}$

    $= \dfrac{\$3000}{1 + 0.0675\left(\frac{2}{12}\right)} = \underline{\$2966.63 \text{ in 4 months}}$

    $= \underline{\$3000 \text{ in 6 months}}$

    $= P(1 + rt) = \$3000\left[1 + 0.0675\left(\dfrac{2}{12}\right)\right] = \underline{\$3033.75 \text{ in 8 months}}$

    $= \$3000\left[1 + 0.0675\left(\dfrac{4}{12}\right)\right] = \underline{\$3067.50 \text{ in 10 months}}$

    $= \$3000\left[1 + 0.0675\left(\dfrac{6}{12}\right)\right] = \underline{\$3101.25 \text{ in 12 months}}$

Exercise 6.4 *(continued)*

23. The present value of Brian's scholarship 9 months earlier is

$$P = \frac{S}{(1+rt)} = \frac{\$2100}{1 + 0.0825\left(\frac{9}{12}\right)} = \$1977.63 < \$2000$$

The <u>economic value of Jody's scholarship is $22.37 larger</u>.

25. The time period from March 29 to August 20 is 232 − 88 = 144 days.
For $1348 to earn $1389 − $1348 = $41 in 144 days,

$$r = \frac{I}{Pt} = \frac{\$41}{\$1348\left(\frac{144}{365}\right)} = 0.0771 = \underline{7.71\%}$$

Money must earn 7.71% for the two payments to be equivalent.

Concept Questions (Section 6.5)

1. The economic value of a nominal amount of money depends on the date when it is paid. This property of money is called the time value of money.

3. Calculate the sum of the equivalent values of the payments on the chosen date.

5. Today's economic value is <u>lower</u>. This economic value is the lump amount today that is equivalent to the payment stream. In other words, the lump amount along with its interest earnings could pay the series of scheduled payments. (The last payment would reduce the remaining funds to zero.) When interest rates are higher, a smaller lump amount will be sufficient to generate the payment stream because more interest will be earned to help meet the payments.

Exercise 6.5

1. Equivalent value 6 months from now $= \$500\left[1 + 0.095\left(\frac{6}{12}\right)\right] + \$300\left[1 + 0.095\left(\frac{3}{12}\right)\right]$

$$= \$523.75 + \$307.13$$
$$= \underline{\$830.88}$$

3. Equivalent value 270 days from now $= \$900\left[1 + 0.0775\left(\frac{60}{365}\right)\right] + \dfrac{\$1000}{1 + 0.0775\left(\frac{120}{365}\right)}$

$$= \$911.466 + \$975.154$$
$$= \underline{\$1886.62}$$

5. Equivalent value 60 days from now

$$= \$1000\left[1 + 0.085\left(\frac{60}{365}\right)\right] + \frac{\$1500}{1 + 0.085\left(\frac{10}{365}\right)} + \frac{\$2000}{1 + 0.085\left(\frac{150}{365}\right)}$$

$$= \$1013.97 + \$1496.51 + \$1932.50$$
$$= \underline{\$4442.98}$$

7. a. Equivalent value today $= \dfrac{\$2000}{1+0.10\left(\frac{6}{12}\right)} + \dfrac{\$2000}{1+0.10(1)} = \$1904.76 + \$1818.18 = \underline{\$3722.94}$

    b. Equivalent value 6 months from today $= \$2000 + \dfrac{\$2000}{1+0.10\left(\frac{6}{12}\right)}$

    $$= \$2000 + \$1904.76$$
    $$= \underline{\$3904.76}$$

    c. The equivalent value of a specified payment stream will be greater at a later date than at an earlier date because of the time value of money.

9. Equivalent payment today $= \$850 + \dfrac{\$1140}{1+0.0825\left(\frac{9}{12}\right)} = \$850.00 + \$1073.57 = \underline{\$1923.57}$

11. a. Stream 1's economic value today $= \$900\left[1+0.095\left(\dfrac{150}{365}\right)\right] + \$1400\left[1+0.095\left(\dfrac{80}{365}\right)\right]$

    $$= \$935.14 + \$1429.15$$
    $$= \underline{\$2364.29}$$

    b. Stream 2's economic value today $= \dfrac{\$800}{1+0.095\left(\frac{30}{365}\right)} + \dfrac{\$600}{1+0.095\left(\frac{75}{365}\right)} + \dfrac{\$1000}{1+0.095\left(\frac{125}{365}\right)}$

    $$= \$793.80 + \$588.51 + \$968.49$$
    $$= \underline{\$2350.80}$$

    Stream 1 payments have a $13.49 greater economic value (in today's dollars).

13. Maturity value of the $750 obligation $= \$750\left[1+0.095\left(\dfrac{6}{12}\right)\right] = \$785.63$

    Maturity value of the $950 obligation $= \$950\left[1+0.095(1)\right] = \$1040.25$
    Equivalent value of the scheduled payments 4 months from now

    $$= \$785.63\left[1+0.0775\left(\dfrac{6}{12}\right)\right] + \$1040.25$$
    $$= \$816.07 + \$1040.25$$
    $$= \underline{\$1856.32}$$

    Thelma should be willing to accept a payment of $1856.32 four months from now.

15. Let x represent the size of the second replacement payment.
    The equivalent value of the scheduled payments on the focal date is

    $$\$2600\left[1+0.0825\left(\dfrac{80}{365}\right)\right] + \dfrac{\$3100}{1+0.0825\left(\frac{10}{365}\right)} = \$2647.01 + \$3093.01 = \$5740.02$$

    The equivalent value of the replacement payments on the focal date is

    $$\$3000\left[1+0.0825\left(\dfrac{30}{365}\right)\right] + x = \$3020.34 + x$$

    For equivalence of the two streams,
    $$\$3020.34 + x = \$5740.02$$
    $$x = \underline{\$2719.68}$$

    The second payment must be $2719.68.

Exercise 6.6

1. Let x represent the unknown payment.

Payment	Date	No. of days	Present value
$1000	May 1	31 + 30 = 61	$981.95 ①
1000	June 1	61 + 31 = 92	973.02
x	July 1	92 + 30 = 122	0.9645368x ②

① $P = \dfrac{\$1000}{1+0.11\left(\frac{61}{365}\right)} = \$981.95$

② $P = \dfrac{x}{1+0.11\left(\frac{122}{365}\right)} = 0.9645368x$

Original loan = Sum of present values of the payments
$$\$3000 = \$981.95 + \$973.02 + 0.9645368x$$
$$\$1045.03 = 0.9645368x$$
$$x = \underline{\$1083.45}$$
The July 1 payment should be $1083.45.

3. Let x represent the unknown payment.

Payment	Date	No. of days	Present value
x	April 13	31 + 12 = 43	0.9881262x ①
$1100	May 27	43 + 18 + 26 = 87	$1073.89 ②
1100	July 13	87 + 5 + 30 + 12 = 134	1060.30

① $P = \dfrac{x}{1+0.102\left(\frac{43}{365}\right)} = 0.9881262x$ ② $P = \dfrac{\$1100}{1+0.102\left(\frac{87}{365}\right)} = \$1073.89$

Original loan = Present value of all payments
$$\$3000 = 0.9881262x + \$1073.89 + \$1060.30$$
$$\$865.81 = 0.9881262x$$
$$x = \underline{\$876.21}$$
The April 13 payment should be $876.21.

5. Let x represent the size of each loan payment. Since the original loan equals the sum of the present values of all loan payments, then

$$\$1000 = \dfrac{x}{1+0.09\left(\frac{30}{365}\right)} + \dfrac{x}{1+0.09\left(\frac{60}{365}\right)}$$
$$= 0.9926571x + 0.9854212x$$
$$= 1.9780783x$$
$$x = \underline{\$505.54}$$
Each loan payment is $505.54.

7. Let x represent the size of each payment. Then

$$\$2500 = \dfrac{x}{1+0.0875\left(\frac{2}{12}\right)} + \dfrac{x}{1+0.0875\left(\frac{4}{12}\right)} + \dfrac{x}{1+0.0875\left(\frac{7}{12}\right)}$$
$$= 0.9856263x + 0.9716599x + 0.9514371x$$
$$= 2.9087233x$$
$$x = \underline{\$859.48}$$
Each loan payment is $859.48.

Exercise 6.6 *(continued)*

9. Let x represent the size of each payment. Then

$$\$5000 = \frac{x}{1+0.07\left(\frac{100}{365}\right)} + \frac{x}{1+0.07\left(\frac{150}{365}\right)} + \frac{x}{1+0.07\left(\frac{200}{365}\right)} + \frac{x}{1+0.07\left(\frac{250}{365}\right)}$$

$$= 0.98118280x + 0.97203728x + 0.96306069x + 0.95424837x$$

$$= 3.87052913x$$

$$x = \underline{\$1291.81}$$

Each loan payment is $1291.81.

11. Let x represent the third payment.

Payment	Date	No. of days	Present value
$2000	June 1	8 + 31 = 39	$1978.86
2000	Aug 1	39 + 30 + 31 = 100	1946.67
x	Oct 1	100 + 31 + 30 = 161	0.9577539x

Since the original loan = Sum of present values of all payments,

$$\$6000 = \$1978.86 + \$1946.67 + 0.95775387x$$

$$\$2074.47 = 0.95775387x$$

$$x = \underline{\$2165.97}$$

The third payment is $2165.97.

13. Let x represent the size of each payment. Then

$$\$4000 = \frac{x}{1+0.13\left(\frac{4}{12}\right)} + \frac{x}{1+0.13\left(\frac{6}{12}\right)} + \frac{x}{1+0.13\left(\frac{8}{12}\right)}$$

$$= 0.9584665x + 0.9389671x + 0.9202454x$$

$$= 2.8176790x$$

$$x = \underline{\$1419.61}$$

Each loan payment is $1419.61.

Review Problems.

1. $r = \dfrac{I}{Pt} = \dfrac{\$327.95}{\$21,000\left(\frac{120}{365}\right)} = 0.0475 = \underline{4.75\%}$

3. Number of days from November 15, 2004 to June 3, 2005

$$= (366 - 320) + 154$$

$$= 200$$

Interest owed = $Prt = \$1750(0.074)\left(\frac{200}{365}\right) = \underline{\$70.96}$

Mary owed Jason $70.96 for interest.

5. Number of days from March 16 to November 1 = 305 − 75 = 230
The amount invested in the term deposit should be

$$P = \frac{S}{(1+rt)} = \frac{\$45,000}{1+0.0575\left(\frac{230}{365}\right)} = \underline{\$43,426.53}$$

Review Problems *(continued)*

7. Number of days from August 18 to January 23 is 14 + 30 + 31 + 30 + 31 + 22 = 158
    Equivalent value on January 23 is

$$P(1 + rt) = \$1000\left[1 + 0.065\left(\frac{158}{365}\right)\right] = \underline{\$1028.14}$$

9. The equivalent value 2 months from now of the scheduled payments is

$$\$1000\left[1 + 0.0625\left(\frac{7}{12}\right)\right] + \frac{\$7500}{1 + 0.0625\left(\frac{2}{12}\right)} = \$1036.46 + \$7422.68 = \$8459.14$$

A single payment of $8459.14 two months from now will place the payee
in an equivalent financial position.

11. The size of the payment due 3 months ago is
$$\$1200\left[1 + 0.085\left(\tfrac{6}{12}\right)\right] = \$1251.00$$

The size of the payment due 3 months from now is
$$\$800\left[1 + 0.085\left(\tfrac{12}{12}\right)\right] = \$868.00$$

The equivalent value 4 months from now of these scheduled payments is
$$\$1251\left[1 + 0.0675\left(\tfrac{7}{12}\right)\right] + \$868\left[1 + 0.0675\left(\tfrac{1}{12}\right)\right] = \$1300.26 + \$872.88 = \underline{\$2173.14}$$
Tanya should be willing to accept a payment of $2173.14 four months from now.

Self-Test Exercise

1. The number of days from September 17, 2004 to March 11, 2005 was
    $$(366 - 261) + 70 = 175$$
    The interest rate earned was
    $$r = \frac{I}{Pt} = \frac{\$212.45}{\$3702.40\left(\frac{175}{365}\right)} = 0.1197 = \underline{11.97\%}$$

2. The duration of the loan was
    $$t = \frac{I}{Pr} = \frac{\$137.99}{\$3300(0.0925)} = 0.45206 \text{ year} = 165 \text{ days}$$
    September 8 comes 165 days after March 27. The loan was repaid on <u>September 8</u>.

3. The number of days from November 19, 2003 to March 3, 2004 is
    $$(365 - 323) + 63 = 105 \text{ days}$$
    The amount that had to be invested on November 19, 2003 was
    $$P = \frac{S}{(1 + rt)} = \frac{\$10,000}{1 + 0.045\left(\frac{105}{365}\right)} = \underline{\$9872.20}$$

4. Number of days from April 29 to June 14 = 2 + 31 + 13 = 46 days
    The economically equivalent payment on April 29 is
    $$P = \frac{S}{(1 + rt)} = \frac{\$60,000}{1 + 0.036\left(\frac{46}{365}\right)} = \underline{\$59,729.01}$$
    Sheldrick Contracting should propose to pay $59,729.01.

5. *a.* The economic value today of the full price due in 4 months is

$$P = \frac{S}{(1+rt)} = \frac{\$3995}{1+0.0525\left(\frac{4}{12}\right)} = \underline{\$3926.29}$$

Peter and Reesa will save $3926.29 – $3900 = $25.51 in current dollars <u>by paying the early-booking price</u>.

b. They will be indifferent between the alternatives if $3900 can earn $3995 – $3900 = $95 interest in 4 months. The corresponding interest rate would be

$$r = \frac{I}{Pt} = \frac{\$95}{\$3900\left(\frac{4}{12}\right)} \times 100\% = \underline{7.31\%}$$

It money can earn 7.31% pa, Peter and Reesa would be indifferent between the two prices.

6. The sum of the equivalent values of the scheduled payments at the focal date 10 months from now is

$$\$1200\left[1+0.059\left(\frac{10}{12}\right)\right] + \$900\left[1+0.059\left(\frac{5}{12}\right)\right] + \$1500\left[1+0.059\left(\frac{2}{12}\right)\right]$$

$$= \$1259.00 + \$922.12 + \$1514.75$$
$$= \underline{\$3695.87}$$

The equivalent replacement payment 10 months from now is $3695.87.

7. *a.* The economic value of the payments today is

$$\frac{\$5000}{1+0.06\left(\frac{4}{12}\right)} + \frac{\$5000}{1+0.06\left(\frac{8}{12}\right)} = \$4901.96 + \$4807.69 = \underline{\$9709.65}$$

b. The economic value today is

$$\frac{\$5000}{1+0.04\left(\frac{4}{12}\right)} + \frac{\$5000}{1+0.04\left(\frac{8}{12}\right)} = \$4934.21 + \$4870.13 = \underline{\$9804.34}$$

Today's economic value of the future payments is the amount of money paid today that can generate the future scheduled payments. At *lower* prevailing interest rates, you will need *more* money today to deliver the scheduled payments.

7 Applications of Simple Interest

Exercise 7.1

1. a. Maturity value, $S = P(1 + rt) = \$15,000\left[1 + 0.0225\left(\dfrac{120}{365}\right)\right] = \underline{\$15,110.96}$

   b. Maturity value $= \$15,110.96\left[1 + 0.0215\left(\dfrac{90}{365}\right)\right] = \underline{\$15,191.07}$

3. The investor will earn an interest rate differential of 3.2% – 3.0% = 0.2% on $60,000 for 270 days. The amount of additional interest on the single $60,000 GIC will then be

$$I = Prt = \$60,000(0.002)\left(\dfrac{270}{365}\right) = \underline{\$88.77}$$

5. Maturity value of the 180-day GIC $= \$15,000\left[1 + 0.0285\left(\dfrac{180}{365}\right)\right] = \$15,210.82$

   Maturity value of the first 90-day GIC $= \$15,000\left[1 + 0.0265\left(\dfrac{90}{365}\right)\right] = \$15,098.01$

   Maturity value of the second 90-day GIC $= \$15,098.01\left[1 + 0.0265\left(\dfrac{90}{365}\right)\right] = \$15,196.66$

   Therefore, the investor will earn
   $15,210.82 – $15,196.66 = $14.16 more from the 180-day GIC.

7. Number of days from June 1 to September 1 = 30 + 31 + 31 = 92 days
   The value of the term deposit on September 1

$$= \$12,000\left[1 + 0.028\left(\dfrac{92}{365}\right)\right] = \$12,084.69$$

Date	Amount in savings account
July 1	$\$12,000\left[1 + 0.0225\left(\dfrac{30}{365}\right)\right] = \$12,022.19$
August 1	$\$12,022.19\left[1 + 0.0225\left(\dfrac{31}{365}\right)\right] = \$12,045.16$
Sept. 1	$\$12,045.16\left[1 + 0.0225\left(\dfrac{31}{365}\right)\right] = \$12,068.18$

Joan will earn $12,084.69 – $12,068.18 = $16.51 more
from the term deposit up to September 1.

Exercise 7.1 (continued)

9.

Period (inclusive)	No. of days	Balance	Amount subject to a rate of: 1.25%	1.5%	1.75%
April 1-9	9	$2439	$1000	$1439	
April 10-22	13	3389	1000	2000	$389
April 23-30	8	2889	1000	1889	

Interest earned from April 1-9 inclusive

$$= [\$1000(0.0125) + \$1439(0.015)]\left(\frac{9}{365}\right) = \$0.840$$

Interest earned from April 10-22 inclusive

$$= [\$1000(0.0125) + \$2000(0.02)15 + \$389(0.0175)]\left(\frac{13}{365}\right) = \$1.756$$

Interest earned from April 23-30 inclusive

$$= [\$1000(0.0125) + \$1889(0.015)]\left(\frac{8}{365}\right) = \$0.895$$

Total interest for April = $0.840 + $1.756 + $0.895 = <u>$3.49</u>

11.

Period (inclusive)	No. of days	Balance (for interest calculation)	Interest rate	Interest
Sept. 1-6	6	$ 8572	1.25%	$ 1.761
Sept. 7-14	8	18,072	1.50%	5.941
Sept. 15-22	8	26,672	1.75%	10.230
Sept. 23-30	8	1672	0.50%	<u>0.183</u>
		Interest credited for September =		<u>$18.12</u>

Concept Questions (Section 7.2)

1. We need to know:
   - The amounts of the future payments;
   - The dates of the future payments;
   - The prevailing (or market) rate or return on similar investments.

3. Estimate the amounts and dates of the future cash flows from the investment. Decide on the *minimum* rate of return you are prepared to accept from the investment. Calculate the sum of the present values of the forecast cash flows, discounting them at the minimum acceptable rate of return.

Exercise 7.2

1. a. Price = Present value of payments

$$= \frac{\$500}{1 + 0.09\left(\frac{3}{12}\right)} + \frac{\$500}{1 + 0.09\left(\frac{6}{12}\right)}$$

$$= \$489.00 + \$478.47$$

$$= \underline{\$967.47}$$

1. *b.* Price in 1 month = Present value, 1 month from now, of the payments

$$= \frac{\$500}{1+0.09\left(\frac{2}{12}\right)} + \frac{\$500}{1+0.09\left(\frac{5}{12}\right)}$$

$$= \$492.61 + \$481.93$$

$$= \underline{\$974.54}$$

c. The shorter the time interval until receipt of a specified payment, the closer the economic value will be to the nominal amount of the payment.

3. *a.* Value of certificate A = Sum of the present values of the payments.

$$= \frac{\$1000}{1+0.0575\left(\frac{4}{12}\right)} + \frac{\$1000}{1+0.0575\left(\frac{8}{12}\right)}$$

$$= \$981.194 + \$963.082$$

$$= \underline{\$1944.28}$$

b. Value of certificate B $= \dfrac{\$1000}{1+0.0575\left(\frac{5}{12}\right)} + \dfrac{\$1000}{1+0.0575\left(\frac{9}{12}\right)}$

$$= \$976.60 + \$958.66$$

$$= \underline{\$1935.26}$$

c. Since the payments from B are received a month after the respective payments from A, certificate B is not as valuable as certificate A.

5. Maximum price = Sum of the present values of the payments

$$= \frac{\$4000}{1+0.0925\left(\frac{3}{12}\right)} + \frac{\$2500}{1+0.0925\left(\frac{6}{12}\right)} + \frac{\$5000}{1+0.0925\left(\frac{9}{12}\right)}$$

$$= \$3909.59 + \$2389.49 + \$4675.63$$

$$= \underline{\$10,974.71}$$

7. Number of days from:
   March 20 to July 1 = 182 − 79 = 103 days
   March 20 to September 1 = 244 − 79 = 165 days

Payment on July 1 $= \$3000\left[1+0.11\left(\dfrac{103}{365}\right)\right] = \$3093.12$

Payment on September 1 $= \$5000\left[1+0.11\left(\dfrac{165}{365}\right)\right] = \$5248.63$

Sale proceeds = Sum of present values of payments

$$= \frac{\$3093.12}{1+0.16\left(\frac{103}{365}\right)} + \frac{\$5248.63}{1+0.16\left(\frac{165}{365}\right)}$$

$$= \$2959.50 + \$4894.61$$

$$= \underline{\$7854.11}$$

Concept Questions (Section 7.3)

1. The price of the 98-day T-bill is higher because less time remains until the $100,000 face value is received. You do not need as large a difference between the face value and the purchase price to provide the required rate of return.

3. The fair market value will steadily rise, reaching the T-bill's face value on the maturity date.

Exercise 7.3

1. Price $= \dfrac{S}{(1+rt)} = \dfrac{\$25,000}{1+0.03672\left(\frac{91}{365}\right)} = \underline{\$24,773}$

3. Time remaining until maturity = 62 days

    Price $= \dfrac{S}{(1+rt)} = \dfrac{\$1,000,000}{1+0.0410\left(\frac{62}{365}\right)} = \underline{\$993,084}$

5.

Term	Price
30 days	$\dfrac{\$100,000}{1+0.055\left(\frac{30}{365}\right)} = \underline{\$99,550}$
60 days	$\dfrac{\$100,000}{1+0.055\left(\frac{60}{365}\right)} = \underline{\$99,104}$
90 days	$\dfrac{\$100,000}{1+0.055\left(\frac{90}{365}\right)} = \underline{\$98,662}$

   The longer the term of the commercial paper issue, the lower the price paid on the issue date.

7. Time remaining until maturity = 364 – 60 = 304 days

    Selling price $= \dfrac{S}{(1+rt)} = \dfrac{\$100,000}{1+0.049\left(\frac{304}{365}\right)} = \underline{\$96,079}$

9. Effectively, the interest earned by the buyer was
    $$I = S - P = \$50,000 - \$48,880 = \$1120$$
    The corresponding annual yield rate was
    $$r = \dfrac{I}{Pt} = \dfrac{\$1120}{\$48,880\left(\frac{182}{365}\right)} = 0.04595 = \underline{4.595\%}$$
    The annual yield on the T-bill was 4.595%.

11. If purchased for $99,000, the T-bill will effectively pay $1000 interest when it matures at $100,000. The time remaining until maturity (when the T-bill will have a market value of $99,000) is
    $$t = \dfrac{I}{Pr} = \dfrac{\$1000}{\$99,000(0.0519)} = 0.19462 \text{ year} = 0.19462 \times 365 \text{ days} = 71.0 \text{ days}$$
    The T-bill's price will first exceed $99,000 $\underline{71 \text{ days}}$ before its maturity date.

13. *a.* Purchase price $= \dfrac{\$100,000}{1+0.031\left(\frac{168}{365}\right)} = \underline{\$98,593}$

    b. (i) Market value $= \dfrac{\$100,000}{1+0.034\left(\frac{83}{365}\right)} = \underline{\$99,233}$

    (ii) Market value $= \dfrac{\$100,000}{1+0.031\left(\frac{83}{365}\right)} = \underline{\$99,300}$

    (iii) Market value $= \dfrac{\$100,000}{1+0.028\left(\frac{83}{365}\right)} = \underline{\$99,367}$

Exercise 7.3 *(continued)*

13. *c.* The amount earned in each case was:

(i) $I = S - P = \$99{,}233 - \$98{,}593 = \$640$

(ii) $I = S - P = \$99{,}300 - \$98{,}593 = \$707$

(iii) $I = S - P = \$99{,}367 - \$98{,}593 = \$774$

The rate of return actually realized in each case was:

(i) $r = \dfrac{I}{Pt} = \dfrac{\$640}{\$98{,}593\left(\frac{85}{365}\right)} = 0.02787 = \underline{2.787\%}$

(ii) $r = \dfrac{\$707}{\$98{,}593\left(\frac{85}{365}\right)} = 0.03079 = \underline{3.079\%}$

(iii) $r = \dfrac{\$774}{\$98{,}593\left(\frac{85}{365}\right)} = 0.03371 = \underline{3.371\%}$

Exercise 7.4

1.

Date	Number of days	Interest rate	Interest	Accrued interest	Payment (Advance)	Principal portion	Balance
5-Feb	--	--	--	--	($15,000)	($15,000)	$15,000
29-Feb	24	8.50%	$83.84	~~$83.84~~	83.84		15,000
15-Mar	15	8.50	52.40	52.40	10,000	10,000	5000
31-Mar	16	8.50	18.63	~~71.03~~	71.03		5000
30-Apr	30	8.50	34.93	~~34.93~~	34.93		5000
1-May	1	8.50	1.16	1.16	(7000)	(7000)	12,000
31-May	30	8.50	83.84	~~85.00~~	85.00		12,000

The interest charged to Dr. Robillard's account was $83.84 on February 29, $71.03 on March 31, $34.93 on April 30, and $85.00 on May 31.

3.

Date	Number of days	Interest rate	Interest	Accrued interest	Payment (Advance)	Principal portion	Balance
3-Jul	--	--	--	--	($25,000)	($25,000)	$25,000
20-Jul	17	10.00%	$116.44	~~$116.44~~	116.44		25,000
29-Jul	9	10.00	61.64	61.64	(30,000)	(30,000)	55,000
5-Aug	7	10.00	105.48	167.12			55,000
20-Aug	15	9.75	220.38	~~387.50~~	387.50		55,000

The amounts of interest charged on July 20 and August 20 were $116.44 and $387.50, respectively.

5.

Date	Number of days	Interest rate	Interest	Accrued interest	Payment (Advance)	Principal portion	Balance
7-Oct	--	--	--	--	($30,000)	($30,000)	$30,000
15-Oct	8	7.75%	$50.96	~~$50.96~~	$50.96		30,000
15-Nov	31	7.75%	197.47	~~197.47~~	197.47		30,000
24-Nov	9	7.75%	57.33	57.33	($15,000)	(15,000)	45,000
15-Dec	21	7.75%	200.65	~~257.98~~	257.98		45,000
17-Dec	2	7.75%	19.11	19.11			45,000
23-Dec	6	7.50%	55.48	74.59	(20,000)	(20,000)	65,000
15-Jan	23	7.50%	307.19	~~381.78~~	381.78		65,000

Exercise 7.4 *(continued)*

7.

Date	Number of days	Interest rate	Interest	Accrued interest	Payment (Advance)	Principal portion	Balance
31-Mar	--	--	--	--	($30,000.00)	($30,000)	$30,000
18-Apr	18	7.50%	$110.96	$110.96	110.96		30,000
28-Apr	10	7.50	61.64	61.64	(10,000.00)	(10,000)	40,000
14-May	16	7.50	131.51	193.15			40,000
18-May	4	7.75	33.97	227.12	227.12		40,000
1-Jun	14	7.75	118.90	118.90	(15,000.00)	(15,000)	55,000
18-Jun	17	7.75	198.53	317.43	5317.43	5000	50,000
3-Jul	15	7.75	159.25	159.25	10,000.00	10,000	40,000
18-Jul	15	7.75	127.40	286.65	286.65		40,000

9.

Date	Number of days	Interest rate	Interest	Accrued interest	Payment (Advance)	Principal portion	Balance
15-Aug	--	--	--	--	--	--	$3589.80
31-Aug	16	8.75%	$13.77	$13.77	$300.00	$300.00	3289.80
15-Sep	15	8.75	11.83	25.60	100.00	74.40	3215.40
30-Sep	15	8.75	11.56	11.56	300.00	300.00	2915.40
11-Oct	11	8.75	7.69	19.25			2915.40
15-Oct	4	8.50	2.72	21.97	100.00	78.03	2837.37
31-Oct	16	8.50	10.57	10.57	300.00	300.00	2537.37
15-Nov	15	8.50	8.86	19.43	100.00	80.57	2456.80

11.

Date	Number of days	Interest rate	Interest	Accrued interest	Payment (Advance)	Principal portion	Balance
1-Apr	--	--	--	--	--	--	$6000.00
1-May	30	8.25%	$40.68	$40.68	$1000.00	$959.32	5040.68
1-Jun	31	8.25	35.32	35.32	1000.00	964.68	4076.00
7-Jun	6	8.25	5.53	5.53			4076.00
1-Jul	24	8.00	21.44	26.97	1000.00	973.03	3102.97
1-Aug	31	8.00	21.08	21.08	1000.00	978.92	2124.05
27-Aug	26	8.00	12.10	12.10			2124.05
1-Sep	5	8.25	2.40	14.50	1000.00	985.50	1138.55
1-Oct	30	8.25	7.72	7.72	1000.00	992.28	146.27
1-Nov	31	8.25	1.02	1.02	147.29	146.27	0.00

Total of the interest charges = $147.29

13.

Date	Number of days	Interest rate	Interest	Accrued interest	Payment (Advance)	Principal portion	Balance
23-Feb	--	--	--	--	--	--	$5000.00
15-Apr	51	5.25%	$36.68	$36.68	$1000.00	$963.32	4036.68
15-May	30	5.25	17.42	17.42	1000.00	982.58	3054.10
15-Jun	31	5.25	13.62	13.62	1000.00	986.38	2067.72
15-Jul	30	5.50	9.35	9.35	1000.00	990.65	1077.07
31-Jul	16	5.50	2.60	2.60			1077.07
15-Aug	15	5.75	2.55	5.15	1000.00	994.85	82.22
15-Sep	31	5.75	0.40	0.40	82.62	82.22	0.00

Exercise 7.5

1. Number of days from June 1 to September 3 = 246 − 152 = 94
   Number of days from Sept. 3 to (and including) Nov. 30 = 334 + 1 − 246 = 89
   Interest accrued during the 6-month grace period

$$= \$9400(0.0925)\frac{94}{365} + \$9400(0.09)\frac{89}{365} = \$430.21$$

Date	Number of days	Interest rate	Interest	Accrued interest	Payment (Advance)	Principal portion	Balance
1-Dec	---	---	---	---	---	---	$9830.21
31-Dec	30	9.00%	$72.72	~~$72.72~~	$135.00	$62.28	9767.93
17-Jan	17	9.00	40.95	40.95		0.00	9767.93
31-Jan	14	9.25	34.66	~~75.61~~	135.00	59.39	9708.54
28-Feb	28	9.25	68.89	~~68.89~~	135.00	66.11	9642.43

3. Number of days from July 1 to September 22 = 265 − 182 = 83
   Number of days from Sept. 22 to (and including) Dec. 31 = 365 + 1 − 265 = 101
   Interest accrued during the 6-month grace period

$$= \$6800(0.085)\frac{83}{365} + \$6800(0.0825)\frac{101}{365} = \$286.67$$

Date	Number of days	Interest rate	Interest	Accrued interest	Payment (Advance)	Principal portion	Balance
1-Jan	---	---	---	---	---	---	$7086.67
31-Jan	30	8.25%	$48.05	~~$48.05~~	$200.00	$151.95	6934.72
28-Feb	28	8.25	43.89	~~43.89~~	200.00	156.11	6778.61
2-Mar	2	8.25	3.06	3.06			6778.61
25-Mar	23	7.75	33.10	36.16	500.00	500.00	6278.61
31-Mar	6	7.75	8.00	~~44.16~~	200.00	155.84	<u>6122.77</u>

5. Number of days from June 1 to (and including) Nov. 30 = 334 + 1 − 152 = 183
   Interest accrued during the 6-month grace period

$$= \$5200(0.0975)\frac{183}{365} = \$254.19$$

Date	Number of days	Interest rate	Interest	Accrued interest	Payment (Advance)	Principal portion	Balance
1-Dec	---	---	---	---	---	---	$5454.19
31-Dec	30	9.75%	$43.71	~~$43.71~~	$110.00	$66.29	5387.90
31-Jan	31	9.75	44.62	~~44.62~~	110.00	65.38	5322.52
14-Feb	14	9.50	19.39	19.39	300.00	300.00	5022.52
28-Feb	14	9.50	18.30	~~37.69~~	110.00	72.31	4950.21

Review Problems

1. The maximum price will be the sum of the present values of the payments discounted at the minimum required rate of return. That is,

$$\text{Price} = \frac{\$4500}{1+0.105\left(\frac{4}{12}\right)} + \frac{\$3000}{1+0.105\left(\frac{8}{12}\right)} + \frac{\$5500}{1+0.105(1)}$$

$$= \$4347.826 + \$2803.738 + \$4977.376$$
$$= \underline{\$12,128.94}$$

The highest price the investor should pay is $12,128.95.

3. $$\text{Price} = \frac{S}{(1+rt)} = \frac{\$50,000}{1+0.04273\left(\frac{91}{365}\right)} = \underline{\$49,472.95}$$

5. The earnings from the certificate will be
$$I = S - P = \$100,000 - \$98,950 = \$1050$$
The corresponding annual rate of return is

$$r = \frac{I}{Pt} = \frac{\$1050}{\$98,950\left(\frac{90}{365}\right)} = 0.04304 = \underline{4.304\%}$$

The investment will yield the buyer 4.304%.

7. In effect, the investor will earn a 0.25% higher rate of return on the single $80,000 GIC. The dollar amount of extra interest earned will be

$$I = Prt = \$80,000(0.0025)\left(\frac{180}{365}\right) = \underline{\$98.63}$$

9.

Period (inclusive)	No. of days	Balance	Amount subject to a rate of:		
			1.00%	1.75%	2.25%
Jan. 1-13	13	$3678	$1000	$2000	$678
Jan. 14-24	11	878	878		
Jan. 25-31	7	1828	1000	828	

I (Jan. 1-13) = $\left[\$1000(0.01) + \$2000(0.0175) + \$678(0.0225)\right]\left(\frac{13}{365}\right) = \$2.146$

I (Jan. 14-24) = $\$878(0.01)\frac{11}{365} = \$0.265$

I (Jan. 25-31) = $\left[\$1000(0.01) + \$828(0.0175)\right]\left(\frac{7}{365}\right) = \$0.470$

Total interest for January = $2.146 + $0.265 + $0.470 = $\underline{\$2.88}$

11.

Date	Number of days	Interest rate	Interest	Accrued interest	Payment (Advance)	Principal portion	Balance
8-Mar	--	--	--	--	($40,000)	($40,000)	$40,000
24-Mar	16	7.25%	$127.12	$~~127.12~~	$127.12		40,000
2-Apr	9	7.25	71.51	71.51	(15,000.00)	(15,000)	55,000
24-Apr	22	7.25	240.34	~~311.85~~	311.85		55,000
13-May	19	7.25	207.57	207.57			55,000
24-May	11	7.50	124.32	~~331.89~~	331.89		55,000
5-Jun	12	7.50	135.62	135.62	25,000.00	25,000	30,000
24-Jun	19	7.50	117.12	~~252.74~~	252.74		30,000

The first four interest deductions were $\underline{\$127.12, \$311.85, \$331.89, \text{ and } \$252.74}$.

Self-Test Exercise

1. Size of the first payment = $P(1 + rt) = \$1900\left[1 + 0.125\left(\frac{3}{12}\right)\right] = \$1959.38$

    Size of the second payment = $\$1900\left[1 + 0.125\left(\frac{6}{12}\right)\right] = \$2018.75$

    Price = Sum of present values of the payments (discounted at 18%)

    $$= \frac{\$1959.38}{1 + 0.18\left(\frac{2}{12}\right)} + \frac{\$2018.75}{1 + 0.18\left(\frac{5}{12}\right)}$$

    $$= \$1902.31 + \$1877.91$$
    $$= \underline{\$3780.22}$$

    The finance company should pay \$3780.22 if it requires an 18% rate of return.

2. a. Price = $\dfrac{S}{(1 + rt)} = \dfrac{\$25,000}{1 + 0.05438\left(\frac{91}{365}\right)} = \underline{\$24,665.59}$

    b. Time left until maturity = 91 − 34 = 57 days
        The amount earned by the second investor will be
        $$I = S - P = \$25,000 - \$24,775 = \$225$$
        This will provide a rate of return of
        $$r = \frac{I}{Pt} = \frac{\$225}{\$24,775\left(\frac{57}{365}\right)} = 0.05815 = \underline{5.815\%}$$

    c. During his 34-day holding period, the first investor earned
        $$I = S - P = \$24,775 - \$24,665.59 = \$109.41$$
        This amount provided a rate of return of
        $$r = \frac{I}{Pt} = \frac{\$109.41}{\$24,665.59\left(\frac{34}{365}\right)} = 0.04762 = \underline{4.762\%}$$

3. Maturity value of the 180-day GIC = $\$20,000\left[1 + 0.035\left(\dfrac{180}{365}\right)\right] = \$20,345.21$

    Maturity value of the first 90-day GIC = $\$20,000\left[1 + 0.033\left(\dfrac{90}{365}\right)\right] = \$20,162.74$

    Maturity value of the second 90-day GIC = $\$20,162.74\left[1 + 0.063\left(\dfrac{90}{365}\right)\right] = \$20,326.80$

    Therefore, Paul will earn \$20,345.21 − \$20,326.80 = $\underline{\$18.41}$ more by purchasing the 180-day GIC.

4.

Date	Number of days	Interest rate	Interest	Accrued interest	Payment (Advance)	Principal portion	Balance
3-Jun	--	--	--	--	($50,000)	($50,000)	$50,000
26-Jun	23	9.00%	$283.56	$283.56	$283.56		50,000
30-Jun	4	9.00	49.32	49.32	(40,000)	(40,000)	90,000
5-Jul	5	9.00	110.96	160.28			90,000
17-Jul	12	9.25	273.70	433.98	(25,000)	(25,000)	115,000
26-Jul	9	9.25	262.29	696.27	696.27		115,000
31-Jul	5	9.50	149.66	149.66	30,000	30,000	85,000
18-Aug	18	9.50	398.22	547.88	35,000	35,000	50,000
26-Aug	8	9.50	104.11	651.99	651.99		50,000

Self-Test Exercise *(continued)*

5.

Date	Number of days	Interest rate	Interest	Accrued interest	Payment (Advance)	Principal portion	Balance
23-May	---	---	---	---	---	---	$15,000.00
15-Jun	23	9.50%	$89.79	$89.79	$700.00	$610.21	14,389.79
15-Jul	30	9.50%	112.36	112.36	700.00	587.64	13,802.15
26-Jul	11	9.50%	39.52	39.52			13,802.15
15-Aug	20	9.25%	69.96	109.48	700.00	590.52	13,211.63
14-Sep	30	9.25%	100.44	100.44			13,211.63
15-Sep	1	9.75%	3.53	103.97	700.00	596.03	12,615.60

Exercise 7A

1. Issue date = May 19 = 139th day of the year (Table 6.2)
    Legal due date = 139 + 120 + 3 = 262nd day of the year = <u>September 19</u>

3. Term = October 17 – 3 days – July 6 = 290 – 3 – 187 = <u>100 days</u>

5. Issue date = Feb. 28 – 3 days – 4 months = <u>October 25</u>

7. Issue date = September 2 – 3 days – 180 days
    = 245 – 183
    = 62nd day of the year
    = <u>March 3</u>

9. Interest period = August 30 + 3 days – April 30 = 242 + 3 – 120 = 125 days

    Maturity value, $S = P(1 + rt) = \$1000\left[1 + 0.095\left(\dfrac{125}{365}\right)\right]$ = <u>$1032.53</u>

11. Face value, $P = \dfrac{S}{(1+rt)} = \dfrac{\$2667.57}{1 + 0.102\left(\frac{93}{365}\right)}$ = <u>$2600.00</u>

13. $I = S - P = \$6388.04 - \$6200 = \$188.04$

    $r = \dfrac{I}{Pt} = \dfrac{\$188.04}{\$6200\left(\frac{123}{365}\right)} = 0.090 = $ <u>9.00%</u>

15. $I = S - P = \$5275.22 - \$5200 = \$75.22$

    $t = \dfrac{I}{Pr} = \dfrac{\$75.22}{\$5200(0.11)} = 0.131504$ year = 48 days

    Term = 48 – 3 = <u>45 days</u>

17. Time until maturity = 50 + 3 – 9 = 44 days

    Proceeds = $\dfrac{S}{(1+rt)} = \dfrac{\$1000}{1 + 0.10\left(\frac{44}{365}\right)}$ = <u>$988.09</u>

19. Maturity value = $P(1 + rt) = \$2700\left[1 + 0.10\left(\dfrac{185}{365}\right)\right]$ = $2836.85

    Time from sale date until maturity = 84 days

    Proceeds = $\dfrac{S}{(1+rt)} = \dfrac{\$2836.85}{1 + 0.12\left(\frac{84}{365}\right)}$ = <u>$2760.61</u>

21. Maturity value = $P(1 + rt) = \$9000\left[1+0.08\left(\dfrac{94}{365}\right)\right] = \$9185.42$

    Time from date of sale until maturity = 94 − 35 = 59 days

    Discount rate, $r = \dfrac{I}{Pt} = \dfrac{\$9185.42 - \$9075.40}{\$9075.40\left(\frac{59}{365}\right)} = 0.075 = \underline{7.50\%}$

23. *a.* Legal due date = February 28, 2006 + 3 days
    = <u>March 3, 2006</u>

    b. Legal due date = September 29, 2005 + 153 days
    = 272nd day + 153 days
    = (425 − 365) days into 2006
    = 60th day in 2006
    = <u>March 1, 2006</u>

25. Maturity value, $S = P(1 + rt) = \$1000\left[1+0.1075\left(\dfrac{123}{365}\right)\right] = \underline{\$1036.23}$

27. Time from sale date until due date = 93 − 31 = 62 days

    Fair selling price = $\dfrac{S}{(1+rt)} = \dfrac{\$3300}{1+0.0775\left(\frac{62}{365}\right)} = \underline{\$3257.12}$

29. Maturity value = $\$750\left[1+0.125\left(\dfrac{103}{365}\right)\right] = \$776.46$

    Time from settlement date until legal due date = 103 − 26 = 77 days

    Settlement amount = $\dfrac{\$776.46}{1+0.0825\left(\frac{77}{365}\right)} = \underline{\$763.17}$

31. Legal due date = December 30 + 3 days = January 2
    Total interest period = 365 + 2 − 181 = 186 days

    Maturity value = $\$2900\left[1+0.135\left(\dfrac{186}{365}\right)\right] = \$3099.50$

    Time from September 1 to January 2 = 186 − 63 = 123 days

    Proceeds = $\dfrac{\$3099.50}{1+0.0975\left(\frac{123}{365}\right)} = \underline{\$3000.90}$

8   Compound Interest: Future Value and Present Value

Concept Questions (Section 8.1)

1. We compound interest when we convert it to principal and calculate subsequent interest on both the principal and the converted interest.

3. The "periodic rate of interest" is the percent interest earned in a single compounding period. The "nominal rate of interest" is the *annual* interest rate you obtain if you *extend* the periodic interest rate to a full year. This extension is done by multiplying the periodic rate of interest by the number of compounding periods in a year.

Exercise 8.1

1. $i = \dfrac{j}{m} = \dfrac{10.8\%}{4} = \underline{2.7\%}$ (per quarter)

3. $i = \dfrac{j}{m} = \dfrac{10.5\%}{12} = \underline{0.875\%}$ (per month)

5. $j = mi = 12(0.91667\%) = \underline{11.0\%}$ compounded monthly

7. $m = \dfrac{j}{i} = \dfrac{9.5\%}{2.375\%} = 4$ (that is, <u>quarterly compounding</u>)

9. $m = \dfrac{j}{i} = \dfrac{13.5\%}{1.125\%} = 12$ (that is, <u>monthly compounding</u>)

Concept Questions (Section 8.2)

1. The future value of an investment at a future date is the combined value of the investment's principal and interest on that date.

3. The more frequent the compounding of the 6% nominal rate, the more interest will be earned by the investment. Therefore, 6% compounded quarterly is the preferred rate. (The other two rates both earn 3% interest in the 6-month term.)
   (1) 6% compounded quarterly; (2) 6% compounded semiannually and 6% pa (tied)

5. Quadrupling is the result of from two successive doublings. If an investment doubles in 9 years, it will quadruple in <u>18 years</u>.

7. Inflation is not the fundamental reason—$100 received today would be worth more than $100 received at a future date even if the inflation rate were 0%. The fundamental reason is that money can be invested to earn interest. $100 received today can earn interest for a longer period than $100 received at a future date.

Exercise 8.2

1. $i = \dfrac{j}{m} = \dfrac{6\%}{2} = 3\%$ (per half year)

   $n = m(\text{Term in years}) = 2(7) = 14$ compounding periods

   Maturity value, $FV = PV(1+i)^n = \$5000(1.03)^{14} = \underline{\$7562.95}$

3. $i = \dfrac{j}{m} = \dfrac{7.5\%}{12} = 0.625\%$ (per month)

   $n = m(\text{Term in years}) = 12(3.25) = 39$ compounding periods

   Maturity value, $FV = PV(1+i)^n = \$12,100(1.00625)^{39} = \underline{\$15,428.20}$

5.

	m	i	n	Maturity amount
a.	1	$\dfrac{9\%}{1} = 9\%$	25	$\$1000(1.09)^{25} = \underline{\$8623.08}$
b.	2	$\dfrac{9\%}{2} = 4.5\%$	$2(25) = 50$	$\$1000(1.045)^{50} = \underline{\$9032.64}$
c.	4	$\dfrac{9\%}{4} = 2.25\%$	$4(25) = 100$	$\$1000(1.0225)^{100} = \underline{\$9254.05}$
d.	12	$\dfrac{9\%}{12} = 0.75\%$	$12(25) = 300$	$\$1000(1.0075)^{300} = \underline{\$9408.41}$

7.

	i	n	Maturity amount
a.	$\dfrac{8\%}{12} = 0.\overline{6}\%$	12	$\$100(1.00\overline{6})^{12} = \$108.30$
b.	$\dfrac{8.1\%}{4} = 2.025\%$	4	$\$100(1.02025)^{4} = \$108.35$
c.	$\dfrac{8.2\%}{2} = 4.1\%$	2	$\$100(1.041)^{2} = \$108.37$
d.		8.3%	1	$\$100(1.083)^{1} = \$108.30$

   The investor would prefer <u>8.2% compounded semiannually</u> since it produces the highest maturity value.

9. $PV = \$3000;\ i = \dfrac{9.5\%}{2} = 4.75\%;\ n = 2(1.5) = 3$

   Maturity value, $FV = PV(1+i)^n = \$3000(1.0475)^3 = \underline{\$3448.13}$

   Interest charged $= FV - PV = \$3448.13 - \$3000 = \underline{\$448.13}$

11. Maturity value at 11% $= PV(1+i)^n = \$1000(1.11)^{25} = \$13,585.46$

    Maturity value at 10% $= PV(1+i)^n = \$1000(1.10)^{25} = \underline{\$10,834.71}$

    Difference: $\underline{\$\ 2750.75}$

    The difference is $\dfrac{\$2750.75}{\$10,834.71} \times 100\% = \underline{25.39\%}$ of the

    maturity value at 10% compounded annually.

13. Maturity value after 25 years = $PV(1+i)^n = \$1000(1.09)^{25} = \$8623.08$

    Maturity value after 20 years = $PV(1+i)^n = \$1000(1.09)^{20} = \underline{\$5604.41}$

    Difference: $\underline{\$3018.67}$

    The difference is $\dfrac{\$3018.67}{\$5604.41} \times 100\% = \underline{53.86\%}$ of the amount after 20 years.

    Note: The equality of the answers in problems 13 and 14 is not coincidence. The percent change in the value of the investment in any 5-year period will be the same (53.86%). It is a property of compound interest that, for a given interest rate, the percent change in value is the same in all intervals of a given length.

15.

Interest rate	20 years	25 years	30 years
8%	$4660.96	$6848.48	$10,062.66
10%	$6727.50	$10,834.71	$17,449.40

17. Equivalent value = $FV = PV(1+i)^n = \$5000(1.0825)^4 = \underline{\$6865.65}$

19. For the first payment, $PV = \$1300$, $i = \frac{6\%}{4} = 1.5\%$; $n = 4(4) = 16$

    For the second payment, $PV = \$1800$, $i = \frac{6\%}{4} = 1.5\%$; $n = 4(2.25) = 9$

    The combined equivalent value 4 years from now is

    $\$1300(1.015)^{16} + \$1800(1.015)^9 = \$1649.681 + \$2058.102 = \underline{\$3707.78}$

21. Equivalent amount $= FV = PV(1+i)^n = \$2000(1.0275)^8 = \underline{\$2484.76}$

23.

Principal	i	n	Maturity amount
$3000	2.5%	6	$3000(1.025)^6 = \$$ 3479.08
$3500	2.5%	4	$3500(1.025)^4 = \$$ 3863.35
$4000	2.5%	2	$4000(1.025)^2 = \$$ 4202.50

Total amount owed = $\underline{\$11,544.93}$

25. $PV = \$5000$ and $i = \dfrac{8\%}{12} = 0.\overline{6}\%$ in each case.

Grand-child	Age	Time until 19th birthday	n
Donna	12 yr, 7 mo	6 yr, 5 mo	77
Tim	10 yr, 3 mo	8 yr, 9 mo	105
Gary	7 yr, 11 mo	11 yr, 1 mo	133

Donna will receive $\$5000(1.00\overline{6})^{77} = \underline{\$8340.04}$

Tim will receive $\$5000(1.00\overline{6})^{105} = \underline{\$10,045.40}$

Gary will receive $\$5000(1.00\overline{6})^{133} = \underline{\$12,099.48}$

Exercise 8.2 *(continued)*

27. For the current GIC, $i = \dfrac{6\%}{2} = 3.00\%$; $n = 5(2) = 10$

    Maturity value $= FV = PV(1+i)^n = \$60{,}000\,(1.03)^{10} = \$80{,}634.98$
    Maturity value of the second GIC will be:

    a. $FV = \$80{,}634.98\,(1.03)^{10} = \underline{\$108{,}366.67}$

    b. $FV = \$80{,}634.98\,(1.035)^{10} = \underline{\$113{,}743.60}$

    c. $FV = \$80{,}634.98\,(1.025)^{10} = \underline{\$103{,}219.59}$

29. For the first 15 months, $PV = \$7000$; $i = \dfrac{9.5\%}{4} = 2.375\%$; $n = \dfrac{15}{3} = 5$

    $$FV = PV(1+i)^n = \$7000\,(1.02375)^5 = \$7871.68$$

    For the next 6 months, $PV = \$7871.68$; $i = \dfrac{8.5\%}{2} = 4.25\%$; $n = 1$

    Total amount owed $= \$7871.68\,(1.0425)^1 = \underline{\$8206.23}$

31. Amount owed after $2\frac{1}{2}$ years $= PV(1+i)^n = \$3000\,(1.025)^5 = \$3394.22$
    Balance owed after \$1000 payment $= \$2394.22$
    Amount owed after another 6 months $= \$2394.22\,(1.025)^1 = \$2454.08$
    Amount owing today (after another 2 years) $= \$2454.08\,(1.005)^{24} = \underline{\$2766.14}$

33. Amount owed after the \$2500 payment $= PV(1+i)^n - \$2500$

    $$= \$10{,}000\,(1.0055)^9 - \$2500$$
    $$= \$8006.03$$

    Amount owed 3 months later $= \$8006.03\,(1.0055)^3 = \$8138.86$

    Amount owed after the \$3000 payment $= \$8138.86\,(1.0175)^2 - \$3000$
    $$= \$5426.21$$

    Amount owed 6 months later $= \$5426.21\,(1.0175)^2$
    $$= \underline{\$5617.79}$$

Concept Questions (Section 8.3)

1. The "discount rate" is the interest rate used in a present value calculation.

3. Discounting is the opposite of compounding.

5. We are told that the present value of any payment discounted back 8 years is just half of the payment. Since 16 years contains two 8-year intervals, there will be two "halvings" of the payment amount. The present value, 16 years earlier, of X will be $\frac{1}{2} \times \frac{1}{2} X = \underline{\underline{\frac{1}{4} X}}$.

Exercise 8.3

1. Given: $i = \frac{4.5\%}{1} = 4.5\%$ (per year); $n = 1(10) = 10$ periods

   Principal, $PV = FV(1+i)^{-n} = \$10{,}000\,(1.045)^{-10} = \underline{\$6439.28}$

3. Given: $i = \frac{7.5\%}{2} = 3.75\%$ (per half year); $n = 2(3.5) = 7$ periods

   Principal, $PV = FV(1+i)^{-n} = \$9704.61(1.0375)^{-7} = \underline{\$7500.00}$

5. Given: $i = \frac{7.5\%}{2} = 3.75\%$; $n = 2(8) = 16$; $FV = \$10{,}000$

   Required investment $= PV = FV(1+i)^{-n} = \$10{,}000(1.0375)^{-16} = \underline{\$5548.69}$

7. Equivalent amount today $= PV = FV(1+i)^{-n} = \$3500\,(1.011)^{-14} = \underline{\$3002.98}$

9. The creditor should accept the economically equivalent amount, that is, the present value of the scheduled payment.
   $$PV = FV(1+i)^{-n} = \$4000\,(1.03)^{-10} = \underline{\$2976.38}$$
   The creditor should accept \$2976.38 today instead of \$5000 five years from now.

11. Today's economic value of the Jorgensen offer is
    $$\$10{,}000 + \$51{,}000(1.0325)^{-2} = \$57{,}839.88$$
    Therefore, Gwen should <u>accept the Araki offer</u> because it is <u>worth \$160.12 more</u>.

13. The appropriate price to pay is the present value of the future cash flows.
    $$\begin{aligned}
    \text{Combined present value} &= \$100(1.08)^{-1} + \$600(1.08)^{-2} + \$400(1.08)^{-3} \\
    &= \$92.593 + \$514.403 + \$317.533 \\
    &= \$924.53
    \end{aligned}$$
    You <u>should not pay more than \$924.53</u> if you want a rate of return of 8%.

15. Given: $i = \frac{5.5\%}{4} = 1.375\%$; $n = 4(2.75) = 11$

    Equivalent value $= PV = FV(1+i)^{-n} = \$1300\,(1.01375)^{-11} = \underline{\$1118.67}$

17. Sum of the equivalent values of the payments, 18 months from now,
    $$\begin{aligned}
    &= \$900\left(1.004\overline{16}\right)^{18} + \$500\left(1.004\overline{16}\right)^{-4} \\
    &= \$969.944 + \$491.753 \\
    &= \underline{\$1461.70}
    \end{aligned}$$

19. Sum of the equivalent values of the payments, 2.25 years from now,
    $$\begin{aligned}
    &= \$1500\,(1.0225)^{12} + \$2500\,(1.0225)^{-9} \\
    &= \$1959.07 + \$2046.30 \\
    &= \underline{\$4005.37}
    \end{aligned}$$

21. Sum of the equivalent values of the payments, 18 months from now,
    $$\begin{aligned}
    &= \$750\,(1.0475)^{3} + \$1000\,(1.0475)^{-1} + \$1250\,(1.0475)^{-5} \\
    &= \$862.032 + \$954.654 + \$991.151 \\
    &= \underline{\$2807.84}
    \end{aligned}$$

23. Equivalent payment 1 year from now $= \$2500\,(1.0175)^{3} + \$2500\,(1.0175)^{-4}$
    $$\begin{aligned}
    &= \$2633.56 + \$2332.40 \\
    &= \underline{\$4965.96}
    \end{aligned}$$

25. The data for the three certificates are presented in the following table.

Maturity Value	Term	j	m	i	n
$4000	3.5 years	5%	2	2.5%	7
$5000	4.5 years	5%	2	2.5%	9
$6000	5.5 years	5.6%	4	1.4%	22

Michelle should invest:

$$PV = FV(1+i)^{-n} = \$4000(1.025)^{-7} = \underline{\$3365.06} \text{ in a } 3\tfrac{1}{2}\text{-year certificate}$$

$$= \$5000(1.025)^{-9} = \underline{\$4003.64} \text{ in a } 4\tfrac{1}{2}\text{-year certificate}$$

$$= \$6000(1.014)^{-22} = \underline{\$4418.92} \text{ in a } 5\tfrac{1}{2}\text{-year certificate}$$

27. Total price = Sum of the present values

$$= \$950(1.01375)^{-4} + \$780(1.01375)^{-6} + \$1270(1.01375)^{-5}$$
$$= \$899.498 + \$718.637 + \$1186.177$$
$$= \underline{\$2804.31}$$

29. Let x represent the final loan payment.

Loan = Present value of all payments

$$\$15,000 = \$4000(1.0575)^{-2} + \$4000(1.0575)^{-6} + x(1.0575)^{-10}$$
$$\$15,000 = \$3576.84 + \$2860.08 + 0.57173692x$$
$$x = \underline{\$14,977.31}$$

The third loan payment will be $14,977.31.

31. Let x represent the size of each loan payment.

$$\$10,000 = x(1.04)^{-5} + x(1.04)^{-8} + x(1.04)^{-14}$$
$$= 0.82192711x + 0.73069021x + 0.57747508x$$
$$= 2.1300924x$$
$$x = \underline{\$4694.63}$$

The amount of each loan payment is $4694.63.

33. Let x represent the size of the first payment.

$$\$7500 = x(1.0075)^{-5} + 2x(1.0075)^{-10} + 4x(1.0075)^{-15}$$
$$= 0.9633292x + 1.8560063x + 3.5758902x$$
$$= 6.3952257x$$
$$x = \underline{\$1172.75}$$

The second payment is $2x = \underline{\$2345.50}$.

35. The scheduled payments are:

$$FV = PV(1+i)^n = \$950(1.01)^4 = \$988.57 \text{ due in 4 months,}$$

$$= \$780(1.01)^6 = \$827.99 \text{ due in 6 months, and}$$

$$= \$1270(1.01)^5 = \$1334.78 \text{ due in 5 months.}$$

The total price to be paid for these scheduled payments is the sum of their present values.

Total price $= \$988.57(1.01375)^{-4} + \$827.99(1.01375)^{-6} + \$1334.78(1.01375)^{-5}$
$$= \underline{\$2945.55}$$

Exercise 8.3 (continued)

37. Interest $= FV - PV = PV(1+i)^n - PV$

$\$1175.98 = PV(1.041)^{17} - PV = PV(1.9799873) - PV = 0.9799873PV$

Original investment, $PV = \dfrac{\$1175.98}{0.9799873} = \underline{\$1200.00}$

Exercise 8.4

Financial Calculator Solutions to Odd-Numbered Problems in Exercise 8.2

1. Given: $PV = \$5000$; $j = 6\%$; $m = 2$
   $n = m$(Term in years)
   $= 2(7)$
   $= 14$ compounding periods
   Maturity value, $FV = \underline{\$7562.95}$

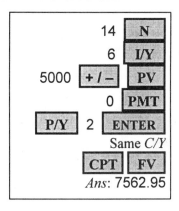

3. Given: $PV = \$12{,}100$; $j = 7.5\%$; $m = 12$
   $n = m$(Term in years)
   $= 12(3.25)$
   $= 39$ compounding periods
   Maturity value, $FV = \underline{\$15{,}428.20}$

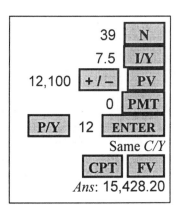

5. Given: $PV = \$1000$; $j = 9\%$ for all parts
   a. $m = 1$; $n = 1(25) = 25$

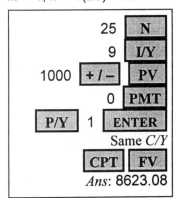

Maturity amount, $FV = \underline{\$8623.08}$

   b. $m = 2$; $n = 2(25) = 50$

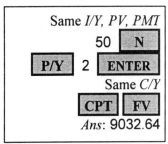

Maturity amount, $FV = \underline{\$9032.64}$

Exercise 8.4 *(financial calculator solutions to Exercise 8.2 continued)*

5. c. $m = 4$; $n = 4(25) = 100$

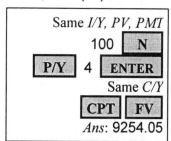

Maturity amount, $FV = \underline{\$9254.05}$

d. $m = 12$; $n = 12(25) = 300$

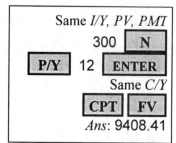

Maturity amount, $FV = \underline{\$9408.41}$

7. Given: $PV = \$100$; Term = 1 year for all parts

   a. $j = 8.0\%$; $m = 12$; $n = 12(1) = 12$

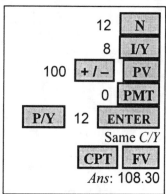

   b. $j = 8.1\%$; $m = 4$; $n = 4(1) = 4$

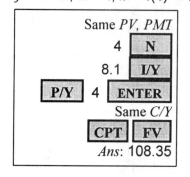

   c. $j = 8.2\%$; $m = 2$; $n = 2(1) = 2$

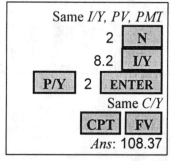

   d. $j = 8.3\%$; $m = 1$; $n = 1(1) = 1$

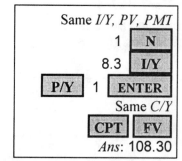

   Choose <u>8.2% compounded semiannually</u> since it produces the highest maturity value.

9. Given: $PV = \$3000$; Term = 18 months = 1.5 years;
   $\qquad j = 9.5\%$; $m = 2$
   $n = m(\text{Term}) = 2(1.5) = 3$ compounding periods
   Maturity value, $FV = \underline{\$3448.13}$
   Interest charged = $FV - PV$
   $\qquad\qquad\qquad = \$3448.13 - \$3000$
   $\qquad\qquad\qquad = \underline{\$448.13}$

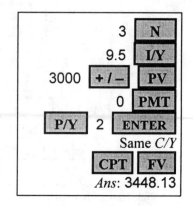

11. Given: PV = $1000; Term = 25 years
     Maturity value at j =11%, m = 1:   Maturity value at j =10%, m = 1:

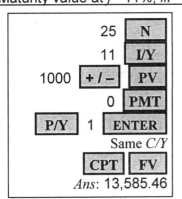

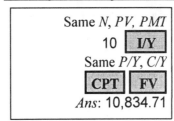

Ans: 13,585.46

The difference is $13,585.46 − $10,834.71 = $2750.75

which is $\dfrac{\$2750.75}{\$10,834.71}$ ×100% = 25.39% of the maturity

value at 10% compounded annually.

13. Given: PV = $1000; j =9%, m = 1
     Maturity value after 25 years: Maturity value after 20 years:

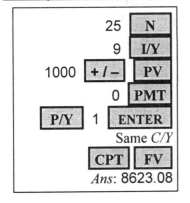

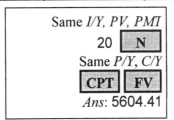

Ans: 5604.41

The difference is $8623.08 − $5604.41 = $3018.67

which is $\dfrac{\$3018.67}{\$5604.41}$ ×100% = 53.86% of the amount

after 20 years.

Note: The equality of the answers in problems 13 and 14 is not coincidence. The
     percent change in the value of the investment in any 5-year period will be the
     same (53.86%). It is a property of compound interest that, for a given interest
     rate, the percent change in value is the same in all intervals of a given length.

15. The solution for the case PV = $1000, j = 8%, m = 1,
     and n = 1(20) is presented in the box to the right.

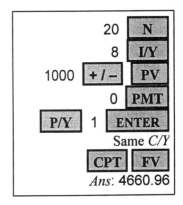

Interest rate	20 years	25 years	30 years
8%	$4660.96	$6848.48	$10,062.66
10%	$6727.50	$10,834.71	$17,449.40

Exercise 8.4 *(financial calculator solutions to Exercise 8.2 continued)*

17. Given: $PV = \$5000$; $j = 8.25\%$; $m = 1$
    Term $= 1.5 + 2.5 = 4$ years
    $n = 1(4) = 4$ compounding periods

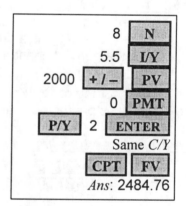

Equivalent value, $FV = \underline{\$6865.65}$

19. For both payments, $j = 6\%$; $m = 4$

    For the first payment:
    $PV = \$1300$, Term $= 4$ years
    $n = 4(4) = 16$

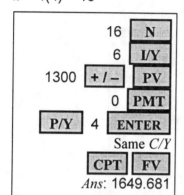

    For the second payment:
    $PV = \$1800$, Term $= 4 - 1.75 = 2.25$ years
    $n = 4(2.25) = 9$

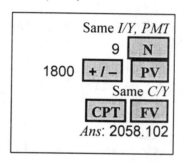

The combined equivalent value 4 years from now is $1649.681 + $2058.102 = $\underline{\$3707.78}$

21. Given: $PV = \$2000$; $j = 5.5\%$; $m = 2$
    Term $= 4$ years
    $n = 2(4) = 8$ compounding periods

Equivalent value, $FV = \underline{\$2484.76}$

Exercise 8.4 *(financial calculator solutions to Exercise 8.2 continued)*

23. The amount owed will be the combined future value.
For each amount borrowed, $j = 5\%$, $m = 2$

$\underline{PV = \$3000; \; n = 3(2) = 6:}$ $\underline{PV = \$3500; \; n = 4:}$ $\underline{PV = \$4000; \; n = 2:}$

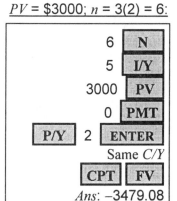

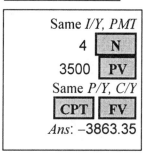

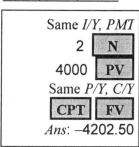

Total amount owed = $3479.08 + $3863.35 + $4202.50
= $11,544.93

25. $PV = \$5000$, $j = 8\%$, and $m = 12$ in each case.

Grand-child	Age	Time until 19th birthday	n
Donna	12 yr, 7 mo	6 yr, 5 mo	$6(12) + 5 = 77$
Tim	10 yr, 3 mo	8 yr, 9 mo	$8(12) + 9 = 105$
Gary	7 yr, 11 mo	11 yr, 1 mo	$11(12) + 1 = 133$

Donna: Tim: Gary:

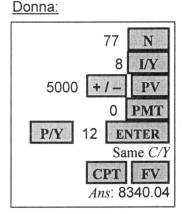

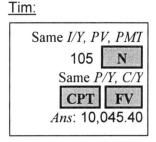

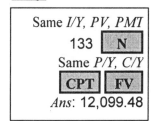

Donna will receive $8340.04, Tim will receive $10,045.40,
and Gary will receive $12,099.48.

27. Maturity value of current GIC
having $j = 6\%$, $m = 2$, $n = 2(5) = 10$

     a. Maturity value of second GIC:
having $j = 6\%$, $m = 2$, $n = 2(5) = 10$

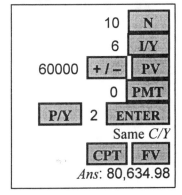

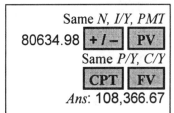

27. *b.* Maturity value of second GIC:
 having $j = 7\%$, $m = 2$, $n = 2(5) = 10$

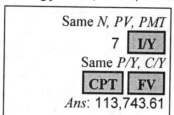

Same *N, PV, PMT*

7 **I/Y**

Same *P/Y, C/Y*

CPT **FV**

Ans: 113,743.61

c. Maturity value of second GIC:
 having $j = 5\%$, $m = 2$, $n = 2(5) = 10$

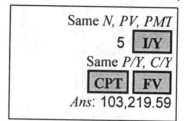

Same *N, PV, PMT*

5 **I/Y**

Same *P/Y, C/Y*

CPT **FV**

Ans: 103,219.59

29. For the first 15 months, $j = 9.5\%$
 $m = 4$, $PV = \$7000$; $n = \frac{15}{3} = 5$

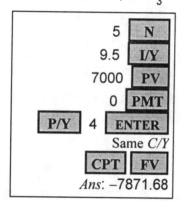

5 **N**

9.5 **I/Y**

7000 **PV**

0 **PMT**

P/Y 4 **ENTER**

Same *C/Y*

CPT **FV**

Ans: −7871.68

For the next 6 months, $j = 8.5\%$
 $m = 2$, $PV = \$7871.68$, $n = 1$

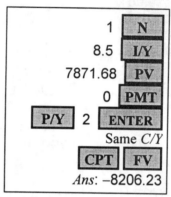

1 **N**

8.5 **I/Y**

7871.68 **PV**

0 **PMT**

P/Y 2 **ENTER**

Same *C/Y*

CPT **FV**

Ans: −8206.23

Total amount owed = $\$7871.68\,(1.0425)^{1}$ = <u>$\$8206.23$</u>

31. The solution requires three steps:
 Step 1: Calculate the amount owed after 2.5 years;
 Step 2: Calculate the amount owed after an additional 6 months;
 Step 3: Calculate the amount owed after an additional 2 years.

Step 1:
$PV = \$3000$, $j = 5\%$,
$m = 2$, $n = 2(2.5) = 5$

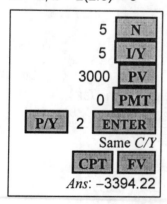

5 **N**

5 **I/Y**

3000 **PV**

0 **PMT**

P/Y 2 **ENTER**

Same *C/Y*

CPT **FV**

Ans: −3394.22

Step 2:
$PV = \$2394.22$, $j = 5\%$,
$m = 2$, $n = 2(0.5) = 1$

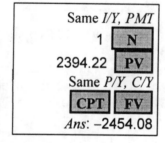

Same *I/Y, PMT*

1 **N**

2394.22 **PV**

Same *P/Y, C/Y*

CPT **FV**

Ans: −2454.08

Step 3:
$PV = \$2454.08$, $j = 6\%$,
 $m = 12$, $n = 12(2) = 24$

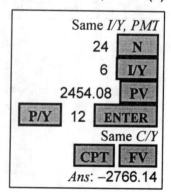

Same *I/Y, PMT*

24 **N**

6 **I/Y**

2454.08 **PV**

P/Y 12 **ENTER**

Same *C/Y*

CPT **FV**

Ans: −2766.14

Total amount now owed = <u>$\$2766.14$</u>

Exercise 8.4 *(financial calculator solutions to* Exercise 8.2 *continued)*

33. The solution requires four steps:
    Step 1: Calculate the amount owed after 9 months;
    Step 2: Calculate the amount owed after an additional 3 months;
    Step 3: Calculate the amount owed after an additional 6 months;
    Step 4: Calculate the amount owed after an additional 6 months.

<u>Step 1</u>:
$PV = \$10,000$, $j = 6.6\%$,
$m = 12$, $n = 9$

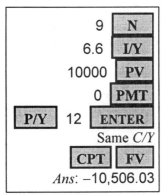

Ans: −10,506.03

<u>Step 2</u>:
$PV = \$10,506.03 − \$2500 = \$8006.03$
$n = 3$

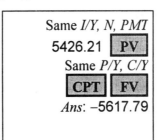

Ans: −8138.86

<u>Step 3</u>:
$PV = \$8138.86$, $j = 7\%$,
$m = 4$, $n = 2$

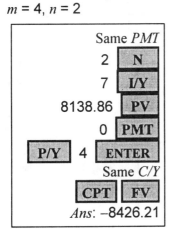

Ans: −8426.21

<u>Step 4</u>:
$PV = \$8426.21 − \$3000 = \$5426.21$
$n = 2$

Same *I/Y, N, PMT*
5426.21 **PV**
Same *P/Y, C/Y*
CPT **FV**
Ans: −5617.79

The amount owed after two years was <u>$5617.79</u>.

Exercise 8.4

Financial Calculator Solutions to Odd-Numbered Problems in Exercise 8.3

1. Given: $FV = \$10,000$; $j = 4.5\%$; $m = 1$
    $n = m(\text{Term in years})$
    $\quad = 1(10)$
    $\quad = 10$ compounding periods
    Principal $= PV = \underline{\$6439.28}$

    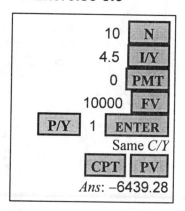

3. Given: $FV = \$9704.61$; $j = 7.5\%$; $m = 2$
    $n = m(\text{Term in years})$
    $\quad = 2\left(\frac{42}{12}\right)$
    $\quad = 7$ compounding periods
    Principal $= PV = \underline{\$7500.00}$

    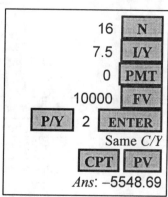

5. Given: $FV = \$10,000$; $j = 7.5\%$; $m = 2$
    $n = m(\text{Term in years})$
    $\quad = 2(8)$
    $\quad = 16$ compounding periods
    Principal $= PV = \underline{\$5548.69}$

    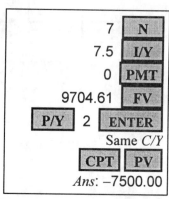

7. Given: $FV = \$3500$; $j = 4.4\%$; $m = 4$
    $n = m(\text{Term in years})$
    $\quad = 4(3.5)$
    $\quad = 14$ compounding periods
    Equivalent amount today $= PV = \underline{\$3002.98}$

    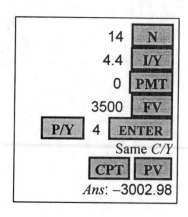

9. The creditor should accept the economically equivalent amount, that is, the present value of the scheduled payment. Given: $FV = \$4000$; $j = 6\%$; $m = 2$

$n = m$(Term in years)

= 2(5)

= 10 compounding periods

The creditor should accept <u>$2976.38</u> today instead of $5000 five years from now.

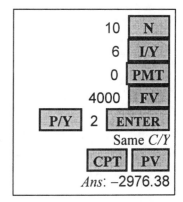

11. The economic value today of an offer is the present value of all payments. For the $51,000 future payment under the Jorgensen offer,

$FV = \$51,000$; $j = 6.5\%$; $m = 2$

$n = m$(Term in years)

= 2(1)

= 2 compounding periods

The economic value of the Jorgensen offer is

$10,000 + $47,839.88 = $57,839.88

Therefore, Gwen should <u>accept the Araki offer</u> because it is <u>worth $160.12 more</u>.

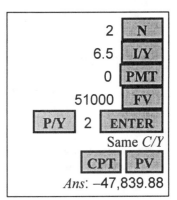

13. The appropriate price to pay is the sum of the present value of the future cash flows.

$100 payment: $600 payment: $40 payment::

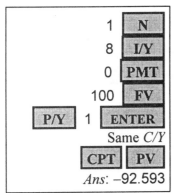

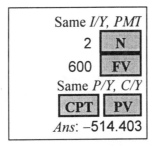

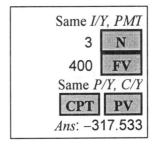

Combined present value = $92.593 + $514.403 + $317.533
= $924.53

<u>Do not take the deal</u>—you <u>should not pay more than $924.53</u> if you want a rate of return of at least 8%.

15. Given: $FV = \$1300$; $j = 5.5\%$; $m = 4$

$n = m$(Term in years)

= 4(3.5 − 0.75)

= 11 compounding periods

Equivalent value nine months from now = <u>$1118.67</u>

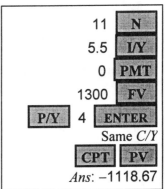

---

17. *First payment*:
$PV = \$900, j = 5\%,$
$m = 12, n = 18$

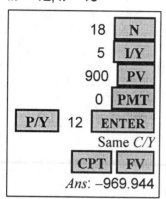

Ans: −969.944

Second payment:
$FV = \$500, j = 5\%,$
$m = 12, n = 22 - 18 = 4$

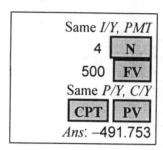

Ans: −491.753

Sum of the equivalent values of the payments, 18 months from now,
= \$969.944 + \$491.753
= <u>\$1461.70</u>

19. *First payment*:
$PV = \$1500, j = 9\%,$
$m = 4, n = 4(2.25 + 0.75) = 12$

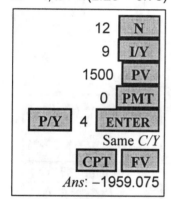

Ans: −1959.075

Second payment:
$FV = \$2500, j = 9\%,$
$m = 4, n = 4(4.5 - 2.25) = 9$

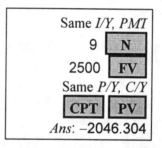

Ans: −2046.304

Sum of the equivalent values of the payments, 2.25 yr from now
= \$1959.075 + \$2046.304
= <u>\$4005.38</u>

21. *First payment*:
$PV = \$750, j = 9.5\%,$
$m = 2, n = 2(1.5) = 3$

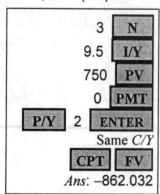

Ans: −862.032

Second payment:
$FV = \$1000, j = 9.5\%,$
$m = 2, n = 2(05) = 1$

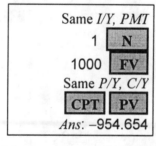

Ans: −954.654

Third payment:
$FV = \$1250, j = 9.5\%,$
$m = 2, n = 2(2.5) = 5$

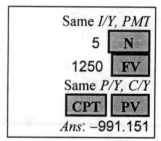

Ans: −991.151

Sum of the equivalent values of the payments
= \$862.032 + \$954.654 + \$991.151
= <u>\$2807.84</u>

Exercise 8.4 *(financial calculator solutions to Exercise 8.3 continued)*

23. *First payment*:
$PV = \$2500, j = 7\%,$
$m = 4, n = 4(1 - 0.25) = 3$

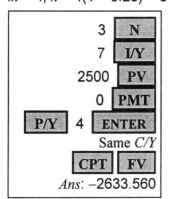

Ans: −2633.560

Second payment:
$FV = \$2500, j = 7\%,$
$m = 4, n = 4(2 - 1) = 4$

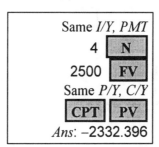

Ans: −2332.396

Equivalent payment one year from now
= $2633.560 + $2332.396
= **$4965.96**

25. The data for the three certificates are presented in the following table.

Maturity Value	Term	j	m	n
$4000	3.5 years	5%	2	2(3.5) = 7
$5000	4.5 years	5%	2	2(4.5) = 9
$6000	5.5 years	5.6%	4	4(5.5) = 22

In each type of certificate, Michelle should invest a principal amount equal to the present value of the maturity value.

First certificate:

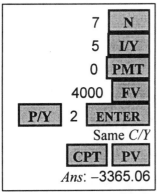

Ans: −3365.06

Second certificate:

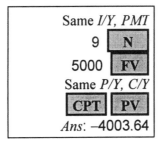

Ans: −4003.64

Third certificate:

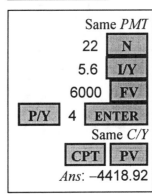

Ans: −4418.92

Michelle should invest <u>$3365.06</u> in a 3.5-year certificate, <u>$4003.64</u> in a 4.5-year certificate, and <u>$4418.92</u> in a 5.5-year certificate.

27. Total price = Sum of the present values of the three contracts.

First contract:

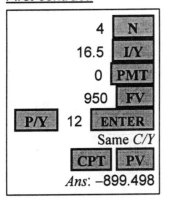

Ans: −899.498

Second contract:

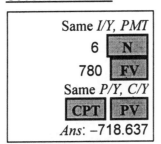

Ans: −718.637

Third contract:

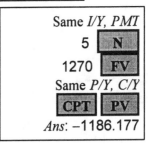

Ans: −1186.177

Total price = $899.498 + $718.637 + $1186.177
= **$2804.31**

Exercise 8.4 *(financial calculator solutions to Exercise 8.3 continued)*

29. Let x represent the final loan payment.

Loan = Present value of all payments

PV of *first payment*:

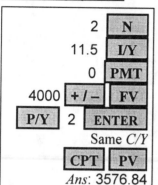

Ans: 3576.84

PV of *second payment*:

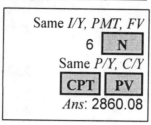

Same *I/Y, PMT, FV*

6 — N

Same *P/Y, C/Y*

CPT   PV

Ans: 2860.08

PV of *third payment*:

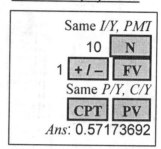

Same *I/Y, PMT*

10 — N

1 +/− FV

Same *P/Y, C/Y*

CPT   PV

Ans: 0.57173692

Hence, $15,000 = \$3576.84 + \$2860.08 + 0.57173692x$

$x = \underline{\$14,977.31}$

The third loan payment will be $14,977.31.

31. Let x represent the size of each loan payment.

PV of *first payment*:

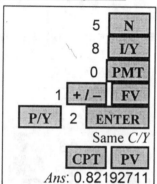

Ans: 0.82192711

PV of *second payment*:

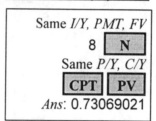

Same *I/Y, PMT, FV*

8 — N

Same *P/Y, C/Y*

CPT   PV

Ans: 0.73069021

PV of *third payment*:

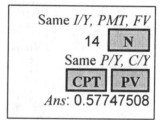

Same *I/Y, PMT, FV*

14 — N

Same *P/Y, C/Y*

CPT   PV

Ans: 0.57747508

Hence, $10,000 = 0.82192711x + 0.73069021x + 0.57747508x$

$= 2.1300924x$

$x = \underline{\$4694.63}$

The amount of each loan payment is $4694.63.

33. Let x represent the size of the first payment.

$7500 = Present value of all three payments

PV of *first payment*:

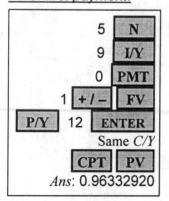

Ans: 0.96332920

PV of *second payment*:

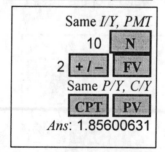

Same *I/Y, PMT*

10 — N

2 +/− FV

Same *P/Y, C/Y*

CPT   PV

Ans: 1.85600631

PV of *third payment*:

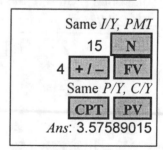

Same *I/Y, PMT*

15 — N

4 +/− FV

Same *P/Y, C/Y*

CPT   PV

Ans: 3.57589015

Hence, $7500 = 0.9633292x + 1.85600631x + 3.57589015x$

$= 6.39522566x$

$x = \underline{\$1172.75}$

The second payment is $2x = \underline{\$2345.50}$.

35. Scheduled payments:

First contract:

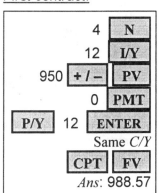

Ans: 988.57

Second contract:

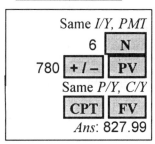

Ans: 827.99

Third contract:

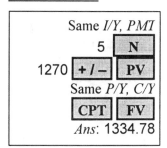

Ans: 1334.78

The total price to be paid for these scheduled payments is the sum of their present values.

First contract:

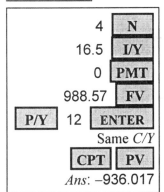

Ans: −936.017

Second contract:

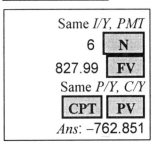

Ans: −762.851

Third contract:

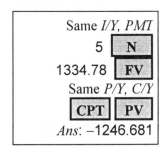

Ans: −1246.681

Total price = $936.017 + $762.851 + $1246.681
= $2945.55

37. First calculate how much interest $1 would earn if invested for 8.5 years at 8.2% compounded semiannually. The future value of $1 is $1.9799873. Therefore, each $1 earns $0.9799873 interest. The number of dollars that had to be invested to earn total interest of $1175.98 was

$$\frac{\$1175.98}{0.9799873} = \$1200.00$$

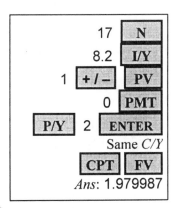

Ans: 1.979987

Concept Questions (Section 8.5)

1. The future value will be the <u>same</u> in both cases. Mathematically, this happens because the order of multiplication in a product does not matter. In this particular case,
$$(1.04)(1.05)(1.06) = (1.06)(1.05)(1.04)$$

3. <u>We should not reach this conclusion</u>. It is true that the strip bond owner does not receive any payments from year to year. However, the market value of the bond increases as the time remaining until maturity decreases. This year-to-year change in market value is the owner's return on investment. The investor can choose to capture the increased value at any time by selling the bond.

5. The overall decrease will be <u>less than $2x$%</u> because the second x% percent decrease acts on a smaller base than the first x% decrease. Consider, for example, two successive 50% decreases. These do not make the final value zero (corresponding to a decrease of $2 \times 50\% = 100\%$). Rather, we reduce the original amount by half twice leaving $\frac{1}{2} \times \frac{1}{2} = \frac{1}{4}$ or 25% of the initial value.

Exercise 8.5

1. Semiannual interest payment $= i(PV) = \dfrac{0.042}{2} \times \$18{,}000 = \underline{\$378.00}$

3. $i = \frac{5.25\%}{2} = 2.625\%$; $n = 2(7) = 14$; $PV = \$30{,}000$

   Maturity value $= FV = PV(1+i)^n = \$30{,}000(1.02625)^{14} = \underline{\$43{,}118.70}$

5. Suppose that \$1000 is invested for 3 years at each rate.
   The maturity value at 4.8% compounded monthly is
   $$FV = PV(1+i)^n = \$1000(1.004)^{36} = \$1154.55$$
   The maturity value at 4.9% compounded semiannually is
   $$FV = PV(1+i)^n = \$1000(1.0245)^6 = \$1156.30$$
   An investor should choose <u>4.9% compounded semiannually</u> since it will produce the larger maturity value.

7. The maturity value at 5.00% compounded annually will be
   $$FV = PV(1+i)^n = \$10{,}000(1.05)^5 = \$12{,}762.82$$
   The maturity value at 4.875% compounded semiannually will be
   $$\$10{,}000(1.024375)^{10} = \$12{,}723.01$$
   The maturity value at 4.75% compounded monthly will be
   $$\$10{,}000\left(1.003958\overline{3}\right)^{60} = \$12{,}674.81$$
   An investor will earn
   $$\$12{,}762.82 - \$12{,}674.81 = \underline{\$88.01}$$
   more at 5.00% compounded annually than at 4.75% compounded monthly.

9. The value of the Canada Premium Bond after 2 years will be
   $$FV = PV(1+i_1)(1+i_2) = \$10{,}000(1.025)(1.03) = \$10{,}557.50$$
   Interest earned in Year 3 $= 0.035(\$10{,}557.50) = \underline{\$369.51}$.
   The value of the Ontario Savings Bond after 2 years will be
   $$\$10{,}000(1.0275)(1.0325) = \$10{,}608.94$$
   Interest earned in Year 3 $= 0.035(\$10{,}608.94) = \underline{\$371.31}$.

Exercise 8.5 *(continued)*

11. Series S60 Bonds were issued on November 1, 1999.

    a. Value of a $5000 S60 bond on November 1, 2003 was

    $$FV = PV(1+i_1)(1+i_2)(1+i_3)(1+i_4)$$
    $$= \$5000(1.046)(1.0485)(1.018)(1.02) \qquad \text{(from Table 8.2)}$$
    $$= \underline{\$5694.01}$$

    b. The bondholder received all accrued interest up to August 1, 2004.
    To the amount in part *a*, we need to add 9 months' interest at 1.75% per year.

    $$I = Prt = \$5694.01(0.0175)\left(\tfrac{9}{12}\right) = \$74.73$$

    The owner received $5694.01 + $74.73 = $\underline{\$5768.74}$ on August 21, 2004
    when she redeemed a $5000 denomination S60 bond.

13. The bondholder received interest from the date of issue (November 1, 1998)
to March 1, 2004. This period was 5 years plus 4 months long. After 5 years,

    $$FV = PV\,(1+i_1)\cdots(1+i_5)$$
    $$= \$300(1.04)(1.046)(1.0485)(1.018)(1.02)$$
    $$= \$355.31$$

    The redemption value includes an additional 4 months' interest at 1.75% per year.
    Redemption value = $355.31 + $355.31(0.0175)$\left(\tfrac{4}{12}\right)$ = $\underline{\$357.38}$

	Value at the end of Year 3 ①	*Interest earned in Year 4* ②	*Maturity value at the end of Year 5* ③
15.	$2256.22	$\underline{\$92.51}$	$\underline{\$2445.03}$
17.	$9129.12	$\underline{\$502.10}$	$\underline{\$10,209.09}$

① Value at end of Year 3 = $PV(1+i_1)(1+i_2)(1+i_3)$

② Interest earned in Year 4 = i_4 (Value at end of Year 3)

$$= i_4 \times ①$$

③ Maturity value = (Value at end of Year 3)$(1+i_4)(1+i_5)$

$$= ① \times (1+i_4)(1+i_5)$$

19. Maturity value of the compound-interest RateOptimizer GIC

    $$= PV\,(1+i_1)\cdots(1+i_5)$$
    $$= \$5000(1.018)(1.0225)(1.026)(1.03)(1.0325)$$
    $$= \$5678.79$$

    Interest earned on RateOptimizer GIC = $5678.79 – $5000 = $\underline{\$678.79}$
    Maturity value of fixed-rate compound-interest GIC

    $$= PV(1+i)^5 = \$5000\,(1.0275)^5 = \$5726.37$$

    Interest earned on fixed-rate GIC = $5726.37 – $5000.00 = $\underline{\$726.38}$

21. Interest earned in Year 4 = i_4 (Value at end of Year 3)

    $$= (i_4)PV(1+i_1)(1+i_2)(1+i_3)$$

    Year 4 interest on Escalating Rate GIC = 0.0325($10,000)(1.02)(1.025)(1.03) = $\underline{\$349.98}$
    Year 4 interest on fixed-rate GIC = 0.0275($10,000)$(1.0275)^3$ = $\underline{\$298.32}$

---

23. After 20 years, the cost of goods that cost $100 today will be the future value of $100 (compounded at the rate of inflation.)

    a. $j = 2\%$, $m = 1$:

$$FV = PV(1+i)^n$$
$$= \$100(1.02)^{20}$$
$$= \underline{\$148.59}$$

    b. $j = 3\%$, $m = 1$:

$$FV = PV(1+i)^n$$
$$= \$100(1.03)^{20}$$
$$= \underline{\$180.61}$$

    c. $j = 4\%$, $m = 1$:

$$FV = PV(1+i)^n$$
$$= \$100(1.04)^{20}$$
$$= \underline{\$219.11}$$

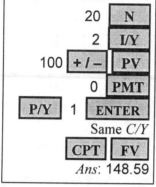

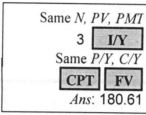

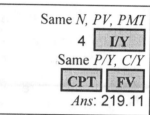

25. To keep pace with inflation, the hourly rate should also grow at $j = 3.5\%$ compounded annually.
Ten years from now, the hourly rate would then be

$$FV = PV(1+i)^n$$
$$= \$15(1.035)^{10}$$
$$= \underline{\$21.16 \text{ per hour}}$$

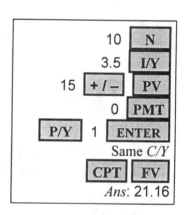

27. The retirement income goal is $35,000 adjusted for 15 years' nominal growth at the projected annual rate of inflation.

    a. $j = 2\%$, $m = 1$:

$$FV = PV(1+i)^n$$
$$= \$35,000(1.02)^{20}$$
$$= \underline{\$47,105.39}$$

    b. $j = 3\%$, $m = 1$:

$$FV = PV(1+i)^n$$
$$= \$35,000(1.03)^{20}$$
$$= \underline{\$54,528.86}$$

    c. $j = 5\%$, $m = 1$:

$$FV = PV(1+i)^n$$
$$= \$35,000(1.04)^{20}$$
$$= \underline{\$72,762.49}$$

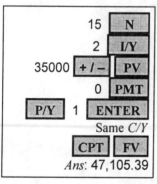

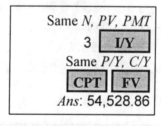

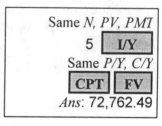

29. Sales for Year 3 = $FV = PV(1+i)^n = \$28,600,000[1+(-0.04)]^3 = \$25,303,450$

    Sales for Year 7 = $\$25,303,450(1.08)^4 = \underline{\$34,425,064}$

Exercise 8.5 *(continued)*

31. Price = Present value of the face value discounted at the market rate of return

$$= FV(1+i)^{-n}$$
$$= \$1000(1.0325)^{-44}$$
$$= \underline{\$244.81}$$

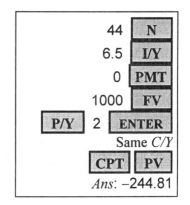

44 **N**
6.5 **I/Y**
0 **PMT**
1000 **FV**
P/Y 2 **ENTER**
Same *C/Y*
CPT **PV**
Ans: −244.81

33. Current market value = *PV* of the $10,000 face value

$$= FV(1+i)^{-n}$$
$$= \$10,000(1.0295)^{-10}$$
$$= \underline{\$7477.16}$$

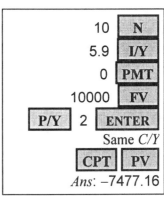

10 **N**
5.9 **I/Y**
0 **PMT**
10000 **FV**
P/Y 2 **ENTER**
Same *C/Y*
CPT **PV**
Ans: −7477.16

35. *a.* With 10 years until maturity,

$n = 2(10) = 20; \; i = \frac{5.99\%}{2} = 2.995\%$

$$PV = FV(1+i)^{-n}$$
$$= \$1000(1.02995)^{-20}$$
$$= \underline{\$554.21}$$

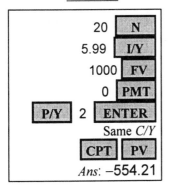

20 **N**
5.99 **I/Y**
1000 **FV**
0 **PMT**
P/Y 2 **ENTER**
Same *C/Y*
CPT **PV**
Ans: −554.21

b. With 6 years until maturity,

$n = 2(6) = 12$

$$PV = FV(1+i)^{-n}$$
$$= \$1000(1.02995)^{-12}$$
$$= \underline{\$701.79}$$

Same *I/Y, FV, PV, PMT*
12 **N**
Same *P/Y, C/Y*
CPT **PV**
Ans: −701.79

c. With *PV* = $554.21, *n* = 2(4) = 8, *i* = 2.995%,

$$FV = PV(1+i)^{n}$$
$$= \$554.21(1.02995)^{8}$$
$$= \underline{\$701.78}$$

d. A bond's market value on any date impounds a rate of return equal to 5.99% compounded semiannually (csa) to the investor. The investor can earn this either in the bond or in another investment earning 5.99% csa.

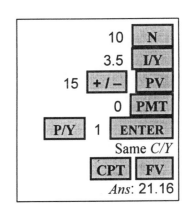

10 **N**
3.5 **I/Y**
15 **+ / −** **PV**
0 **PMT**
P/Y 1 **ENTER**
Same *C/Y*
CPT **FV**
Ans: 21.16

---

37. Market price of one strip bond = $FV(1+i)^{-n}$

$$= \$1000(1.03125)^{-26}$$
$$= \$449.30$$

The number of strip bonds that may be purchased with $12,830 is the integer portion of

$$\frac{\$12,830}{\$449.30} = 28.56$$

That is, <u>28</u> $1000 face value strip bonds can be purchased.

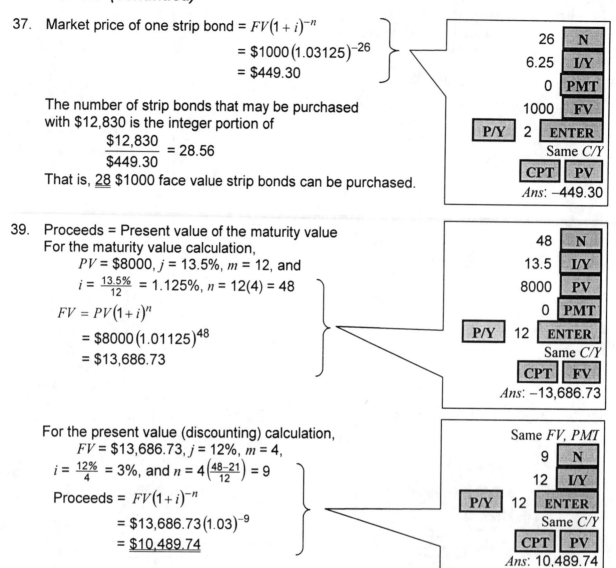

39. Proceeds = Present value of the maturity value
For the maturity value calculation,
$PV = \$8000$, $j = 13.5\%$, $m = 12$, and
$i = \frac{13.5\%}{12} = 1.125\%$, $n = 12(4) = 48$

$$FV = PV(1+i)^n$$
$$= \$8000(1.01125)^{48}$$
$$= \$13,686.73$$

For the present value (discounting) calculation,
$FV = \$13,686.73$, $j = 12\%$, $m = 4$,
$i = \frac{12\%}{4} = 3\%$, and $n = 4\left(\frac{48-21}{12}\right) = 9$

Proceeds = $FV(1+i)^{-n}$

$$= \$13,686.73(1.03)^{-9}$$
$$= \underline{\$10,489.74}$$

41. The appropriate price to pay is the present value, on the date of purchase, of the scheduled payments.
    Step 1: Calculate the balance after the first payment.
    Step 2: Calculate the second payment.
    Step 3: Calculate the present value (on the date of purchase) of the two payments.

    Step 1:
    $PV = \$4000$, $j = 9\%$, $m = 4$,
    $i = \frac{9\%}{4} = 2.25\%$, $n = 4(2) = 8$

    $FV = \$4000(1.0225)^8 = \$4779.32$

    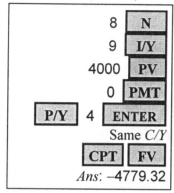

    Step 2:
    $PV = \$2779.32$;
    same j, m, and i ; $n = 4(1) = 4$

    $FV = \$2779.32(1.0225)^4 = \$3038.03$

    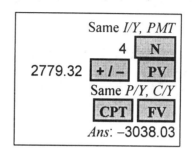

    Balance after $2000 payment
    = $4779.32 – $2000 = $2779.32

    Step 3: Calculate PVs discounting at $j = 10\%$, $m = 2$, $i = \frac{10\%}{2} = 5\%$,

    PV of first payment:
    $FV = \$2000.00$; $n = 2(1.5) = 3$
    $PV = \$2000(1.05)^{-3} = \$1727.675$

    PV of second payment:
    $FV = \$3038.03$; $n = 2(2.5) = 5$
    $PV = \$3038.03(1.05)^{-5} = \$2380.376$

    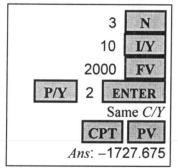

    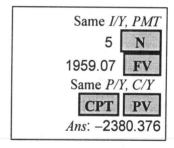

    The appropriate price is the sum of the present values, that is, <u>$4108.05</u>

Concept Questions (Section 8.6)

1. <u>No</u>. Think of the simplest case where one payment stream consists of a single payment and the other payment stream consists of a single (different) payment on a different date. These two payments are equivalent at only one interest rate.

3. Compare the future values of the two streams at a focal date 5 (or more) years from now (assuming that money is invested at 7% compounded semiannually as soon as it is received). The two future values will be equal.

Exercise 8.6

1. Let x represent the replacement payment due in 24 months. The equivalent value of the scheduled payments at a focal date 24 months from today is

    $$\$3000\,(1.015)^8 + \$2000\,(1.015)^3 = \$3379.48 + \$2091.36 = \$5470.84$$

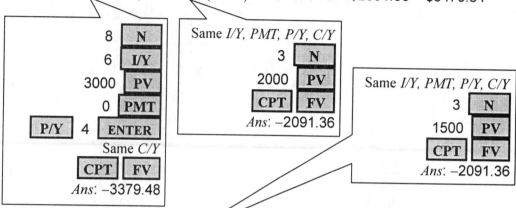

    The equivalent value of the replacement payments on the same date is

    $$\$1500\,(1.015)^3 + x = \$1568.52 + x$$

    For equivalence of the two payment streams,

    $$\$1568.52 + x = \$5470.84$$
    $$x = \underline{\$3902.32}$$

    The second payment due in 24 months is $3902.32.

3. Let x represent the amount of each replacement payment.
    For equivalence at a focal date 9 months from now,

    $$\$1400\,(1.0325)^1 + \$2300\,(1.0325)^{-2} = x + x\,(1.0325)^{-3}$$

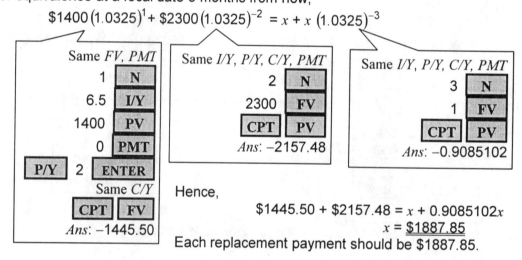

    Hence,

    $$\$1445.50 + \$2157.48 = x + 0.9085102x$$
    $$x = \underline{\$1887.85}$$

    Each replacement payment should be $1887.85.

5. Let x represent the size of the first replacement payment.
   For equivalence at a focal date 2 months from now,

$$\$400(1.00875)^{10} + \$650(1.00875)^5 = x + 2x(1.00875)^{-5}$$

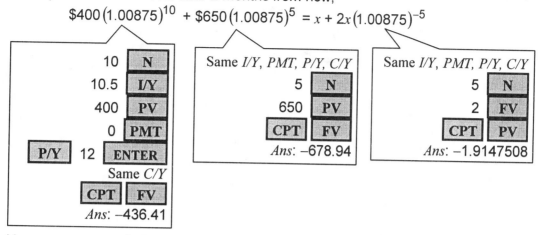

Hence, $\$436.41 + \$678.94 = x + 1.9147508x$
$$x = \$382.66$$

The replacement payments are <u>$382.66</u> in 2 months and <u>$765.32</u> in 7 months.

7. Let x represent the size of each replacement payment.
   For equivalence at a focal date today,

$$\$4000 = x + x(1.006)^{-4} + x(1.006)^{-9}$$

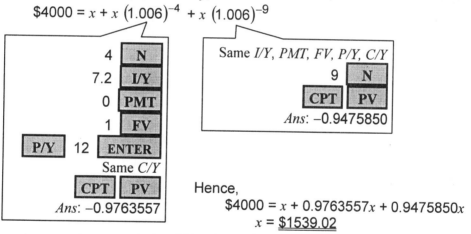

Hence,
$$\$4000 = x + 0.9763557x + 0.9475850x$$
$$x = \underline{\$1539.02}$$

Each replacement payment should be $1539.02.

9. The scheduled payments are

$$FV = PV(1+i)^n$$
$$= \$1400(1.02)^1$$
$$= \$1428.00 \text{ in 3 months}$$

and

$$FV = \$2300(1.02)^7$$
$$= \$2641.98$$
in 21 months.

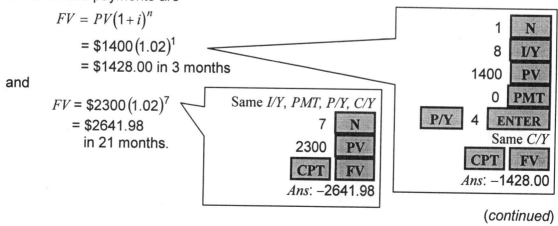

(continued)

Exercise 8.6 *(continued)*

9. *(continued)*
   Let x represent the amount of each replacement payment.
   For equivalence at a focal date 9 months from now,

   $$\$1428.00(1.0325)^1 + \$2641.98(1.0325)^{-2} = x + x(1.0325)^{-3}$$

   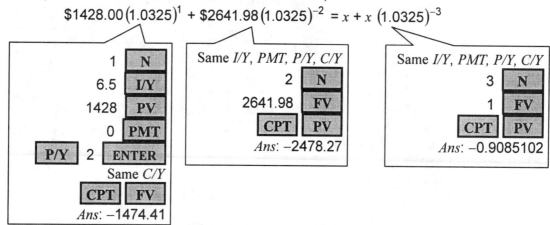

   Hence, $\$1474.41 + \$2478.27 = x + 0.9085102x$
   $$x = \underline{\$2071.08}$$
   Each replacement payment should be $2071.08.

11. Furniture City should be willing to accept a cash price that equals the down payment plus
    the discounted balance that would otherwise be received from the finance company.

    Cash price = $0.25(\$1595) + 0.75(\$1595)(1.15)^{-6} = \underline{\$1492.77}$

13. The winner should choose the alternative having
    the larger current economic value.

    a. Economic value of (1) = $\$10,000 + \$10,000(1.06)^{-5}$
       $$= \$17,472.58$$

    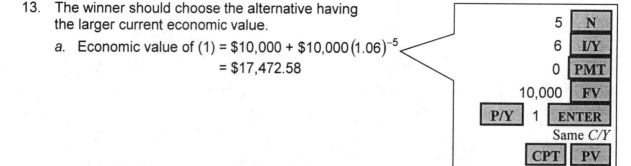

    The economic value of alternative (2) is
    $$\$6700 + \$6700(1.06)^{-5} + \$6700(1.06)^{-10} + \$6700(1.06)^{-15} = \$18,243.55$$

    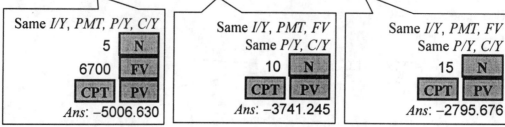

    Alternative (2) should be chosen since it <u>is worth $770.97 more</u>.

    b. Economic value of (1) = $\$10,000 + \$10,000(1.085)^{-5} = \$15,934.51$
       The economic value of alternative (2) is
       $$\$6700 + \$6700(1.085)^{-5} + \$6700(1.085)^{-10} + \$6700(1.085)^{-15} = \$16,089.85$$
       Alternative (1) should be chosen since it <u>is worth $560.60 more</u>.

15. Let x represent the amount of the second replacement payment due 4 years from today. For equivalence at a focal date 4 years from today,

$$\$5000(1.0375)^2 + \$7000(1.0375)^{-2} = 0.5x(1.0375)^5 + x$$

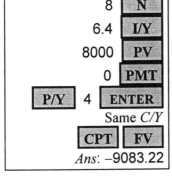

2	**N**
7.5	**I/Y**
5000	**PV**
0	**PMT**
P/Y 2	**ENTER**

Same *C/Y*

CPT	**FV**

Ans: −5382.03

Same *I/Y, PMT, P/Y, C/Y*

2	**N**
7000	**FV**
CPT	**PV**

Ans: −6503.12

Same *I/Y, PMT, P/Y, C/Y*

5	**N**
0.5	**PV**
CPT	**FV**

Ans: −0.6010499

Hence, $\$5382.03 + \$6503.12 = 0.6010499x + x$
$$x = \$7423.35$$

The replacement payments are $\underline{\$3711.68}$ due in $1\frac{1}{2}$ years and $\underline{\$7423.35}$ due in 4 years.

17. Let x represent the size of the second replacement payment.
For equivalence at a focal date 9 months from today,

$$\$8000(1.016)^8 + \$6000(1.016) = \$4000(1.016)^3 + x + 3x(1.016)^{-3}$$

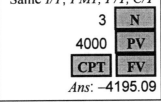

8	**N**
6.4	**I/Y**
8000	**PV**
0	**PMT**
P/Y 4	**ENTER**

Same *C/Y*

CPT	**FV**

Ans: −9083.22

Same *I/Y, PMT, P/Y, C/Y*

3	**N**
4000	**PV**
CPT	**FV**

Ans: −4195.09

Same *I/Y, PMT, P/Y, C/Y*

3	**N**
3	**FV**
CPT	**PV**

Ans: −2.8604880

Hence, $\$9083.22 + \$6096.00 = \$4195.09 + x + 2.8604880x$
$$x = \$2845.27$$

The last two replacement payments are $\underline{\$2845.27}$ due in 9 months and
$\underline{\$8535.81}$ due in $1\frac{1}{2}$ years.

Exercise 8.6 *(continued)*

19. The scheduled payments to Andrea are:

$2000(1.045)^8 = \$2844.20$ in 1 year and $1000(1.04)^7 = \$1315.93$ in 2 years.

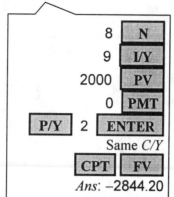

8 | N
9 | I/Y
2000 | PV
0 | PMT
P/Y | 2 | ENTER
Same C/Y
CPT | FV
Ans: −2844.20

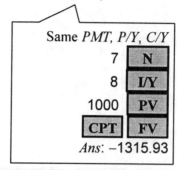

Same *PMT, P/Y, C/Y*

7 | N
8 | I/Y
1000 | PV
CPT | FV
Ans: −1315.93

Let x represent the size of each replacement payment.
For equivalence at a focal date 1 year from now,

$$\$2844.20 + \$1315.93(1.015)^{-4} = x + x(1.015)^{-8}$$

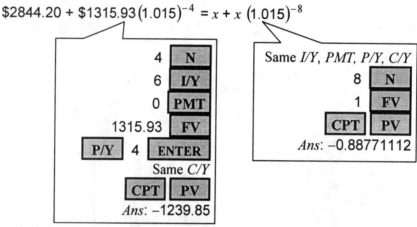

4 | N
6 | I/Y
0 | PMT
1315.93 | FV
P/Y | 4 | ENTER
Same C/Y
CPT | PV
Ans: −1239.85

Same *I/Y, PMT, P/Y, C/Y*

8 | N
1 | FV
CPT | PV
Ans: −0.88771112

Hence, $\$2844.20 + \$1239.85 = x + 0.88771112x$

$$x = \underline{\$2163.49}$$

The two replacement payments should each be $2163.49.

Review Problems

1. Value of compound-interest CSB after 3 years
$$= PV(1+i_1)(1+i_2)(1+i_3)$$
$$= \$4000(1.0525)(1.06)(1.0675)$$
$$= \$4763.83$$
Maturity value of 3-year Bond-Beater GIC
$$= \$4000(1.0575)(1.065)(1.0725)$$
$$= \$4831.56$$
The Bond-Beater GIC earns $4831.56 − $4763.83 = $\underline{\$67.73}$ more than the CSB in the first 3 years.

3. *a.* Maturity value $= PV(1+i_1)^2(1+i_2)^2(1+i_3)^2$
$$= \$12,000(1.02)^2(1.025)^2(1.03)^2$$
$$= \underline{\$13,915.66}$$

3. *b.* Interest earned in the second year

$$= \text{Value after 2 years} - \text{Value after 1 year}$$
$$= \$12{,}000(1.02)^2(1.025)^2 - \$12{,}000(1.02)^2$$
$$= \$13{,}116.84 - \$12{,}484.80$$
$$= \underline{\$632.04}$$

5. Original principal, $PV = FV(1+i)^{-n} = \$2297.78(1.007)^{-19} = \underline{\$2012.56}$

Interest portion $= \$2297.78 - \$2012.56 = \underline{\$285.22}$

7. *Step 1:* Amount owed after 2.5 yr.   *Step 2:* Amount owed after 5 yr.

$j = 9\%$, $m = 12$, $n = 12(2.5) = 30$ $j = 8.25,\%$, $m = 2$, $n = 2(2.5) = 5$

$FV = \$25{,}000(1.0075)^{30} = \$31{,}281.794$ $FV = \$31{,}281.794(1.04125)^5 = \underline{\$38{,}288.36}$

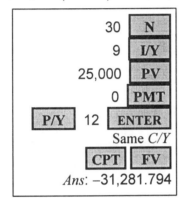

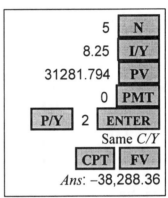

9. Equivalent amount $= FV(1+i)^{-n}$

$$= \$4800(1.04)^{-9}$$
$$= \underline{\$3372.42}$$

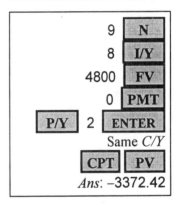

11. The sum of the scheduled payments' equivalent values 6 months from now is

$$\$2400(1.015)^2 + \$1200(1.015)^{-4} + \$3000(1.015)^{-9} = \underline{\$6226.94}$$

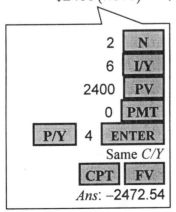

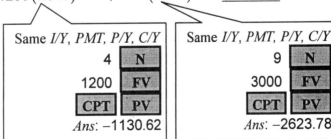

A single payment of $6226.94 six months from now is equivalent to the three scheduled payments.

13. For an initial investment PV, the maturity value at 5.5% compounded semiannually will be
$$PV(1.0275)^{12} = 1.38478(PV)$$
and at 5.6% compounded annually will be
$$PV(1.056)^6 = 1.38670(PV)$$
The <u>5.6% compound annual</u> rate will result in the larger maturity value.

15. <u>*Current price:*</u>
$$PV = FV(1+i)^{-n}$$
$$= \$1000(1.0295)^{-38}$$
$$= \underline{\$331.28}$$

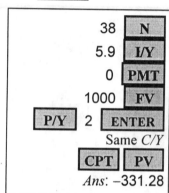

P/Y | 2 | ENTER
Same *C/Y*
CPT | PV
Ans: −331.28

<u>*Price in 4 years:*</u>
$$PV = \$1000(1.0295)^{-30}$$
$$= \underline{\$418.03}$$

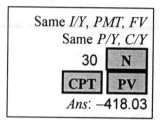

Same *I/Y, PMT, FV*
Same *P/Y, C/Y*
30 | N
CPT | PV
Ans: −418.03

<u>*Price in 5 years:*</u>
$$PV = \$1000(1.0295)^{-28}$$
$$= \underline{\$443.06}$$

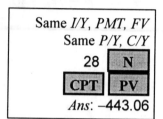

Same *I/Y, PMT, FV*
Same *P/Y, C/Y*
28 | N
CPT | PV
Ans: −443.06

or $FV = PV(1+i)^n$
$$= \$331.28(1.0295)^8$$
$$= \$418.03$$

or $FV = PV(1+i)^n$
$$= \$331.28(1.0295)^{10}$$
$$= \$443.06$$

Hence, the increase in value during the fifth year will be
$$\$443.06 - \$418.03 = \underline{\$25.03}$$

17. <u>*Payment due in 2 yr.:*</u>
$$FV = PV(1+i)^n$$
$$= \$1500(1.02)^8$$
$$= \$1757.49$$

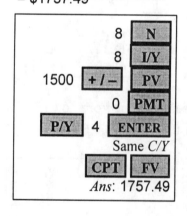

8 | N
8 | I/Y
1500 | +/− | PV
0 | PMT
P/Y | 4 | ENTER
Same *C/Y*
CPT | FV
Ans: 1757.49

<u>*Payment due in 4 yr.:*</u>
$$FV = \$2500(1.02)^{16}$$
$$= \$3431.96$$

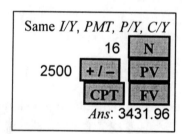

Same *I/Y, PMT, P/Y, C/Y*
16 | N
2500 | +/− | PV
CPT | FV
Ans: 3431.96

(continued)

17. *(continued)*

The fair market value of the note, 18 months after the issue date, is the present value on the date of sale of the scheduled payments. That is,

Price = 1757.49(1.0525)^{-1}$ + 3431.96(1.0525)^{-5}$ = $1669.82 + $2657.25 = <u>$4327.07</u>

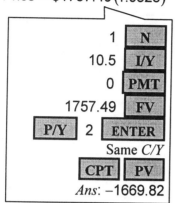

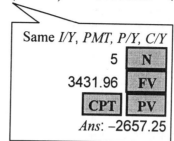

19. Choose any value, say 10,000, for the number employed in 1995. The forecast number of employees 5 years later was:

$$FV = PV(1+i)^n$$
$$= 10,000$$
$$= 10,000[1+(-0.035)]^5$$
$$= 10,000(0.965)^5$$
$$= 8368$$

Number of jobs lost = 10,000 − 8368 = 1632

That is, $\dfrac{1632}{10,000} \times 100\%$ = <u>16.32%</u>

of base metal mining jobs were expected to be lost.

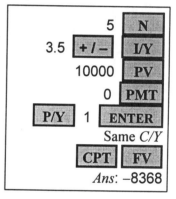

21. The original loan equals the combined present value of the payments and the balance. Let x represent the size of each of the three equal payments.

$$\$10,000 = x(1.00875)^{-12} + x(1.00875)^{-24} + x(1.00875)^{-36} + \$5326.94(1.00875)^{-36}$$

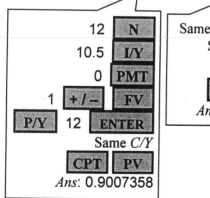

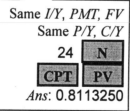

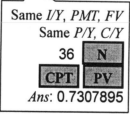

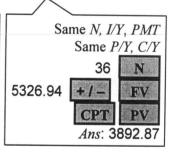

Hence, $10,000 = 0.9007358x + 0.8113250x + 0.7307895x + $3892.87

2.4428503x = $6107.13

x = <u>$2500.00</u>

Each of the three payments was $2500.00.

23. *Maturity value of $3000 loan:*

$$FV = PV(1+i)^n$$

$$= \$3000(1.05)^{12}$$

$$= \$5387.57 \text{ due 2 yr. from now}$$

Maturity value of $1500 loan:

$$FV = \$1500(1.0225)^{14}$$

$$= \$2048.23 \text{ due } 2\tfrac{1}{4} \text{ yr. from now}$$

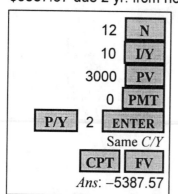

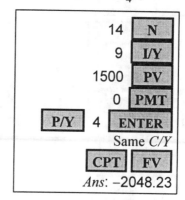

Let x represent the amount of each replacement payment.
For equivalence at a focal date 2 years from now,

$$\$5387.57 + \$2048.23(1.02)^{-1} = x + x(1.02)^{-6}$$

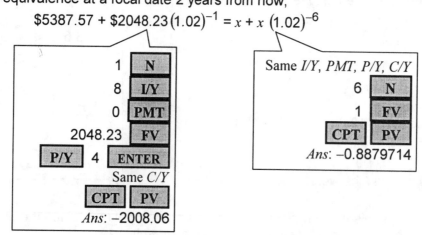

Hence, $\$5387.57 + \$2008.06 = x + 0.8879714x$

$$x = \underline{\$3917.24}$$

The two replacement payments should each be $3917.24.

Self-Test Exercise

1. a. Maturity value of Springboard GIC = $PV(1+i_1)\cdots(1+i_5)$

$$= \$10,000(1.0225)(1.03)(1.0375)(1.045)(1.065)$$

$$= \underline{\$12,160.59}$$

Maturity value of fixed-rate GIC = $PV(1+i)^5 = \$10,000(1.035)^5 = \underline{\$11,876.86}$

   b. Interest earned in the third year on the Springboard GIC

$$= (i_3)PV(1+i_1)(1+i_2)$$

$$= 0.0375(\$10,000)(1.0225)(1.03)$$

$$= \underline{\$394.94}$$

Interest earned in the third year by the fixed-rate GIC

$$= i(PV)(1+i)^2 = 0.035(\$10,000)(1.035)^2 = \underline{\$374.93}$$

2. a. Portfolio value = *FV* of $1000

    $$= \$1000\,(1.1192)^{20}$$

    $$= \underline{\$9509.42}$$

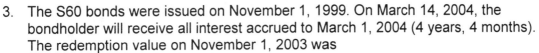

    b. Amount required on December 31, 1998 to
        have the same purchasing power as $1000
        on December 31, 1978

    $$= PV(1+i)^n = \$1000\,(1.045)^{20} = \underline{\$2411.71}$$

    c. The percent increase in purchasing power of the
        funds originally invested in the S&P/TSX portfolio is

    $$\frac{\$9509.42 - \$2411.71}{\$2411.71} \times 100\% = \underline{294.3\%}$$

3. The S60 bonds were issued on November 1, 1999. On March 14, 2004, the
    bondholder will receive all interest accrued to March 1, 2004 (4 years, 4 months).
    The redemption value on November 1, 2003 was

    $$= PV\,(1+i_1)\cdots(1+i_4)$$

    $$= \$1000(1.046)(1.0485)(1.018)(1.02)$$

    $$= \$1130.80$$

    Additional interest to March 1, 2004 = $1130.80(0.0175)\left(\frac{4}{12}\right)$ = $6.64

    Redemption value on March 14, 2004 = $1130.80 + $6.64 = $\underline{\$1145.44}$

4. According to the Valuation Principle, the finance company will pay the present
    value of the two payments discounted at the required rate of return.

    $$\text{Present value} = \$542.50\,(1.035)^{-2} + \$542.50\,(1.035)^{-4}$$

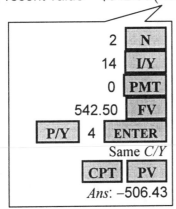

Hence, Present value = $506.43 + $472.76 = $\underline{\$979.19}$

Self-Test Exercise *(continued)*

5. *Value after 1 year:*

$FV = PV(1+i)^n$

$= \$3000(1.0075)^{12}$

$= \$3281.42$

Value after 2 years:

Initial investment

$= \$3281.42 + \$4000$

$FV = \$7281.42(1.02125)^4$

$= \$7920.35$

Value after 3 years:

Initial investment

$= \$7920.35 + \$3500$

$FV = \$11,420.35(1.03875)^2 =$

$= \underline{\$12,322.58}$

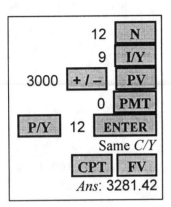

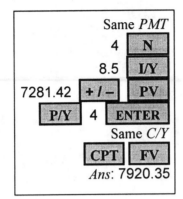

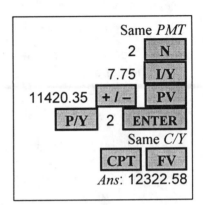

6. Amount owed just before first payment

$\quad = \$10,000(1.0575)^3$

$\quad = \$11,826.09$

Amount owed just after first payment

$\quad = \$11,826.09 - \$1800$

$\quad = \$10,026.09$

Amount owed after 2 years

$\quad = \$10,026.09(1.0575)$

$\quad = \$10,602.59$

Amount owed just before second payment

$\quad = \$10,602.59(1.00895)^6$

$\quad = \$11,184.84$

Amount owed just after second payment

$\quad = \$11,184.84 - \$2400$

$\quad = \$8784.84$

Amount owed after 3 years

$\quad = \$8784.84(1.00895)^6$

$\quad = \underline{\$9267.27}$

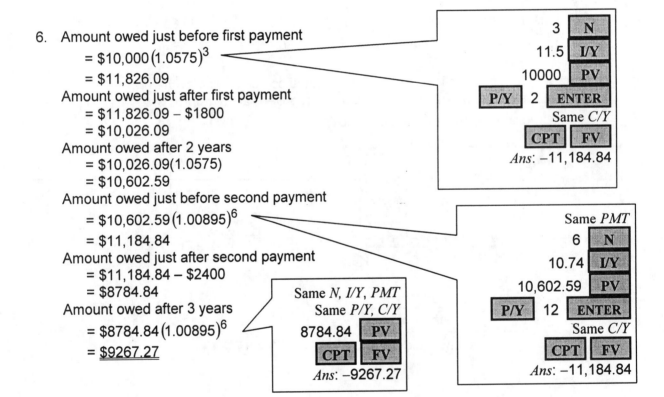

7. Today's economic value of Offer 1 = $10,000 + $15,000 $(1.05125)^{-1}$ + $15,000 $(1.05125)^{-3}$

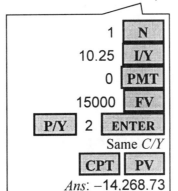

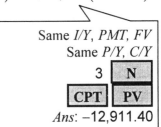

Hence,

Economic value of Offer 1 = $10,000 + $14,268.73 + $12,911.40 = <u>$37,180.13</u>

Today's economic value of Offer 2 = $8000 + $17,500 $(1.05125)^{-2}$ + $17,500 $(1.05125)^{-4}$

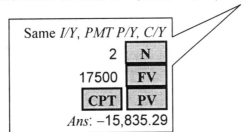

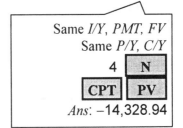

Hence,

Economic value of Offer 2 = $8000 + $15,835.29 + $14,328.94 = <u>$38,164.23</u>

Donnelly should accept <u>Offer 2</u>. Its current economic value is almost $1000 more than that of Offer 1.

8. The value on December 31, 2003 of $1000 invested in the Sprott Canadian Equity Fund on December 31, 1998 was

$$FV = PV(1+i)^n = \$1000(1.419)^5 = \$5733.23$$

The value on December 31, 2003 of $1000 invested at 6.8% compounded annually on December 31, 1998 was

$$FV = \$1000(1.068)^5 = \$1389.49$$

The Sprott Canadian Equity Fund earned $5733.23 − $1389.49 = <u>$4363.74</u> more.

9. Suppose the current level of waste discharge is 100 units. The target level after 5 years is the future value of 100 units compounded at $j = -10\%$ compounded annually.

That is, $FV = 100(1+i)^n$

$= 100[1+(-0.10)]^5$

$= 100(0.9)^5$

$= 59.05$ units

The target level is <u>59.05%</u> of the current level.

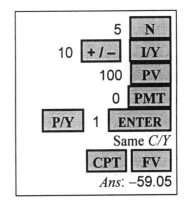

10. Let x represent the size of the replacement payments due 2 and 4 years from now. For equivalence at a focal date 2 years from now,

$$\$2300(1.04875)^7 + \$3100(1.04875)^{-2} = \$2000(1.04875)^4 + x + x(1.04875)^{-4}$$

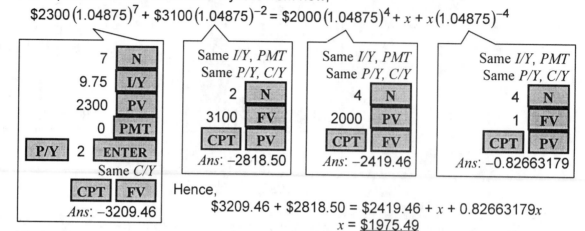

Hence,

$$\$3209.46 + \$2818.50 = \$2419.46 + x + 0.82663179x$$
$$x = \underline{\$1975.49}$$

The second and third payments should be $1975.49.

11. Let x represent the size of each loan payment.

$$\$6500 = x(1.009375)^{-3} + x(1.009375)^{-6} + x(1.009375)^{-12}$$
$$= 0.9723942x + 0.9455505x + 0.8940658x$$
$$= 2.8120105x$$
$$x = \underline{\$2311.51}$$

Each loan payment should be $2311.51.

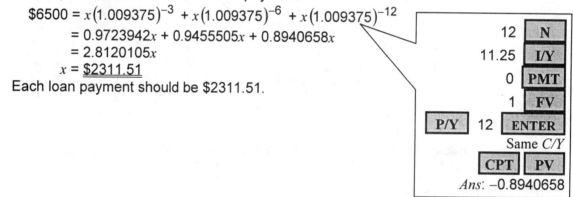

9 Compound Interest: Further Topics and Applications

Concept Questions (Section 9.1)

1. If $FV < PV$, the quantity is decreasing in size as time passes. Therefore, the rate of growth is negative. That is, the value for i is <u>negative</u>.

3. Since the time interval is the same for both cases, the relative size of the periodic rates of return is indicated by the overall *percent* increase rather than the overall *dollar* increase. In the case "$1 grew to $2", the final value is twice the initial value (100% increase). In the case "$3 grew to $5", the final value is 1.667 times the initial value (66.7% increase). Therefore, the periodic rate of return was higher in the <u>"$1 grew to $2"</u> scenario.

Exercise 9.1

1. $PV = \$3400$, $FV = \$4297.91$, $n = 3$

$$i = \left(\frac{FV}{PV}\right)^{1/n} - 1$$

$$= \left(\frac{\$4297.91}{\$3400}\right)^{1/3} - 1$$

$= 0.08125 = 8.125\%$ per year
Nominal rate, $j = mi = 1(8.125\%)$
$\qquad = $ <u>8.125% compounded annually</u>.

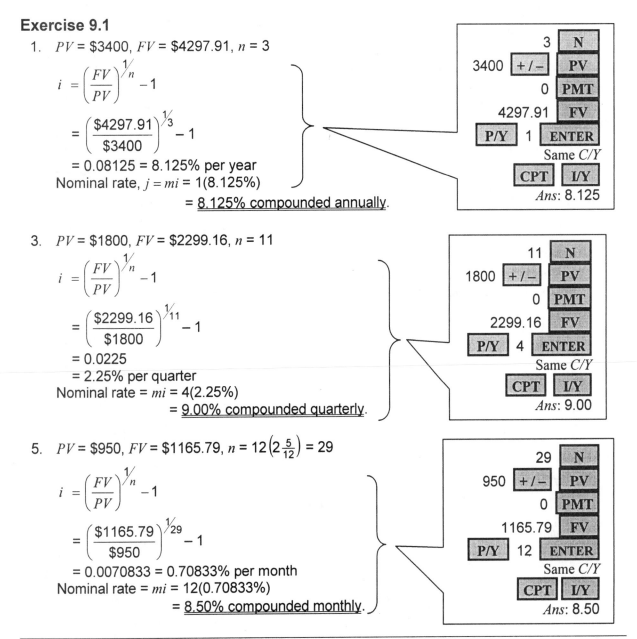

3. $PV = \$1800$, $FV = \$2299.16$, $n = 11$

$$i = \left(\frac{FV}{PV}\right)^{1/n} - 1$$

$$= \left(\frac{\$2299.16}{\$1800}\right)^{1/11} - 1$$

$= 0.0225$
$= 2.25\%$ per quarter
Nominal rate $= mi = 4(2.25\%)$
$\qquad = $ <u>9.00% compounded quarterly</u>.

5. $PV = \$950$, $FV = \$1165.79$, $n = 12\left(2\tfrac{5}{12}\right) = 29$

$$i = \left(\frac{FV}{PV}\right)^{1/n} - 1$$

$$= \left(\frac{\$1165.79}{\$950}\right)^{1/29} - 1$$

$= 0.0070833 = 0.70833\%$ per month
Nominal rate $= mi = 12(0.70833\%)$
$\qquad = $ <u>8.50% compounded monthly</u>.

7. $PV = \$4600$, $FV = \$332,000$, $n = 100$

$$i = \left(\frac{FV}{PV}\right)^{1/n} - 1$$

$$= \left(\frac{\$332,000}{\$4600}\right)^{1/100} - 1$$

$= 0.0437$

$= 4.37\%$

The bequest earned $j = mi = \underline{4.37\%\ \text{compounded annually}}$.

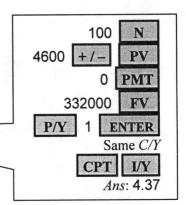

9. $PV = \$2550$ per month, $FV = \$4475$ per month, $n = 11$

$$i = \left(\frac{FV}{PV}\right)^{1/n} - 1$$

$$= \left(\frac{\$4475}{\$2550}\right)^{1/11} - 1$$

$= 0.0525 = 5.25\%$

Ander's salary has grown at the rate of
$j = mi = \underline{5.25\%\ \text{compounded annually}}$.

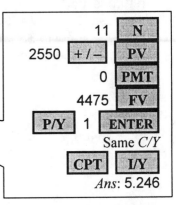

11. $PV = \$70,000$, $FV = \$260,000$, $n = 17$

$$i = \left(\frac{FV}{PV}\right)^{1/n} - 1$$

$$= \left(\frac{\$260,000}{\$70,000}\right)^{1/17} - 1$$

$= 0.0802$

$= 8.02\%$

The value of the home increased at the rate of
$j = mi = \underline{8.02\%\ \text{compounded annually}}$.

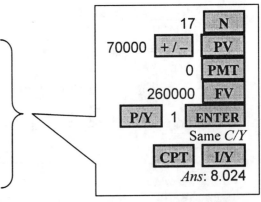

13. For all cases, let $PV = \$1$ and $FV = \$2$.
    a. With $n = 12$,

$$i = \left(\frac{FV}{PV}\right)^{1/n} - 1$$

$$= \left(\frac{\$2}{\$1}\right)^{1/12} - 1$$

$= 0.0595 = 5.95\%$

and $j = mi = 1(5.95\%)$

$= 5.95\%$ <u>compounded annually</u>.

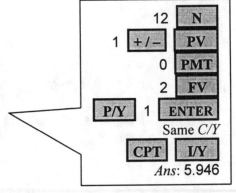

    b. With $n = 10$,

$i = 2^{1/10} - 1 = 0.0718 = 7.18\%$

and $j = mi = 1(7.18\%)$

$= \underline{7.18\%\ \text{compounded annually}}$.

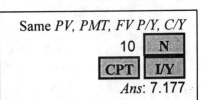

Exercise 9.1 *(continued)*

13. c. With $n = 8$,

$$i = 2^{1/8} - 1$$
$$= 0.0905 = 9.05\%$$
and $j = mi = 1(9.05\%)$
$$\underline{= 9.05\% \text{ compounded annually.}}$$

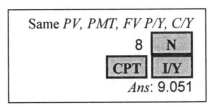
Same *PV, PMT, FV P/Y, C/Y*
8 **N**
CPT **I/Y**
Ans: 9.051

d. With $n = 6$,

$$i = 2^{1/6} - 1$$
$$= 0.1225 = 12.25\%$$
and $j = mi = 1(12.25\%)$
$$\underline{= 12.25\% \text{ compounded annually.}}$$

Same *PV, PMT, FV P/Y, C/Y*
6 **N**
CPT **I/Y**
Ans: 12.246

j	Years	$j \times$ Years
5.95%	12	71.4
7.18%	10	71.8
9.05%	8	72.4
12.25%	6	73.5

Average = 72.3

The products of the annual rate of return (in %) and the doubling time (in years) are similar. As an approximation, <u>the product is close to 72</u>.

15. $PV = 100$, $FV = 70$, $n = 6$

$$i = \left(\frac{FV}{PV}\right)^{1/n} - 1$$

$$= \left(\frac{70}{100}\right)^{1/6} - 1$$

$$= -0.0577$$
$$\underline{= -5.77\%}$$

The number of forestry workers <u>declined at</u> the rate of <u>5.77% compounded annually</u>.

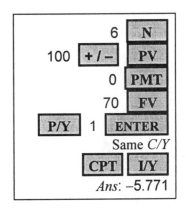
6 **N**
100 **+/−** **PV**
0 **PMT**
70 **FV**
P/Y 1 **ENTER**
Same *C/Y*
CPT **I/Y**
Ans: −5.771

17. $PV = 67.2$, $FV = 119.5$, $n = 10$

$$i = \left(\frac{FV}{PV}\right)^{1/n} - 1$$

$$= \left(\frac{119.5}{67.2}\right)^{1/10} - 1$$

$$= 0.0593$$
$$= 5.93\%$$

The average rate of inflation during the 1980's was <u>5.93% compounded annually</u>.

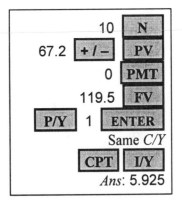
10 **N**
67.2 **+/−** **PV**
0 **PMT**
119.5 **FV**
P/Y 1 **ENTER**
Same *C/Y*
CPT **I/Y**
Ans: 5.925

19. In problems 16 and 17, we found that the equivalent annual inflation rate was 8.04% in the 1970s and 5.93% in the 1980s. This means that a basket of goods purchased for $100 in 1970, cost

$$100(1.0804)^{10}(1.0593)^{10} = \$385.51$$

in 1990. The average annual rate of inflation for the entire 20 years was

$$i = \left(\frac{FV}{PV}\right)^{1/n} - 1$$

$$= \left(\frac{\$385.51}{\$100}\right)^{1/20} - 1$$

$$= 0.0698$$

= <u>6.98% compounded annually</u>

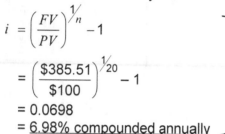

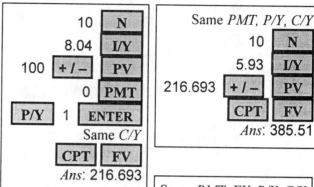

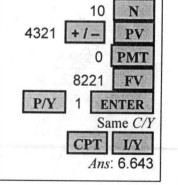

21. Maturity value of the note $= PV(1+i)^n$

$$= \$3800(1.0475)^8$$

$$= \$5508.28$$

Based on proceeds of $4481 paid 18 months ($n = 6$ quarters) before maturity,

$$i = \left(\frac{FV}{PV}\right)^{1/n} - 1$$

$$= \left(\frac{\$5508.28}{\$4481}\right)^{1/6} - 1$$

$$= 0.0350 = 3.50\%$$

The buyer will realize a rate of return of $mi = 4(3.50\%) =$ <u>14.0% compounded quarterly</u> on her investment.

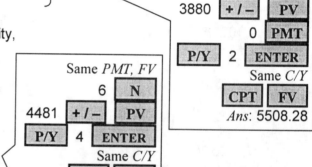

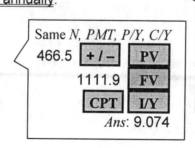

23. *a.* For the S&P/TSX Index,

$$i = \left(\frac{FV}{PV}\right)^{1/n} - 1 = \left(\frac{8221}{4321}\right)^{1/10} - 1 = 6.64\%$$

The S&P/TSX stock portfolio grew by <u>6.64% compounded annually</u>.

For the S&P 500 Index,

$$i = \left(\frac{1111.9}{466.5}\right)^{1/10} - 1 = 9.07\%$$

The S&P 500 stock portfolio grew by <u>9.07% compounded annually</u>.

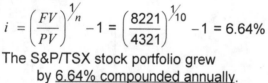

23. *b.* Value of S&P/TSX portfolio at end of 2003 = $10,000 \times \dfrac{8221}{4321} = \$19,025.69$

Value of S&P 500 portfolio at end of 2003 = $10,000 \times \dfrac{1111.9}{466.5} = \$23,834.94$

The US portfolio was worth $23,834.94 – $19,025.69 = <u>$4809.25</u> more.

25. To simply maintain purchasing power,

$100 must grow to $100 \times \dfrac{115.3}{95.6} = \$120.607$

A $100 investment actually grew to $193 in 7 years.

Real periodic rate, $i = \left(\dfrac{FV}{PV}\right)^{\frac{1}{n}} - 1$

$= \left(\dfrac{\$193}{\$120.607}\right)^{\frac{1}{7}} - 1$

$= 0.0695$

Hence, $j = mi = $ <u>6.95% compounded annually</u>

27. Suppose the amount initially invested was $100. The future value 2 years later was

$FV = PV(1+i)^n$

$= \$100(1.06)^4$

$= \$126.248$

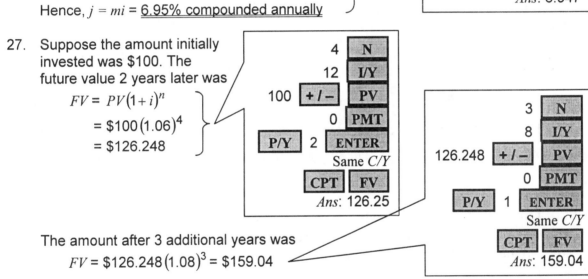

The amount after 3 additional years was

$FV = \$126.248(1.08)^3 = \$159.04$

The equivalent rate of return that would produce the same maturity amount after 5 years is

$i = \left(\dfrac{FV}{PV}\right)^{\frac{1}{n}} - 1 = \left(\dfrac{\$159.04}{\$100}\right)^{\frac{1}{5}} - 1 = 0.0972$

$j = mi = 1(9.72\%) = $ <u>9.72% compounded annually</u>

29. Suppose the initial investment in the portfolio was $100. Its value after 5 years would have been

$FV = PV(1+i_1)(1+i_2)(1+i_3)\cdots(1+i_n)$

$= \$100(1.20)(1.15)(0.90)(1.25)(0.95)$

$= \$147.4845$

The annually compounded return that would produce the same value after 5 years is

$i = \left(\dfrac{FV}{PV}\right)^{\frac{1}{n}} - 1 = \left(\dfrac{\$147.4875}{\$100}\right)^{\frac{1}{5}} - 1 = 0.0808 = 8.08\%$

The equivalent rate of return was <u>8.08% compounded annually</u>.

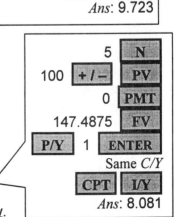

31. Suppose the initial investment for each holding period was $100. For the last 3-year period,

$$FV = PV(1+i_1)(1+i_2)(1+i_3)\cdots(1+i_n)$$
$$= \$100(1.244)(1.402)(1.269)$$
$$= \$221.325$$

$$i = \left(\frac{FV}{PV}\right)^{1/n} - 1 = \left(\frac{\$221.325}{\$100}\right)^{1/3} - 1 = 0.3032 = 30.32\%$$

The 3-year equivalent rate of return was
$$j = mi = 1(30.32\%) = \underline{30.32\% \text{ compounded annually}}.$$

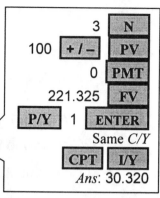

For the last 5 years,
$$FV = \$221.325(1.299)(1.762) = \$506.577$$

$$i = \left(\frac{FV}{PV}\right)^{1/n} - 1 = \left(\frac{\$506.577}{\$100}\right)^{1/5} - 1 = 0.3833 = 38.33\%$$

The 5-year equivalent rate of return was
$$j = mi = 1(38.33\%) = \underline{38.33\% \text{ compounded annually}}.$$

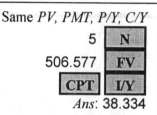

For the entire 10 years,
$$FV = \$506.577(1-0.05)(1.085)(1.491)(1-0.054)(1-0.122)$$
$$= \$646.64$$

$$i = \left(\frac{FV}{PV}\right)^{1/n} - 1 = \left(\frac{\$646.64}{\$100}\right)^{1/10} - 1 = 0.2052 = 20.52\%$$

The 10-year equivalent rate of return was
$$j = mi = 1(23.07\%) = \underline{20.52\% \text{ compounded annually}}.$$

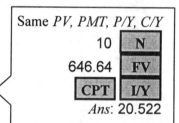

Concept Questions (Section 9.2)

1. In the case of <u>annual compounding</u>, the value calculated for n will equal the number of years in the term of the loan or investment.

Exercise 9.2

1. $$n = \frac{\ln\left(\dfrac{FV}{PV}\right)}{\ln(1+i)} = \frac{\ln\left(\dfrac{\$4483.92}{\$1100}\right)}{\ln(1.063)}$$
$$= \frac{1.4052}{0.061095}$$
$$= 23.00 \text{ periods}$$

Since the compounding period is 1 year, the term is <u>23 years</u>.

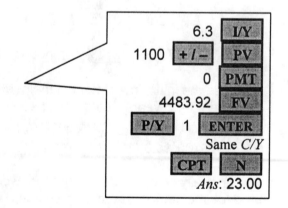

Exercise 9.2 *(continued)*

3. $n = \dfrac{ln\left(\dfrac{FV}{PV}\right)}{ln(1+i)} = \dfrac{ln\left(\dfrac{\$10,365.39}{\$5670}\right)}{ln(1.0475)}$

$= \dfrac{0.603283}{0.046406}$

$= 13.0$ periods

Total time $= 13(0.5 \text{ year})$

$\qquad = 6.5$ years

$\qquad = \underline{6 \text{ years, 6 months}}$

9.5	**I/Y**
5670 **+ / −**	**PV**
0	**PMT**
10365.39	**FV**
P/Y 2	**ENTER**

Same C/Y

CPT	**N**

Ans: 13.00

5. $n = \dfrac{ln\left(\dfrac{FV}{PV}\right)}{ln(1+i)} = \dfrac{ln\left(\dfrac{\$3837.30}{\$2870}\right)}{ln(1.008\overline{3})}$

$= \dfrac{0.290457}{0.0082988}$

$= 35.00$ periods

Total time $= 35(1 \text{ month})$

$\qquad = 35$ months

$\qquad = \underline{2 \text{ years, 11 months}}$

10	**I/Y**
2870 **+ / −**	**PV**
0	**PMT**
3837.30	**FV**
P/Y 12	**ENTER**

Same C/Y

CPT	**N**

Ans: 35.00

7. $n = \dfrac{ln\left(\dfrac{FV}{PV}\right)}{ln(1+i)} = \dfrac{ln\left(\dfrac{\$3252}{\$2640}\right)}{ln(1.015)} = 14.00$ periods

Total time before the scheduled payment
$= 14(3 \text{ months}) = 42 \text{ months} = \underline{3 \text{ years, 6 months}}$

6	**I/Y**
2640 **+ / −**	**PV**
0	**PMT**
3252	**FV**
P/Y 4	**ENTER**

Same C/Y

CPT	**N**

Ans: 14.003

9. $n = \dfrac{ln\left(\dfrac{FV}{PV}\right)}{ln(1+i)} = \dfrac{ln\left(\dfrac{\$10,000}{\$4011.33}\right)}{ln(1.032)} = 29.00$ periods

The time remaining until the maturity date is
$29(\tfrac{1}{2} \text{ year}) = \underline{14 \text{ years, 6 months}}$.

6.4	**I/Y**
4011.33 **+ / −**	**PV**
0	**PMT**
10000	**FV**
P/Y 2	**ENTER**

Same C/Y

CPT	**N**

Ans: 29.000

11. a.
$$n = \frac{ln\left(\frac{FV}{PV}\right)}{ln(1+i)} = \frac{ln(2)}{ln(1.084)} = 8.5937 \text{ periods}$$

Each period is 1 year. The partial period is
0.5937(12 months) = 7.12 months.
Rounded to the nearest month,
the investment will double in <u>8 years, 7 months</u>.

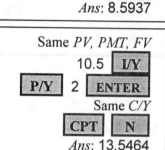

8.4   **I/Y**
1   **+/−**   **PV**
0   **PMT**
2   **FV**
P/Y   1   **ENTER**
Same *C/Y*
CPT   **N**
Ans: 8.5937

b.
$$n = \frac{ln\left(\frac{FV}{PV}\right)}{ln(1+i)} = \frac{ln(2)}{ln(1.0525)} = 13.5464 \text{ periods}$$

Each period is 6 months. The partial period is
0.5464(6 months) = 3.28 months.
Rounded to the nearest month,
the investment will double in
13(0.5 year) + 3 months = 6.5 years + 3 months
= <u>6 years, 9 months</u>.

Same *PV, PMT, FV*
10.5   **I/Y**
P/Y   2   **ENTER**
Same *C/Y*
CPT   **N**
Ans: 13.5464

13. a.
$$n = \frac{ln\left(\frac{FV}{PV}\right)}{ln(1+i)} = \frac{ln(4)}{ln(1.08)} = 18.013 \text{ periods}$$

Since each period is 1 year,
the fractional period is
(4 quarters /year) × (0.013 year) = 0.052 quarter
Rounded to the nearest quarter, it will take
<u>18 years</u> for the investment to quadruple.

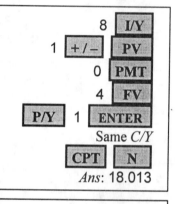

8   **I/Y**
1   **+/−**   **PV**
0   **PMT**
4   **FV**
P/Y   1   **ENTER**
Same *C/Y*
CPT   **N**
Ans: 18.013

b.
$$n = \frac{ln(4)}{ln(1.045)} = 31.495 \text{ periods}$$

Each period is 6 months (2 quarters).
The investment will quadruple in
31.495(2 quarters) = 62.99 quarters
Rounded to quarter, the time period is
63 quarters = $\frac{63}{4}$ years
= <u>15 years, 9 months</u>

Same *PV, PMT, FV*
9   **I/Y**
P/Y   2   **ENTER**
Same *C/Y*
CPT   **N**
Ans: 31.495

15. If money loses 25% of its purchasing power, a nominal
$100 (*FV*) at the end of the period will buy only 75% as
much as a nominal $100 at the beginning of the period.
That is, $100 at the end will buy the same amount as
$75 (*PV*) at the beginning of the period.

a.
$$n = \frac{ln\left(\frac{FV}{PV}\right)}{ln(1+i)} = \frac{ln\left(\frac{\$100}{\$75}\right)}{ln(1+0.02)} = 14.527 \text{ periods}$$

Each period is 1 year. The partial period is
0.527(12 months) = 6.32 months.
Rounded to the nearest month, money will lose 25%
of its purchasing power in <u>14 years, 6 months</u>.

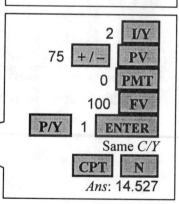

2   **I/Y**
75   **+/−**   **PV**
0   **PMT**
100   **FV**
P/Y   1   **ENTER**
Same *C/Y*
CPT   **N**
Ans: 14.527

15. *b.* $\quad n = \dfrac{ln\left(\dfrac{\$100}{\$75}\right)}{ln\left(1+0.04\right)} = 7.335$ periods

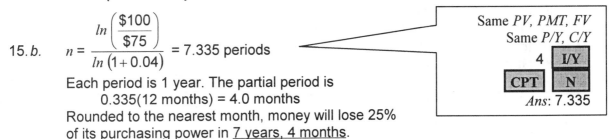

Same *PV, PMT, FV*
Same *P/Y, C/Y*

4 | I/Y

CPT | N

Ans: 7.335

    Each period is 1 year. The partial period is
       0.335(12 months) = 4.0 months
    Rounded to the nearest month, money will lose 25%
    of its purchasing power in <u>7 years, 4 months</u>.

17.   Maturity value $= FV = PV(1+i)^n$

                 $= \$2600(1.1225)^3$

                 $= \$3677.33$

Discounted price $= \$3283.57$
The number of compounding periods between
the discount date and maturity is

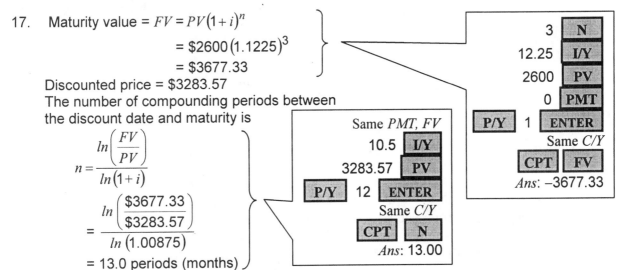

3 | N

12.25 | I/Y

2600 | PV

0 | PMT

P/Y | 1 | ENTER

Same *C/Y*

CPT | FV

Ans: −3677.33

$$n = \dfrac{ln\left(\dfrac{FV}{PV}\right)}{ln\left(1+i\right)}$$

$$= \dfrac{ln\left(\dfrac{\$3677.33}{\$3283.57}\right)}{ln\left(1.00875\right)}$$

    $= 13.0$ periods (months)

Same *PMT, FV*

10.5 | I/Y

3283.57 | PV

P/Y | 12 | ENTER

Same *C/Y*

CPT | N

Ans: 13.00

Hence, the discounting took place 36 − 13 = <u>23 months</u> after the issue date.

19.   The number of months required for $4000 borrowed
at 7.5% compounded monthly to grow to $5000 is

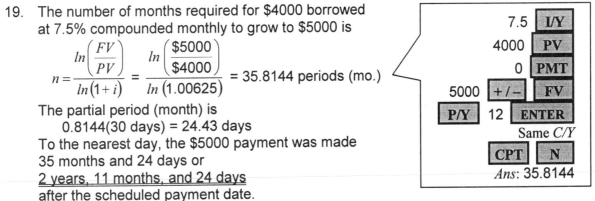

$$n = \dfrac{ln\left(\dfrac{FV}{PV}\right)}{ln\left(1+i\right)} = \dfrac{ln\left(\dfrac{\$5000}{\$4000}\right)}{ln\left(1.00625\right)} = 35.8144 \text{ periods (mo.)}$$

7.5 | I/Y

4000 | PV

0 | PMT

5000 | +/− | FV

P/Y | 12 | ENTER

Same *C/Y*

CPT | N

Ans: 35.8144

The partial period (month) is
    0.8144(30 days) = 24.43 days
To the nearest day, the $5000 payment was made
35 months and 24 days or
<u>2 years, 11 months, and 24 days</u>
after the scheduled payment date.

21. $557.05 represents the present value of $1000
on the purchase date. The number of half-years
between the purchase date and maturity date was

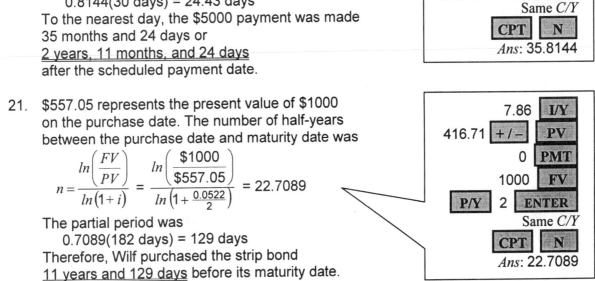

$$n = \dfrac{ln\left(\dfrac{FV}{PV}\right)}{ln\left(1+i\right)} = \dfrac{ln\left(\dfrac{\$1000}{\$557.05}\right)}{ln\left(1+\dfrac{0.0522}{2}\right)} = 22.7089$$

7.86 | I/Y

416.71 | +/− | PV

0 | PMT

1000 | FV

P/Y | 2 | ENTER

Same *C/Y*

CPT | N

Ans: 22.7089

The partial period was
    0.7089(182 days) = 129 days
Therefore, Wilf purchased the strip bond
<u>11 years and 129 days</u> before its maturity date.

Exercise 9.2 *(continued)*

23. The $9380.24 payout figure represents the present value on the prepayment date of the loan's maturity value (discounted at 10% compounded quarterly). The maturity value was

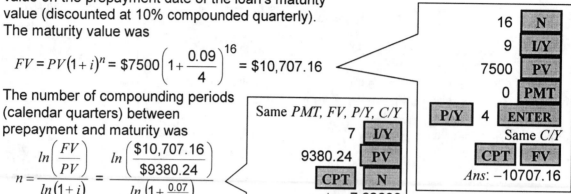

$$FV = PV(1+i)^n = \$7500\left(1+\frac{0.09}{4}\right)^{16} = \$10{,}707.16$$

The number of compounding periods (calendar quarters) between prepayment and maturity was

$$n = \frac{\ln\left(\dfrac{FV}{PV}\right)}{\ln(1+i)} = \frac{\ln\left(\dfrac{\$10{,}707.16}{\$9380.24}\right)}{\ln\left(1+\dfrac{0.07}{4}\right)} = 7.62639$$

The partial period (quarter) was
0.62639(91 days) = 57.0 days long
Hence, the loan was prepaid <u>1 year, 9 months, and 57 days</u> before maturity.

25. *a.* Number of days from September 8, 2003 to March 8, 2004 = 182
Number of days from January 27, 2004 to March 8, 2004 = 41
Number of compounding periods to maturity, $n = 47\frac{41}{182} = 47.225275$

$$\text{Price on January 27, 2004} = \frac{FV}{(1+i)^n} = \frac{\$100}{1.02925^{47.225275}} = \underline{\$25.63}$$

b. Number of compounding periods to maturity, $n = 15\frac{41}{182} = 15.225275$

$$\text{Price on January 27, 2020} = \frac{\$100}{1.02975^{15.225275}} = \underline{\$64.47}$$

27. *a.* Number of days from December 1, 2003 to June 1, 2004 = 183
Number of days from January 27, 2004 to June 1, 2004 = 126
Number of compounding periods to maturity, $n = 56\frac{126}{183} = 56.688525$

$$\frac{\text{Yield}}{2} = i = \left(\frac{FV}{PV}\right)^{1/n} - 1 = \left(\frac{\$100}{\$19.79}\right)^{1/56.688525} - 1 = 1.028989 - 1 = 2.8989\%$$

Yield on January 27, 2004 = 2(2.8989%) = <u>5.798% compounded semiannually</u>.

b.
$$\frac{\text{Yield}}{2} = i = \left(\frac{\$100}{\$19.79}\right)^{1/54.688525} - 1 = 1.030065 - 1 = 3.0065\%$$

Yield on January 27, 2005 = 2(3.0065%) = <u>6.013% compounded semiannually</u>.

Concept Questions (Section 9.3)

1. The effective rate of interest is the *equivalent annually compounded* rate.

3. Yes. The effective interest rate equals the nominal rate for annual compounding.

5. If compounding is more frequent than annual, the effective rate exceeds the nominal rate. Lenders would prefer to disclose the lower <u>nominal rate</u> since most borrowers do not understand the distinction between nominal and effective rates.

Exercise 9.3

1. $f = (1+i)^m - 1$

   $= (1 + \frac{0.105}{2})^2 - 1$

   $= 0.1078$

   $= \underline{10.78\%}$

Using the calculator's financial functions, find the future value of $100 after 1 year.

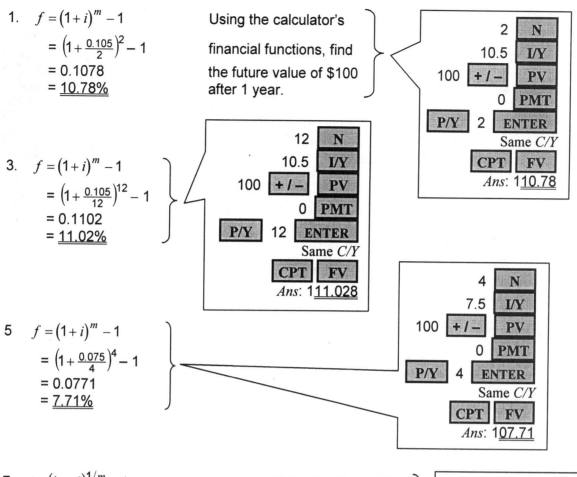

3. $f = (1+i)^m - 1$

   $= (1 + \frac{0.105}{12})^{12} - 1$

   $= 0.1102$

   $= \underline{11.02\%}$

5. $f = (1+i)^m - 1$

   $= (1 + \frac{0.075}{4})^4 - 1$

   $= 0.0771$

   $= \underline{7.71\%}$

7. $i = (1+f)^{1/m} - 1$

   $= (1.105)^{1/2} - 1$

   $= 0.05119$

   $= 5.119\%$

   $j = mi$

   $= 2(5.119\%)$

   $= \underline{10.24\% \text{ compounded semiannually}}$

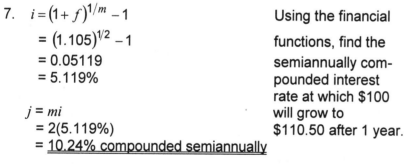

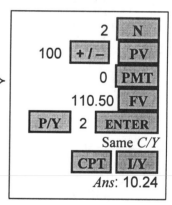

Using the financial functions, find the semiannually compounded interest rate at which $100 will grow to $110.50 after 1 year.

9. $i = (1+f)^{1/m} - 1$

   $= (1.105)^{1/12} - 1$

   $= 0.00836$

   $= 0.836\%$

   $j = mi$

   $= 12(0.836\%)$

   $= \underline{10.03\% \text{ compounded monthly}}$

Using the financial functions, find the monthly compounded interest rate at which $100 will grow to $110.50 after 1 year.

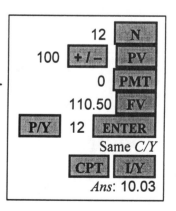

Chapter 9: Compound Interest: Further Topics and Applications

Exercise 9.3 *(continued)*

11. $i = (1+f)^{1/m} - 1$

   $= (1.075)^{1/4} - 1$

   $= 0.01824$

   $= 1.824\%$

   $j = mi$

   $= 4(1.824\%)$

   $= \underline{7.30\% \text{ compounded quarterly}}$

Using the financial functions, find the quarterly compounded interest rate at which $100 will grow to $107.50 after 1 year.

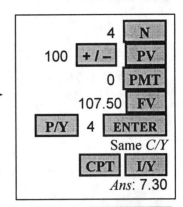

13. $f = (1+i)^m - 1$

   $= \left(1 + \frac{0.12}{12}\right)^{12} - 1$

   $= 0.1268$

   $= \underline{12.68\%}$

Using the calculator's financial functions, find the future value of $100 after 1 year.

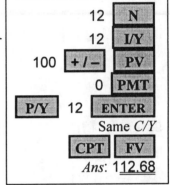

15. $f = (1+i)^m - 1$

   $= \left(1 + \frac{0.115}{4}\right)^4 - 1$

   $= 0.1201$

   $= \underline{12.01\%}$

Using the calculator's financial functions, find the future value of $100 after 1 year.

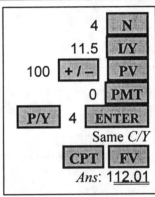

17. $i = (1+f)^{1/m} - 1$

   $= (1.1025)^{1/2} - 1$

   $= 0.0500$

   $= 5.00\%$

   $j = mi$

   $= 2(5.00\%)$

   $= \underline{10.00\% \text{ compounded semiannually}}$

Using the financial functions, find the semiannually compounded interest rate at which $100 will grow to $110.25 after 1 year.

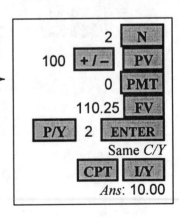

Exercise 9.3 *(continued)*

19. $i = (1+f)^{1/m} - 1$

    $= (1.10)^{1/12} - 1$

    $= 0.007974$

    $= 0.7974\%$

    $j = mi$

    $= 12(0.7974\%)$

    $= \underline{9.57\% \text{ compounded monthly}}$

Using the financial functions, find the find the monthly compounded interest rate at which \$100 will grow to \$110 after 1 year.

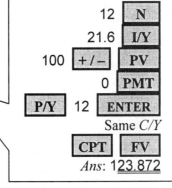

Ans: 9.57

21. Since the interest is collected each month, we have monthly compounding. The nominal annual rate charged is
    $j = mi = 12(1.8\%) = 21.6\%$ compounded monthly
    The effective interest rate charged is

    $f = (1+i)^m - 1 = (1.018)^{12} - 1 = 0.2387 = \underline{23.87\%}$

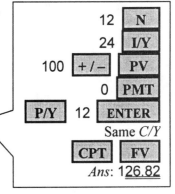

Ans: 1<u>23.872</u>

23. Since the interest is charged each month, we have monthly compounding. The nominal annual rate charged is
    $j = mi = 12(2\%) = 24\%$ compounded monthly
    The effective interest rate charged is

    $f = (1+i)^m - 1 = (1.02)^{12} - 1 = 0.2682 = \underline{26.82\%}$

    Using the calculator's financial functions, find the future value of \$100 after 1 year.

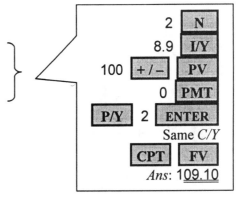

Ans: 1<u>26.82</u>

25. $f = (1+i)^m - 1$

    $= \left(1 + \frac{0.089}{2}\right)^2 - 1$

    $= 0.0910$

    $= \underline{9.10\%}$

    Using the calculator's financial functions, find the future value of \$100 after 1 year.

Ans: 1<u>09.10</u>

Exercise 9.3 *(continued)*

27. The fundamental question is: "What annually compounded rate of return would produce the same growth in $2\frac{1}{2}$ years (30 months)?" In this case,

$$f = j = mi = 1(i) = i$$

where $\quad i = \left(\dfrac{FV}{PV}\right)^{1/n} - 1$

$$= \left(\dfrac{\$6450}{\$5000}\right)^{1/2.5} - 1$$

$$= 0.1072$$

$$= 10.72\%$$

Hence, $\quad f = j = \underline{10.72\%}$

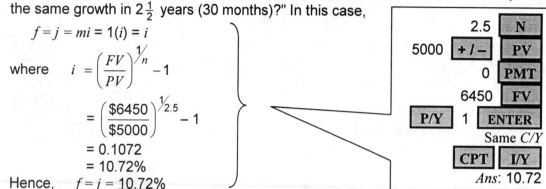

29.

Bank	Credit union
$f = (1+i)^m - 1$	$f = (1+i)^m - 1$
$= \left(1 + \dfrac{0.072}{12}\right)^{12} - 1$	$= \left(1 + \dfrac{0.074}{2}\right)^2 - 1$
$= 0.0744$	$= 0.0754$
$= 7.44\%$	$= 7.54\%$

Using the calculator's financial functions, find the future value of $100 after 1 year.

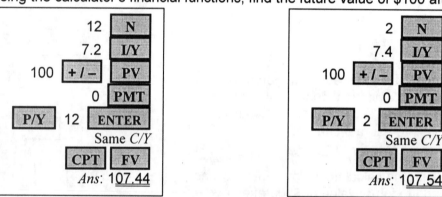

Lisa should <u>choose the bank loan</u> since it has a 0.1% lower effective interest rate.

31.

Bank	Mortgage broker
$f = (1+i)^m - 1$	$f = (1+i)^m - 1$
$= \left(1 + \dfrac{0.065}{2}\right)^2 - 1$	$= \left(1 + \dfrac{0.064}{12}\right)^{12} - 1$
$= 0.0661$	$= 0.0659$
$= 6.61\%$	$= 6.59\%$

Using the calculator's financial functions, find the future value of $100 after 1 year.

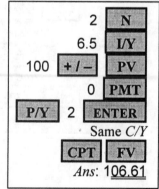

Exercise 9.3 *(continued)*

33. For the annually compounded rate,
    $j = i = f = $ <u>5.75% compounded annually</u>

    Semiannual compounding

    $i = (1 + f)^{1/m} - 1$

    $\quad = (1.0575)^{1/2} - 1$

    $\quad = 0.02835$

    $\quad = 2.835\%$

    $j = 2i$

    $\quad = $ <u>5.67% compounded semiannually</u>

    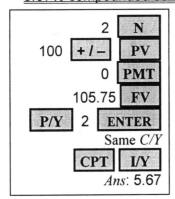

    Monthly compounding

    $i = (1 + f)^{1/m} - 1$

    $\quad = (1.0575)^{1/12} - 1$

    $\quad = 0.00467$

    $\quad = 0.467\%$

    $j = 12i$

    $\quad = $ <u>5.60% compounded monthly</u>

    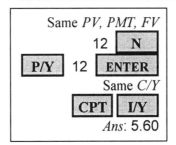

35. $f \text{(old)} = (1 + i)^m - 1$

    $\quad = \left(1 + \frac{0.18}{12}\right)^{12} - 1$

    $\quad = 0.1956$

    $f \text{(new)} = 0.1956 + 0.02 = 0.2156$

    $i \text{(new)} = (1 + f)^{1/m} - 1$

    $\quad = (1.2156)^{1/12} - 1$

    $\quad = 0.01640$

    The annual rate should be changed to
    $j = 12i = $ <u>19.68%</u> compounded monthly.

    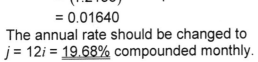

    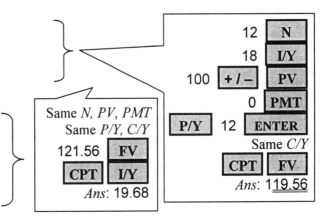

Concept Questions (Section 9.4)

1. If two nominal interest rates are equivalent, they will produce the same future value of an investment after 1 year.

3. The equivalent periodic rate for 6 months is more than six times the equivalent periodic rate for 1 month because the 1-month rate achieves extra growth through the compounding of interest earnings at the end of each month. Therefore, the answer is <u>(iii) Greater than 3%</u>.

Exercise 9.4

Note: We will use the abbreviations:

ca = compounded annually	cq = compounded quarterly
csa = compounded semiannually	cm = compounded monthly

Problem	j_1	m_1	m_2	$i_2 = (1+i_1)^{m_1/m_2} - 1$	$j_2 = m_2 i_2$
1.	10%	1	2	$\left(1+\frac{0.10}{1}\right)^{1/2} - 1 = 0.04881$	$2(0.04881) = \underline{9.76\% \text{ csa}}$
3.	10%	1	12	$(1+0.10)^{1/12} - 1 = 0.007974$	$12(0.007974) = \underline{9.57\% \text{ cm}}$
5.	10%	2	4	$\left(1+\frac{0.10}{2}\right)^{2/4} - 1 = 0.02470$	$4(0.02470) = \underline{9.88\% \text{ cq}}$
7.	10%	4	1	$\left(1+\frac{0.10}{4}\right)^{4/1} - 1 = 0.1038$	$1(0.1038) = \underline{10.38\% \text{ ca}}$
9.	10%	4	12	$\left(1+\frac{0.10}{4}\right)^{4/12} - 1 = 0.008264$	$12(0.008264) = \underline{9.92\% \text{ cm}}$
11.	10%	12	2	$\left(1+\frac{0.10}{12}\right)^{12/2} - 1 = 0.05105$	$2(0.05105) = \underline{10.21\% \text{ csa}}$
13.	9%	2	1	$\left(1+\frac{0.09}{2}\right)^{2/1} - 1 = 0.0920$	$1(0.0920) = \underline{9.20\% \text{ ca}}$
15.	8.25%	1	12	$(1+0.0825)^{1/12} - 1 = 0.006628$	$12(0.006628) = \underline{7.95\% \text{ cm}}$
17.	7.5%	2	4	$\left(1+\frac{0.075}{2}\right)^{2/4} - 1 = 0.01858$	$4(0.01858) = \underline{7.43\% \text{ cq}}$
19.	8.5%	4	2	$\left(1+\frac{0.085}{4}\right)^{4/2} - 1 = 0.004293$	$2(0.004293) = \underline{8.59\% \text{ csa}}$
21. a.	6%	2	1	$\left(1+\frac{0.06}{2}\right)^{2/1} - 1 = 0.0609$	$1(0.0609) = \underline{6.09\% \text{ ca}}$
b.	6%	4	1	$\left(1+\frac{0.06}{4}\right)^{4/1} - 1 = 0.06136$	$1(0.06136) = \underline{6.14\% \text{ ca}}$
c.	6%	12	1	$\left(1+\frac{0.06}{12}\right)^{12/1} - 1 = 0.06168$	$1(0.06168) = \underline{6.17\% \text{ ca}}$
23.	5.5%	2	12	$\left(1+\frac{0.055}{2}\right)^{2/12} - 1 = 0.004532$	$12(0.004532) = \underline{5.44\% \text{ cm}}$
25.	9%	12	2	$\left(1+\frac{0.09}{12}\right)^{12/2} - 1 = 0.04585$	$2(0.04585) = \underline{9.17\% \text{ csa}}$
27.	5.25%	1	2	$\left(1+\frac{0.0525}{1}\right)^{1/2} - 1 = 0.02591$	$2(0.02591) = \underline{5.18\% \text{ csa}}$
	5.25%	1	12	$(1+0.0525)^{1/12} - 1 = 0.004273$	$12(0.004273) = \underline{5.13\% \text{ cm}}$

Review Problems

1. $PV = \$10,000$; $FV = \$5432$, $n = 5$, $m = 1$

$$i = \left(\frac{FV}{PV}\right)^{1/n} - 1$$

$$= \left(\frac{\$5432}{\$10,000}\right)^{1/5} - 1$$

$$= -0.1149$$

$$= -11.49\%$$

The fund earned $j = mi = 1(-11.49\%) = -11.49\%$ compounded annually during the five years.

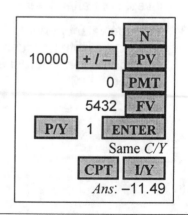

Review Problems *(continued)*

3. $PV = \$165,000$; $FV = \$485,000$, $n = 8$, $m = 1$

$$i = \left(\frac{FV}{PV}\right)^{1/n} - 1$$

$$= \left(\frac{\$485,000}{\$165,000}\right)^{1/8} - 1$$

$$= 0.1443$$

$$= \underline{14.43\%}$$

Sales grew at a compound annual rate of
14.43% during the 8-year period.

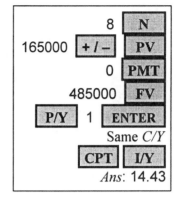

Ans: 14.43

5. The value, after 5 years, of an initial $100 investment was

$$FV = PV(1 + i_1)\cdots(1 + i_5)$$

$$= \$100(1 - 0.13)(1 + 0.18)(1 + 0.05)(1 + 0.24)(1 - 0.05)$$

$$= \$126.98$$

The 5-ear compound annual return was

$$j = mi = 1(i) = i = \left(\frac{FV}{PV}\right)^{1/n} - 1$$

$$= \left(\frac{\$126.98}{\$100}\right)^{1/5} - 1$$

$$= 0.0489$$

$$= \underline{4.89\%}$$

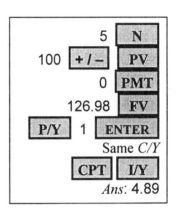

Ans: 4.89

7. $$n = \frac{ln\left(\dfrac{FV}{PV}\right)}{ln(1 + i)} = \frac{ln\left(\dfrac{\$895.67}{\$800}\right)}{ln(1.00\overline{6})}$$

$$= \frac{0.11296}{0.0066445}$$

$$= 17.00 \text{ periods}$$

Terry made the payment 17 months after March 1,
that is, on <u>August 1 of the following year</u>.

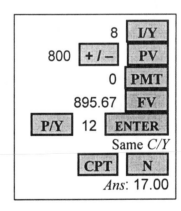

Ans: 17.00

Chapter 9: Compound Interest: Further Topics and Applications

9. Maturity value $= PV(1+i)^n$

$\qquad = \$4500(1.0575)^8$

$\qquad = \$7038.10$

The number of compounding periods between
the discount date and the maturity date is

$n = \dfrac{ln\left(\dfrac{FV}{PV}\right)}{ln(1+i)}$

$\quad = \dfrac{ln\left(\dfrac{\$7038.10}{\$5697.84}\right)}{ln(1.02375)}$

$\quad = \dfrac{0.21125}{0.023472}$

$\quad = 9.00$ periods

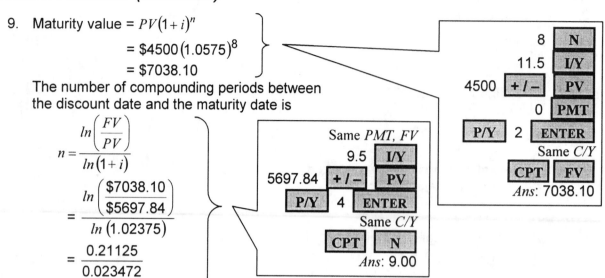

8 N

11.5 I/Y

4500 +/− PV

0 PMT

P/Y 2 ENTER

Same C/Y

CPT FV

Ans: 7038.10

Same *PMT, FV*

9.5 I/Y

5697.84 +/− PV

P/Y 4 ENTER

Same *C/Y*

CPT N

Ans: 9.00

Therefore, the discounting took place

$\qquad 16 - 9 = 7$ periods $= 21$ months <u>1 year and 9 months</u> after the issue date.

11. The number of half years for $10,000 invested at 8%
compounded semiannually to grow to $12,000 is

$n = \dfrac{ln\left(\dfrac{FV}{PV}\right)}{ln(1+i)} = \dfrac{ln\left(\dfrac{\$12,000}{\$10,000}\right)}{ln\left(1+\dfrac{0.08}{2}\right)} = \dfrac{0.18232}{0.039221} = 4.6486$

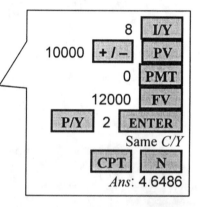

8 I/Y

10000 +/− PV

0 PMT

12000 FV

P/Y 2 ENTER

Same C/Y

CPT N

Ans: 4.6486

The number of days in the partial half year is

$\qquad 0.6486(182$ days$) = 118.0$ days.

To the nearest day, it will take <u>2 years and 118 days</u>
for the $10,000 to grow to $12,000.

13. The effective interest rate is

$f = (1+i)^m - 1$

$\quad = (1.00875)^{12} - 1$

$\quad = 0.1102$

$\quad = 11.02\%$

Using a calculator's
financial functions,
determine the
future value of
$100 after 1 year.

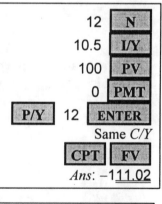

12 N

10.5 I/Y

100 PV

0 PMT

P/Y 12 ENTER

Same C/Y

CPT FV

Ans: −1<u>11.02</u>

The periodic rate 6-month rate having
the same effective rate is the value of i in

$0.1102 = (1+i)^2 - 1$

$(1+i)^2 = 1.1102$

$\qquad i = (1.1102)^{1/2} - 1 = 0.05366 = 5.366\%$

The equivalent nominal rate is

$\qquad j = 2i = 10.73\%$ compounded semiannually

For any nominal interest rate <u>below 10.73% compounded
semiannually</u>, you should choose semiannual compounding.

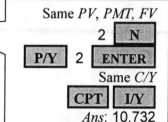

Same *PV, PMT, FV*

2 N

P/Y 2 ENTER

Same *C/Y*

CPT I/Y

Ans: 10.732

Review Problems *(continued)*

15. Given: $i = 1.5\%$, $m = 12$

$$f = (1+i)^m - 1 = (1.015)^{12} - 1$$
$$= 0.1956$$
$$= \underline{19.56\%}$$

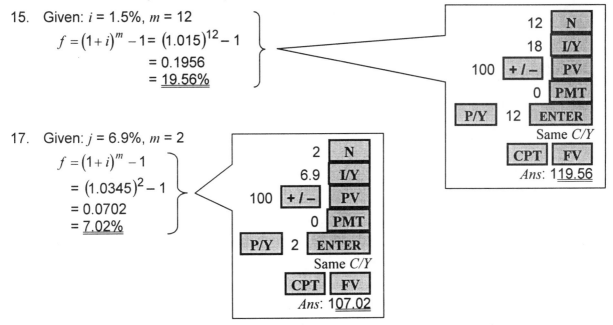

12	N
18	I/Y
100 [+/−]	PV
0	PMT
P/Y 12	ENTER

Same *C/Y*

CPT	FV

Ans: 1<u>19.56</u>

17. Given: $j = 6.9\%$, $m = 2$

$$f = (1+i)^m - 1$$
$$= (1.0345)^2 - 1$$
$$= 0.0702$$
$$= \underline{7.02\%}$$

2	N
6.9	I/Y
100 [+/−]	PV
0	PMT
P/Y 2	ENTER

Same *C/Y*

CPT	FV

Ans: 1<u>07.02</u>

19.

Bank

$$f(\text{bank}) = (1+i)^m - 1$$
$$= (1.04375)^2 - 1$$
$$= 0.08941$$
$$= 8.94\%$$

2	N
8.75	I/Y
100 [+/−]	PV
0	PMT
P/Y 2	ENTER

Same *C/Y*

CPT	FV

Ans: 1<u>08.941</u>

Broker

$$f(\text{broker}) = (1.007 1\overline{6})^{12} - 1$$
$$= 0.08947$$
$$= 8.95\%$$

12	N
8.6	I/Y
100 [+/−]	PV
0	PMT
P/Y 12	ENTER

Same *C/Y*

CPT	FV

Ans: 1<u>08.947</u>

Camille should take the <u>bank mortgage</u> since its effective interest rate is lower.

Self-Test Exercise

1. Given: $PV = \$85{,}000$, $FV = \$215{,}000$, $n = 13$
   The compound annual rate of appreciation of the home has been

$$i = \left(\frac{FV}{PV}\right)^{1/n} - 1$$
$$= \left(\frac{\$215{,}000}{\$85{,}000}\right)^{1/13} - 1$$
$$= 0.0740$$
$$= \underline{7.40\%}$$

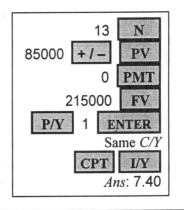

13	N
85000 [+/−]	PV
0	PMT
215000	FV
P/Y 1	ENTER

Same *C/Y*

CPT	I/Y

Ans: 7.40

2. $PV = 109.6$, $FV = 133.8$, $n = 8.5$
    The average compound annual inflation rate was

$$i = \left(\frac{FV}{PV}\right)^{1/n} - 1$$

$$= \left(\frac{133.8}{109.6}\right)^{1/8.5} - 1$$

$$= 0.0237$$

$$= \underline{2.37\%}$$

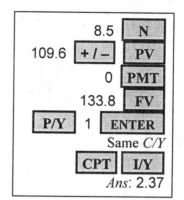

3. Suppose the company began the 5-year period with sales of 1000 units per year. (The answer to the problem will not depend on the initial number chosen because the given information is in terms of percentage changes.)
    After the first 5 years, annual sales will be

$$FV = PV(1+i)^n = 1000(1-0.10)^5 = 590.49 \text{ units per year}$$

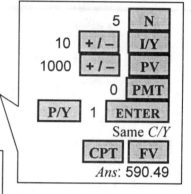

a. To return to 1000 units per year over the subsequent 5 years, the compound annual growth of sales must be

$$i = \left(\frac{FV}{PV}\right)^{1/n} - 1$$

$$= \left(\frac{1000}{590.45}\right)^{1/5} - 1$$

$$= 0.1111$$

$$= \underline{11.11\%}$$

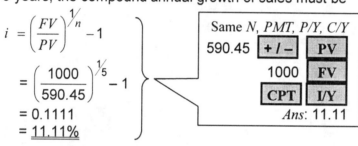

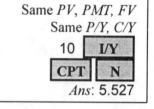

b. If sales grow at 10% per year, it will take

$$n = \frac{ln\left(\dfrac{FV}{PV}\right)}{ln(1+i)} = \frac{ln\left(\dfrac{1000}{590.45}\right)}{ln(1.1111)} = 5.527 \text{ years}$$

or <u>5 years and 6 months</u> (to the nearest month) to return to the original level of sales.

4. In terms of beginning dollars, the ending $54,230 has a purchasing power of only

$$\$54,230 \times \frac{\text{Beginning CPI}}{\text{Ending CPI}} = \$54,230 \times \frac{100}{126.5} = \$42,869.57$$

The portfolio's annually compounded real rate of return was

$$i = \left(\frac{FV}{PV}\right)^{1/n} - 1 = \left(\frac{\$42,869.57}{\$35,645}\right)^{1/6} - 1 = 0.0312 = \underline{3.12\%}$$

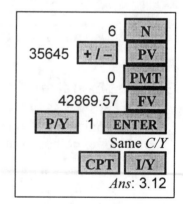

5. Suppose the initial investment in the mutual fund was $100. Its value after 6 years was
   $$\$100(1+i_1)\cdots(1+i_6) = \$100(1-0.259)(1.829)(1-0.253)(1-0.049)(1-0.129)(1.409)$$
   $$= \$130.33$$
   The annually compounded rate of return that would
   have produced the same final value is

   $$i = \left(\frac{FV}{PV}\right)^{\frac{1}{n}} - 1$$

   $$= \left(\frac{\$130.33}{\$100}\right)^{\frac{1}{6}} - 1$$

   $$= 0.0451$$
   $$= \underline{4.51\%}$$

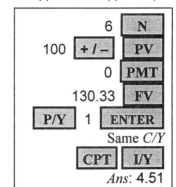

6. The number of compounding periods (quarters) for $100
   to grow to $250 at 9% compounded quarterly is

   $$n = \frac{ln\left(\frac{FV}{PV}\right)}{ln(1+i)} = \frac{ln\left(\frac{\$250}{\$100}\right)}{ln(1.0225)} = 41.180$$

   The partial period is
   $\quad$ 0.180(3 months) = 0.54 months.
   Rounded to the nearest month, it will take an investment
   $\quad$ 3(41) + 1 = 124 months
   $\quad\quad\quad\quad\quad$ = <u>10 years and 4 months</u>
   to increase by 150% if it earns 9% compounded quarterly.

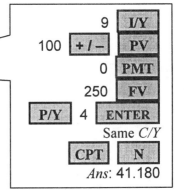

7. If money loses one-third of its purchasing power, $100 (*FV*) at
   the end will buy only two-thirds as much as $100 bought at
   the beginning. That is, $100 at the end buys what
   $66.67 (*PV*) bought at the beginning.

   $$n = \frac{ln\left(\frac{FV}{PV}\right)}{ln(1+i)} = \frac{ln\left(\frac{\$100}{\$66.67}\right)}{ln(1+0.03)} = 13.716 \text{ periods}$$

   Each period is 1 year. The partial period is
   $\quad$ 0.716(12 months) = 8.59 months.
   Rounded to the nearest month, money will lose one-third
   of its purchasing power in <u>13 years, 9 months</u>.

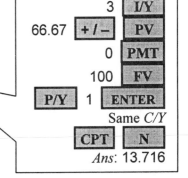

8. The purchase price is the present value of the $10,000 face
   value discounted at 6.47% compounded semiannually.
   The number of half years until maturity is

   $$n = \frac{ln\left(\frac{FV}{PV}\right)}{ln(1+i)} = \frac{ln\left(\frac{\$10,000}{\$4271.17}\right)}{ln\left(1+\frac{0.0647}{2}\right)} = 26.7198$$

   The partial period is 0.7198(182 days) = 131.00 days
   Therefore, the bond will mature
   $\quad \frac{26}{2}$ years and 131 days = <u>13 years and 131 days</u>
   after the date of purchase.

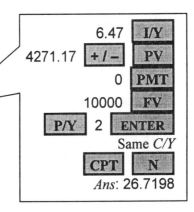

9. Given: $f = 5.375\%$

Hence, $j_1 = m_1 i_1 = 1(5.375\%) = 5.375\%$ compounded annually.

The equivalent periodic rate for 6 months ($m_2 = 2$) is

$$i_2 = \left(1 + i_1\right)^{m_1/m_2} - 1 = \left(1.05375\right)^{1/2} - 1 = 0.02652$$

The corresponding nominal rate is

$$j_2 = m_2 i_2 = 2i_2 = 2(2.652\%) = 5.30\% \text{ compounded semiannually}$$

Choose a semiannually compounded GIC if the nominal
rate <u>exceeds 5.30% compounded semiannually</u>.

10. The preferred loan is the one with the lowest effective rate.

<u>$j = 7.6\%$ c.q.</u>	<u>$j = 7.5\%$ c.m.</u>	<u>$j = 7.7\%$ c.sa.</u>
$f = \left(1 + i\right)^m - 1$	$f = \left(1 + i\right)^m - 1$	$f = \left(1 + i\right)^m - 1$
$= \left(1.019\right)^4 - 1$	$= \left(1.00625\right)^{12} - 1$	$= \left(1.0385\right)^2 - 1$
$= 0.07819$	$= 0.07763$	$= 0.07848$
$= 7.82\%$	$= 7.76\%$	$= 7.85\%$

Using the calculator's financial functions, find the future value of $100 after 1 year.

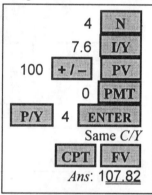

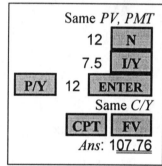

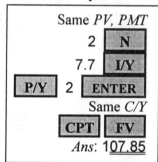

<u>7.5% compounded monthly</u> has the lowest effective rate.

11. The effective interest rate is the annually
compounded rate that will also cause $6000 to
grow to $7900 in 33 months (2.75 years.)

$$f = i = \left(\frac{FV}{PV}\right)^{1/n} - 1 = \left(\frac{\$7900}{\$6000}\right)^{1/2.75} - 1$$

$$= 0.1052$$

$$= \underline{10.52\%} \text{ per year}$$

The investment earned an effective rate of 10.52%
during the 33-month period.

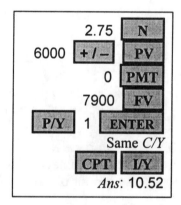

Exercise 9A

1. The simple annualized rate of inflation was
$$\frac{12\,\text{months}}{2\,\text{months}} \times 0.5\% = \underline{3\%}$$
The effective annualized rate of inflation was
$$f = (1+i)^m - 1 = (1.005)^{12/2} - 1 = 0.0304 = \underline{3.04\%}$$

3. Increase in 1 month $= \dfrac{\$333.81 - \$331.12}{\$331.12} \times 100\% = 0.81239\%$

   Simple annualized rate $= \dfrac{12\,\text{months}}{1\,\text{month}} \times 0.81239\% = \underline{9.75\%}$

   Effective annualized rate $= (1.0081239)^{12/1} - 1 = 0.10196 = \underline{10.20\%}$

5. The compound or effective increase in house prices for the year will be
$$f = (1+i)^m - 1 = (1.08)^{12/7} - 1 = 0.1410 = \underline{14.10\%}$$

7. Holding-period return $= \dfrac{125}{365} \times 4.6\% = 1.5753\%$

   The corresponding effective annualized rate of return is
$$f = (1+i)^m - 1 = (1.015753)^{365/125} - 1 = 0.04670 = \underline{4.67\%}$$

9. Percent change during 3 months $= \dfrac{\$12.56 - \$12.86}{\$12.86} \times 100\% = -2.3328\%$

   Simple annualized rate $= \dfrac{12\,\text{months}}{3\,\text{months}} (-2.3328\%) = \underline{-9.33\%}$

   Effective annualized rate, $f = (1+i)^m - 1 = (1 - 0.023328)^{12/3} - 1 = \underline{-9.01\%}$

   The shares in the mutual fund declined at a simple annual rate of 9.33% and an effective annual rate of 9.01%.

11. Current (simple) yield $= \dfrac{1\,\text{year}}{\text{Holding period}} \times$ Holding-period return

   $= \dfrac{365\,\text{days}}{7\,\text{days}} \times 0.097\%$

   $= \underline{5.06\%}$

   Effective annualized yield, $f = (1+i)^m - 1 = (1.00097)^{365/7} - 1 = 0.05185 = \underline{5.19\%}$

13. The return for the most recent 7 days was
$$4.54\% \times \frac{7\,\text{days}}{365\,\text{days}} = 0.08707\%$$
The corresponding effective (annualized) yield is
$$f = (1+i)^m - 1 = (1.0008707)^{365/7} - 1 = 0.04643 = \underline{4.64\%}$$

Exercise 9A *(continued)*

15. The discounter pays out $170 now and gets back the full $200 when the tax refund is received. The holding-period return is

$$\frac{\$30}{\$170} \times 100\% = 17.647\%$$

a. If the holding period is 25 days, the discounter's effective annualized rate of return is

$$f = (1+i)^m - 1 = (1.17647)^{365/25} - 1 = 9.727 = \underline{972.7\%}$$

b. It the holding period is 50 days,

$$f = (1.17647)^{365/50} - 1 = 2.275 = \underline{227.5\%}$$

10 Ordinary Annuities: Future Value and Present Value

Concept Questions (Section 10.1)

1. The two types of annuities are distinguished by comparing the payment interval to the compounding interval. If the payment interval *equals* the compounding interval, the annuity is a *simple* annuity. Otherwise, it is a general annuity.

3. <u>No</u>. Insurance premiums are paid at the beginning of the period of coverage. In the present case, the monthly payments will be made at the beginning of each month of coverage. To qualify as an ordinary annuity, the monthly payments would have to occur at the end of each month of coverage.

Concept Questions (Section 10.2)

1. Subtract the nominal sum of the payments from the annuity's future value.

3. G's future value will be <u>(ii) more than double</u> H's future value. From the pattern of the contributions of individual payments to the annuity's future value, we see that the earlier half of an annuity's payments contribute more to the future value than the later half of the payments. It follows that doubling the number of payments will more than double an annuity's future value.

Exercise 10.2

1. Given: $PMT = \$500$, $n = 1(13) = 13$, $i = \frac{6.75\%}{1} = 6.75\%$

$$FV = PMT\left[\frac{(1+i)^n - 1}{i}\right]$$

$$= \$500\left(\frac{1.0675^{13} - 1}{0.0675}\right)$$

$$= \underline{\$9908.64}$$

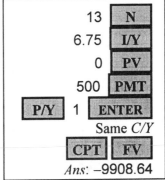

3. Given: $PMT = \$75$, $n = 12(2.5) = 30$, $i = \frac{8\%}{12} = 0.6\overline{6}\%$

$$FV = PMT\left[\frac{(1+i)^n - 1}{i}\right]$$

$$= \$75\left(\frac{1.00\overline{6}^{30} - 1}{0.00\overline{6}}\right)$$

$$= \underline{\$2481.66}$$

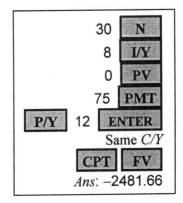

5. Given: $PMT = \$175$, $n = 12(8.25) = 99$, $i = \frac{6\%}{12} = 0.5\%$

$$FV = PMT\left[\frac{(1+i)^n - 1}{i}\right]$$

$$= \$175\left(\frac{1.005^{99} - 1}{0.005}\right)$$

$$= \underline{\$22,346.66}$$

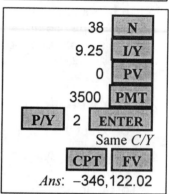

99	**N**
6	**I/Y**
0	**PV**
175	**PMT**
P/Y 12	**ENTER**

Same *C/Y*

CPT **FV**

Ans: −22,346.66

7. Given: $PMT = \$3500$, $n = 2(19) = 38$, $i = \frac{9.25\%}{2} = 4.625\%$

$$FV = PMT\left[\frac{(1+i)^n - 1}{i}\right]$$

$$= \$3500\left(\frac{1.04625^{38} - 1}{0.04625}\right)$$

$$= \underline{\$346,122.02}$$

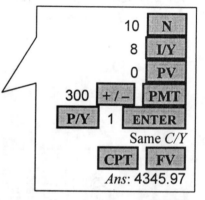

38	**N**
9.25	**I/Y**
0	**PV**
3500	**PMT**
P/Y 2	**ENTER**

Same *C/Y*

CPT **FV**

Ans: −346,122.02

9. Given: $PMT = \$300$, $n = 1(10) = 10$, $i = \frac{8\%}{1} = 8\%$

$$FV = PMT\left[\frac{(1+i)^n - 1}{i}\right] = \$300\left(\frac{1.08^{10} - 1}{0.08}\right) = \underline{\$4345.97}$$

	10	**N**
	8	**I/Y**
	0	**PV**
300	**+/−**	**PMT**
P/Y	1	**ENTER**

Same *C/Y*

CPT **FV**

Ans: 4345.97

11. Given: $PMT = \$3000$, $n = 1(18) = 18$, $i = \frac{11.75\%}{1} = 11.75\%$

$$FV = PMT\left[\frac{(1+i)^n - 1}{i}\right]$$

$$= \$3000\left(\frac{1.1175^{18} - 1}{0.1175}\right)$$

$$= \underline{\$163,066.90}$$

Jeremy's investments are worth \$163,066.90 today.

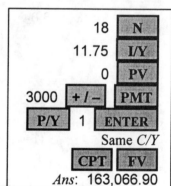

	18	**N**
	11.75	**I/Y**
	0	**PV**
3000	**+/−**	**PMT**
P/Y	1	**ENTER**

Same *C/Y*

CPT **FV**

Ans: 163,066.90

Exercise 10.2 *(continued)*

13. Given: $PMT = \$60$, $n = 12(5) = 60$, $i = \frac{6\%}{12} = 0.5\%$

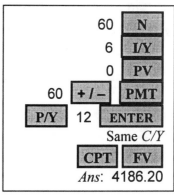

$$FV = PMT\left[\frac{(1+i)^n - 1}{i}\right]$$

$$= \$60\left(\frac{1.005^{60} - 1}{0.005}\right)$$

$$= \underline{\$4186.20}$$

Josie will have $4186.20 after 5 years.

15. a. Given: $PMT = \$1000$, $i = \frac{10\%}{1} = 10\%$, $n = 5$ payments

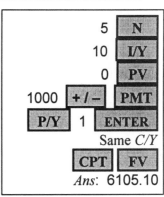

$$FV = PMT\left[\frac{(1+i)^n - 1}{i}\right] = \$1000\left(\frac{1.10^5 - 1}{0.10}\right) = \underline{\$6105.10}$$

Similarly,

   b. $FV = \underline{\$15{,}937.43}$ for $n = 10$
   c. $FV = \underline{\$31{,}772.48}$ for $n = 15$
   d. $FV = \underline{\$57{,}275.00}$ for $n = 20$
   e. $FV = \underline{\$98{,}347.06}$ for $n = 25$
   f. $FV = \underline{\$164{,}494.02}$ for $n = 30$

17. a.   (i)   (ii)   (iii)

$$FV = PV(1+i)^n \qquad FV = PMT\left[\frac{(1+i)^n - 1}{i}\right] \qquad FV = \$1675\left(\frac{1.08^5 - 1}{0.08}\right)$$

$$= \$5000(1.08)^8 \qquad\qquad = \$910\left(\frac{1.08^8 - 1}{0.08}\right) \qquad\qquad = \underline{\$9826.56}$$

$$= \underline{\$9254.65} \qquad\qquad = \underline{\$9679.33}$$

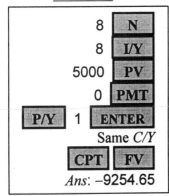

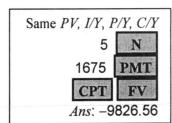

   b. Similarly, at 10% compounded annually,

      (i)   (ii)   (iii)

$$FV = \$5000(1.10)^8 \qquad FV = \$910\left(\frac{1.10^8 - 1}{0.10}\right) \qquad FV = \$1675\left(\frac{1.10^5 - 1}{0.10}\right)$$

$$= \underline{\$10{,}717.94} \qquad\qquad = \underline{\$10{,}406.66} \qquad\qquad = \underline{\$10{,}226.04}$$

At the lower (8%) interest rate, the five-payment annuity has the largest economic value while the lump payment has the lowest economic value. At the higher (10%) interest rate, the ranking of the economic values is reversed.

19. For the first 2 years, $PMT = \$1200$,
    $n = 2(4) = 8$, $i = \frac{10\%}{4} = 2.5\%$.
    The future value after 2 years is

    $$FV = PMT\left[\frac{(1+i)^n - 1}{i}\right]$$

    $$= \$1200\left(\frac{1.025^8 - 1}{0.025}\right)$$

    $$= \$10,483.34$$

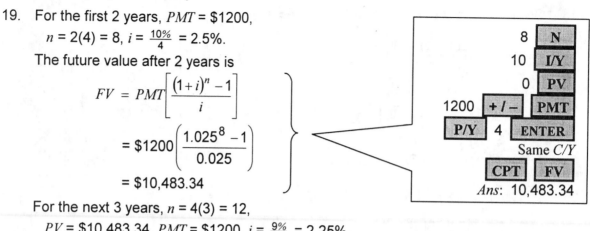

For the next 3 years, $n = 4(3) = 12$,
    $PV = \$10,483.34$, $PMT = \$1200$, $i = \frac{9\%}{4} = 2.25\%$
    The combined future value of these amounts
    at the end of the 3 years is

    $$FV = PMT\left[\frac{(1+i)^n - 1}{i}\right] + PV(1+i)^n$$

    $$= \$1200\left(\frac{1.0225^{12} - 1}{0.0225}\right) + \$10,483.34(1.0225)^{12}$$

    $$= \$16,322.67 + \$13,691.77$$

    $$= \underline{\$30,014.43}$$

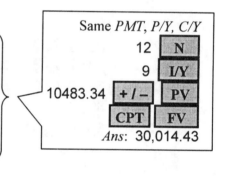

21. After 10 years, Marika's RRSP will be worth

    $$FV = PV(1+i)^n + PMT\left[\frac{(1+i)^n - 1}{i}\right]$$

    $$= \$18,000(1.045)^{20} + \$2000\left(\frac{1.045^{20} - 1}{0.045}\right)$$

    $$= \$43,410.85 + \$62,742.85$$

    $$= \$106,153.70$$

After a further 5 years, it will be worth

    $$FV = \$106,153.70(1.0075)^{60} + \$300\left(\frac{1.0075^{60} - 1}{0.0075}\right)$$

    $$= \$166,202.83 + \$22,627.24$$

    $$= \underline{\$188,830.07}$$

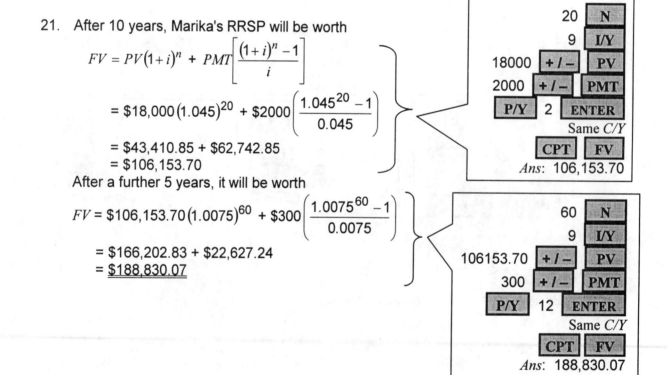

Exercise 10.2 *(continued)*

23. If contributions start this year, the amount in the RRSP 30 years from now will be

$$FV = PMT\left[\frac{(1+i)^n - 1}{i}\right]$$

$$= \$1000\left(\frac{1.08^{30} - 1}{0.08}\right)$$

$$= \$113{,}283$$

If contributions start in the sixth year and continue for 25 years, the RRSP will be worth

$$FV = \$1000\left(\frac{1.08^{25} - 1}{0.08}\right) = \$73{,}106$$

The RRSP will be worth
$\$113{,}283 - \$73{,}106 = \underline{\$40{,}177}$ more
as a result of the first 5 years' contributions.

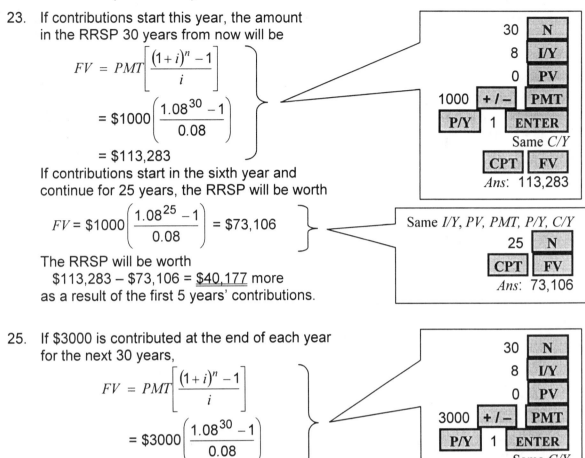

30	N
8	I/Y
0	PV
1000 +/–	PMT
P/Y 1	ENTER

Same *C/Y*

CPT   FV
Ans: 113,283

Same *I/Y, PV, PMT, P/Y, C/Y*

25	N

CPT   FV
Ans: 73,106

25. If $3000 is contributed at the end of each year for the next 30 years,

$$FV = PMT\left[\frac{(1+i)^n - 1}{i}\right]$$

$$= \$3000\left(\frac{1.08^{30} - 1}{0.08}\right)$$

$$= \$339{,}850$$

If $6000 is contributed at the end of each of the last 15 years,

$$FV = \$6000\left(\frac{1.08^{15} - 1}{0.08}\right) = \$162{,}913$$

The $3000 contribution for 30 years will result in
$\$339{,}850 - \$162{,}913 = \underline{\$176{,}937}$
more in the RRSP. (The first plan's future value is more than twice the second plan's future value.)

30	N
8	I/Y
0	PV
3000 +/–	PMT
P/Y 1	ENTER

Same *C/Y*

CPT   FV
Ans: 339,850

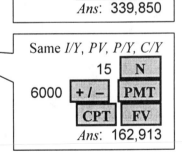

Same *I/Y, PV, P/Y, C/Y*

15	N
6000 +/–	PMT

CPT   FV
Ans: 162,913

Concept Questions (Section 10.3)

1. A's present value will be <u>(i) double</u> B's present value. When we inspect the present value formula

$$PV = PMT\left[\frac{1-(1+i)^{-n}}{i}\right]$$

we note that, for given values of i and n, the present value is proportional to *PMT*. Therefore, doubling the size of the payment will double the annuity's present value.

3. G's present value is <u>(iii) less than double</u> H's present value. The later half of G's payments will be discounted more heavily (and therefore contribute less to G's present value) than the earlier half of G's payments.

Exercise 10.3

1. Given: $PMT = \$500$; $n = 1(13) = 13$,
   $i = \frac{6.5\%}{1} = 6.5\%$

   $$PV = PMT\left[\frac{1-(1+i)^{-n}}{i}\right]$$

   $$= \$500\left(\frac{1-1.065^{-13}}{0.065}\right)$$

   $$= \underline{\$4299.87}$$

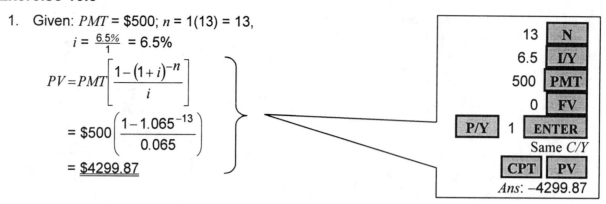

13 N
6.5 I/Y
500 PMT
0 FV
P/Y 1 ENTER
Same C/Y
CPT PV
Ans: −4299.87

3. Given: $i = \frac{8\%}{12} = 0.\overline{6}\,\%$; $PMT = \$75$,
   $n = 12(2.5) = 30$

   $$PV = PMT\left[\frac{1-(1+i)^{-n}}{i}\right]$$

   $$= \$75\left(\frac{1-1.00\overline{6}^{-30}}{0.00\overline{6}}\right)$$

   $$= \underline{\$2033.16}$$

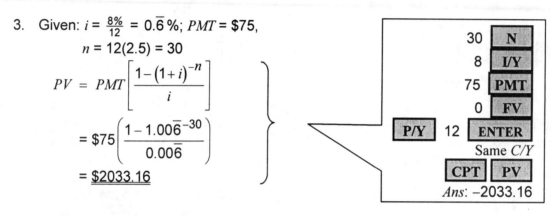

30 N
8 I/Y
75 PMT
0 FV
P/Y 12 ENTER
Same C/Y
CPT PV
Ans: −2033.16

5. Given: $i = \frac{6\%}{12} = 0.5\%$; $PMT = \$175$,
   $n = 12(8.25) = 99$

   $$PV = PMT\left[\frac{1-(1+i)^{-n}}{i}\right]$$

   $$= \$175\left(\frac{1-1.005^{-99}}{0.005}\right)$$

   $$= \underline{\$13,638.69}$$

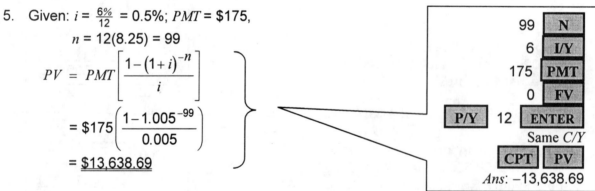

99 N
6 I/Y
175 PMT
0 FV
P/Y 12 ENTER
Same C/Y
CPT PV
Ans: −13,638.69

7. Given: $i = \frac{9.9\%}{2} = 4.95\%$;
   $PMT = \$1240$, $n = 2(9.5) = 19$

   $$PV = PMT\left[\frac{1-(1+i)^{-n}}{i}\right]$$

   $$= \$1240\left(\frac{1-1.0495^{-19}}{0.0495}\right)$$

   $$= \underline{\$15,047.05}$$

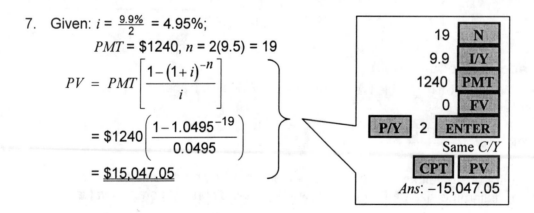

19 N
9.9 I/Y
1240 PMT
0 FV
P/Y 2 ENTER
Same C/Y
CPT PV
Ans: −15,047.05

Exercise 10.3 (continued)

9. Given: $i = \frac{6\%}{4} = 1.5\%$; $PMT = \$1000$, $n = 4(4) = 16$

$$PV = PMT\left[\frac{1-(1+i)^{-n}}{i}\right]$$

$$= \$1000\left(\frac{1-1.015^{-16}}{0.015}\right)$$

$$= \underline{\$14,131.26}$$

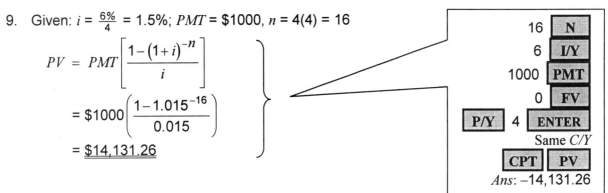

16	N
6	I/Y
1000	PMT
0	FV

P/Y 4 ENTER
Same *C/Y*

CPT PV
Ans: −14,131.26

11. $PMT = \$1000$ and $i = 7\%$ in all parts.

a. For $n = 5$,

$$PV = PMT\left[\frac{1-(1+i)^{-n}}{i}\right]$$

$$= \$1000\left(\frac{1-1.07^{-5}}{0.07}\right)$$

$$= \underline{\$4100.20}$$

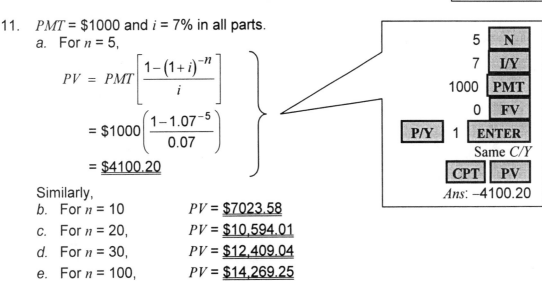

5	N
7	I/Y
1000	PMT
0	FV

P/Y 1 ENTER
Same *C/Y*

CPT PV
Ans: −4100.20

Similarly,

b. For $n = 10$ $PV = \underline{\$7023.58}$
c. For $n = 20$, $PV = \underline{\$10,594.01}$
d. For $n = 30$, $PV = \underline{\$12,409.04}$
e. For $n = 100$, $PV = \underline{\$14,269.25}$
f. For $n = 1000$, $PV = \underline{\$14,285.71}$

13. The amount required to purchase an annuity is the present value of the payments discounted at the rate of return earned by the purchase price.
If $j = 6\%$ compounded monthly for a 20-year term,
$i = \frac{6\%}{12} = 0.5\%$ and $n = 20(12) = 240$,

$$PV = PMT\left[\frac{1-(1+i)^{-n}}{i}\right]$$

$$= \$3000\left(\frac{1-1.005^{-240}}{0.005}\right)$$

$$= \underline{\$418,742.32}$$

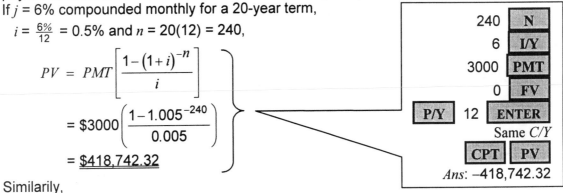

240	N
6	I/Y
3000	PMT
0	FV

P/Y 12 ENTER
Same *C/Y*

CPT PV
Ans: −418,742.32

Similarily,

i	Term	n	PV
$i = \frac{6\%}{12} = 0.5\%$	25 years	12(25) = 300	$\underline{\$465,620.59}$
$i = \frac{7\%}{12} = 0.58\overline{3}\%$	20 years	12(20) = 240	$\underline{\$386,947.52}$
$i = \frac{7\%}{12} = 0.58\overline{3}\%$	25 years	12(25) = 300	$\underline{\$424,460.71}$

Exercise 10.3 *(continued)*

15. For the first 6 years , $i = \frac{6\%}{2}$ = 3%; for the subsequent 9 years, $i = \frac{8\%}{2}$ = 4%. The present value, 6 years from now, of the last 18 payments is

$$PV = PMT\left[\frac{1-(1+i)^{-n}}{i}\right]$$

$$= \$2000\left(\frac{1-1.04^{-18}}{0.04}\right)$$

$$= \$25,318.59$$

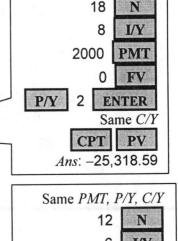

18 N
8 I/Y
2000 PMT
0 FV
P/Y 2 ENTER
Same *C/Y*
CPT PV
Ans: –25,318.59

The present value (today) of the preceding amount and the first 12 payments is

$$PV = \$25,318.59(1.03)^{-12} + \$2000\left(\frac{1-1.03^{-12}}{0.03}\right)$$

$$= \underline{\$37,665.96}$$

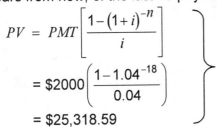

Same *PMT, P/Y, C/Y*
12 N
6 I/Y
25,318.59 FV
CPT PV
Ans: –37,665.96

17. The fair market value (*FMV*) of a share is the present value of future dividends and the redemption payment, discounted at the market's required rate of return.

   a. Given: $PMT = \$1.00$, $n = 4(15.25) = 61$, $FV = \$50$, and $i = \frac{7\%}{4}$ = 1.75%

$$FMV = PMT\left[\frac{1-(1+i)^{-n}}{i}\right] + FV(1+i)^{-n}$$

$$= \$1.00\left(\frac{1-1.0175^{-61}}{0.0175}\right) + \$50(1.0175)^{-61}$$

$$= \underline{\$54.66}$$

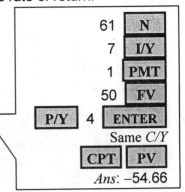

61 N
7 I/Y
1 PMT
50 FV
P/Y 4 ENTER
Same *C/Y*
CPT PV
Ans: –54.66

Similarly,

   b. For $i = \frac{6\%}{4}$ = 1.5%,

$$FMV = \$1.00\left(\frac{1-1.015^{-61}}{0.015}\right) + \$50(1.015)^{-61} = \underline{\$59.95}$$

Same *N, PMT, FV, P/Y, C/Y*
6 I/Y
CPT PV
Ans: –59.95

   c. For $i = \frac{5\%}{4}$ = 1.25%

$$FMV = \$1.00\left(\frac{1-1.0125^{-61}}{0.0125}\right) + \$50(1.0125)^{-61} = \underline{\$65.94}$$

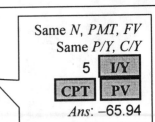

Same *N, PMT, FV*
Same *P/Y, C/Y*
5 I/Y
CPT PV
Ans: –65.94

19. *a.*   Original loan = Present value of all payments

Original loan = $PMT\left[\dfrac{1-(1+i)^{-n}}{i}\right]$

$= \$1333.28\left(\dfrac{1-1.05375^{-40}}{0.05375}\right)$

$= \underline{\$21,750.01}$

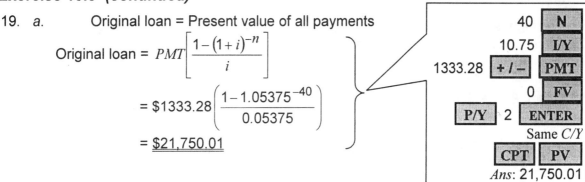

40	N
10.75	I/Y
1333.28 +/−	PMT
0	FV

P/Y   2   ENTER

Same *C/Y*

CPT   PV

Ans: 21,750.01

b.   Balance = Present value of the remaining

40 − 2(8.5) = 23 payments

$= \$1333.28\left(\dfrac{1-1.05375^{-23}}{0.05375}\right)$

$= \underline{\$17,365.12}$

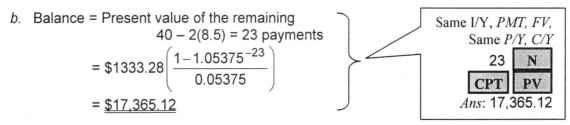

Same I/Y, *PMT, FV,*
Same *P/Y, C/Y*

| 23 | N |

CPT   PV

Ans: 17,365.12

21.   Selling price = Down payment
           + Present value of the monthly payments

$PMT = \$160.70$, $n = 12(3.5) = 42$, $i = \dfrac{12\%}{12} = 1\%$

PV of monthly payments $= PMT\left[\dfrac{1-(1+i)^{-n}}{i}\right]$

$= \$160.70\left(\dfrac{1-1.01^{-42}}{0.01}\right)$

$= \underline{\$5489.21}$

Thus, the selling price was $2000 + \$5489.21 = \underline{\$7489.21}$

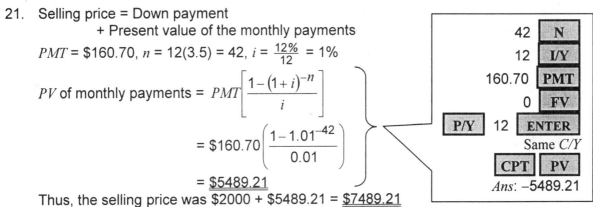

42	N
12	I/Y
160.70	PMT
0	FV

P/Y   12   ENTER

Same *C/Y*

CPT   PV

Ans: −5489.21

23.   Household Finance paid the present value of the
    scheduled payments discounted at the required rate
    of return (19.5% compounded monthly).

Given: $PMT = \$250$, $n = 15$, $i = \dfrac{19.5\%}{12} = 1.625\%$

Price $= PMT\left[\dfrac{1-(1+i)^{-n}}{i}\right]$

$= \$250\left(\dfrac{1-1.01625^{-15}}{0.01625}\right)$

$= \underline{\$3304.30}$

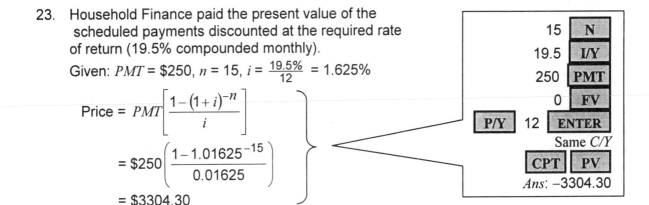

15	N
19.5	I/Y
250	PMT
0	FV

P/Y   12   ENTER

Same *C/Y*

CPT   PV

Ans: −3304.30

---

25. The highest price is the price that provides the lowest acceptable rate of return (10.5%
    compounded monthly). This price is the present
    value of all mortgage payments discounted at 10.5%
    compounded monthly.

    Given: $PMT = \$800$, $i = \frac{7.5\%}{12} = 0.625\%$,

    $n = 12(3.5) = 42$, and $FV = \$45,572$

    $$Price = PMT\left[\frac{1-(1+i)^{-n}}{i}\right] + FV(1+i)^{-n}$$

    $$= \$800\left(\frac{1-1.00625^{-42}}{0.00625}\right) + \$45,572(1.00625)^{-42}$$

    $$= \underline{\$64,550.64}$$

    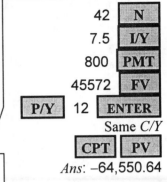

42	N
7.5	I/Y
800	PMT
45572	FV

    P/Y 12 ENTER
    Same *C/Y*
    CPT PV
    Ans: −64,550.64

27. The economic value of the contract at the date of termination
    is the present value of the remaining payments.

    Given: $PMT = \$90,000$, $n = 12(3) = 36$, $i = \frac{7.5\%}{12} = 0.625\%$

    $$PV = PMT\left[\frac{1-(1+i)^{-n}}{i}\right]$$

    $$= \$90,000\left(\frac{1-1.00625^{-36}}{0.00625}\right)$$

    $$= \underline{\$2,893,312.18}$$

    The settlement amount is $2,893,312.18.

    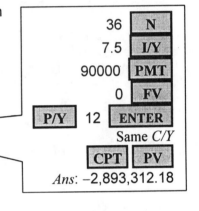

36	N
7.5	I/Y
90000	PMT
0	FV

    P/Y 12 ENTER
    Same *C/Y*
    CPT PV
    Ans: −2,893,312.18

29. Colin and Marie should accept the offer that has the
    higher current economic value; that is, the one with
    the larger present value. The present value of the
    four payments of $2000 is

    $$PV = \$2000\left(\frac{1-1.05^{-4}}{0.05}\right) = \$7091.90$$

    They should <u>accept the multiple-payment offer</u>
    since <u>it is worth</u>
    $1000 + $7091.90 − $7900 = <u>$191.90 more</u>

    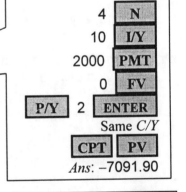

4	N
10	I/Y
2000	PMT
0	FV

    P/Y 2 ENTER
    Same *C/Y*
    CPT PV
    Ans: −7091.90

31. The offer having the higher current economic value is
    preferred. The present value of the five payments
    of $1900 is

    $$PV = \$1900\left(\frac{1-1.05^{-4}}{0.05}\right) = \$6737.31$$

    Therefore, <u>Mrs. Martel's offer is worth</u>
    $1900 + $6737.31 − $8500 = <u>$137.31 more</u>
    in current dollars.

    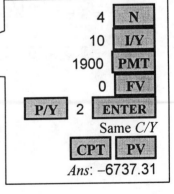

4	N
10	I/Y
1900	PMT
0	FV

    P/Y 2 ENTER
    Same *C/Y*
    CPT PV
    Ans: −6737.31

33. Consider a $1000 purchase. It requires a $100 down payment plus 12 monthly payments of $900/12 = $75. Flemmings should be willing to accept a cash amount equal to the present value of the payments discounted at the rate of return that Flemmings can earn on this money. The present value of the payments is

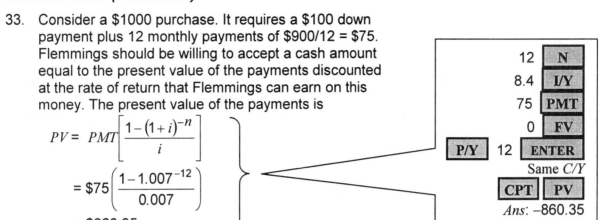

$$PV = PMT\left[\frac{1-(1+i)^{-n}}{i}\right]$$

$$= \$75\left(\frac{1-1.007^{-12}}{0.007}\right)$$

$$= \$860.35$$

Cash price = $100 + $860.35 = $960.35

This is a $39.65 or <u>3.97% discount</u> from the $1000 list price.

35. Let represent the normal monthly pension payment at age 60. The choice at age 55 is between:
    (i) receiving 0.85*PMT* per month for 28 years, or
    (ii) waiting 5 years and then receiving *PMT* per month for 28 − 5 = 23 years.
    The economic values of the two alternatives are their present values at age 55. For option (i),

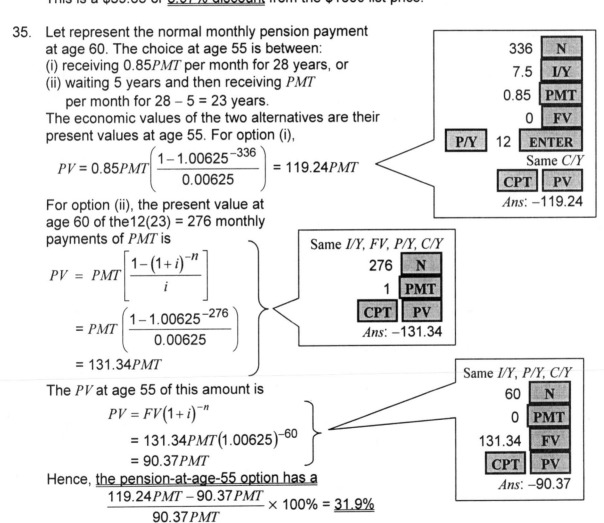

$$PV = 0.85PMT\left(\frac{1-1.00625^{-336}}{0.00625}\right) = 119.24PMT$$

For option (ii), the present value at age 60 of the 12(23) = 276 monthly payments of *PMT* is

$$PV = PMT\left[\frac{1-(1+i)^{-n}}{i}\right]$$

$$= PMT\left(\frac{1-1.00625^{-276}}{0.00625}\right)$$

$$= 131.34PMT$$

The *PV* at age 55 of this amount is

$$PV = FV(1+i)^{-n}$$

$$= 131.34PMT(1.00625)^{-60}$$

$$= 90.37PMT$$

Hence, <u>the pension-at-age-55 option has a</u>

$$\frac{119.24PMT - 90.37PMT}{90.37PMT} \times 100\% = \underline{31.9\%}$$

<u>higher economic value</u>

Concept Questions (Exercise 10.4)

1. A deferred annuity is an ordinary annuity that does not begin until a specified time period (called the period of deferral) has passed.

3. The payments form an ordinary annuity when viewed from a focal date at the end of the period of deferral. We can then use the formula for the present value of an ordinary annuity to obtain the present value of the payments at the *end* of the period of deferral.

5. The future values of both annuities are calculated at a focal date coinciding with the final payment. The future values are the <u>same</u> since the deferred annuity payments form an ordinary annuity when viewed from a focal date at the final payment.

Exercise 10.4

1. Given: $PMT = \$2000$, $i = \frac{7\%}{2} = 3.5\%$, $n = 2(10) = 20$, $d = 2(5) = 10$

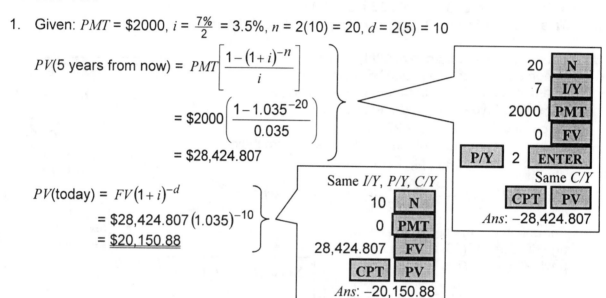

$$PV\text{(5 years from now)} = PMT\left[\frac{1-(1+i)^{-n}}{i}\right]$$

$$= \$2000\left(\frac{1-1.035^{-20}}{0.035}\right)$$

$$= \$28,424.807$$

$$PV\text{(today)} = FV(1+i)^{-d}$$

$$= \$28,424.807\,(1.035)^{-10}$$

$$= \underline{\$20,150.88}$$

3. Given: $PMT = \$500$, $i = \frac{9\%}{12} = 0.75\%$,
    $n = 12(3.5) = 42$, $d = 12(2.75) = 33$

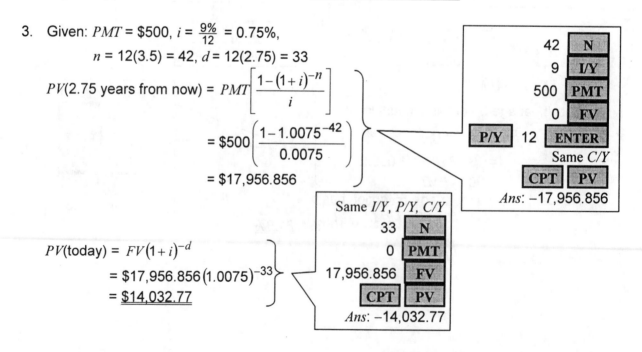

$$PV\text{(2.75 years from now)} = PMT\left[\frac{1-(1+i)^{-n}}{i}\right]$$

$$= \$500\left(\frac{1-1.0075^{-42}}{0.0075}\right)$$

$$= \$17,956.856$$

$$PV\text{(today)} = FV(1+i)^{-d}$$

$$= \$17,956.856\,(1.0075)^{-33}$$

$$= \underline{\$14,032.77}$$

Exercise 10.4 *(continued)*

5. Given: $PMT = \$1076.71$, $i = \frac{7\%}{4} = 1.75\%$,

$n = 4(12.5) = 50$, and $PV = \$30,000$

At a focal date at the end of the period of deferral,
FV of $\$30,000 = PV$ of ordinary annuity

Right hand side $= \$1076.71\left(\dfrac{1-1.0175^{-50}}{0.0175}\right)$

$= \$35,683.47$

Left hand side $= \$30,000(1.0175)^d$

Hence, $\$30,000(1.0175)^d = \$35,683.47$
Using formula (9-2) to calculate d,

$d = \dfrac{\ln\left(\dfrac{FV}{PV}\right)}{\ln(1+i)} = \dfrac{\ln\left(\dfrac{\$35,683.47}{\$30,000}\right)}{\ln(1.0175)}$

$= 10.00$ payment intervals

The period of deferral is 10 quarters
or <u>2 years and 6 months</u>.

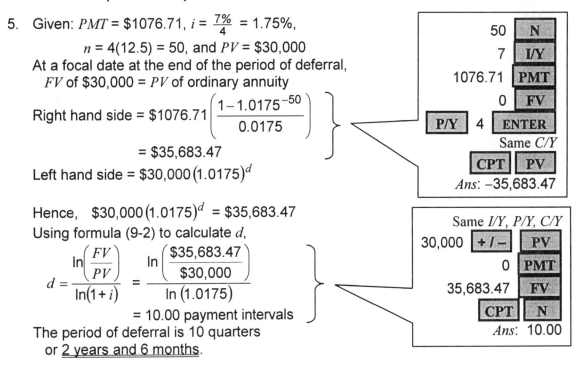

7. The amount that must be invested now to generate
the future payments is the present value of the payments.
Given: $PMT = \$200$, $n = 12(5) = 60$,

$d = 12(3.5) = 42$, and $i = \frac{7.5\%}{12} = 0.625\%$,

$PV(3.5 \text{ years from now}) = PMT\left[\dfrac{1-(1+i)^{-n}}{i}\right]$

$= \$200\left(\dfrac{1-1.00625^{-60}}{0.00625}\right)$

$= \$9981.06$

$PV(\text{today}) = FV(1+i)^{-d}$

$= \$9981.06(1.00625)^{-42}$

$= \underline{\$7682.97}$

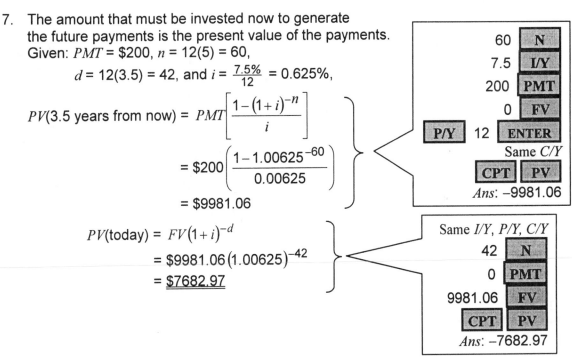

9. Today's economic value of the future payments is their present value (discounted at the time value of money). Viewing the payments as a deferred ordinary simple annuity,

$PMT = \$1500$, $n = 4(11) = 44$, $d = 4(5.75) = 23$,

and $i = \frac{6.5\%}{4} = 1.625\%$

$$PV(\text{5.75 years from now}) = PMT\left[\frac{1-(1+i)^{-n}}{i}\right]$$

$$= \$1500\left(\frac{1-1.01625^{-44}}{0.01625}\right)$$

$$= \$46{,}891.229$$

$$PV(\text{today}) = FV(1+i)^{-d}$$

$$= \$46{,}891.229(1.01625)^{-23}$$

$$= \underline{\$32{,}365.23}$$

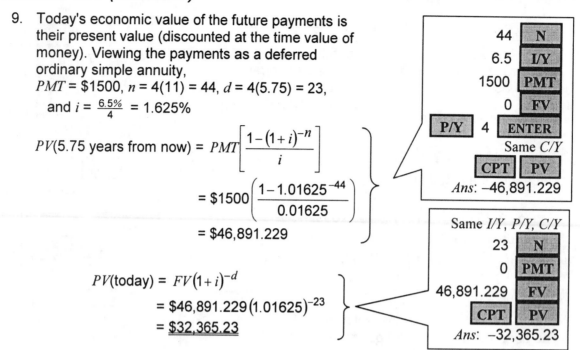

44 N
6.5 I/Y
1500 PMT
0 FV
P/Y 4 ENTER
Same C/Y
CPT PV
Ans: −46,891.229

Same I/Y, P/Y, C/Y
23 N
0 PMT
46,891.229 FV
CPT PV
Ans: −32,365.23

11. Today's economic value economic is the present value. For the $1000 annuity,

$$PV(\text{today}) = PMT\left[\frac{1-(1+i)^{-n}}{i}\right]$$

$$= \$1000\left(\frac{1-1.065^{-10}}{0.065}\right)$$

$$= \$7188.83$$

For the $2000 annuity,

$PV(\text{10 years from now})$

$$= \$2000\left(\frac{1-1.065^{-10}}{0.065}\right)$$

$$= \$14{,}377.66$$

$$PV(\text{today}) = \frac{\$14{,}377.66}{1.065^{10}} = \$7659.35$$

<u>The $1000 annuity has the greater economic value</u>.

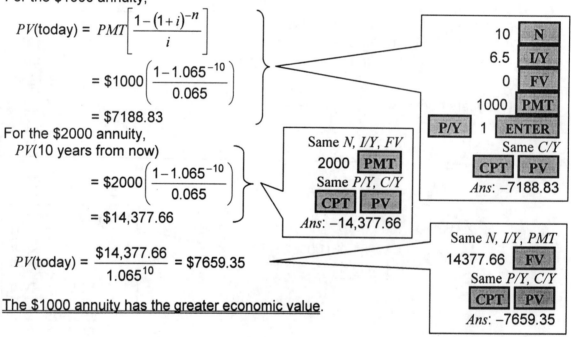

10 N
6.5 I/Y
0 FV
1000 PMT
P/Y 1 ENTER
Same C/Y
CPT PV
Ans: −7188.83

Same N, I/Y, FV
2000 PMT
Same P/Y, C/Y
CPT PV
Ans: −14,377.66

Same N, I/Y, PMT
14377.66 FV
Same P/Y, C/Y
CPT PV
Ans: −7659.35

13. The price paid will be the present value of the payments discounted at the required rate of return. Since the first payment is due in 6 months, the period of deferral is 5 months (in order to treat the payments as a deferred ordinary annuity).

Given: $PMT = \$231$, $n = 15$, $d = 5$, and $i = \frac{18\%}{12} = 1.5\%$

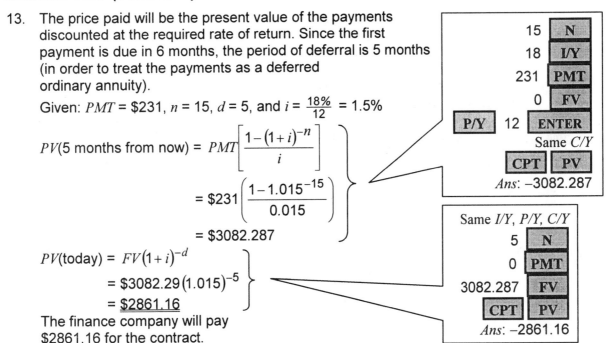

$PV(5 \text{ months from now}) = PMT\left[\dfrac{1-(1+i)^{-n}}{i}\right]$

$= \$231\left(\dfrac{1-1.015^{-15}}{0.015}\right)$

$= \$3082.287$

$PV(\text{today}) = FV(1+i)^{-d}$

$= \$3082.29(1.015)^{-5}$

$= \underline{\$2861.16}$

The finance company will pay $2861.16 for the contract.

15. The original loan equals the present value of the payments. Thus,

$PV = \$35,000$ with $PMT = \$1573.83$, $n = 4(12) = 48$, and $i = \frac{10\%}{4} = 2.5\%$.

At a focal date at the end of the period of deferral,

FV of $35,000 = PV of ordinary annuity

$\$35,000(1.025)^d = \$1573.83\left(\dfrac{1-1.025^{-48}}{0.025}\right)$

$= \$43,710.22$

Using formula (9-2) to calculate d,

$d = \dfrac{\ln\left(\dfrac{FV}{PV}\right)}{\ln(1+i)} = \dfrac{\ln\left(\dfrac{\$43,710.22}{\$35,000}\right)}{\ln(1.025)} = 9.00$

The period of deferral was 9 quarters long. The interval between the date of the loan and the first payment was 10 quarters or <u>2 years and 6 months</u>.

17. Given: For the initial investment, $PV = \$10,000$, $i = \frac{8.5\%}{2} = 4.25\%$.

For the deferred annuity, $PMT = \$1000$, $n = 40$, and $i = 4.25\%$.

At a focal date at the end of the period of deferral,

FV of $10,000 = PV of ordinary annuity

$\$10,000(1.0425)^d = \$1000\left(\dfrac{1-1.0425^{-40}}{0.0425}\right) = \$19,077.27$

Using formula (9-2) to calculate d,

$d = \dfrac{\ln\left(\dfrac{FV}{PV}\right)}{\ln(1+i)} = \dfrac{\ln\left(\dfrac{\$19,077.27}{\$10,000}\right)}{\ln(1.0425)} = 15.52$

The period of deferral is 15.52 half years or 7 years and 9 months (rounded to the nearest month. Since, the first withdrawal occurs 6 months after the period of deferral, the $10,000 deposit must be made <u>8 years and 3 months</u> before the first withdrawal.

Concept Questions (Section 10.5)

1. The payments are at the end of each payment interval (*ordinary* annuity) and the payment interval is not equal to the compounding interval (*general* annuity).

3. $c = \dfrac{\text{Number of compoundings per year}}{\text{Number of payments per year}} = \dfrac{2}{12} = 0.1\overline{6}$

   i_2 is the interest rate per payment interval. In this case, it is the interest rate per month. It will be <u>approximately equal to</u> $\dfrac{\text{Nominal annual rate}}{12} = \dfrac{6\%}{12} = \underline{0.5\%}$ per month. The correct value will be <u>smaller</u> than 0.5% because i_2 compounded 6 times must equal $i = \frac{6\%}{2} = 3\%$ per half year.

Exercise 10.5

1. $i = \dfrac{5\%}{4} = 1.25\%$; $c = \dfrac{\text{Number of compoundings per year}}{\text{Number of payments per year}} = \dfrac{4}{1} = 4$

   $i_2 = (1+i)^c - 1 = (1.0125)^4 - 1 = 0.05095 = \underline{5.095\%}$ (per year)

3. $i = \dfrac{8\%}{4} = 2\%$; $c = \dfrac{\text{Number of compoundings per year}}{\text{Number of payments per year}} = \dfrac{4}{2} = 2$

   $i_2 = (1+i)^c - 1 = (1.02)^2 - 1 = 0.0404 = \underline{4.040\%}$ (per half year)

5. $i = \dfrac{6.5\%}{4} = 1.625\%$; $c = \dfrac{\text{Number of compoundings per year}}{\text{Number of payments per year}} = \dfrac{4}{12} = 0.\overline{3}$

   $i_2 = (1+i)^c - 1 = (1.01625)^{0.\overline{3}} - 1 = 0.00539 = \underline{0.539\%}$ (per month)

7. $i = \dfrac{7.75\%}{1} = 7.75\%$; $c = \dfrac{\text{Number of compoundings per year}}{\text{Number of payments per year}} = \dfrac{1}{4} = 0.25$

   $i_2 = (1+i)^c - 1 = (1.0775)^{0.25} - 1 = 0.01884 = \underline{1.884\%}$ (per quarter)

9. $i = \dfrac{6\%}{1} = 6\%$; $c = \dfrac{\text{Number of compoundings per year}}{\text{Number of payments per year}} = \dfrac{1}{12} = 0.08\overline{3}$

   $i_2 = (1+i)^c - 1 = (1.06)^{0.08\overline{3}} - 1 = 0.00487 = \underline{0.487\%}$ (per month)

11. $i = \frac{6.5\%}{1} = 6.5\%$; $n = 4(11) = 44$;

    $c = \dfrac{\text{Number of compoundings per year}}{\text{Number of payments per year}} = \dfrac{1}{4} = 0.25$

    $i_2 = (1+i)^c - 1 = (1.065)^{0.25} - 1 = 0.015868285$

    $FV = PMT \left[\dfrac{(1+i)^n - 1}{i} \right]$

    $= \$400 \left(\dfrac{1.015868285^{44} - 1}{0.015868285} \right)$

    $= \underline{\$25,186.12}$

44	N
6.5	I/Y
0	PV
400	PMT
P/Y 4	ENTER
C/Y 1	ENTER
CPT	FV

Ans: –25,186.12

13. $i = \frac{8\%}{12} = 0.\overline{6}\%$; $n = 2(3.5) = 7$;

$$c = \frac{\text{Number of compoundings per year}}{\text{Number of payments per year}} = \frac{12}{2} = 6$$

$$i_2 = (1+i)^c - 1 = (1.00\overline{6})^6 - 1 = 0.040672622$$

$$FV = PMT\left[\frac{(1+i)^n - 1}{i}\right] = \$2750\left(\frac{1.040672622^7 - 1}{0.040672622}\right)$$

$$= \underline{\$21,764.70}$$

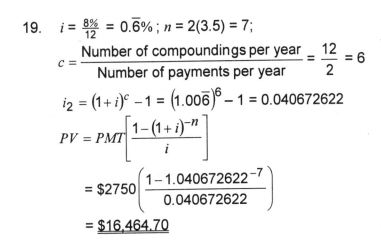

7	N
8	I/Y
0	PV
2750	PMT

P/Y 2 ENTER
C/Y 12 ENTER
CPT FV

Ans: −21,764.70

15. $i = \frac{5.25\%}{12} = 0.4375\%$; $n = 17$;

$$c = \frac{\text{Number of compoundings per year}}{\text{Number of payments per year}} = \frac{12}{1} = 12$$

$$i_2 = (1+i)^c - 1 = (1.00875)^{12} - 1 = 0.0537818867$$

$$FV = PMT\left[\frac{(1+i)^n - 1}{i}\right]$$

$$= \$3500\left(\frac{1.0537818867^{17} - 1}{0.0537818867}\right)$$

$$= \underline{\$93,482.61}$$

17	N
5.25	I/Y
0	PV
3500	PMT

P/Y 1 ENTER
C/Y 12 ENTER
CPT FV

Ans: −93,482.61

17. $i = \frac{6.5\%}{1} = 6.5\%$; $n = 4(11) = 44$;

$$c = \frac{\text{Number of compoundings per year}}{\text{Number of payments per year}} = \frac{1}{4} = 0.25$$

$$i_2 = (1+i)^c - 1 = (1.065)^{0.25} - 1 = 0.015868285$$

$$PV = PMT\left[\frac{1-(1+i)^{-n}}{i}\right]$$

$$= \$400\left(\frac{1.015868285^{-44} - 1}{0.015868285}\right)$$

$$= \underline{\$12,598.41}$$

44	N
6.5	I/Y
400	PMT
0	FV

P/Y 4 ENTER
C/Y 1 ENTER
CPT PV

Ans: −12,598.41

19. $i = \frac{8\%}{12} = 0.\overline{6}\%$; $n = 2(3.5) = 7$;

$$c = \frac{\text{Number of compoundings per year}}{\text{Number of payments per year}} = \frac{12}{2} = 6$$

$$i_2 = (1+i)^c - 1 = (1.00\overline{6})^6 - 1 = 0.040672622$$

$$PV = PMT\left[\frac{1-(1+i)^{-n}}{i}\right]$$

$$= \$2750\left(\frac{1-1.040672622^{-7}}{0.040672622}\right)$$

$$= \underline{\$16,464.70}$$

7	N
8	I/Y
2750	PMT
0	FV

P/Y 2 ENTER
C/Y 12 ENTER
CPT PV

Ans: −16,464.70

21. $i = \frac{5.25\%}{12} = 0.4375\%$; $n = 17$;

$$c = \frac{\text{Number of compoundings per year}}{\text{Number of payments per year}} = \frac{12}{1} = 12$$

$$i_2 = (1+i)^c - 1 = = (1.00875)^{12} - 1 = 0.0537818867$$

$$PV = PMT\left[\frac{1-(1+i)^{-n}}{i}\right]$$

$$= \$3500\left(\frac{1-1.0537818867^{-17}}{0.0537818867}\right)$$

$$= \underline{\$38,367.94}$$

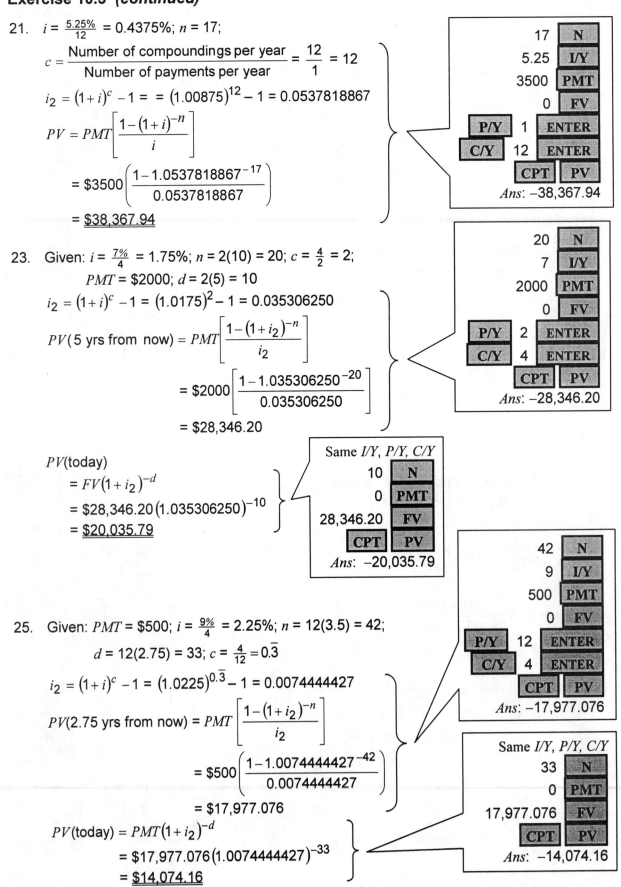

17	**N**
5.25	**I/Y**
3500	**PMT**
0	**FV**
P/Y 1	**ENTER**
C/Y 12	**ENTER**
CPT	**PV**

Ans: −38,367.94

23. Given: $i = \frac{7\%}{4} = 1.75\%$; $n = 2(10) = 20$; $c = \frac{4}{2} = 2$;

$PMT = \$2000$; $d = 2(5) = 10$

$$i_2 = (1+i)^c - 1 = (1.0175)^2 - 1 = 0.035306250$$

$$PV(5 \text{ yrs from now}) = PMT\left[\frac{1-(1+i_2)^{-n}}{i_2}\right]$$

$$= \$2000\left[\frac{1-1.035306250^{-20}}{0.035306250}\right]$$

$$= \$28,346.20$$

20	**N**
7	**I/Y**
2000	**PMT**
0	**FV**
P/Y 2	**ENTER**
C/Y 4	**ENTER**
CPT	**PV**

Ans: −28,346.20

$PV(\text{today})$

$$= FV(1+i_2)^{-d}$$

$$= \$28,346.20(1.035306250)^{-10}$$

$$= \underline{\$20,035.79}$$

Same *I/Y, P/Y, C/Y*

10	**N**
0	**PMT**
28,346.20	**FV**
CPT	**PV**

Ans: −20,035.79

25. Given: $PMT = \$500$; $i = \frac{9\%}{4} = 2.25\%$; $n = 12(3.5) = 42$;

$d = 12(2.75) = 33$; $c = \frac{4}{12} = 0.\overline{3}$

$$i_2 = (1+i)^c - 1 = (1.0225)^{0.\overline{3}} - 1 = 0.0074444427$$

$$PV(2.75 \text{ yrs from now}) = PMT\left[\frac{1-(1+i_2)^{-n}}{i_2}\right]$$

$$= \$500\left(\frac{1-1.0074444427^{-42}}{0.0074444427}\right)$$

$$= \$17,977.076$$

$$PV(\text{today}) = PMT(1+i_2)^{-d}$$

$$= \$17,977.076(1.0074444427)^{-33}$$

$$= \underline{\$14,074.16}$$

42	**N**
9	**I/Y**
500	**PMT**
0	**FV**
P/Y 12	**ENTER**
C/Y 4	**ENTER**
CPT	**PV**

Ans: −17,977.076

Same *I/Y, P/Y, C/Y*

33	**N**
0	**PMT**
17,977.076	**FV**
CPT	**PV**

Ans: −14,074.16

27. Given: $PMT = \$356.83$; $i = \frac{7\%}{4} = 1.75\%$; $c = \frac{4}{12} = 0.\overline{3}$;

   $n = 12(12.5) = 150$; $PV = \$30,000$

   $i_2 = (1+i)^c - 1 = (1.0175)^{0.\overline{3}} - 1 = 0.005799633$

   At a focal date at the end of the period of deferral,
   FV of $\$30,000 = PV$ of ordinary annuity

   Right hand side $= \$356.83\left(\dfrac{1 - 1.0057996326^{-150}}{0.0057996326}\right)$

   $= \$35,683.49$

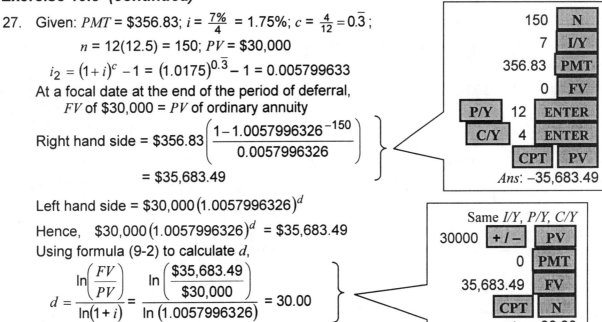

   Left hand side $= \$30,000(1.0057996326)^d$

   Hence, $\$30,000(1.0057996326)^d = \$35,683.49$

   Using formula (9-2) to calculate d,

   $d = \dfrac{\ln\left(\dfrac{FV}{PV}\right)}{\ln(1+i)} = \dfrac{\ln\left(\dfrac{\$35,683.49}{\$30,000}\right)}{\ln(1.0057996326)} = 30.00$

   The period of deferral is 30 payment intervals, that is,
   30 months or <u>2 years and 6 months</u>.

29. a. $PMT = \$1000$, $n = 25$, $i = 6\%$, $m = 1$

   $FV = PMT\left[\dfrac{(1+i)^n - 1}{i}\right]$

   $= \$1000\left(\dfrac{1.06^{25} - 1}{0.06}\right)$

   $= \underline{\$54,864.51}$

   b. $i = \frac{6\%}{4} = 1.5\%$; $n = 25$; $c = \frac{4}{1} = 4$

   $i_2 = (1+i)^c - 1 = (1.015)^4 - 1$

   $\qquad = 0.061363551$

   $FV = \$1000\left(\dfrac{1.061363551^{25} - 1}{0.061363551}\right) = \underline{\$55,929.71}$

   c. $i = \frac{6\%}{12} = 0.75\%$; $n = 25$; $c = \frac{12}{1} = 12$

   $i_2 = (1+i)^c - 1 = (1.005)^{12} - 1$

   $\qquad = 0.061677812$

   $FV = \$1000\left(\dfrac{1.061677812^{25} - 1}{0.061677812}\right) = \underline{\$56,178.55}$

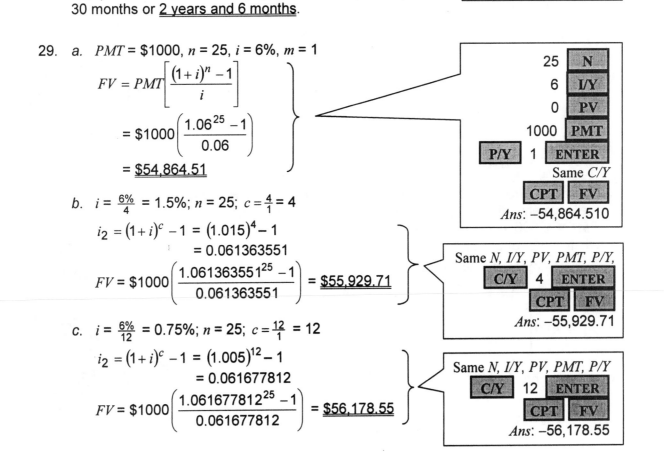

Exercise 10.5 *(continued)*

31. Given: $i = \frac{9\%}{2} = 4.5\%$

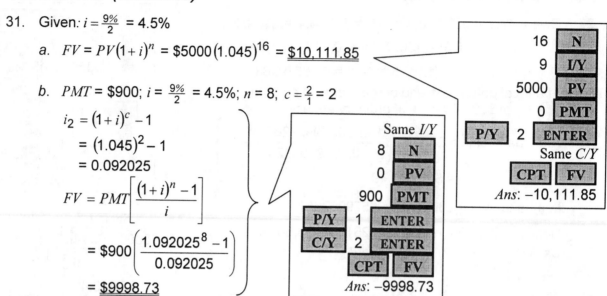

a. $FV = PV(1+i)^n = \$5000(1.045)^{16} = \underline{\$10,111.85}$

16 N
9 I/Y
5000 PV
0 PMT
P/Y 2 ENTER
Same *C/Y*
CPT FV
Ans: −10,111.85

b. $PMT = \$900$; $i = \frac{9\%}{2} = 4.5\%$; $n = 8$; $c = \frac{2}{1} = 2$

$i_2 = (1+i)^c - 1$

$ = (1.045)^2 - 1$

$ = 0.092025$

$FV = PMT\left[\dfrac{(1+i)^n - 1}{i}\right]$

$ = \$900\left(\dfrac{1.092025^8 - 1}{0.092025}\right)$

$ = \underline{\$9998.73}$

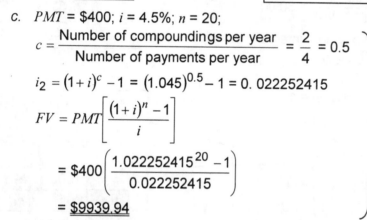

Same *I/Y*
8 N
0 PV
900 PMT
P/Y 1 ENTER
C/Y 2 ENTER
CPT FV
Ans: −9998.73

c. $PMT = \$400$; $i = 4.5\%$; $n = 20$;

$c = \dfrac{\text{Number of compoundings per year}}{\text{Number of payments per year}} = \dfrac{2}{4} = 0.5$

$i_2 = (1+i)^c - 1 = (1.045)^{0.5} - 1 = 0.022252415$

$FV = PMT\left[\dfrac{(1+i)^n - 1}{i}\right]$

$ = \$400\left(\dfrac{1.022252415^{20} - 1}{0.022252415}\right)$

$ = \underline{\$9939.94}$

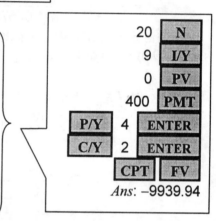

20 N
9 I/Y
0 PV
400 PMT
P/Y 4 ENTER
C/Y 2 ENTER
CPT FV
Ans: −9939.94

33. The amount required to purchase the annuity is the present value of the payments discounted at the rate of return on the annuity.
$PMT = \$2500$, $n = 12(20) = 240$, $i = 6.75\%$,

$c = \dfrac{\text{Number of compoundings per year}}{\text{Number of payments per year}} = \dfrac{1}{12} = 0.08\overline{3}$

$i_2 = (1+i)^c - 1 = (1.0675)^{0.08\overline{3}} - 1 = 0.00545813044$

$PV = PMT\left[\dfrac{1-(1+i)^{-n}}{i}\right]$

$ = \$2500\left(\dfrac{1-1.00545813044^{-240}}{0.00545813044}\right)$

$ = \underline{\$333,998.96}$

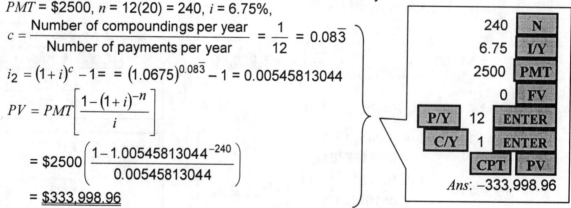

240 N
6.75 I/Y
2500 PMT
0 FV
P/Y 12 ENTER
C/Y 1 ENTER
CPT PV
Ans: −333,998.96

Exercise 10.5 *(continued)*

35. Selling price = Down payment + Present value of the monthly payments

$PMT = \$160.70$, $n = 12(3.5) = 42$, $i = \frac{12\%}{4} = 3\%$, $c = \frac{4}{12} = 0.\overline{3}$

$i_2 = (1+i)^c - 1 = (1.03)^{0.\overline{3}} - 1 = 0.0099016340$

$PV = PMT\left[\dfrac{1-(1+i)^{-n}}{i}\right]$

$= \$160.70\left(\dfrac{1-1.0099016340^{-42}}{0.0099016340}\right)$

$= \$5499.94$

Thus, the selling price was $2000 + \$5499.94 = \underline{\$7499.94}$.

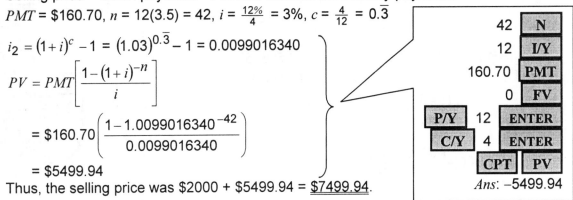

42	N
12	I/Y
160.70	PMT
0	FV

P/Y	12	ENTER
C/Y	4	ENTER
	CPT	PV

Ans: –5499.94

37. a. The value placed on a 25% interest in the partnership was the present value of all payments (discounted at the interest rate charged on the purchase price). The payments form an ordinary general annuity with

$PMT = \$537.66$, $n = 144$, $i = \frac{8\%}{2} = 4\%$,

$c = \dfrac{\text{Number of compoundings per year}}{\text{Number of payments per year}} = \dfrac{2}{12} = 0.1\overline{6}$

$i_2 = (1+i)^c - 1 = (1.04)^{0.1\overline{6}} - 1 = 0.0065581969$

$PV = PMT\left[\dfrac{1-(1+i)^{-n}}{i}\right]$

$= \$537.66\left(\dfrac{1-1.0065581969^{-144}}{0.0065581969}\right)$

$= \$49,999.61$

The implied value of the entire partnership is

$4(\$49,999.61) = \underline{\$199,998}$ (to the nearest dollar)

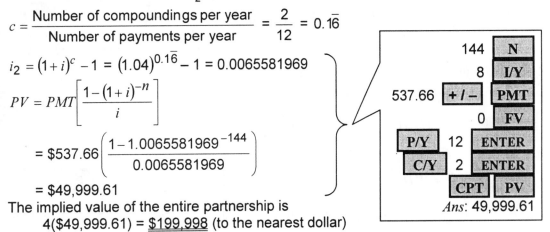

144	N
8	I/Y
537.66	+/–	PMT
0	FV

P/Y	12	ENTER
C/Y	2	ENTER
	CPT	PV

Ans: 49,999.61

b. Total interest = Total payments – Principal

$= 144(\$537.66) - \$49,999.61$

$= \underline{\$27,423}$

---

39. For the first 8.5 years, $i = \frac{9\%}{4} = 2.25\%$;

$PMT = \$600$; $n = 2(8.5) = 17$; $c = \frac{4}{2} = 2$

$i_2 = (1 + i)^c - 1 = (1.0225)^2 - 1 = 0.045506250$
and the future value at the end of the 8.5 years is

$FV = PMT\left[\dfrac{(1+i)^n - 1}{i}\right]$

$= \$600\left(\dfrac{1.045506250^{17} - 1}{0.045506250}\right)$

$= \$14,910.252$

For the next 11.5 years, $PMT = \$600$;

$n = 2(11.5) = 23$; $i = \frac{8\%}{2} = 4\%$; $PV = \$14,910.252$

The combined future value at the end of the 20 years is

$\$14,910.252\,(1.04)^{23} + \$600\left(\dfrac{1.04^{23} - 1}{0.04}\right)$

$= \$36,749.531 + \$21,970.733$
$= \underline{\$58,720.26}$

41. For the first 10 years, $i = \frac{7.5\%}{12} = 0.625\%$;

$PMT = \$1000$; $n = 10$; $c = \frac{12}{1} = 12$

and $\quad i_2 = (1 + i)^c - 1 = (1.00625)^{12} - 1$
$= 0.077632599$

$FV = PMT\left[\dfrac{(1+i)^n - 1}{i}\right]$

$\doteq \$1000\left(\dfrac{1.077632599^{10} - 1}{0.077632599}\right) - 1$

$= \$14,324.71$

For the next 15 years, $PV = \$14,324.71$; $PMT = \$1000$;

$i = \frac{8\%}{2} = 4\%$; $c = \frac{2}{1} = 2$; $n = 15$

and $i_2 = (1 + i)^c - 1 = (1.04)^2 - 1 = 0.0816$
The combined future value after 25 years will be

$\$14,324.71\,(1.04)^{30} + \$1000\left(\dfrac{1.0816^{15} - 1}{0.0816}\right) = \underline{\$73,953.35}$

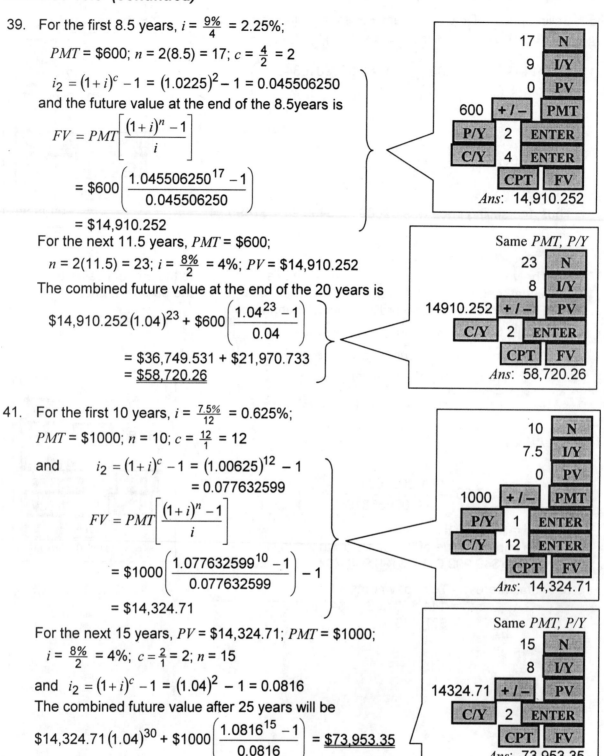

43. For the past 9 years,

$i = \frac{8\%}{4} = 2\%$; $PMT = \$2000$; $n = 9$; $c = \frac{4}{1} = 4$; and

$i_2 = (1+i)^c - 1 = (1.02)^4 - 1 = 0.082432160$

The current value of Gloria's RRSP is

$$FV = PMT\left[\frac{(1+i)^n - 1}{i}\right]$$

$$= \$2000\left(\frac{1.08243216^9 - 1}{0.08243216}\right) - 1$$

$$= \$25,230.137$$

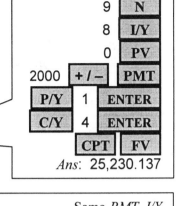

9   N
8   I/Y
0   PV
2000   +/−   PMT
P/Y   1   ENTER
C/Y   4   ENTER
CPT   FV
Ans: 25,230.137

For the next 15 years, $PMT = \$2000$; $n = 30$;

$i = 2\%$; $c = \frac{4}{2} = 2$; $PV = \$25,230.137$;

and $i_2 = (1+i)^c - 1 = (1.02)^2 - 1 = 0.0404$

The total amount 15 years from now will be

$$\$25,230.137\,(1.02)^{60} + \$2000\left(\frac{1.0404^{30} - 1}{0.0404}\right)$$

$$= \underline{\$195,703.17}$$

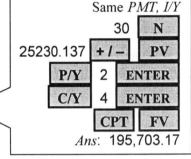

Same *PMT, I/Y*
30   N
25230.137   +/−   PV
P/Y   2   ENTER
C/Y   4   ENTER
CPT   FV
Ans: 195,703.17

45. For the last 10 years of the 15-year period,

$j = 9\%$, $m = 1$, $c = \frac{1}{2} = 0.5$, $n = 2(10) = 20$, and

$i_2 = (1+i)^c - 1 = (1.09)^{0.5} - 1 = 0.044030651$

The PV, 5 years from now, of the last 20 payments is

$$PV = PMT\left[\frac{1-(1+i)^{-n}}{i}\right] = \$2000\left(\frac{1-1.044030651^{-20}}{0.044030651}\right)$$

$$= \$26,235.778$$

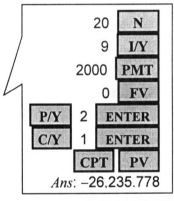

20   N
9   I/Y
2000   PMT
0   FV
P/Y   2   ENTER
C/Y   1   ENTER
CPT   PV
Ans: −26,235.778

For the first 5 years,

$i = \frac{7.5\%}{12} = 0.625\%$, $c = \frac{12}{2} = 6$, $n = 10$, and

$i_2 = (1+i)^c - 1 = (1.00625)^6 - 1 = 0.038090843$

The present value (today) of all payments is

$$\frac{\$26,235.778}{1.00625^{60}} + \$2000\left(\frac{1-1.038090843^{-10}}{0.038090843}\right)$$

$$= \$18,052.624 + \$16,377.069$$

$$= \underline{\$34,429.69}$$

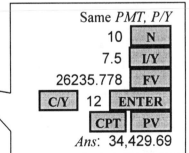

Same *PMT, P/Y*
10   N
7.5   I/Y
26235.778   FV
C/Y   12   ENTER
CPT   PV
Ans: 34,429.69

Exercise 10.5 *(continued)*

49. The inheritance's current economic value is the present value of the deferred general annuity. Since the first quarterly payment is 4.5 years from now, the period of deferral is 4.25 years (if we wish to treat the payments as a deferred ordinary annuity).

Given: $PMT = \$2000$, $n = 4(20) = 80$,

$$d = 4(4.25) = 17, \ i = \frac{6\%}{12} = 0.5\%, \ c = \frac{12}{4} = 3$$

$$i_2 = (1+i)^c - 1 = (1.005)^3 - 1 = 0.015075125$$

$$PV(4.25 \text{ yrs. from now}) = PMT\left[\frac{1-(1+i_2)^{-n}}{i_2}\right]$$

$$= \$2000\left(\frac{1-1.015075125^{-80}}{0.015075125}\right)$$

$$= \$92,590.13$$

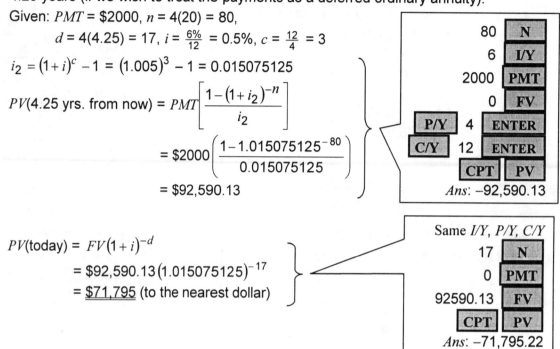

$$PV(\text{today}) = FV(1+i)^{-d}$$

$$= \$92,590.13\,(1.015075125)^{-17}$$

$$= \underline{\$71,795} \text{ (to the nearest dollar)}$$

51. The initial investment equals the present value of the withdrawals.

Given: $PV = \$19,665$, $PMT = \$1000$, $n = 60$,

$$i = \frac{9.5\%}{2} = 4.75\%, \text{ and } c = \frac{2}{4} = 0.5.$$

$$i_2 = (1+i)^c - 1 = (1.0475)^{0.5} - 1 = 0.023474475$$

With the focal date at the end of the period of deferral,
FV of $\$19,665 = PV$ of ordinary annuity

$$\text{Right hand side} = \$1000\left(\frac{1-1.023474475^{-60}}{0.023474475}\right)$$

$$= \$32,012.21$$

Left hand side $= \$19,665\,(1.0475)^d$

Hence, $\$19,665\,(1.0475)^d = \$32,012.21$

Using formula (9-2) to calculate d,

$$d = \frac{\ln\left(\dfrac{FV}{PV}\right)}{\ln(1+i)} = \frac{\ln\left(\dfrac{\$32,012.21}{\$19,665}\right)}{\ln(1.023474475)} = 21.00$$

The period of deferral is 21 quarters long.
The investment must be made 22 quarters
or <u>5 years and 6 months</u> before the first withdrawal.

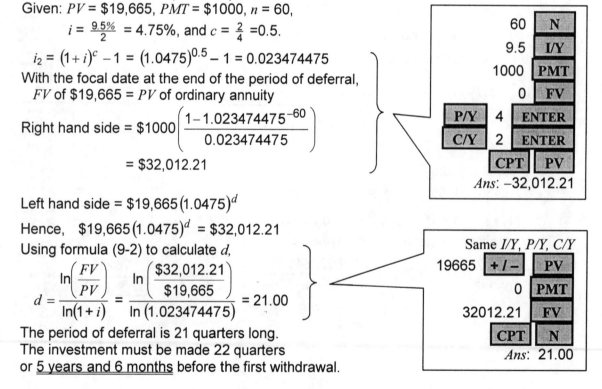

53. For the first 7 years, $i = \frac{8\%}{4} = 2\%$, $PMT = \$3000$,

$n = 1(7) = 7$, $c = \frac{4}{1} = 4$, and

$i_2 = (1+i)^c - 1 = (1.02)^4 - 1 = 0.082432160$

Amount in the RRSP after 7 years will be

$FV = \$3000 \left(\dfrac{1.08243216^7 - 1}{0.08243216} \right) = \$26{,}968.51$

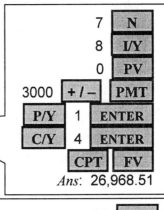

```
          7  N
          8  I/Y
          0  PV
3000 +/-    PMT
   P/Y  1  ENTER
   C/Y  4  ENTER
        CPT   FV
   Ans: 26,968.51
```

For the next 5 years, $PMT = \$500$, $i = \frac{8\%}{4} = 2\%$,

$n = 12(5) = 60$, $c = \frac{4}{12} = 0.\overline{3}$, and

$i_2 = (1+i)^c - 1 = (1.02)^{0.\overline{3}} - 1 = 0.0066227096$

Amount in the RRSP after 12 years will be

$FV = PV(1+i)^n + PMT \left[\dfrac{(1+i)^n - 1}{i} \right]$

$= \$26{,}968.51 (1.02)^{20} + \$500 \left(\dfrac{1.0066227096^{60} - 1}{0.0066227096} \right)$

$= \$76{,}761.75$

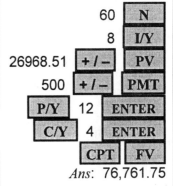

```
            60  N
             8  I/Y
26968.51 +/-   PV
    500  +/-   PMT
   P/Y  12  ENTER
   C/Y   4  ENTER
        CPT   FV
   Ans: 76,761.75
```

For the last 13 years, $PMT = \$500$, $n = 12(13) = 156$,

$i = \frac{7\%}{2} = 3.5\%$, $c = \frac{2}{12} = 0.1\overline{6}$, and

$i_2 = (1+i)^c - 1 = (1.035)^{0.1\overline{6}} - 1 = 0.00575003948$

Amount in the RRSP after 25 years will be

$FV = PV(1+i)^n + PMT \left[\dfrac{(1+i)^n - 1}{i} \right]$

$= \$76{,}761.75 (1.035)^{26} + \$500 \left(\dfrac{1.00575003948^{156} - 1}{0.00575003948} \right)$

$= \underline{\$313{,}490.72}$

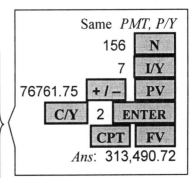

```
   Same PMT, P/Y
           156  N
             7  I/Y
76761.75 +/-   PV
   C/Y   2  ENTER
        CPT   FV
   Ans: 313,490.72
```

Review Problems

1. Since it is a purchase transaction, choose the option having the lower current economic value—that is, the lower present value. The present value of the 60 payments of $1000 is

$PV = PMT \left[\dfrac{1 - (1+i)^{-n}}{i} \right]$

$= \$1000 \left(\dfrac{1 - 1.00625^{-60}}{0.00625} \right)$

$= \$49{,}905.31$

The current economic value of the 5-year-payment option is
$\$10{,}000 + \$49{,}905.31 = \$59{,}905.31$
Choose the 5-year-payment option since its economic value
is $94.69 lower (in current dollars.)

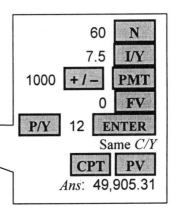

```
           60  N
          7.5  I/Y
1000  +/-    PMT
            0  FV
   P/Y  12  ENTER
       Same C/Y
        CPT   PV
   Ans: 49,905.31
```

Review Problems *(continued)*

3. a. The value placed on half of the partnership is the present value of Dr. Wilson's
        payments discounted at 7% compounded semiannually.
        Given: $PMT = \$714.60$, $n = 12(15) = 180$,

$$i = \frac{7\%}{2} = 3.5\%, c = \frac{2}{12} = 0.1\overline{6}$$

$$i_2 = (1+i)^c - 1 = (1.035)^{0.1\overline{6}} - 1 = 0.0057500395$$

$$PV = PMT\left[\frac{1-(1+i)^{-n}}{i}\right]$$

$$= \$714.60\left(\frac{1-1.0057500395^{-180}}{0.0057500395}\right)$$

$$= \$80,000.05$$

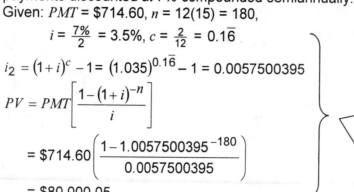

Ans: 80,000.05

The implied value of the partnership was 2($80,000) = $160,000.

   b. Total interest = 180($714.60) − $80,000 = $48,628.

5. a. The original amount of the loan is the present
        value of all the payments.

$$\text{Original loan} = PMT\left[\frac{1-(1+i)^{-n}}{i}\right]$$

$$= \$587.33\left(\frac{1-1.007^{-180}}{0.007}\right)$$

$$= \$59,999.80$$

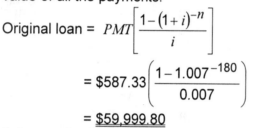

180 N
8.4 I/Y
587.33 +/− PMT
0 FV
P/Y 12 ENTER
Same C/Y
CPT PV
Ans: 59,999.80

   b. Balance after 7½ years
        = Present value of the remaining payments

$$= \$587.33\left(\frac{1-1.007^{-90}}{0.0007}\right)$$

$$= \$39,119.37$$

Same *I/Y, PMT, FV, P/Y, C/Y*
90 N
CPT PV
Ans: 39,119.37

7. The finance company will pay the present value of the
    payments discounted at the required rate of return.
    The payments form a deferred annuity having
    $PMT = \$249$, $n = 12$, $d = 5$, and $i = \frac{16.5\%}{12} = 1.375\%$
    The present value 5 months from now is

$$PV = PMT\left[\frac{1-(1+i)^{-n}}{i}\right]$$

$$= \$249\left(\frac{1-1.01375^{-12}}{0.01375}\right)$$

$$= \$2737.237$$

Price = PV(today) = $FV(1+i)^{-d}$

$$= \$2737.237(1.01375)^{-5}$$

$$= \$2556.57$$

The finance company will pay $2556.57 for the contract.

12 N
16.5 I/Y
249 PMT
0 FV
P/Y 12 ENTER
Same C/Y
CPT PV
Ans: 2737.237

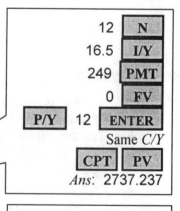

Same *I/Y, P/Y, C/Y*
5 N
0 PMT
2737.237 FV
CPT PV
Ans: 2556.57

Review Problems *(continued)*

9. The amount in the RRSP will be the future value of the payments.
   For monthly contributions,

   $PMT = \$500$, $n = 12(20) = 240$, $i = \frac{7.5\%}{2} = 3.75\%$, $c = \frac{2}{12} = 0.1\overline{6}$

   and $i_2 = (1+i)^c - 1 = (1.0375)^{0.1\overline{6}} - 1 = 0.0061545239$

   $$FV = PMT\left[\frac{(1+i)^n - 1}{i}\right]$$

   $$= \$500\left(\frac{1.0061545239^{240} - 1}{0.0061545239}\right)$$

   $$= \$273,000.71$$

   For annual contributions,

   $PMT = \$6000$, $n = 20$, $i = 3.75\%$, $c = \frac{2}{1} = 2$

   and $i_2 = (1.0375)^2 - 1 = 0.076406250$

   $$FV = \$6000\left(\frac{1.076406250^{20} - 1}{0.076406250}\right) = \$263,882.50$$

   The value of the RRSP will be
   $\$273,000.71 - \$263,882.50 = \underline{\$9118.21}$ larger
   for the case of monthly contributions.

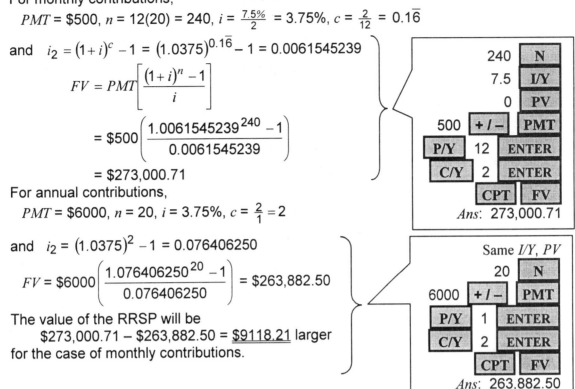

11. If \$3000 is contributed every 6 months for 20 years,

    $$FV = PMT\left[\frac{(1+i)^n - 1}{i}\right]$$

    $$= \$3000\left(\frac{1.04^{40} - 1}{0.04}\right)$$

    $$= \$285,076.55$$

    If \$6000 is contributed every 6 months for the final 10 years,

    $$FV = \$6000\left(\frac{1.04^{20} - 1}{0.04}\right) = \$178,668.47$$

    The early start results in
    $$\frac{\$285,076.55 - \$178,668.47}{\$178,668.47} \times 100\% = \underline{59.56\%} \text{ more}$$
    funds in the RRSP after 20 years.

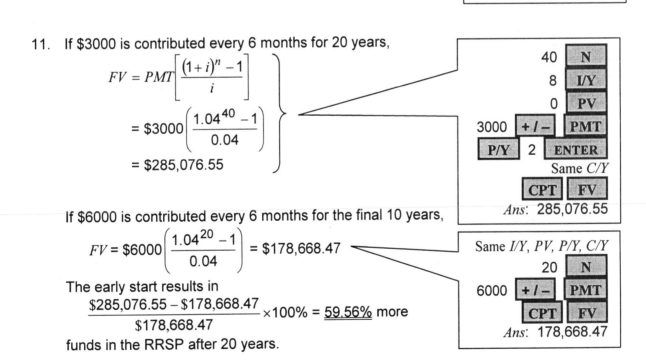

13. The appropriate price to pay is the present value of the payments discounted at the required rate of return. The present value, 5 years from now, of the last 7 years' payments is

$$PV = PMT\left[\frac{1-(1+i)^{-n}}{i}\right]$$

$$= \$1500\left(\frac{1-1.0175^{-28}}{0.0175}\right)$$

$$= \$32,980.43$$

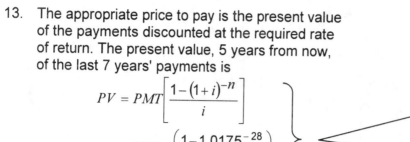

Today's present value of this amount and the first 5 years' payments is

$$\$32,980.43(1.015)^{-20} + \$1500\left(\frac{1-1.015^{-20}}{0.015}\right)$$

$$= \$24,486.99 + \$25,752.96$$
$$= \underline{\$50,239.95}$$

The appropriate price to pay is $50,239.95.

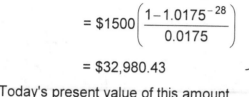

15. The current economic value equals today's present value of the future payments. The payments form a deferred general annuity having

$PMT = \$2500$, $n = 4(20) = 80$, $d = 4(5) = 20$,

$i = \frac{6\%}{12} = 0.5\%$, $c = \frac{12}{4} = 3$, and

$$i_2 = (1+i)^c - 1 = (1.005)^3 - 1 = 0.015075125$$

$$PV(5 \text{ years from now}) = PMT\left[\frac{1-(1+i)^{-n}}{i}\right]$$

$$= \$2500\left(\frac{1-1.015075125^{-80}}{0.015075125}\right)$$

$$= \$115,737.657$$

$$PV(\text{today}) = FV(1+i)^{-d}$$

$$= \$115,737.657(1.015075125)^{-20}$$

$$= \underline{\$85,804.68}$$

The current economic value of the inheritance is $85,804.68.

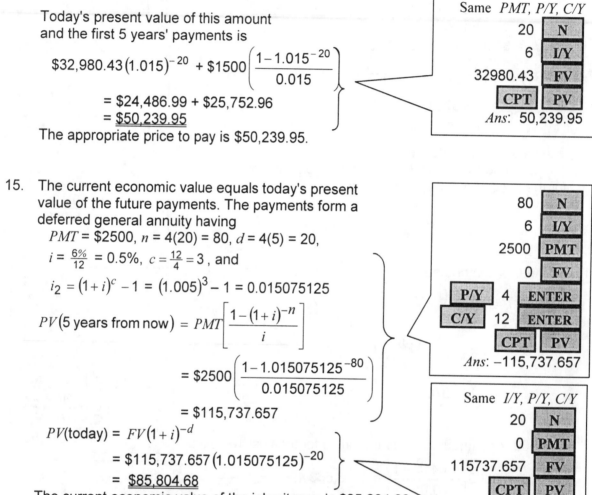

Self-Test Exercise

1. a. $PMT = \$1000$, $n = 2(20) = 40$, $i = \frac{8.5\%}{2} = 4.25\%$

$$FV = PMT\left[\frac{(1+i)^n - 1}{i}\right]$$

$$= \$1000\left(\frac{1.0425^{40} - 1}{0.0425}\right)$$

$$= \underline{\$100{,}822.83}$$

b. $PMT = \$2000$, $n = 20$, $i = 8.5\%$

$$FV = \$2000\left(\frac{1.085^{20} - 1}{0.085}\right)$$

$$= \underline{\$96{,}754.03}$$

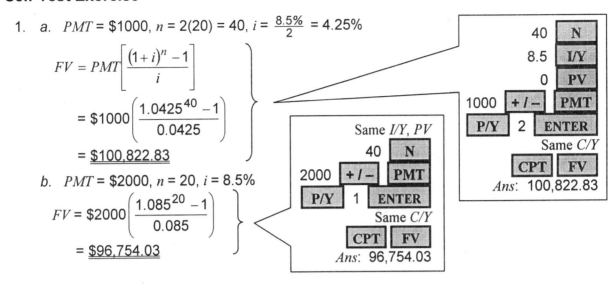

2. a. Amount borrowed = Present value of the monthly payments

$$= \$812.47\left(\frac{1 - 1.00875^{-60}}{0.00875}\right)$$

$$= \$37{,}800.03$$

Purchase price = $\$9000 + \$37{,}800.03$

$$= \underline{\$46{,}800.03}$$

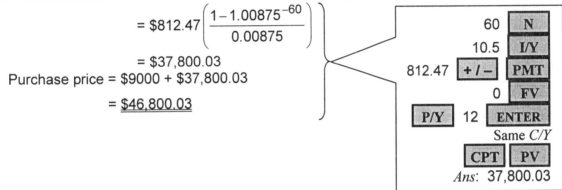

b. Payout amount = Principal balance after 24 payments
= PV of the remaining 36 payments

$$= \$812.47\left(\frac{1 - 1.00875^{-36}}{0.00875}\right)$$

$$= \underline{\$24{,}997.20}$$

3. The finance company will pay an amount equal to the present value of the 15 payments discounted at its required rate of return.

$PMT = \$180.50$, $n = 15$, $i = \frac{21\%}{2} = 10.5\%$, $c = \frac{2}{12} = 0.1\overline{6}$

$$i_2 = (1+i)^c - 1 = (1.105)^{0.1\overline{6}} - 1 = 0.016780120$$

Price $= PV = PMT\left[\frac{1 - (1+i)^{-n}}{i}\right]$

$$= \$180.50\left(\frac{1 - 1.01678012^{-15}}{0.01678012}\right)$$

$$= \underline{\$2376.15}$$

The finance company will pay $2376.15 for the contract.

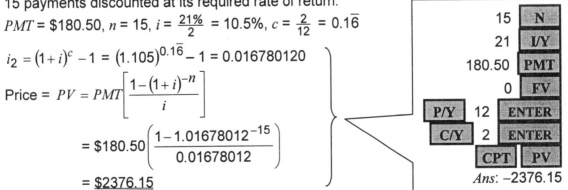

4. The amount (future value) in Dr. Krawchuk's RRSP when he left general practice was

$$FV = PMT\left[\frac{(1+i)^n - 1}{i}\right]$$

$$= \$2000\left(\frac{1.025^{24} - 1}{0.025}\right)$$

$$= \$64,698.08$$

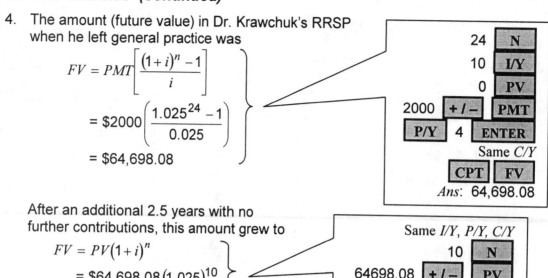

After an additional 2.5 years with no further contributions, this amount grew to

$$FV = PV(1+i)^n$$

$$= \$64,698.08\,(1.025)^{10}$$

$$= \underline{\$82,819.01}$$

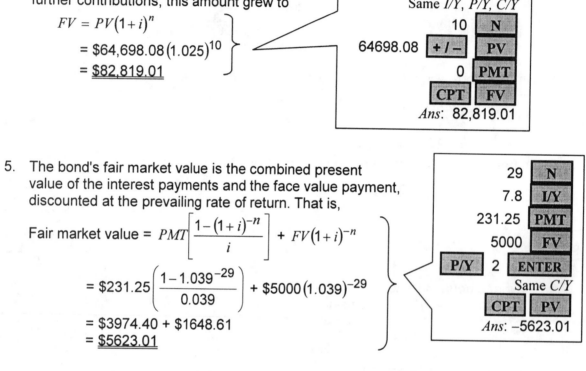

5. The bond's fair market value is the combined present value of the interest payments and the face value payment, discounted at the prevailing rate of return. That is,

$$\text{Fair market value} = PMT\left[\frac{1-(1+i)^{-n}}{i}\right] + FV(1+i)^{-n}$$

$$= \$231.25\left(\frac{1-1.039^{-29}}{0.039}\right) + \$5000\,(1.039)^{-29}$$

$$= \$3974.40 + \$1648.61$$

$$= \underline{\$5623.01}$$

6. The current economic value of the award is the present value of all the payments discounted at the time value of money. The present value, 5 years from now, of the 120 monthly payments of $1000 is

$$PV = PMT\left[\frac{1-(1+i)^{-n}}{i}\right]$$

$$= \$1000\left(\frac{1-1.005^{-120}}{0.005}\right)$$

$$= \underline{\$90,073.45}$$

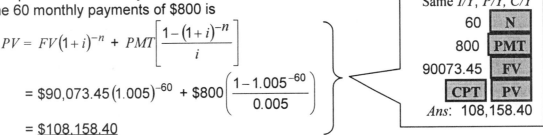

The present value today of this amount and the 60 monthly payments of $800 is

$$PV = FV(1+i)^{-n} + PMT\left[\frac{1-(1+i)^{-n}}{i}\right]$$

$$= \$90,073.45\,(1.005)^{-60} + \$800\left(\frac{1-1.005^{-60}}{0.005}\right)$$

$$= \underline{\$108,158.40}$$

The economic value of the award, 1 month before the first payment, is $108,158.40.

7. For the first 30 months,
$PMT = \$800$, $n = 4(2.5) = 10$, $i = \frac{10\%}{4} = 2.5\%$

The future value, 30 months from now, of the first 10 payments is

$$FV = PMT\left[\frac{(1+i)^n - 1}{i}\right]$$

$$= \$800\left(\frac{1.025^{10} - 1}{0.025}\right)$$

$$= \$8962.71$$

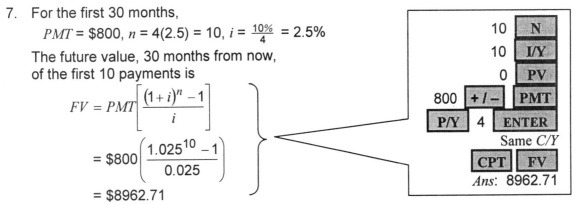

For the subsequent $7(12) - 30 = 54$ months,
$PMT = \$800$, $n = 4(4.5) = 18$, $i = \frac{9\%}{2} = 4.5\%$, $c = \frac{2}{4} = 0.5$

$$i_2 = (1+i)^c - 1 = (1.045)^{0.5} - 1 = 0.022252415$$

The combined future value, 7 years from now, of this amount and the last 18 payments is

$$FV = PV(1+i)^n + PMT\left[\frac{(1+i)^n - 1}{i}\right]$$

$$= \$8962.71\,(1.045)^9 + \$800\left(\frac{1.022252415^{18} - 1}{0.022252415}\right)$$

$$= \$13,319.44 + \$17,475.68$$

$$= \underline{\$30,795.12}$$

Self-Test Exercise *(continued)*

8. The selling price (original loan) equals the present value of the payments. The payments form a deferred simple annuity having

$PMT = \$226.51$, $n = 12$, $d = 3$, and $i = \frac{16.5\%}{12} = 1.375\%$.

$$PV(\text{3 months from now}) = PMT\left[\frac{1-(1+i)^{-n}}{i}\right]$$

$$= \$226.51\left(\frac{1-1.01375^{-12}}{0.01375}\right)$$

$$= \$2490.006$$

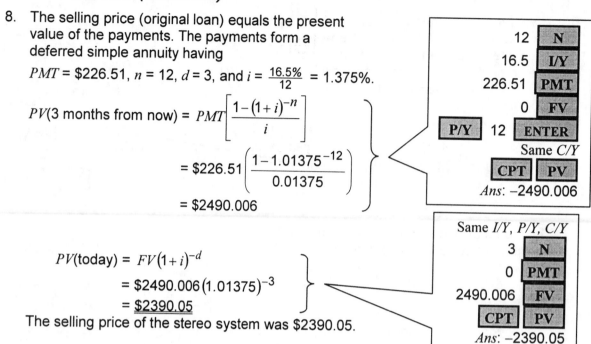

$$PV(\text{today}) = FV(1+i)^{-d}$$

$$= \$2490.006\,(1.01375)^{-3}$$

$$= \underline{\$2390.05}$$

The selling price of the stereo system was $2390.05.

11   Ordinary Annuities: Payment Size, Term, and Interest Rate

Concept Questions (Section 11.1)

1. The monthly payments will be (ii) *more* than half as large because you will pay more total interest if you pay off the loan over 10 years instead of 5 years. (The total of the principal components of the payments will be the same in both cases.)

Exercise 11.1

1. Given: $FV = \$54{,}511$, $n = 1(13) = 13$, $i = j = 5.4\%$

   Substitute into $FV = PMT\left[\dfrac{(1+i)^n - 1}{i}\right]$

   $$\$54{,}511 = PMT\left(\dfrac{1.054^{13} - 1}{0.054}\right)$$

   $PMT = \underline{\$3000.00}$

3. Given: $FV = \$4357$, $n = 12(2.5) = 30$, $i = \dfrac{7.5\%}{12} = 0.625\%$

   $$\$4357 = PMT\left(\dfrac{1.00625^{30} - 1}{0.00625}\right)$$

   $PMT = \underline{\$132.50}$

5. Given: $PV = \$27{,}277$, $n = 12(8.25) = 99$, $i = \dfrac{6\%}{12} = 0.5\%$

   Substitute into $PV = PMT\left[\dfrac{1-(1+i)^{-n}}{i}\right]$

   $$\$27{,}277 = PMT\left(\dfrac{1-1.005^{-99}}{0.005}\right)$$

   $PMT = \underline{\$350.00}$

7. Given: $PV = \$20{,}049$, $n = 2(19) = 38$, $i = \dfrac{9.25\%}{2} = 4\,625\%$

   $$\$20{,}049 = PMT\left(\dfrac{1-1.04625^{-38}}{0.04625}\right)$$

   $PMT = \underline{\$1130.00}$

9. Given: $PV = \$25,000$, $n = 4(8.5) = 34$,

   $i = \frac{9.5\%}{2} = 4.75\%$, $c = \frac{2}{4} = 0.5$

   $i_2 = (1+i)^c - 1 = (1.0475)^{0.5} - 1 = 0.023474475$

   $\$25,000 = PMT \left(\dfrac{1 - 1.023474475^{-34}}{0.023474475} \right)$

   $PMT = \underline{\$1075.51}$

34	N
9.5	I/Y
25000 +/−	PV
0	FV
P/Y 4	ENTER
C/Y 2	ENTER
CPT	PMT

   Ans: 1075.51

11. Given: $FV = \$100,000$, $n = 15$, $i = \frac{9\%}{4} = 2.25\%$, $c = \frac{4}{1} = 4$

    $i_2 = (1+i)^c - 1 = (1.0225)^4 - 1 = 0.093083319$

    $\$100,000 = PMT \left(\dfrac{1.093083319^{15} - 1}{0.093083319} \right)$

    $PMT = \underline{\$3324.24}$

13. At a focal date 4 years from now,

    FV of $\$20,000 = PV$ of ordinary annuity

    For the FV calculation, $PV = \$20,000$, $i = 7.75\%$, and $n = 4$.

    For the PV calculation, $i = 7.75\%$ and $n = 10$.

    $\$20,000(1.0775)^4 = PMT \left(\dfrac{1 - 1.0775^{-10}}{0.0775} \right)$

    $PMT = \dfrac{\$26,958.71}{6.7864085} = \underline{\$3972.46}$

15. At a focal date 2.25 years from now,

    FV of $\$50,000 = PV$ of ordinary annuity

    For the FV calculation, $PV = \$50,000$, $i = \frac{6.4\%}{4} = 1.6\%$, and $n = 4(2.25) = 9$.

    For the PV calculation, $i = 2.5\%$ and $n = 4(20) = 80$.

    $\$50,000(1.016)^9 = PMT \left(\dfrac{1 - 1.016^{-80}}{0.016} \right)$

    $PMT = \dfrac{\$57,678.42}{44.945705} = \underline{\$1283.29}$

17. At a focal date 6 years from now,

    FV of $\$25,000 = PV$ of ordinary annuity

    For the FV calculation, $PV = \$25,000$, $i = \frac{9.5\%}{2} = 4.75\%$, and $n = 2(6) = 12$.

    For the PV calculation, $i = 4.75\%$, $n = 12(7.5) = 90$, $c = \frac{2}{12} = 0.1\overline{6}$, and

    $i_2 = (1+i)^c - 1 = (1.0475)^{0.1\overline{6}} - 1 = 0.007764383$

    $\$25,000(1.0475)^{12} = PMT \left(\dfrac{1 - 1.007764383^{-90}}{0.007764383} \right)$

    $PMT = \dfrac{\$43,630.32}{64.586204} = \underline{\$675.54}$

Exercise 11.1 *(continued)*

19. a. Given: $FV = \$200{,}000$, $n = 25$, $i = 8\%$

$$\$200{,}000 = PMT\left(\frac{1.08^{25} - 1}{0.08}\right)$$

$$PMT = \underline{\$2735.76}$$

b. Given: $FV = \$200{,}000$, $n = 25$, $i = 10\%$

$$\$200{,}000 = PMT\left(\frac{1.10^{25} - 1}{0.10}\right)$$

$$PMT = \underline{\$2033.61}$$

21. a. Given: $PV = \$20{,}000$, $n = 12(10) = 120$, $i = \frac{5.4\%}{12} = 0.45\%$

$$\$20{,}000 = PMT\left(\frac{1 - 1.0045^{-120}}{0.0045}\right)$$

$$PMT = \underline{\$216.06}$$

b. Given: $PV = \$20{,}000$, $n = 12(20) = 240$, $i = 0.45\%$

$$\$20{,}000 = PMT\left(\frac{1 - 1.0045^{-240}}{0.0045}\right)$$

$$PMT = \underline{\$136.45}$$

23. Original loan = Present value of all the payments
For every case, $PV = \$20{,}000$, $i = \frac{9\%}{12} = 0.75\%$

a. For $n = 12(5) = 60$, $\$20{,}000 = PMT\left(\frac{1 - 1.0075^{-60}}{0.0075}\right)$

$$PMT = \underline{\$415.17}$$

Total interest $60(\$415.17) - \$20{,}000 = \underline{\$4910.20}$

Similarly,

b. For $n = 120$, $PMT = \underline{\$253.35}$, Total interest = $\underline{\$10{,}402.00}$
c. For $n = 180$, $PMT = \underline{\$202.85}$, Total interest = $\underline{\$16{,}513.00}$
d. For $n = 240$, $PMT = \underline{\$179.95}$, Total interest = $\underline{\$23{,}188.00}$
e. For $n = 300$, $PMT = \underline{\$167.84}$, Total interest = $\underline{\$30{,}352.00}$

25. Original loan = Present value of all payments
The payments in this case form a general annuity having
$PV = \$20{,}000$, $n = 2(7.5) = 15$, $i = \frac{9\%}{12} = 0.75\%$, $c = \frac{12}{2} = 6$

$$i_2 = (1 + i)^c - 1 = (1.0075)^6 - 1 = 0.045852235$$

$$\$20{,}000 = PMT\left(\frac{1 - 1.045852235^{-15}}{0.045852235}\right)$$

$$PMT = \underline{\$1873.20}$$

The semiannual payment is $1873.20.
Total interest Karen will pay
$15(\$1873.20) - \$20{,}000 = \underline{\$8098.00}$.

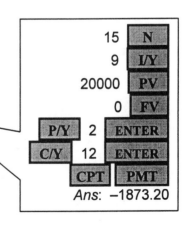

27. The $600,000 balance is the present value of the payments which form an ordinary general annuity.

$PV = \$600,000,\ n = 4(20) = 80,\ i = 8\%,\ c = \frac{1}{4} = 0.25$

$i_2 = (1+i)^c - 1 = (1.08)^{0.25} - 1 = 0.019426547$

$\$600,000 = PMT\left(\dfrac{1-1.019426547^{-80}}{0.019426547}\right)$

$PMT = \underline{\$14,839.78}$

Henry's quarterly payments will be $14,839.78.

Total interest Henry will pay = 80($14,839.78) − $600,000 = $\underline{\$587,182.40}$.

29. The future value of the replacement payments is $25,000.

$FV = \$25,000,\ n = 11,\ i = \frac{5.4\%}{12} = 0.45\%$

$\$25,000 = PMT\left(\dfrac{1.0045^{11}-1}{0.0045}\right)$

$PMT = \underline{\$2222.05}$

Eleven monthly payments of $2222.05 are economically equivalent to the scheduled payment of $25,000.

31. *a.* Original loan = Present value of all payments

$PV = \$7500,\ n = 12(3) = 36,\ i = \frac{9\%}{12} = 0.75\%$

$\$7500 = PMT\left(\dfrac{1-1.0075^{-36}}{0.0075}\right)$

$PMT = \underline{\$238.50}$

b. $f = (1+i)^m - 1 = (1.0075)^{12} - 1 = 0.09381 = \underline{9.38\%}$

c. Balance = Present value of the 12 remaining payments

$= \$238.50\left(\dfrac{1-1.0075^{-12}}{0.0075}\right)$

$= \underline{\$2727.23}$

33. With a focal date at age 65,

FV of amount in RRSP at age 56 = PV of the annuity

For the FV calculation, $PV = \$195,000,\ n = 12(9) = 108,\ i = \frac{8.4\%}{12} = 0.7\%$

For the PV calculation, $n = 12(20) = 240$, and $i = \frac{7.2\%}{12} = 0.6\%$.

$\$195,000\,(1.007)^{108} = PMT\left(\dfrac{1-1.006^{-240}}{0.006}\right)$

$\$414,207.00 = PMT\left(\dfrac{1-1.006^{-240}}{0.006}\right)$

$PMT = \underline{\$3261.26}$

Exercise 11.1 *(continued)*

35. At a focal date 10 years from now,

        Future value of the retiring allowance = Present value of the 15-year annuity

Viewed from the focal date, the annuity is an ordinary simple annuity.

Putting the word equation into mathematics,

$$\$25,000\,(1.07)^{10} = PMT\left(\frac{1-1.013^{-60}}{0.013}\right)$$

$$PMT = \underline{\$1185.51}$$

Elizabeth can expect payments of $1185.51 at the beginning of each quarter.

37. At a focal date 4 years from now,

        Future value of quarterly savings = Present value of the monthly withdrawals

$$PMT\left(\frac{1.015^{16}-1}{0.015}\right) = \$3000\left(\frac{1-1.0035^{-12}}{0.0035}\right)$$

The solution is $PMT = \underline{\$1962.61}$. Tim and Justine must contribute $1962.61 to the fund at the end of every calendar quarter for the next 4 years.

39. a. The nominal amount in the RRSP should be

$$FV = PV(1+i)^n = \$500,000\,(1.02)^{30} = \underline{\$905,680.79}$$

    b. The contributions form an ordinary general annuity having

$$FV = \$905,680.79,\ n = 4(30) = 120,\ i = \frac{8.5\%}{2} = 4.25\%,\ c = \frac{2}{4} = 0.5,$$

$$i_2 = (1+i)^c - 1 = (1.0425)^{0.5} - 1 = 0.021028893$$

$$\$905,680.79 = PMT\left(\frac{1.021028893^{120}-1}{0.021028893}\right)$$

$$PMT = \underline{\$1708.17}$$

Dr. Collins should make quarterly contributions of $1708.17.

41. At a focal date on Brice's 65th birthday,

        FV of $154,000 = PV of ordinary simple annuity payments

For the FV calculation, $PV = \$154,000$, $n = 12(11) = 132$, and $i = \frac{8.25\%}{12} = 0.6875\%$.

For the PV calculation, $n = 12(20) = 240$ and $i = 0.6875\%$.

Hence, $$\$154,000\,(1.006875)^{132} = PMT\left(\frac{1-1.006875^{-240}}{0.006875}\right)$$

$$PMT = \frac{\$380,447.16}{117.361849} = \underline{\$3241.66}$$

The annuity payments will be $3241.66 per month.

43.   *a.*   The original loan equals the present value of the loan payments. Shifting the focal date to the date 2.5 years from now,

$$FV \text{ of } \$3,000,000 = PV \text{ of ordinary annuity}$$

For the FV calculation, $PV = \$3,000,000$, $n = 2(2.5) = 5$, and $i = \frac{6\%}{2} = 3\%$.

For the PV calculation, $n = 2(15) = 30$, and $i = 3\%$.
Hence,

$$\$3,000,000(1.03)^5 = PMT\left(\frac{1-1.03^{-30}}{0.03}\right)$$

$$PMT = \frac{\$3,477,822.22}{19.60044135} = \underline{\$177,435.91}$$

The semiannual loan payments will be $177,435.91.

  b.   Total interest = Total of payments − Principal
$$= 30(\$177,435.91) - \$3,000,000$$
$$= \underline{\$2,323,077.30}$$

45.   The present value (on the purchase date) of the deferred annuity payments equals $85,000. Alternatively, at a focal date 9 years from now,

$$FV \text{ of } \$85,000 = PV \text{ of ordinary annuity}$$

For the FV calculation, $PV = \$85,000$, $n = 9$, and $i = 5.5\%$.

For the PV calculation, $n = 2(20) = 40$, $i = 5.5\%$, $c = \frac{1}{2} = 0.5$, and

$$i_2 = (1+i)^c - 1 = (1.055)^{0.5} - 1 = 0.027131929$$

Hence, $\$85,000(1.055)^9 = PMT\left(\dfrac{1-1.027131929^{-40}}{0.027131929}\right)$

$$PMT = \frac{\$137,623.01}{24.2250019} = \underline{\$5681.03}$$

The semiannual payments will be $5681.03.

47.   At a focal date 28 years from now,

$$FV \text{ of RRSP contributions} = PV \text{ of the annuity payments.}$$

The amount in the RRSP 10 years from now will be

$$FV = PMT\left[\frac{(1+i)^n - 1}{i}\right] = \$7000\left(\frac{1.075^{10} - 1}{0.075}\right) = \$99,029.61$$

The left side of the word equation is the future value, 28 years from now, of the preceding amount and the contributions for years 11 to 28 inclusive. That is,

$$\$99,029.61(1.075)^{18} + PMT\left(\frac{1.075^{18} - 1}{0.075}\right) = \$364,013.45 + PMT(35.677388)$$

The present value, 28 years from now, of the $6000 per month annuity is

$$\$6000\left(\frac{1-1.00625^{-300}}{0.00625}\right) = \$811,917.68$$

Substituting these amounts in the original word equation gives
$$\$364,013.45 + PMT(35.677388) = \$811,917.68$$
The solution is $PMT = \underline{\$12,554.29}$. Mr. Groman must contribute $12,554.29 at each year-end for years 11 to 28 inclusive.

Exercise 11.1 *(continued)*

49. The amount, 20 years from now, that will have the purchasing power of $6000 (in today's dollars) is
$$FV = PV(1+i)^n = \$6000(1.025)^{20} = \$9831.70$$
At a focal date 20 years from now,
$$FV \text{ of the RRSP} = PV \text{ of the 25-year annuity}$$
For the FV calculation, $PV = \$54,000$, $i = \frac{8\%}{2} = 4\%$, and $n = 40$.

For the PV calculation, $PMT = \$9831.70$, $i = \frac{5.5\%}{4} = 1.375\%$, and $n = 4(25) = 100$.

$$\$54,000(1.04)^{40} + PMT\left(\frac{1.04^{40}-1}{0.04}\right) = \$9831.70\left(\frac{1-1.01375^{-100}}{0.01375}\right)$$

$$\$259,255.11 + PMT(95.0255157) = \$532,542.67$$
$$PMT = \underline{\$2875.94}$$

Semiannual RRSP contributions of $2875.94 are needed to reach the retirement goal.

Concept Questions (Section 11.2)

1. You will pay off the loan in <u>(ii) less than half the time</u>. If payments are doubled, you will pay less interest over the life of the loan. Therefore, the total of the nominal payments (principal + interest) will be reduced and you will pay off the loan in less than half the time.

Exercise 11.2

1. Given: $PV = \$50,000$, $PMT = \$3874.48$, $i = \frac{6.5\%}{2} = 3.25\%$

$$n = -\frac{\ln\left(1 - \frac{i \times PV}{PMT}\right)}{\ln(1+i)} = -\frac{\ln\left(1 - \frac{0.0325 \times \$50,000}{\$3874.48}\right)}{\ln(1.0325)} = -\frac{-0.54371}{0.031983} = 17.00$$

The annuity consists of 17 semiannual payments. Its term is
$$\frac{17}{2} \text{ years} = 8.5 \text{ years} = \underline{8 \text{ years and 6 months}}.$$

3. Given: $PV = \$200,000$, $PMT = \$5807.91$, $i = \frac{9\%}{4} = 2.25\%$

$$n = -\frac{\ln\left(1 - \frac{i \times PV}{PMT}\right)}{\ln(1+i)} = -\frac{\ln\left(1 - \frac{0.0225 \times \$200,000}{\$5807.91}\right)}{\ln(1.0225)} = 67.00$$

There are 67 payments in the annuity requiring 67 calendar quarters. The term is $\frac{67}{4}$ years = 16.75 years = <u>16 years and 9 months</u>.

5. Given: $PV = \$100,000$, $PMT = \$10,000$, $i = 8.75\%$

$$n = -\frac{\ln\left(1 - \frac{i \times PV}{PMT}\right)}{\ln(1+i)} = -\frac{\ln\left(1 - \frac{0.0875 \times \$100,000}{\$10,000}\right)}{\ln(1.0875)} = 24.79$$

The annuity consists of 25 annual payments with the last payment smaller than $10,000. The annuity's term is <u>25 years</u>.

Exercise 11.2 *(continued)*

7. Given: $FV = \$100,000$, $PMT = \$5000$, $i = \frac{7.5\%}{2} = 3.75\%$

$$n = \frac{\ln\left(1 + \dfrac{i \times FV}{PMT}\right)}{\ln(1+i)} = \frac{\ln\left(1 + \dfrac{0.0375 \times \$100,000}{\$5000}\right)}{\ln(1.0375)} = 15.20$$

The annuity consists of 16 semiannual payments with the last payment smaller than $5000. The term of the annuity is 16 half years = 8 years.

9. Given: $FV = \$74,385$, $PMT = \$1200$, $i = 8.75\%$, $c = \frac{1}{4} = 0.25$

$$i_2 = (1+i)^c - 1 = (1.0875)^{0.25} - 1 = 0.02119179$$

$$n = \frac{\ln\left(1 + \dfrac{i \times FV}{PMT}\right)}{\ln(1+i)} = \frac{\ln\left(1 + \dfrac{0.02119179 \times \$74,385}{\$1200}\right)}{\ln(1.02119179)} = 40.00$$

The 40 quarterly payments have a term of 10 years.

11. Given: $PV = \$5825.85$, $PMT = \$1000$, $i = \frac{7.5\%}{2} = 3.75\%$, $c = \frac{4}{2} = 2$

$$i_2 = (1+i)^c - 1 = (1.0375)^2 - 1 = 0.0764025$$

$$n = -\frac{\ln\left(1 - \dfrac{i \times PV}{PMT}\right)}{\ln(1+i)} = -\frac{\ln\left(1 - \dfrac{0.0764025 \times \$5825.85}{\$1000}\right)}{\ln(1.0764025)} = 8.00$$

The annuity has 8 annual payments. Its term is 8 years.

13. At a focal date 7 years from now,
FV of $40,000 = PV$ of ordinary simple annuity
For the FV calculation, $i = 8.7\%$, $n = 7$, and $PV = \$40,000$

$$FV = PV(1+i)^n = \$40,000(1.087)^7 = \$71,724.38$$

Now substitute $PV = \$71,724.38$, $PMT = \$9427.11$, and $i = 8.7\%$ into formula (10-2n) to obtain n.

$$n = -\frac{\ln\left(1 - \dfrac{i \times PV}{PMT}\right)}{\ln(1+i)} = -\frac{\ln\left(1 - \dfrac{0.087 \times \$71,724.38}{\$9427.11}\right)}{\ln(1.087)} = 13.00 \text{ payments}$$

The term of the annuity is 13 years.

15. At a focal date 5.5 years from now,
FV of $15,000 = PV$ of ordinary simple annuity,
For the FV calculation, $i = \frac{6.75\%}{12} = 0.5625\%$, $n = 12(5.5) = 66$, and $PV = \$15,000$

$$FV = PV(1+i)^n = \$15,000(1.005625)^{66} = \$21,720.57$$

Now substitute $PV = \$21,720.57$, $PMT = \$253.89$, and $i = 0.5625\%$ into formula (10-2n) to obtain n.

$$n = -\frac{\ln\left(1 - \dfrac{i \times PV}{PMT}\right)}{\ln(1+i)} = -\frac{\ln\left(1 - \dfrac{0.005625 \times \$21,720.57}{\$253.89}\right)}{\ln(1.005625)} = 117.00 \text{ payments}$$

The term of the annuity is 117 months or 9 years and 9 months.

Business Mathematics in Canada, 5/e

17. At a focal date 4.5 years from now,

$$FV \text{ of } \$37,958.58 = PV \text{ of ordinary annuity}$$

For the FV calculation, $i = \frac{8.5\%}{2} = 4.25\%$, $n = 2(4.5) = 9$, and $PV = \$37,958.58$

$$FV = PV(1+i)^n = \$37,958.58\,(1.0425)^9 = \$55,207.05$$

For the annuity, $PV = \$55,207.05$, $PMT = \$2500$, $i = 4.25\%$, $c = \frac{2}{4} = 0.5$, and

$$i_2 = (1+i)^c - 1 = (1.0425)^{0.5} - 1 = 0.02102889$$

Substitute these values into formula (10-2n) to obtain n.

$$n = -\frac{\ln\left(1 - \dfrac{i \times PV}{PMT}\right)}{\ln(1+i)} = -\frac{\ln\left(1 - \dfrac{0.02102889 \times \$55,207.05}{\$2500}\right)}{\ln(1.02102889)} = 30.00 \text{ payments}$$

The term of the annuity is 30 quarters or <u>7 years and 6 months</u>.

19. The deposits form an ordinary simple annuity having

$$FV = \$10,000, \quad PMT = \$100 \text{ and } i = \frac{5.25\%}{12} = 0.4375\%$$

$$n = \frac{\ln\left(1 + \dfrac{i \times FV}{PMT}\right)}{\ln(1+i)} = \frac{\ln\left(1 + \dfrac{0.004375 \times \$10,000}{\$100}\right)}{\ln(1.004375)} = 83.131$$

Rounded to the next higher month it will require a total of 84 months or <u>7 years</u> to accumulate $10,000.

21. The purchase price represents the present value of the annuity. Hence,

$$PV = \$300,000 \text{ with } PMT = \$2500 \text{ and } i = \frac{7.5\%}{12} = 0.625\%.$$

$$n = -\frac{\ln\left(1 - \dfrac{i \times PV}{PMT}\right)}{\ln(1+i)} = -\frac{\ln\left(1 - \dfrac{0.00625 \times \$300,000}{\$2500}\right)}{\ln(1.00625)} = 222.50$$

The annuity will have 223 monthly payments. Its term will be 223 months or <u>18 years and 7 months</u>.

23. The original loan equals the present value of the loan payments.
With $PV = \$100,000$, $PMT = \$1000$, and $i = \frac{10.5\%}{12} = 0.875\%$,

$$n = -\frac{\ln\left(1 - \dfrac{i \times PV}{PMT}\right)}{\ln(1+i)}$$

$$= -\frac{\ln\left(1 - \dfrac{0.00875 \times \$100,000}{\$1000}\right)}{\ln(1.00875)} = 238.69$$

That is, it will take 239 months to pay off the loan (with the last payment smaller than the others).

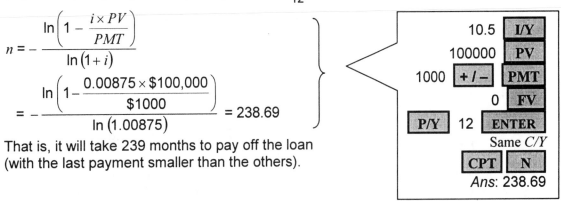

(continued)

Exercise 11.2 (continued)

23. (continued)

With PMT increased to $1100 per month,

$$n = -\frac{\ln\left(1 - \frac{0.00875 \times \$100{,}000}{\$1100}\right)}{\ln(1.00875)} = 182.16$$

The loan will be paid off in only 183 months. Therefore, the $1000 payments will take (239 − 183) months = 56 months = <u>4 years and 8 months</u> longer to pay off the loan.

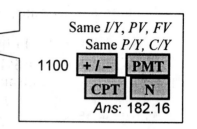

Same *I/Y, PV, FV*
Same *P/Y, C/Y*

1100 | +/− | PMT
CPT | N

Ans: 182.16

25. The purchase price of the annuity is the present value of the annuity payments. In this case, the payments form an ordinary general annuity having

$$PV = \$200{,}000,\ PMT = \$5000,\ i = \frac{5.5\%}{2} = 2.75\%,\ c = \frac{2}{4} = 0.5$$

$$i_2 = (1+i)^c - 1 = (1.0275)^{0.5} - 1 = 0.013656747$$

The number of payments that the annuity will provide is

$$n = -\frac{\ln\left(1 - \frac{i \times PV}{PMT}\right)}{\ln(1+i)} = -\frac{\ln\left(1 - \frac{0.013656747 \times \$200{,}000}{\$5000}\right)}{\ln(1.013656747)} = 58.26$$

The 59 quarterly payments will last for $\frac{59}{4}$ years = 14.75 years = <u>14 years and 9 months</u>

27. In effect, the customer borrows $1395 − $50 = $1345. The loan equals the present value of the payments. Thus,

$$PV = \$1345,\ PMT = \$50,\ i = \frac{13.5\%}{12} = 1.125\%$$

The number of payments will be

$$n = -\frac{\ln\left(1 - \frac{i \times PV}{PMT}\right)}{\ln(1+i)} = -\frac{\ln\left(1 - \frac{0.01125 \times \$1345}{\$50}\right)}{\ln(1.01125)} = 32.22$$

The final payment (smaller than $50) will be the 33rd payment occurring 33 months or <u>2 years and 9 months</u> after the date of purchase.

29. The economic value at age 65 of each annuity is the present value of the payments discounted at the time value of money.

For the 25-year-term annuity, $PMT = \$307,\ n = 12(25) = 300$, and $i = \frac{6\%}{12} = 0.5\%$

$$PV = PMT\left[\frac{1-(1+i)^{-n}}{i}\right] = \$307\left(\frac{1-1.005^{-300}}{0.005}\right) = \$47{,}648.51$$

For payments of $408 per month to have the same economic value,

$$n = -\frac{\ln\left(1 - \frac{i \times PV}{PMT}\right)}{\ln(1+i)} = -\frac{\ln\left(1 - \frac{0.005 \times \$47{,}648.51}{\$408}\right)}{\ln(1.005)} = 175.81$$

Therefore, if the man receives 176 payments, the life annuity will have the higher economic value. He must live at least 176 months (14 years and 8 months) beyond age 65. That is, he must live <u>at least to an age of 79 years and 8 months</u>.

Exercise 11.2 *(continued)*

31. At focal date 41 months from now,

$$FV \text{ of } \$10{,}000 = PV \text{ of ordinary simple annuity payments}$$

For the FV calculation, $PV = \$10{,}000$, $i = \frac{7.5\%}{12} = 0.625\%$, $n = 12(3) + 5 = 41$

$$FV = PV(1+i)^n = \$10{,}000(1.00625)^{41} = \$12{,}910.46$$

Now substitute $PV = \$12{,}910.46$, $PMT = \$300$, and $i = 0.625\%$ into formula (10-2n) to obtain n.

$$n = -\frac{\ln\left(1 - \dfrac{i \times PV}{PMT}\right)}{\ln(1+i)} = -\frac{\ln\left(1 - \dfrac{0.00625 \times \$12{,}910.46}{\$300}\right)}{\ln(1.00625)} = 50.28$$

The fund will provide <u>51</u> monthly withdrawals (with the last one less than $300).

33. At a focal date 3 years ago,

$$FV \text{ of } \$17{,}000 = PV \text{ of the RRIF withdrawals}$$

The amount on the left side is

$$FV = PV(1+i)^n = \$17{,}000(1.05)^{18} = \$40{,}912.53$$

Now substitute $PV = \$40{,}912.53$, $PMT = \$1000$, and $i = \frac{8\%}{4} = 2\%$ into formula (10-2n) to obtain n.

$$n = -\frac{\ln\left(1 - \dfrac{i \times PV}{PMT}\right)}{\ln(1+i)} = -\frac{\ln\left(1 - \dfrac{0.02 \times \$40{,}912.53}{\$1000}\right)}{\ln(1.02)} = 86.11$$

There will be 87 withdrawals in all. 4(3) = 12 withdrawals have already been made and 87 − 12 = 75 withdrawals remain. These will continue for another

$$\frac{75}{4} = 18.75 \text{ years} = \underline{18 \text{ years and 9 months}}$$

35. The original loan equals the present value of the payments. Equivalently, At a focal date 23 months from now,

$$FV \text{ of } \$20{,}000 = PV \text{ of ordinary general annuity payments}$$

For the FV calculation, $PV = \$20{,}000$, $i = 8\%$, $c = \frac{1}{12} = 0.08\overline{3}$, $n = 12 + 11 = 23$, and

$$i_2 = (1+i)^c - 1 = (1.08)^{0.08\overline{3}} - 1 = 0.006434030$$

$$FV = PV(1+i)^n = \$20{,}000(1.006434030)^{23} = \$23{,}178.87$$

Now substitute $PV = \$23{,}178.87$, $PMT = \$300$, and $i_2 = 0.006434030$ into formula (10-2n) to obtain n.

$$n = -\frac{\ln\left(1 - \dfrac{i \times PV}{PMT}\right)}{\ln(1+i)} = -\frac{\ln\left(1 - \dfrac{0.006434030 \times \$23{,}178.87}{\$300}\right)}{\ln(1.006434030)} = 107.18$$

The 108th payment will extinguish the debt. It will occur 23 + 108 = 131 months or <u>10 years and 11 months</u> after the date the $20,000 was originally borrowed.

Exercise 11.2 (continued)

37. At a focal date 6 years from now,

$$FV \text{ of } \$139{,}000 = PV \text{ of the ordinary general annuity payments}$$

The left side is

$$FV = PV(1+i)^n = \$139{,}000\,(1.085)^6 = \$226{,}773.98$$

For the right side of the equation,

$$PV = \$226{,}773.98, \; PMT = \$5000, \; i = \tfrac{7.5\%}{12} = 0.625\%, \; c = \tfrac{12}{4} = 3, \text{ and}$$

$$i_2 = (1+i)^c - 1 = (1.00625)^3 - 1 = 0.01886743$$

Using formula (10-2n) to obtain n, we get

$$n = -\frac{\ln\!\left(1 - \dfrac{i \times PV}{PMT}\right)}{\ln(1+i)} = -\frac{\ln\!\left(1 - \dfrac{0.00625 \times \$226{,}773.98}{\$5000}\right)}{\ln(1.00625)} = 103.58$$

There will be 104 payments lasting 104 quarters or <u>26 years</u> after the purchase of the annuity.

Concept Questions (Section 11.3)

1. If you obtain i using the trial-and-error method presented in Appendix 11B, the calculated periodic rate is for <u>one payment interval</u>. In other words, the trial-and-error method assumes the compounding period equals the payment interval.

   If you use a financial calculator to directly obtain j, the compounding period will correspond to the value entered in the calculator for C/Y. With the Texas Instruments BA II PLUS calculator, you normally just let C/Y take on the value for by P/Y default. Then the compounding period equals the payment interval.

3. It is easiest to explain the conceptual errors in the suggested method by describing the loan scenario to which the method would properly apply. If you borrow $2180 for 1 year and pay $240 interest at the *end* of the year, the interest rate on the loan is

$$\frac{\$240}{\$2180} \times 100\% = 11.01\% \text{ compounded annually}$$

This method should not be used for the installment payment plan because the member does not have the use of the *full* $2180 for the *entire* year and some interest is paid *before* the end of the year. Both factors (but particularly the first factor) raise the effective rate above 11.01%.

Exercise 11.3

1. Given: $PV = \$27{,}207.34, \; PMT = \$4000, \; n = 10$
   Then $\quad j = $ <u>7.70% compounded annually</u>
   Since $\quad m = 1,$
   Then $\quad f = j = $ <u>7.70%</u>

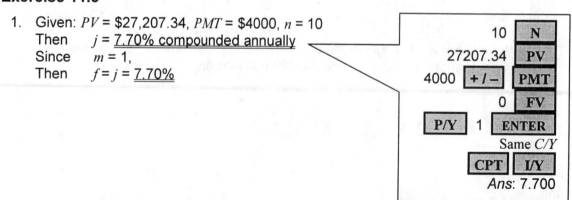

3. Given: $PV = \$50,000$, $PMT = \$1941.01$, $n = 4(7.75) = 31$
   Then $j = \underline{4.80\% \text{ compounded quarterly}}$

   $$i = \frac{j}{m} = \frac{4.80\%}{4} = 1.20\% \text{ per quarter}$$

   and $f = (1+i)^m - 1 = (1.01200)^4 - 1 = \underline{4.89\%}$

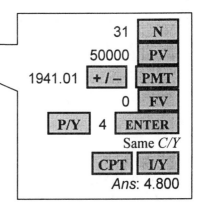

31	**N**
50000	**PV**
1941.01	**+ / −** **PMT**
0	**FV**
P/Y 4	**ENTER**

Same C/Y

CPT	**I/Y**

Ans: 4.800

5. Given: $FV = \$500,000$, $PMT = \$3030.02$, $n = 2(25) = 50$
   Then $j = \underline{8.50\% \text{ compounded semiannually}}$

   $$i = \frac{j}{m} = \frac{8.50\%}{2} = 4.25\% \text{ per half year}$$

   and $f = (1+i)^m - 1 = (1.0425)^2 - 1 = \underline{8.68\%}$

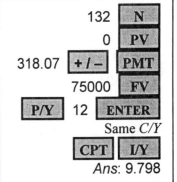

50	**N**
0	**PV**
3030.02	**+ / −** **PMT**
500000	**FV**
P/Y 2	**ENTER**

Same C/Y

CPT	**I/Y**

Ans: 8.500

7. Given: $FV = \$100,000$, $PMT = \$251.33$, $n = 12(15) + 5 = 185$
   Then $j = \underline{9.00\% \text{ compounded monthly}}$

   $$i = \frac{j}{m} = \frac{9.00\%}{12} = 0.75\% \text{ per month}$$

   and $f = (1+i)^m - 1 = (1.0075)^{12} - 1 = \underline{9.38\%}$

9. Given: $FV = \$75,000$, $PMT = \$318.07$, $n = 12(11) = 132$

   Then $j = \underline{9.80\% \text{ compounded monthly}}$

   $$i = \frac{j}{m} = \frac{9.798\%}{12} = 0.8165\% \text{ per month}$$

   and $f = (1+i)^m - 1 = (1.008165)^{12} - 1 = \underline{10.25\%}$

132	**N**
0	**PV**
318.07	**+ / −** **PMT**
75000	**FV**
P/Y 12	**ENTER**

Same C/Y

CPT	**I/Y**

Ans: 9.798

11. The purchase price represents the present value
    of the annuity. That is,
    $PV = \$100,000$ for $PMT = \$830$ and $n = 12(20) = 240$.
    Then $j = \underline{7.90\% \text{ compounded monthly}}$

    $$i = \frac{j}{m} = \frac{7.896\%}{12} = 0.65803\% \text{ per month}$$

    $$f = (1+i)^m - 1 = (1.0065803)^{12} - 1 = \underline{8.19\%}$$

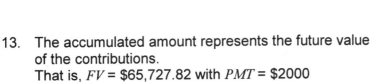

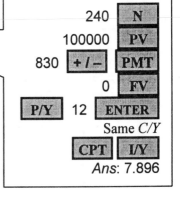

240	**N**
100000	**PV**
830	**+ / −** **PMT**
0	**FV**
P/Y 12	**ENTER**

Same C/Y

CPT	**I/Y**

Ans: 7.896

13. The accumulated amount represents the future value
    of the contributions.
    That is, $FV = \$65,727.82$ with $PMT = \$2000$
    and $n = 2(10.5) = 21$.
    Then $j = \underline{8.50\% \text{ compounded semiannually}}$

    $$i = \frac{j}{m} = \frac{8.50\%}{2} = 4.25\% \text{ per half year}$$

    and $f = (1+i)^m - 1 = (1.0425)^2 - 1 = \underline{8.68\%}$

15. The original loan equals the present value of the loan payments. That is,

    PV = \$9000, PMT = \$220.77, and n = 12(4) = 48.

    Then j = <u>8.25% compounded monthly</u>

    $i = \dfrac{j}{m} = \dfrac{8.249\%}{12} = 0.6874\%$ per month

    and $f = (1+i)^m - 1 = (1.006874)^{12} - 1 = \underline{8.57\%}$

48	**N**
9000	**PV**
220.77 **+/−**	**PMT**
0	**FV**
P/Y 12	**ENTER**
	Same *C/Y*
CPT	**I/Y**
	Ans: 8.249

17. The initial purchase price equals the present value of the annuity payments. That is,

    PV = \$150,000 with PMT = \$1200 and n = 12(20) = 240

    Then j = 7.4083% compounded monthly

    $i = \dfrac{j}{m} = \dfrac{7.4083\%}{12} = 0.61736\%$ per month

    and $f = (1+i)^m - 1 = (1.0061736)^{12} - 1 = \underline{7.67\%}$

19. The interest rate being charged is the discount rate that makes PV = \$260 for n = 12 payments of PMT = \$26. This rate is

    Then j = 35.076% compounded monthly

    $i = \dfrac{j}{m} = \dfrac{35.076\%}{12} = 2.923\%$ per month or

    and $f = (1+i)^m - 1 = (1.02923)^{12} - 1 = \underline{41.30\%}$

21. You can choose between:
    (i) borrowing \$26,198 at 0% compounded monthly;
    (ii) paying a cash price of \$23,498.
    The interest rate under the option (i) loan is the interest rate on a loan

    of \$23,498 loan for which the monthly payment is $\dfrac{\$26,198}{48}$ = \$545.79

    Therefore, determine j for the case
    PV = \$23,498, n = 48, PMT = \$545.79 and FV = 0.
    The solution is j = 5.4355% compounded monthly

    Then $i = \dfrac{j}{m}$ = 0.45296% per month and $f = (1+i)^m - 1 = (1.0045296)^{12} - 1 = \underline{5.57\%}$
    The effective interest rate for "0% financing" loan is <u>5.57%</u>.

23. The customer can choose between:
    (i) borrowing \$20,000 at 1.9% compounded monthly;
    (ii) taking the \$1250 cash rebate and borrowing \$18,750 at market rates.
    The effective interest rate under the option (i) loan is the interest rate on an \$18,750 loan that has the same monthly payment.
    Step 1: Determine the monthly payments under option (i).

    PV = \$20,000, n = 48, $i = \dfrac{1.9\%}{12} = 0.158\overline{3}\%$

    Substitution into formula (10-2) gives PMT = \$433.03.
    Step 2: Calculate j for an option (ii) loan where
    PV = \$18,750, n = 48, PMT = \$433.03.
    The solution is j = 5.1448 compounded monthly.
    Step 3: Obtain i from the value for j, and convert to an effective rate, f.

    $i = \dfrac{j}{m}$ = 0.42873% per month and $f = (1+i)^m - 1 = (1.0042873)^{12} - 1 = \underline{5.27\%}$

    The effective interest rate on the "1.9%" loan was <u>5.27%</u>.

Review Problems

1. Given: $FV = \$500,000$; $i = \frac{7.75\%}{2} = 3.875\%$; $n = 2(20) = 40$

   Substitute these values into formula (10-1) giving

   $$\$500,000 = PMT\left(\frac{1.03875^{40} - 1}{0.03875}\right)$$

   $PMT = \underline{\$5418.78}$

   Semiannual investments of $5418.78 are required.

3. The selling price of the annuity represents the present value of the annuity payments. Hence, $PV = \$100,000$ where $PMT = \$802.76$ and $n = 12(20) = 240$. Substitute into formula (10-2) and solve for i.

   $i = 0.62114\%$ per month

   $j = mi = 12(0.62114\%) = \underline{7.45\% \text{ compounded monthly}}$

   $f = (1+i)^m - 1 = (1.0062114)^{12} - 1 = \underline{7.71\%}$

5. The accumulated amount is the future value of the contributions which form an ordinary annuity. That is, $FV = \$205,064$, $PMT = \$2000$, $n = 4(13.75) = 55$

   Solving formula (10-1) for i gives $i = 2.125\%$ per quarter. Then,

   $f = (1+i)^m - 1 = (1.02125)^4 - 1 = \underline{8.78\%}$

7. The original loan equals the present value of all payments.

   With $PV = \$100,000$, $i = \frac{9\%}{12} = 0.75\%$, and $PMT = \$1000$,

   $$n = -\frac{\ln\left(1 - \dfrac{i \times PV}{PMT}\right)}{\ln(1+i)} = -\frac{\ln\left(1 - \dfrac{0.0075 \times \$100,000}{\$1000}\right)}{\ln(1.0075)} = 185.5$$

   Hence, 186 monthly payments are required to pay off the loan. If the payments are increased to $1050, we obtain $n = 167.7$. That is, only 168 payments will be required to pay off the loan. Therefore, it takes $186 - 168 = \underline{18 \text{ months longer}}$ to pay off the loan with the smaller payments.

9. The purchase price equals the present value of the annuity payments discounted at the rate of return earned by the invested funds. The payments form an ordinary general annuity having

   $$PV = \$175,000, PMT = \$4000, i = \frac{7\%}{2} = 3.5\%, c = \frac{2}{4} = 0.5$$

   $$i_2 = (1+i)^c - 1 = (1.035)^{0.5} - 1 = 0.0173495$$

   $$n = -\frac{\ln\left(1 - \dfrac{i \times PV}{PMT}\right)}{\ln(1+i)} = -\frac{\ln\left(1 - \dfrac{0.0173495 \times \$175,000}{\$4000}\right)}{\ln(1.0173495)} = 82.74$$

   The payments will continue for 83 calendar quarters or $\underline{20 \text{ years and 9 months}}$.

Review Problems (continued)

11. The original loan equals the present value of the loan payments. The payments form an ordinary general annuity having

$$PV = \$90,000, \ n = 2(10) = 20, \ i = \frac{9.75\%}{12} = 0.8125\%, \ c = \frac{12}{2} = 6$$

$$i_2 = (1+i)^c - 1 = (1.008125)^6 - 1 = 0.049751027$$

Solve for PMT in formula (10-2),

$$\$90,000 = PMT \left(\frac{1 - 1.049751027^{-20}}{0.049751027} \right)$$

$$PMT = \underline{\$7206.60}$$

13. a. Use formula (8-2) to adjust $PV = \$400,000$ for $n = 25$ years of inflation at $i = 2.5\%$ per year.

$$FV = PV(1+i)^n = \$400,000 \, (1.025)^{25} = \underline{\$741,577.64}$$

Mr. Braun should have $741,577.64 in his RRSP 25 years from now to have the same purchasing power as $400,000 current dollars.

b. The contributions form an ordinary general annuity having

$$FV = \$741,577.64, \ n = 4(25) = 100, \ i = \frac{7.5\%}{2} = 3.75\%, \ c = \frac{2}{4} = 0.5, \text{ and}$$

$$i_2 = (1+i)^c - 1 = (1.0375)^{0.5} - 1 = 0.01857744$$

Hence,
$$\$741,578 = PMT \left(\frac{1.01857744^{100} - 1}{0.01857744} \right)$$

$$PMT = \underline{\$2598.90}$$

Mr. Braun should make quarterly contributions of $2598.90.

15. The economic value of each annuity is the present value of the payments discounted at the time value of money. For the 20-year-term annuity,

$$PMT = \$394, \ n = 12(20) = 240, \ i = \frac{7.2\%}{12} = 0.6\%$$

$$PV = PMT \left[\frac{1 - (1+i)^{-n}}{i} \right] = \$394 \left(\frac{1 - 1.006^{-240}}{0.006} \right) = \$50,041.32$$

Next calculate n in order for the life annuity ($PMT = \$440$) to have the same present value.

$$n = -\frac{\ln\left(1 - \frac{i \times PV}{PMT}\right)}{\ln(1+i)} = -\frac{\ln\left(1 - \frac{0.006 \times \$50,041.32}{\$440}\right)}{\ln(1.006)} = 191.72$$

The man must live at least 192 months (16 years) beyond age 70. That is, he must live to at least age $\underline{86 \text{ years}}$ of age.

17. With a focal date 2 years and 9 months from today

$$FV \text{ of } \$30,000 = PV \text{ of ordinary simple annuity}$$

The left side of the equation is

$$FV = PV(1+i)^n = \$30,000 \, (1.0175)^{11} = \$36,307.79$$

For the PV calculation, $PV = \$36,307.79$, $i = 1.75\%$, and $PMT = \$2000$.
Then the number of payments is

$$n = -\frac{\ln\left(1 - \frac{i \times PV}{PMT}\right)}{\ln(1+i)} = -\frac{\ln\left(1 - \frac{0.0175 \times \$36,307.79}{\$2000}\right)}{\ln(1.0175)} = 22.035$$

There can be $\underline{23 \text{ withdrawals}}$ (with the last one being only about $0.035 \times \$2000 = \$70$).

Review Problems *(continued)*

19. At a focal date 8 years from now,
$$FV \text{ of } \$120,000 = PV \text{ of ordinary general annuity}$$
For the FV calculation, $PV = \$120,000$, $n = 8$, $i = 7.25\%$.
For the PV calculation, $n = 2(25) = 50$, $i = 7.25\%$, $c = \frac{1}{2} = 0.5$, and

$$i_2 = (1+i)^c - 1 = (1.0725)^{0.5} - 1 = 0.03561576$$

Hence, $\$120,000(1.0725)^8 = PMT\left(\dfrac{1 - 1.03561576^{-50}}{0.03561576}\right)$

$$PMT = \frac{\$210,067.88}{23.1973975} = \underline{\$9055.67}$$

The annuity payments will be $9055.67.

21. The nominal amount desired at age 60 is
$$FV = PV(1+i)^n = \$250,000(1.02)^{29} = \$443,961.17$$
This amount represents the future value of his RRSP contributions. That is,
$$FV = \$443,961.17 \text{ with } n = 29 \text{ and } i = 8\%.$$
Substituting in formula (10-1),

$$\$443,961.17 = PMT\left(\frac{1.08^{29} - 1}{0.08}\right)$$

$$PMT = \underline{\$4270.26}$$

Justin should make annual contributions of $4270.26.

Self-Test Exercise

1. *a.* The loan payments form an ordinary simple annuity having
$$PV = \$30,000, \quad n = 12(8) = 96, \quad i = \tfrac{7.5\%}{12} = 0.625\%$$
Substituting into formula (10-2)

$$\$30,000 = PMT\left(\frac{1 - 1.00625^{-96}}{0.00625}\right)$$

$$PMT = \underline{\$416.52}$$

b. Now, $30,000 is the combined present value of $n = 12(5) = 60$ payments and the $10,000 balance. That is,

$$\$30,000 = PMT\left(\frac{1 - 1.00625^{-60}}{0.00625}\right) + \$10,000(1.00625)^{-60}$$

Solving for PMT gives $PMT = \underline{\$463.26}$.

2. With $PV = \$65,000$, $PMT = \$625$, and $i = \tfrac{7.2\%}{12} = 0.6\%$,

$$n = -\frac{\ln\left(1 - \dfrac{i \times PV}{PMT}\right)}{\ln(1+i)} = \frac{\ln\left(1 - \dfrac{0.006 \times \$65,000}{\$625}\right)}{\ln(1.006)} = 163.52$$

Thus, 164 payments are required to satisfy the loan. With PMT reduced to $600, we obtain $n = 175.49$. That is, 176 payments are required. The larger payments will pay off the loan (176 – 164) months = 12 months = <u>1 year sooner</u>.
The interest savings are approximately
$$175.49(\$600) - 163.52(\$625) \approx \underline{\$3094}.$$

3. Given: $PMT = \$2000$, $n = 2(20) = 40$, $FV = \$250,000$
   Substitute into formula (10-1) and solve for i. The solution is
   $i = 5.140\%$ per half year and

   $$f = (1+i)^m - 1 = (1.0514)^2 - 1 = \underline{10.54\%}$$

4. The payments form an ordinary general annuity having
   $$FV = \$15,000, \ n = 4(8.5) = 34, \ i = 7.5\%, \ c = \frac{1}{4} = 0.25, \text{ and}$$

   $$i_2 = (1+i)^c - 1 = (1.075)^{0.25} - 1 = 0.01824460$$

   Substitute into formula (10-1).

   $$\$15,000 = PMT\left(\frac{1.0182446^{34} - 1}{0.0182446}\right)$$

   $$PMT = \underline{\$322.29}$$

   Quarterly payments of $322.29 are required.

5. *a.* The original loan equals the present value of all payments.
   $$PV = \$90,000, \ n = 12(20) = 240, \ i = \frac{7.9\%}{12} = 3.95\%, \ c = \frac{2}{12} = 0.1\overline{6}, \text{ and}$$

   $$i_2 = (1+i)^c - 1 = (1.0395)^{0.1\overline{6}} - 1 = 0.006477527$$

   Hence, $\quad \$90,000 = PMT\left(\dfrac{1 - 1.006477527^{-240}}{0.006477527}\right)$

   $$PMT = \underline{\$740.13}$$

   b. If $PMT = \$800$ instead of $\$740.13$,

   $$n = -\frac{\ln\left(1 - \dfrac{i \times PV}{PMT}\right)}{\ln(1+i)} = -\frac{\ln\left(1 - \dfrac{0.006477527 \times \$90,000}{\$800}\right)}{\ln(1.006477527)} = 202.06$$

   It will take 203 months or <u>16 years and 11 months</u> to pay off the loan.

6. With the focal date at the date of the last $500 contribution,
   $$FV \text{ of the contributions} = PV \text{ of } \$13,232.56$$

   For the PV calculation, $FV = \$13,232.56$, $i = \frac{7.5\%}{4} = 1.875\%$, $n = 4(3) = 12$

   Then $\quad PV = FV(1+i)^{-n} = \$13,232.56(1.01875)^{-12} = \$10,588.45$
   For the FV calculation, $FV = \$10,588.45$, $PMT = \$500$, and $i = 1.875\%$

   Then $\quad n = \dfrac{\ln\left(1 + \dfrac{i \times FV}{PMT}\right)}{\ln(1+i)} = \dfrac{\ln\left(1 + \dfrac{0.01875 \times \$10,588.45}{\$500}\right)}{\ln(1.01875)} = \underline{18.00}$

   Eighteen contributions of $500 were made.

7. At the focal date 23 months from now,
$$FV \text{ of } \$3,500,000 = PV \text{ of ordinary simple annuity}$$
For the FV calculation, $PV = \$3,500,000$, $i = 0.75\%$, and $n = 23$.
$$FV = \$3,500,000(1.0075)^{23} = \$4,156,275.29$$
On the right side of the word equation, $FV = \$4,156,275.29$, $PMT = \$40,000$, and $i = 0.75\%$. Using formula (10-2n) to obtain n, we have
$$n = -\frac{\ln\left(1 - \dfrac{i \times PV}{PMT}\right)}{\ln(1+i)} = -\frac{\ln\left(1 - \dfrac{0.0075 \times \$4,156,275.29}{\$40,000}\right)}{\ln(1.0075)} = 202.22 \text{ payments}$$
To extinguish the loan, 203 monthly payments will be required. Measured from the date of the *first* payment, it will take 202 months or <u>16 years and 10 months</u>.

8. Viewed from the date each trust is set up, the payments each child will receive form a deferred general annuity whose present value is $20,000. That is,
$$PV = \$20,000, \ n = 4(15) = 60, \ i = \frac{9.25\%}{2} = 4.625\%, \ c = \frac{2}{4} = 0.5 \text{ and}$$
$$i_2 = (1+i)^c - 1 = (1.04625)^{0.5} - 1 = 0.022863627$$
Lena will receive her first payments in 5 years. At a focal date 4.75 years from now,
$$FV \text{ of } \$20,000 = PV \text{ of ordinary annuity}$$
$$\$20,000(1.022863627)^{19} = PMT\left(\frac{1 - 1.022863627^{-60}}{0.022863627}\right)$$
$$PMT = \frac{\$30,730.31}{32.47105} = \underline{\$946.39}$$
Axel will receive his first payment in 9.5 years. At a focal date 9.25 years from now,
$$FV \text{ of } \$20,000 = PV \text{ of ordinary annuity}$$
$$\$20,000(1.022863627)^{37} = PMT\left(\frac{1 - 1.022863627^{-60}}{0.022863627}\right)$$
$$PMT = \$46,162.17 \div 32.471047 = \underline{\$1421.64}$$
Lena will receive quarterly payments of $946.39 and Axel will receive quarterly payments of $1421.64.

12 Annuities: Special Situations

Concept Questions (Section 12.1)

1. The <u>perpetuity has the larger present value</u>. The greater the number of payments in an annuity, the larger the annuity's present value. Hence, PV(perpetuity) $>$ PV(annuity).
   Alternatively, the perpetuity may be viewed as a combination of an annuity identical to the given annuity and a deferred perpetuity. Then
   PV of given perpetuity = (PV of given annuity) + (PV of deferred perpetuity)
   Therefore, PV of given perpetuity $>$ PV of given annuity

3. The market value will <u>rise</u>. The rate of return (dividend yield) is the (fixed) annual dividend calculated as a percentage of the market value. If investors will accept a lower rate of return, they will pay a higher price for the shares.

Exercise 12.1

1. The $125,000 gift is the present value of the payments.
   $PMT = i \times PV = 0.05 \times \$125,000 = \underline{\$6250.00}$

3. Given: $PMT = \$10,000$

   With $i = \frac{6\%}{2} = 3\%$, $PV = \dfrac{PMT}{i} = \dfrac{\$10,000}{0.033} = \$333,333.33$

   With $i = \frac{5\%}{2} = 2.5\%$, $PV = \dfrac{PMT}{i} = \dfrac{\$10,000}{0.025} = \$400,000.00$

   Therefore, $400,000.00 - $333,333.33 = $\underline{\$66,666.67}$ less is required to fund the perpetuity at the higher rate of return.

5. The amount required to fund each case is the present value of the payments.

   For the perpetuity, $PV = \dfrac{PMT}{i} = \dfrac{\$1000}{0.015} = \$66,666.67$

   For the annuity, $PV = PMT\left[\dfrac{1-(1+i)^{-n}}{i}\right] = \$1000\left(\dfrac{1-1.015^{-120}}{0.015}\right) = \$55,498.45$

   You need $66,666.67 - $55,498.45 = $\underline{\$11,168.22}$ more money to fund the perpetuity.

7. The owner should be willing to accept the current economic value of the stream of future payments. This economic value equals the present value of the future payments. On the date of the next scheduled payment, the payments consist of a simple perpetuity plus the payment due on that date. Hence,

   $PV = \$500 + \dfrac{PMT}{i} = \$500 + \dfrac{\$500}{0.058} = \underline{\$9120.69}$

   The landowner should be willing to accept $9120.69.

9. Price = $500 + Present value of quarterly payments
   The quarterly payments form an ordinary general perpetuity having

   $PMT = \$15$, $i = 6.5\%$, and $c = \frac{1}{4} = 0.25$

   $i_2 = (1+i)^c - 1 = (1.065)^{0.25} - 1 = 0.015868285$

   $PV = \dfrac{PMT}{i_2} = \dfrac{\$15}{0.015868285} = \$945.28$

   Price of a plot = $500 + $945.28 = $\underline{\$1445.28}$

Exercise 12.1 *(continued)*

11. *a.* The price equals the present value of the dividends discounted at the required rate of return. Since the next dividend is about to be paid, the dividends form a simple perpetuity *after* the first payment. With $PMT = \$3.00$ and $i = \frac{6.5\%}{2} = 3.25\%$.

$$\text{Price} = \$1.50 + \frac{PMT}{i} = \$1.50 + \frac{\$1.50}{0.0225} = \underline{\$68.17}$$

b. Price = Present value of the payments

$$= PMT + \frac{PMT}{i}$$

$$\$70 = \$1.50 + \frac{\$1.50}{i}$$

$$i = \frac{\$1.50}{\$70 - \$1.50} = 0.02190 = 2.190\% \text{ per half year}$$

$$j = mi = 2(2.190\%) = \underline{4.38\% \text{ compounded semiannually}}$$

13. *a.* The payments form a general perpetuity having

$$PMT = \$1000, \ i = \frac{5.5\%}{2} = 2.75\%, \ c = \frac{2}{4} = 0.5, \text{ and}$$

$$i_2 = (1+i)^c - 1 = (1.0275)^{0.5} - 1 = 0.013656747$$

The initial amount needed to sustain the perpetuity is

$$PV = \frac{PMT}{i_2} = \frac{\$1000}{0.013656747} = \underline{\$73,223.88}$$

b. The present value of the payments 9 months from now is the amount calculated in part *a*, that is, $73,223.88. The present value today is

$$PV = FV(1+i)^{-n} = \$73,223.88\,(1.013656747)^{-3} = \underline{\$70,303.99}$$

15. At a focal date 2 years and 9 months from now,

$$FV \text{ of } \$1 \text{ million donation} = PV \text{ of ordinary simple perpetuity}$$

For the FV calculation, $PV = \$1,000,000$, $n = 4(2.75) = 11$, and $i = \frac{6\%}{4} = 1.5\%$

$$FV = PV(1+i)^n = \$1,000,000\,(1.015)^{11} = \$1,177,948.94$$

For the perpetuity, $PV = \$1,177,948.94$ and $i = 1.5\%$. Hence,

$$PMT = i \times PV = 0.015 \times \$1,177,948.94 = \underline{\$17,669.23}$$

Quarterly payments of $17,669.23 will be made.

17. At a focal date today,

$$FV \text{ of the } \$500,000 \text{ bequest} = PV \text{ of the ordinary perpetuity}$$

For the FV calculation, $PV = \$500,000$, $i = \frac{5\%}{2} = 2.5\%$, and $n = 2(1.5) = 3$. Hence,

$$FV = PV(1+i)^n = \$500,000\,(1.025)^3 = \$538,445.31$$

The quarterly payments form an ordinary general perpetuity having

$$PV = \$538,445.31, \ i = \frac{5.2\%}{2} = 2.6\%, \ c = \frac{2}{4} = 0.5, \text{ and}$$

$$i_2 = (1+i)^c - 1 = (1.026)^{0.5} - 1 = 0.012916581$$

Then $PMT = i_2 \times PV = 0.012916581(\$538,445.31) = \underline{\$6954.87}$

The hospice will receive quarterly payments of $6954.87.

Concept Questions (Section 12.2)

1. <u>No</u>. In this section constant growth means that each successive payment increases by the <u>same percentage</u>.

Exercise 12.2

1. The amount in the RRSP will be the future value of the contributions, which form a constant-growth ordinary simple annuity.
   Given: $PMT = \$3000$, $g = 2.5\%$, $n = 25$, and $i = 9\%$. Then,

$$FV = PMT\left[\frac{(1+i)^n - (1+g)^n}{i-g}\right] = \$3000\left(\frac{1.09^{25} - 1.025^{25}}{0.09 - 0.025}\right) = \underline{\$312{,}421.69}$$

3. Given: $FV = \$750{,}000$, $n = 30$, $g = 3\%$, and $i = 10\%$. Substitute into

$$FV = PMT\left[\frac{(1+i)^n - (1+g)^n}{i-g}\right]$$

$$\$750{,}000 = PMT\left(\frac{1.10^{30} - 1.03^{30}}{0.10 - 0.03}\right) = PMT(214.601997$$

$$PMT = \underline{\$3494.84}$$

5. For the fixed-payment annuity,

$$PMT = \$1000, \ n = 12(25) = 300, \ i = \frac{5.4\%}{12} = 0.45\%, \ \text{and}$$

$$\text{Price} = PV = PMT\left[\frac{1-(1+i)^{-n}}{i}\right] = \$1000\left(\frac{1 - 1.0045^{-300}}{0.0045}\right) = \$164{,}438.55$$

For the indexed annuity, $g = \frac{2.4\%}{12} = 0.2\%$ per month and

$$\text{Price} = PMT\left[\frac{1-(1+g)^n(1+i)^{-n}}{i-g}\right] = \$1000\left[\frac{1 - \left(1.002^{300}\right)\left(1.0045^{-300}\right)}{0.0045 - 0.002}\right] = \$210{,}593.83$$

Indexation of the annuity costs $\$210{,}593.83 - \$164{,}438.55 = \underline{\$46{,}155.28}$ more.

7. The current economic value of future pension payments is their present value.
   Given: $PMT = \$20{,}000$, $n = 25$, $i = 5\%$
   With indexation (at $g = 2.5\%$ per year),

$$PV = PMT\left[\frac{1-(1+g)^n(1+i)^{-n}}{i-g}\right] = \$20{,}000\left[\frac{1 - \left(1.025^{25}\right)\left(1.05^{-25}\right)}{0.05 - 0.025}\right] = \underline{\$362{,}020.14}$$

Without indexation ($g = 0\%$),

$$PV = PMT\left[\frac{1-(1+i)^{-n}}{i}\right] = \$20{,}000\left(\frac{1 - 1.05^{-25}}{0.05}\right) = \$281{,}878.89$$

Hence, $\$362{,}020.14 - \$281{,}878.89 = \underline{\$80{,}141.25}$ (representing 22.1%) of the pension's economic value comes from the indexation feature.

Exercise 12.2 *(continued)*

9. At a focal date at the end of the 30-year contributory period,

$$FV \text{ of RRSP contributions} = PV \text{ of RRIF withdrawals}$$

For the FV calculation,

$PMT = \$2000$, $n = 30$, $g = 3\%$, and $i = 9\%$. Then,

$$FV = PMT\left[\frac{(1+i)^n - (1+g)^n}{i-g}\right] = \$2000\left(\frac{1.09^{30} - 1.03^{30}}{0.09 - 0.03}\right) = \$361,347.20$$

For the PV calculation,

$PV = \$361,347.20$, $n = 12(25) = 300$, $g = \frac{1.8\%}{12} = 0.15\%$, and $i = \frac{6\%}{12} = 0.5\%$

Substitute into

$$PV = PMT\left[\frac{1-(1+g)^n(1+i)^{-n}}{i-g}\right]$$

$$\$361,347.20 = PMT\left[\frac{1-(1.0015^{300})(1.005^{-300})}{0.005 - 0.0015}\right]$$

$$= PMT(185.391515)$$

$$PMT = \underline{\$1949.10}$$

The initial RRIF withdrawal will be $1949.10.

11. Market value of shares = PV of dividends

The dividends in the first 5 years form a constant growth ordinary simple annuity.
The dividends in the next 25 years form another constant growth ordinary simple annuity.

For the first 5 years,

$PMT = \$2.00(1.10) = \$2.20$, $n = 5$, $g = 10\%$, and $i = 9\%$.

For the next 25 years,

$PMT = \$2.00(1.10)^5(1.03) = \$3.318$, $n = 25$, $g = 3\%$, and $i = 9\%$.

At a focal date 5 years from now, the PV of the subsequent 25 years' dividends is

$$PV = PMT\left[\frac{1-(1+g)^n(1+i)^{-n}}{i-g}\right] = \$3.318\left[\frac{1-(1.03^{25})(1.09^{-25})}{0.09 - 0.03}\right] = \$41.873$$

The PV today of this amount and the first 5 years' dividends is

$$PV = \$41.873(1.09)^{-5} + \$2.20\left[\frac{1-(1.10^5)(1.09^{-5})}{0.09 - 0.10}\right]$$

$$= \$27.214 + \$10.279$$

$$= \underline{\$37.49}$$

The fair market value of the shares is $37.49.

Review Problems

1. The amount required to fund an annuity or a perpetuity is the present value of the payments. For a perpetuity having $PMT = \$1000$ and $i = 6\%$,

$$PV = \frac{PMT}{i} = \frac{\$1000}{0.06} = \$16,666.67$$

For the annuity having $PMT = \$1000$, $n = 25$, and $i = 6\%$,

$$PV = PMT\left[\frac{1-(1+i)^{-n}}{i}\right] = \$1000\left(\frac{1-1.06^{-25}}{0.06}\right) = \$12,783.36$$

Therefore,

$$\frac{\$16,666.67 - \$12,783.36}{\$12,783.36} \times 100\% = \underline{30.38\%}$$

more funds are needed to fund the perpetuity.

3. The amount that must be dedicated today is the present value of the future payments.
   a. The payments form an ordinary simple perpetuity having

   $PMT = \$2000$ and $i = \frac{5.6\%}{4} = 1.4\%$.

   $$PV = \frac{PMT}{i} = \frac{\$2000}{0.014} = \underline{\$142,857.14}$$

   b. The payments form a deferred ordinary simple perpetuity having a 4-year plus 9-month period of deferral. The PV of the payments on that date is the amount calculated in part a. The PV of this amount today is

   $$PV = FV(1+i)^{-n} = \$142,857.14(1.014)^{-19} = \underline{\$109,693.48}$$

5. The amount required to fund an annuity or a perpetuity is the present value of the payments. For the perpetuity, $PMT = \$500$, $i = \frac{7\%}{4} = 1.75\%$, $c = \frac{4}{12} = 0.\overline{3}$, and

   $$i_2 = (1+i)^c - 1 = 1.0175^{0.\overline{3}} - 1 = 0.0057996326$$

   $$PV = \frac{PMT}{i_2} = \frac{\$500}{0.0057996326} = \$86,212.36$$

   For the annuity having $PMT = \$500$, $n = 12(25) = 300$, and $i_2 = 0.57996326\%$,

   $$PV = PMT\left[\frac{1-(1+i_2)^{-n}}{i_2}\right] = \$500\left(\frac{1-1.0057996326^{-300}}{0.0057996326}\right) = \$71,002.41$$

   Therefore, $\$86,212.36 - \$71,002.41 = \underline{\$15,209.95}$ more is required to fund the perpetuity.

Self-Test Exercise

1. The payments form a deferred perpetuity having a 4.5-year period of deferral. At a focal date 4.5 years after the donation,

$$FV \text{ of } \$100,000 \text{ donation} = PV \text{ of perpetuity}$$

For the FV calculation, $PV = \$100,000$, $n = 2(4.5) = 9$, and $i = \frac{5\%}{2} = 2.5\%$

$$FV = PV(1+i)^n = \$100,000(1.025)^9 = \$124,886.30$$

For the perpetuity on the right side,

$$PV = \$124,886.30 \text{ and } i = 2.5\%$$

Hence, $\$124,886.30 = \dfrac{PMT}{0.025}$

$$PMT = \underline{\$3122.16}$$

The semiannual payments in perpetuity will be $3122.16.

2. We have a perpetuity with $PV = \$200,000$ and $i = \frac{5.4\%}{12} = 0.45\%$

The monthly payments will be

$$PMT = i \times PV = 0.0045 \times \$200,000 = \underline{\$900}$$

3. The amount required to fund the perpetuity is today's present value of the deferred perpetuity. The present value, 1 year from now, of the annual scholarship is

$$PV = \frac{PMT}{i} = \frac{\$5000}{0.0625} = \$80,000$$

The present value of this amount 1 year earlier is

$$PV = FV(1+i)^{-n} = \frac{\$80,000}{1.0625^1} = \underline{\$75,294.12}$$

Mrs. McTavish must pay $75,294.12 to establish the perpetual scholarship fund.

4. The amount required to fund an annuity or a perpetuity is the present value of the payments. For a perpetuity having $PMT = \$1000$ and $i = \frac{5.8\%}{2} = 2.9\%$,

$$PV = \frac{PMT}{i} = \frac{\$1000}{0.029} = \$34,482.76$$

For the annuity having $PMT = \$1000$, $n = 2(30) = 60$, and $i = 2.9\%$,

$$PV = PMT\left[\frac{1-(1+i)^{-n}}{i}\right] = \$1000\left(\frac{1-1.029^{-60}}{0.029}\right) = \$28,278.65$$

Therefore,

$$\frac{\$34,482.76 - \$28,278.65}{\$28,278.65} \times 100\% = \underline{21.94\%}$$

more funds are needed to fund the perpetuity.

13 Annuities Due

Concept Questions (Section 13.1)

1. Insurance premium payments, rent payments, lease payments, newspaper and magazine subscriptions, membership dues.

3. Each payment in an annuity due earns interest for *one more* payment interval than the corresponding payment in an ordinary annuity.

Exercise 13.1

1. Given: $PMT = \$325$, $n = 12(7.25) = 87$, $i = \frac{6\%}{12} = 0.5\%$

$$FV(\text{due}) = PMT\left[\frac{(1+i)^n - 1}{i}\right] \times (1+i)$$

$$= \$325\left(\frac{1.005^{87} - 1}{0.005}\right)(1.005)$$

$$= \underline{\$35,490.38}$$

BGN mode

87 N
6 I/Y
0 PV
325 PMT
P/Y 12 ENTER
Same C/Y
CPT FV
Ans: −35,490.38

3. Given: $PMT = \$329$, $n = 2(8.5) = 17$, $i = \frac{8.75\%}{2} = 4.375\%$

$$FV(\text{due}) = PMT\left[\frac{(1+i)^n - 1}{i}\right] \times (1+i) = \$329\left(\frac{1.04375^{17} - 1}{0.04375}\right)(1.04375) = \underline{\$8404.79}$$

5. Given: $PMT = \$500$, $n = 12(4) = 48$, $i = j = 6.5\%$, $c = \dfrac{\text{Compoundings per year}}{\text{Payments per year}} = \frac{1}{4} = 0.25$

$$i_2 = (1+i)^c - 1 = (1.065)^{0.25} - 1 = 0.0158682848$$

$$FV(\text{due}) = PMT\left[\frac{(1+i)^n - 1}{i}\right] \times (1+i)$$

$$= \$500\left(\frac{1.0158682848^{48} - 1}{0.0158682848}\right)(1.0158682848)$$

$$= \underline{\$36,141.68}$$

7. Given: $PMT = \$3000$, $n = 2(4.5) = 9$, $i = \frac{8\%}{12} = 0.\overline{6}\%$,

$$c = \frac{\text{Compoundings per year}}{\text{Payments per year}} = \frac{12}{2} = 6; \quad i_2 = (1+i)^c - 1 = (1.00\overline{6})^6 - 1 = 0.04067622$$

$$FV(\text{due}) = PMT\left[\frac{(1+i)^n - 1}{i}\right](1+i) = \$3000\left(\frac{1.04067622^9 - 1}{0.04067622}\right)(1.04067622) = \underline{\$33,130.87}$$

9. Given: $PMT = \$2500$, $n = 16$, $i = \frac{5.25\%}{12} = 0.875\%$,

$$c = \frac{\text{Compoundings per year}}{\text{Payments per year}} = \frac{12}{1} = 12$$

$$i_2 = (1+i)^c - 1 = (1.004375)^{12} - 1 = 0.0537818867$$

$$FV(\text{due}) = \$2500\left(\frac{1.0537818867^{16} - 1}{0.0537818867}\right)(1.0537818867)$$

$$= \underline{\$64,273.29}$$

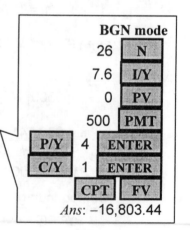

BGN mode

16   N
5.25   I/Y
0   PV
2500   PMT
P/Y   1   ENTER
C/Y   12   ENTER
CPT   FV
Ans: –64,273.29

11. *a.* Given: $PMT = \$100$, $n = 300$, $i = \frac{6\%}{12} = 0.5\%$

$$FV(\text{due}) = PMT\left[\frac{(1+i)^n - 1}{i}\right] \times (1+i)$$

$$= \$100\left(\frac{1.005^{300} - 1}{0.005}\right)(1.005)$$

$$= \underline{\$69,645.89}$$

BGN mode

300   N
6   I/Y
0   PV
100   PMT
P/Y   12   ENTER
Same C/Y
CPT   FV
Ans: –69,645.89

b. If instead, $i = \frac{8\%}{12} = 0.\overline{6}\%$

$$FV(\text{due}) = \$100\left(\frac{1.00\overline{6}^{300} - 1}{0.00\overline{6}}\right)(1.00\overline{6})$$

$$= \underline{\$95,736.66}$$

BGN mode
Same *N, PMT, PV*
8   I/Y
Same *P/Y, C/Y*
CPT   FV
Ans: –95,736.66

13. *a.* Given: $PMT = \$500$, $n = 4(6.5) = 26$, $i = \frac{7.6\%}{1} = 7.6\%$,

$$c = \frac{\text{Compoundings per year}}{\text{Payments per year}} = \frac{1}{4} = 0.25$$

$$i_2 = (1+i)^c - 1 = (1.0076)^{0.25} - 1 = 0.0184813196$$

$$FV(\text{due}) = \$2500\left(\frac{1.0537818867^{16} - 1}{0.0537818867}\right)(1.0537818867)$$

$$= \underline{\$16,803.44}$$

Amount in mutual fund will be $16,803.44.

b. Earnings = $16,803.44 – 26($500) = $\underline{\$3803.44}$

BGN mode

26   N
7.6   I/Y
0   PV
500   PMT
P/Y   4   ENTER
C/Y   1   ENTER
CPT   FV
Ans: –16,803.44

15. Given: $PMT = \$1000$, $n = 12(5) = 60$, $i = \frac{6\%}{12} = 0.5\%$

$$FV(\text{due}) = PMT\left[\frac{(1+i)^n - 1}{i}\right] \times (1+i) = \$1000\left(\frac{1.005^{60} - 1}{0.005}\right)(1.005) = \underline{\$70,118.88}$$

17. With August 1, 2017 as the focal date, the RRSP contributions form a simple annuity due. The amount in the RRSP will be the future value of previous contributions.

With $PMT = \$1500$, $n = 2(27.5) = 55$, and $i = \frac{8.5\%}{2} = 4.25\%$,

$$FV(\text{due}) = PMT\left[\frac{(1+i)^n - 1}{i}\right] \times (1+i) = \$1500\left(\frac{1.0425^{55} - 1}{0.0425}\right)(1.0425) = \underline{\$326,252.08}$$

Interest portion = Amount in RRSP – Contributions
$$= \$326,252.08 - 55(\$1500)$$
$$= \underline{\$243,752.08}$$

19. Given: $PMT = \$2000$, $n = 2(25) = 50$, $i = 8.25\%$, $c = \dfrac{\text{Compoundings per year}}{\text{Payments per year}} = \dfrac{1}{2} = 0.5$

$$i_2 = (1+i)^c - 1 = (1.0825)^{0.5} - 1 = 0.040432602$$

$$FV(\text{due}) = PMT\left[\frac{(1+i)^n - 1}{i}\right] \times (1+i) = \$2000\left(\frac{1.040432602^{50} - 1}{0.040432602}\right) = \underline{\$321,965.55}$$

The value of the RRSP in 25 years will be $321,965.55.

21. a. For the monthly contributions, $PMT = \$400$, $n = 12(25) = 300$, $i = \frac{7.5\%}{12} = 0.625\%$

For the annual contributions, $PMT = \$2000$, $n = 25$, $i = 0.625\%$, and

$$c = \frac{\text{Compoundings per year}}{\text{Payments per year}} = \frac{12}{1} = 12$$

and $i_2 = (1+i)^c - 1 = (1.00625)^{12} - 1 = 0.0776325989$

$$FV(\text{due}) = \$400\left(\frac{1.00625^{300} - 1}{0.00625}\right)(1.00625)$$

$$+ \$2000\left(\frac{1.0776325989^{25} - 1}{0.0776325989}\right)(1.0776325989)$$

$$= \$353,097.50 + \$152,217.77$$
$$= \underline{\$505,315}$$

The plan will be worth $505,315 after 25 years.

b. Earnings = $\$505,315 - 300(\$400) - 25(\$2000) = \underline{\$335,315}$

23. The amount in Fay's RRSP on her 31st birthday was

$$FV(\text{due}) = PMT\left[\frac{(1+i)^n - 1}{i}\right] \times (1+i) = \$3000\left(\frac{1.08^{10} - 1}{0.08}\right)(1.08) = \$46,936.462$$

The future value of this amount at age 65 (34 years later) will be
$$FV = \$46,936.462(1.08)^{34} = \underline{\$642,566.44}$$

The amount in Fred's RRSP on his 65th birthday will be

$$FV(\text{due}) = PMT\left[\frac{(1+i)^n - 1}{i}\right] \times (1+i) = \$3000\left(\frac{1.08^{34} - 1}{0.08}\right)(1.08) = \underline{\$513,950.41}$$

Fay will have
$$\$642,566.44 - \$513,950.41 = \underline{\$128,616.03}$$
more in her RRSP at age 65 than Fred will have at age 65.

Concept Questions (Section 13.2)

1. The focal date is at the beginning of the *first* payment interval. Since payments are at the *beginning* of each payment interval, the focal date <u>coincides with the first payment</u>.

3. Since $\quad\quad PV(\text{due}) = PV \times (1+i)$
   then $PV(\text{due})$ is $i\%$ larger than PV. In the particular case at hand, $PV(\text{due})$ will exceed PV by <u>3%</u>.

Exercise 13.2

1. Given: $PMT = \$325$, $n = 12(7.25) = 87$, $i = \frac{6\%}{12} = 0.5\%$

$$PV(\text{due}) = PMT\left[\frac{1-(1+i)^{-n}}{i}\right] \times (1+i) = \$325\left(\frac{1-1.005^{-87}}{0.005}\right)(1.005) = \underline{\$22,996.58}$$

3. Given: $PMT = \$329$, $n = 2(8.5) = 17$, $i = \frac{8.75\%}{2} = 4.375\%$

$$PV(\text{due}) = PMT\left[\frac{1-(1+i)^{-n}}{i}\right] \times (1+i) = \$329\left(\frac{1-1.04375^{-17}}{0.04375}\right)(1.04375) = \underline{\$4058.70}$$

5. Given: $PMT = \$500$, $n = 4(12) = 48$, $i = j = 6.5\%$,

$$c = \frac{\text{Compoundings per year}}{\text{Payments per year}} = \frac{1}{4} = 0.25$$

$$i_2 = (1+i)^c - 1 = (1.065)^{0.25} - 1 = 0.0158682848$$

$$PV(\text{due}) = PMT\left[\frac{1-(1+i)^{-n}}{i}\right](1+i)$$

$$= \$500\left(\frac{1.0158682848^{-48} - 1}{0.0158682848}\right)(1.0158682848)$$

$$= \underline{\$16,975.13}$$

	BGN mode
48	N
6.5	I/Y
500	PMT
0	FV
P/Y 4	ENTER
C/Y 1	ENTER
CPT	PV

$Ans: -16,975.13$

7. Given: $PMT = \$3000$, $n = 2(4.5) = 9$, $i = \frac{8\%}{12} = 0.\overline{6}\%$, $c = \frac{12}{2} = 6$

$$i_2 = (1+i)^c - 1 = (1.00\overline{6})^6 - 1 = 0.040672622$$

$$PV(\text{due}) = PMT\left[\frac{1-(1+i)^{-n}}{i}\right] \times (1+i)$$

$$= \$3000\left(\frac{1-1.040672622^{-9}}{0.040672622}\right)(1.040672622) = \underline{\$23,142.25}$$

9. Given: $PMT = \$2500$, $n = 16$, $i = \frac{5.25\%}{12} = 0.4375\%$, $c = \frac{12}{1} = 12$

$$i_2 = (1+i)^c - 1 = (1.004375)^{12} - 1 = 0.0537818867$$

$$PV(\text{due}) = PMT\left[\frac{1-(1+i)^{-n}}{i}\right] \times (1+i)$$

$$= \$2500\left(\frac{1-1.0537818867^{-16}}{0.0537818867}\right)(1.0537818867) = \underline{\$27,798.34}$$

Exercise 13.2 *(continued)*

11. a. Given: $PMT = \$1000$, $n = 2(25) = 50$, $i = \frac{6\%}{2} = 3\%$

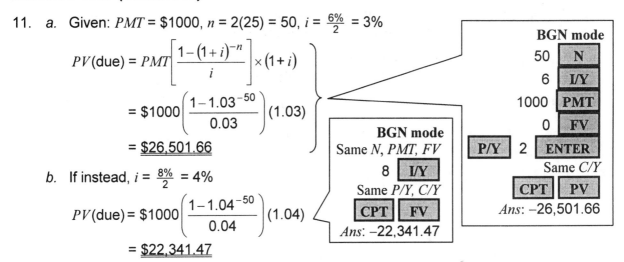

$$PV(\text{due}) = PMT\left[\frac{1-(1+i)^{-n}}{i}\right] \times (1+i)$$

$$= \$1000\left(\frac{1-1.03^{-50}}{0.03}\right)(1.03)$$

$$= \underline{\$26,501.66}$$

b. If instead, $i = \frac{8\%}{2} = 4\%$

$$PV(\text{due}) = \$1000\left(\frac{1-1.04^{-50}}{0.04}\right)(1.04)$$

$$= \underline{\$22,341.47}$$

13. a. Purchase price = Present value of payments (which form a simple annuity due.)
   With $PMT = \$60.26$, $n = 30$, $i = \frac{18\%}{12} = 1.5\%$,

$$PV(\text{due}) = PMT\left[\frac{1-(1+i)^{-n}}{i}\right] \times (1+i) = \$60.26\left(\frac{1-1.015^{-30}}{0.015}\right)(1.015) = \underline{\$1468.90}$$

   The purchase price was $1468.90.

   b. Interest paid = 30($60.26) − $1468.90 = $\underline{\$338.90}$.

15. The economic value of the jackpot on the date of the first payment is the present value of the payments discounted at the time value of money. The twenty payments constitute an annuity due.
   a. Given: $PMT = \$4.38$ million, $n = 20$, $i = 7\%$

$$PV(\text{due}) = PMT\left[\frac{1-(1+i)^{-n}}{i}\right] \times (1+i)$$

$$= (\$4.38 \text{ million})\left(\frac{1-1.07^{-20}}{0.07}\right)(1.07) = \underline{\$49.650 \text{ million}}$$

   If money was worth 7% compounded annually, the economic value of the jackpot was $49.65 million (not 20 × $4.38 million = $87.6 million.)

   b. Similarly, if $i = 6\%$, we obtain
      $PV(\text{due}) = \underline{\$53.253 \text{ million}}$
      for the jackpot's economic value on the date of the first payment.

17. The current economic value of Rosie's offer is the present value of her payments. The payments form a simple annuity due having
   $PMT = \$1900$, $n = 5$, $i = 5\%$

$$PV(\text{due}) = PMT\left[\frac{1-(1+i)^{-n}}{i}\right] \times (1+i) = \$1900\left(\frac{1-1.05^{-5}}{0.05}\right)(1.05) = \$8637.31$$

   Rosie Senario's offer is worth $8637.31 − $8500 = $\underline{\$137.31 \text{ more}}$ in current dollars.

Exercise 13.2 *(continued)*

19. The amount required in the RRIF is the present value of the withdrawals.
    Given: $PMT = \$32{,}500$, $n = 15$, $i = 7\%$

$$PV\text{(due)} = PMT\left[\frac{1-(1+i)^{-n}}{i}\right]\times(1+i) = \$32{,}500\left(\frac{1-1.07^{-15}}{0.07}\right)(1.07) = \underline{\$316{,}727.71}$$

Karsten must have $316,727.71 in his RRIF at age 65.

21. The required amount of money is the present value of the payments.
    The payments form a general annuity due having

$PMT = \$1200$, $n = 12(15) = 180$, $i = \frac{9\%}{2} = 4.5\%$, $c = \frac{2}{12} = 0.1\overline{6}$

$$i_2 = (1+i)^c - 1 = (1.045)^{0.1\overline{6}} - 1 = 0.0073631230$$

$$PV\text{(due)} = PMT\left[\frac{1-(1+i)^{-n}}{i}\right]\times(1+i)$$

$$= \$1200\left(\frac{1-1.0073631230^{-180}}{0.0073631230}\right)(1.0073631230) = \underline{\$120{,}339.78}$$

$120,339.78 is the initial lump amount required to sustain the withdrawals.

23. a. The initial lease liability is the present value of all payments discounted at the cost of borrowing. The payments form a simple annuity due having
    $PMT = \$2700$, $n = 12(5) = 60$, and $i = \frac{9\%}{12} = 0.75\%$

$$\text{Lease liability} = \$2700\left(\frac{1-1.0075^{-60}}{0.0075}\right)(1.0075) = \underline{\$131{,}043.62}$$

   b. After the first year, 48 payments remain and

$$\text{Lease liability} = \$2700\left(\frac{1-1.0075^{-48}}{0.0075}\right)(1.0075) = \$109{,}312.65$$

   The reduction in the liability during the first year is
   $$\$131{,}043.62 - \$109{,}312.65 = \underline{\$21{,}730.97}$$

25. The ranking does not depend on where the focal date is set. The choice of 8 years from now as the focal date will minimize the calculations required to determine each stream's economic value on the focal date.
    a. (i) The $10,000 is already at the focal date.

   (ii) Economic value $= FV\text{(due)} = PMT\left[\frac{(1+i)^n - 1}{i}\right]\times(1+i)$

$$= \$850\left(\frac{1.08^8 - 1}{0.08}\right)(1.08) = \$9764.42$$

   (iii) Economic value $= PV\text{(due)} = PMT\left[\frac{1-(1+i)^{-n}}{i}\right]\times(1+i)$

$$= \$1700\left(\frac{1-1.08^{-8}}{0.08}\right)(1.08) = \$10{,}550.83$$

   The $1700 annuity has the largest economic value and the $850 annuity has the lowest value.

Exercise 13.2 *(continued)*

25. *b.* (i) The $10,000 payment is already at the focal date.

(ii) Economic value = FV(due) = $\$850\left(\dfrac{1.10^8 - 1}{0.10}\right)(1.10) = \$10{,}692.56$

(iii) Economic value = PV(due) = $\$1700\left(\dfrac{1 - 1.10^{-8}}{0.10}\right)(1.10) = \$9976.31$

The ranking in part *a* is reversed. <u>The $850 annuity now has the largest economic value and the $1700 annuity has the lowest value</u>.

27. Heath and Company should choose the lease having the lower economic value. The current economic value of each lease is the present value of the lease payments discounted at the time value of money.

For the lease on the current premises, $PMT = \$2100$, $n = 12(7) = 84$, $i = \frac{7.5\%}{12} = 0.625\%$.

$$PV(\text{due}) = \$2100\left(\dfrac{1 - 1.00625^{-84}}{0.00625}\right)(1.00625) = \$137{,}768.09$$

For the lease on the new premises, the payments form a deferred ordinary annuity having $PMT = \$2500$, $n = 12(6) = 72$, $i = 0.625\%$, and period of deferral = 11 months. At a focal date 11 months from now,

$$PV = PMT\left[\dfrac{1 - (1 + i)^{-n}}{i}\right] = \$2500\left(\dfrac{1 - 1.00625^{-72}}{0.00625}\right) = \$144{,}591.31$$

$$PV(\text{today}) = FV(1 + i)^{-n} = \$144{,}591.31\,(1.00625)^{-11} = \$135{,}013.55$$

Therefore, Heath should <u>accept the lease on the new location</u> since it represents a saving (in current dollars) of
$$\$137{,}768.09 - \$135{,}013.55 = \underline{\$2754.54}$$

Concept Questions (Section 13.3)

1. If PMT, n, and i are the same for an ordinary annuity and an annuity due, the ordinary annuity will have the smaller FV. Therefore, if FV, n, and i are the same, the <u>ordinary annuity</u> has the larger PMT.

3. The larger the down payment, the smaller the lease payments.

5. *a.* The lessee <u>should not exercise the purchase option</u>. If the lessee wishes to purchase the vehicle, an equivalent vehicle can be purchased at a lower price in the "used-car market".

b. The lessee <u>should exercise the purchase option</u>. If the lessee does not wish to own the vehicle, it can be sold for more than the residual value in the "used-car market".

c. If the lessee does the rational thing, the lessor *loses*
Residual value − Market value
in case *a*, but *does not gain* or capture the difference
Market value − Residual value
in case *b*. The lessor's exposure to this market value risk is one reason why the interest rate on a lease contract is normally higher than the interest rate on a loan to purchase the same vehicle.

Exercise 13.3

1. Given: $PV(\text{due}) = \$25,000$, $n = 2(8.5) = 17$, $i = \frac{6.5\%}{2} = 3.25\%$
   Substitute into formula (13-2).

$$\$25,000 = PMT\left(\frac{1 - 1.0325^{-17}}{0.0325}\right)(1.0325)$$

$$PMT = \underline{\$1876.26}$$

3. Given: $PV(\text{due}) = \$45,000$, $n = 12(11) = 132$, $i = 7\%$,

$$c = \frac{\text{Number of compoundings per year}}{\text{Number of payments per year}} = \frac{1}{12} = 0.08\overline{3}$$

$$i_2 = (1 + i)^c - 1 = (1.07)^{0.08\overline{3}} - 1 = 0.00565414539$$

Substitute into formula (13-2).

$$\$45,000 = PMT\left(\frac{1 - 1.00565414539^{-132}}{0.00565414539}\right)(1.00565414539)$$

$$PMT = \underline{\$482.00}$$

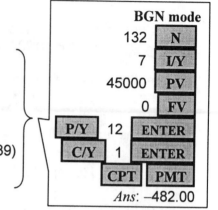

BGN mode

132	N
7	I/Y
45000	PV
0	FV
P/Y 12	ENTER
C/Y 1	ENTER
CPT	PMT

Ans: –482.00

5. Given: $FV(\text{due}) = \$22,500$, $PMT = \$150.75$, $i = \frac{9\%}{12} = 0.75\%$

$$n = \frac{\ln\left[1 + \dfrac{i \times FV(\text{due})}{PMT(1 + i)}\right]}{\ln(1 + i)} = \frac{\ln\left(1 + \dfrac{0.0075 \times \$22,500}{\$150.75(1.0075)}\right)}{\ln(1.0075)} = 100.00 \text{ payments}$$

The annuity has 100 monthly payments requiring
$\frac{100}{12}$ years = $8.\overline{3}$ years = <u>8 years and 4 months</u>.

7. Given: $FV(\text{due}) = \$52,033.58$, $PMT = \$1200$,
   $\quad\quad i = 7.3\%$, $c = \frac{1}{4} = 0.25$

$$i_2 = (1 + i)^c - 1 = (1.073)^{0.25} - 1 = 0.0177706682$$

$$n = \frac{\ln\left[1 + \dfrac{i \times FV(\text{due})}{PMT(1 + i)}\right]}{\ln(1 + i)}$$

$$= \frac{\ln\left(1 + \dfrac{0.0177706682 \times \$52,033.58}{\$1200(1.0177706682)}\right)}{\ln(1.0177706682)}$$

$$= 32.00 \text{ payments}$$

The annuity has 32 quarterly payments. Its term is <u>8 years</u>.

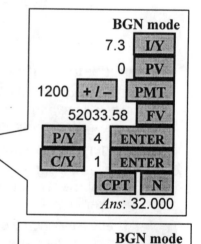

BGN mode

7.3	I/Y
0	PV
1200 +/–	PMT
52033.58	FV
P/Y 4	ENTER
C/Y 1	ENTER
CPT	N

Ans: 32.000

9. Given: $FV(\text{due}) = \$75,000$, $PMT = \$1969.40$,
   $\quad\quad n = 2(11.5) = 23$
   $\quad\quad j = $ <u>8.00% compounded semiannually</u>

$$i = \frac{j}{m} = \frac{8.00\%}{2} = 4.00\% \text{ per half year}$$

$$f = (1 + i)^m - 1 = (1.04)^2 - 1 = \underline{8.16\%}$$

BGN mode

23	N
0	PV
1969.40 +/–	PMT
75000	FV
P/Y 2	ENTER
Same C/Y	
CPT	I/Y

Ans: 8.000

11. Given: $PV(\text{due}) = \$45,000$, $PMT = \$386.83$, $n = 12(13) + 8 = 164$

$j = \underline{5.40\% \text{ compounded monthly}}$

$i = \dfrac{j}{m} = \dfrac{5.40\%}{12} = 0.45\%$ per month

$f = (1+i)^m - 1 = (1.0045)^{12} - 1 = \underline{5.54\%}$

13. $\left(\begin{array}{c}\text{Purchase}\\\text{price}\end{array}\right) - \left(\begin{array}{c}\text{Down}\\\text{payment}\end{array}\right) = \left(\begin{array}{c}\text{Present value of}\\\text{the lease payments}\end{array}\right) + \left(\begin{array}{c}\text{Present value of}\\\text{the residual value}\end{array}\right)$

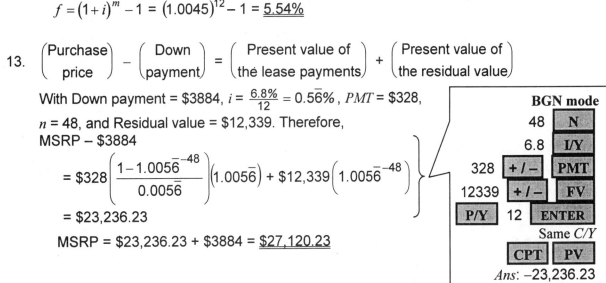

With Down payment = 3884, $i = \dfrac{6.8\%}{12} = 0.56\overline{6}\%$, $PMT = \$328$,

$n = 48$, and Residual value = $12,339$. Therefore,

MSRP − 3884

$= \$328\left(\dfrac{1 - 1.005\overline{6}^{-48}}{0.005\overline{6}}\right)(1.005\overline{6}) + \$12,339\left(1.005\overline{6}^{-48}\right)$

$= \$23,236.23$

MSRP $= \$23,236.23 + \$3884 = \underline{\$27,120.23}$

15. $\left(\begin{array}{c}\text{Purchase}\\\text{price}\end{array}\right) - \left(\begin{array}{c}\text{Down}\\\text{payment}\end{array}\right) = \left(\begin{array}{c}\text{Present value of}\\\text{the lease payments}\end{array}\right) + \left(\begin{array}{c}\text{Present value of}\\\text{the residual value}\end{array}\right)$

With Purchase price = $37,290$, $PMT = \$359$, $i = \dfrac{3.9\%}{12} = 0.325\%$,

$n = 39$, and Residual value = $21,997$,

$\$37,290 - (\text{Down payment}) = \$359\left(\dfrac{1 - 1.00325^{-39}}{0.00325}\right)(1.00325) + \$21,997\left(1.00325^{-39}\right)$

$= \$32,555.01$

Down payment $= \underline{\$4734.99}$

17. $\left(\begin{array}{c}\text{Purchase}\\\text{price}\end{array}\right) - \left(\begin{array}{c}\text{Down}\\\text{payment}\end{array}\right) = \left(\begin{array}{c}\text{Present value of}\\\text{the lease payments}\end{array}\right) + \left(\begin{array}{c}\text{Present value of}\\\text{the residual value}\end{array}\right)$

With Purchase price = $40,040$, Down payment = 5835,
$PMT = \$438$, $n = 48$, and Residual value = $19,400$,

$\$40,040 - \$5835$

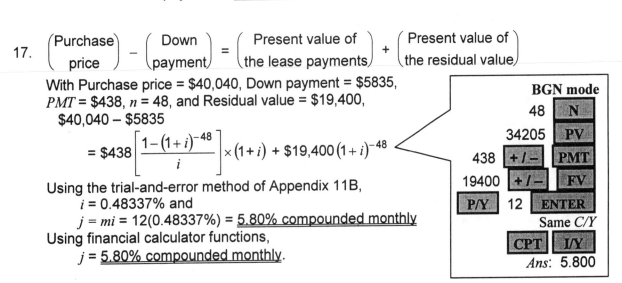

$= \$438\left[\dfrac{1 - (1+i)^{-48}}{i}\right] \times (1+i) + \$19,400(1+i)^{-48}$

Using the trial-and-error method of Appendix 11B,
$i = 0.48337\%$ and
$j = mi = 12(0.48337\%) = \underline{5.80\% \text{ compounded monthly}}$
Using financial calculator functions,
$j = \underline{5.80\% \text{ compounded monthly}}$.

Exercise 13.3 (continued)

19. $\left(\begin{array}{c}\text{Purchase}\\\text{price}\end{array}\right) - \left(\begin{array}{c}\text{Down}\\\text{payment}\end{array}\right) = \left(\begin{array}{c}\text{Present value of}\\\text{the lease payments}\end{array}\right) + \left(\begin{array}{c}\text{Present value of}\\\text{the residual value}\end{array}\right)$

With Down payment = \$5070, $i = \frac{4.8\%}{12} = 0.4\%$, $PMT = \$365$,

$n = 48$, and Residual value = \$13,958. Therefore,

$$MSRP - \$5070 = \$365\left(\frac{1-1.004^{-48}}{0.004}\right)(1.004) + \$13,958\left(1.004^{-48}\right) = \$27,499.59$$

MSRP = \$27,499.59 + \$5070 = $\underline{\$32,569.59}$

21. $\left(\begin{array}{c}\text{Purchase}\\\text{price}\end{array}\right) - \left(\begin{array}{c}\text{Down}\\\text{payment}\end{array}\right) = \left(\begin{array}{c}\text{Present value of}\\\text{the lease payments}\end{array}\right) + \left(\begin{array}{c}\text{Present value of}\\\text{the residual value}\end{array}\right)$

With Purchase price = \$30,210, Down payment = \$2775,

$PMT = \$362$, $i = \frac{3.9\%}{12} = 0.325\%$, and Residual value = \$16,987,

we have

\$30,210 − \$2775

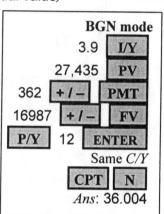

$$= \$362\left[\frac{1-(1.00325)^{-n}}{0.00325}\right] \times (1.00325) + \$16,987(1.00325)^{-n}$$

Using the financial calculator functions,
we obtain $\qquad n = 36.00$
The term of the lease is <u>36 months</u>.

23. a. Given: $PV(\text{due}) = \$200,000$, $n = 20$, $i = 6\%$
    Substitute into formula (13-2) giving

    $$\$200,000 = PMT\left(\frac{1-1.06^{-20}}{0.06}\right)(1.06)$$

    $PMT = \underline{\$16,449.92}$

    b. Given: $PV = \$200,000$, $n = 20$, $i = 6\%$
    Substitute into formula (10-2) giving

    $$\$200,000 = PMT\left(\frac{1-1.06^{-20}}{0.06}\right)$$

    $PMT = \underline{\$17,436.91}$

25. The \$500,000 target is the future value of the semiannual contributions.
    a. The contributions form a simple annuity due having

    $$FV(\text{due}) = \$500,000, \ n = 2(9) = 18, \ i = \frac{7.5\%}{2} = 3.75\%$$

    $$\$500,000 = PMT\left(\frac{1.0375^{18}-1}{0.0375}\right)(1.0375)$$

    $PMT = \underline{\$19,227.29}$

    b. Now $FV = \$500,000$, $n = 18$, $i = 3.75\%$ and

    $$\$500,000 = PMT\left(\frac{1.0375^{18}-1}{0.0375}\right)$$

    $PMT = \underline{\$19,948.31}$

The calculator display (right) shows:

BGN mode

3.9	I/Y
27,435	PV
362 +/−	PMT
16987 +/−	FV
P/Y 12	ENTER
	Same C/Y
CPT	N

Ans: 36.004

27. The future value of the payments is $10,000.
    The payments form a simple annuity due having

    $$FV(\text{due}) = \$10,000, \; n = 12(4) = 48, \; i = \tfrac{6.6\%}{12} = 0.55\%$$

    $$\$10,000 = PMT\left(\frac{1.0055^{48} - 1}{0.0055}\right)(1.0055)$$

    $$PMT = \underline{\$181.61}$$

    Erin must invest $181.61 each month.

29. The present value of the lease payments discounted at the lessor's required rate of return equals the capital cost of the equipment. With

    $$PV(\text{due}) = \$8500, \; n = 12(3) = 36, \; i = \tfrac{13.5\%}{12} = 1.125\%, \text{ and}$$

    $$\$8500 = PMT\left(\frac{1 - 1.01125^{-36}}{0.01125}\right)(1.01125)$$

    $$PMT = \underline{\$285.24}$$

    The lease payments will be $285.24 at the beginning of each month for 3 years.

31. With the contributions at the beginning of each year,

    $$FV(\text{due}) = \$500,000, \; n = 27, \; i = 9\%$$

    $$\$500,000 = PMT\left(\frac{1.09^{27} - 1}{0.09}\right)(1.09)$$

    $$PMT = \$4465.55$$

    With the contributions at the end of each year,

    $$FV = \$500,000, \; n = 27, \; i = 9\%$$

    $$\$500,000 = PMT\left(\frac{1.09^{27} - 1}{0.09}\right)$$

    $$PMT = \$4867.45$$

    The annual contributions must be
    $4867.45 − $4465.55 = $\underline{\$401.90}$
    larger if made at the end of the year instead of the beginning.

33. Initial lease liability = Present value of all lease payments.
    The lease payments form a simple annuity due having

    $$PV(\text{due}) = \$43,000, \; n = 12(5) = 60, \; i = \tfrac{10.5\%}{12} = 0.875\%$$

    $$\$43,000 = PMT\left(\frac{1 - 1.00875^{-60}}{0.00875}\right)(1.00875)$$

    $$PMT = \underline{\$916.22}$$

    The monthly lease payment is $916.22.

35. The future value of Kim's contributions must be $8000. The contributions form a simple annuity due having $FV(\text{due}) = \$15,000$, $PMT = \$700$, and $i = \tfrac{4.2\%}{12} = 0.35\%$.

    The number of contributions will be

    $$n = \frac{\ln\left[1 + \dfrac{i \times FV(\text{due})}{PMT(1+i)}\right]}{\ln(1+i)} = \frac{\ln\left(1 + \dfrac{0.0035 \times \$15,000}{\$700(1.0035)}\right)}{\ln(1.0035)} = 20.629$$

    After 20 months, $FV(\text{due}) = \$14,526.09$. Therefore, the 21st deposit (of $700) occurring <u>20 months from today</u> will reach the goal.

---

37. The purchase price is the present value of the remaining payments discounted at the investor's required rate of return. Viewed from the date of purchase, the payments form a simple annuity due with

PV(due) = \$13,372, PMT = \$500, $i = \frac{9.75\%}{12} = 8.125\%$

The number of remaining payments is

$$n = -\frac{\ln\left[1 - \dfrac{i \times PV(\text{due})}{PMT(1+i)}\right]}{\ln(1+i)} = -\frac{\ln\left(1 - \dfrac{0.08125 \times \$13,372}{\$500(1.08125)}\right)}{\ln(1.08125)} = 30.00$$

The investor will receive <u>30 payments</u>.

39. The monthly deposits form a simple annuity due whose future value is to be \$100,000. With FV(due) = \$100,000, PMT = \$220, and $i = \frac{5.4\%}{12} = 0.45\%$,

$$n = \frac{\ln\left[1 + \dfrac{i \times FV(\text{due})}{PMT(1+i)}\right]}{\ln(1+i)} = \frac{\ln\left(1 + \dfrac{0.0045 \times \$100,000}{\$220(1.0045)}\right)}{\ln(1.0045)} = 247.36$$

That is, 248 deposits of \$220 will be needed to accumulate \$100,000. If the monthly deposits are only \$200,

$$n = \frac{\ln\left(1 + \dfrac{0.0045 \times \$100,000}{\$200(1.0045)}\right)}{\ln(1.0045)} = 261.82$$

That is, 262 deposits of \$200 will be needed to surpass \$100,000. Therefore, (262 − 248) = <u>14 fewer deposits</u> of \$220 will be required.

41. The contributions form an annuity due whose future value is \$223,000. That is, FV(due) = \$223,000 with PMT = \$2500 and n = 2(16) = 32. Use the calculator's financial functions to obtain j = 11.226% compounded semiannually. Alternatively, substitute into formula (13-1) and solve for i using the trial-and-error method of Appendix 11B to obtain i = 5.613% per half year.

Then $f = (1+i)^m - 1 = (1.05613)^2 - 1 = \underline{11.54\%}$

43. The amount in the RRSP represents the future value of the contributions. Hence, FV(due) = \$327,685 with PMT = \$1500 and n = 4(20) = 80. Use the calculator's financial functions to obtain j = <u>8.80% compounded quarterly</u>. Alternatively, substitute into formula (13-1) and solve for i using the trial-and-error method of Appendix 11B to obtain i = 2.20% per quarter.

Then $f = (1+i)^m - 1 = (1.022)^4 - 1 = \underline{9.09\%}$

45. The purchase price is the present value of the payments. That is, PV(due) = \$1195, PMT = \$110, and n = 12. Use the calculator's financial functions to obtain j = 22.356% compounded monthly. Alternatively, substitute into formula (13-2) and solve for i using the trial-and-error method of Appendix 11B to obtain i = 1.863% per month.

Then $f = (1+i)^m - 1 = (1.01863)^{12} - 1 = \underline{24.79\%}$

47. The present value of the lease payments discounted at the required rate of return must equal the capital cost of the equipment.

a. PV(due) = \$25,000, $n = 12(5) = 60$, $i = \frac{15\%}{4} = 3.75\%$, $c = \frac{4}{12} = 0.\overline{3}$

$$i_2 = (1+i)^c - 1 = (1.0375)^{0.\overline{3}} - 1 = 0.012346926$$

$$\$25,000 = PMT\left(\frac{1-1.012346926^{-60}}{0.012346926}\right)(1.012346926)$$

$PMT = \underline{\$585.12}$
The monthly lease payment is \$585.12.

b. PV(due) = \$25,000, $n = 2(5) = 10$, $i = 3.75\%$, $c = \frac{4}{2} = 2$

$$i_2 = (1+i)^c - 1 = (1.0375)^2 - 1 = 0.07640625$$

$$\$25,000 = PMT\left(\frac{1-1.07640625^{-10}}{0.07640625}\right)(1.07640625)$$

$PMT = \underline{\$3405.38}$
The semiannual lease payment is \$3405.38.

49. Present value of instalment payments = \$1900.
For payments at the beginning of each quarter,

$$PV\text{(due)} = \$1900, \; n = 4, \; i = \frac{15\%}{2} = 7.5\%, \; c = \frac{2}{4} = 0.5,$$

$$i_2 = (1+i)^c - 1 = (1.075)^{0.5} - 1 = 0.036822068$$

$$\$1900 = PMT\left(\frac{1-1.036822068^{-4}}{0.036822068}\right)(1.036822068)$$

$PMT = \underline{\$501.07}$
For payments at the beginning of each month,

$$PV\text{(due)} = \$1900, \; n = 12, \; i = \frac{15\%}{2} = 7.5\%, \; c = \frac{2}{12} = 0.1\overline{6}$$

$$i_2 = (1+i)^c - 1 = (1.075)^{0.1\overline{6}} - 1 = 0.012126379$$

$$\$1900 = PMT\left(\frac{1-1.012126379^{-12}}{0.012126379}\right)(1.012126379)$$

$PMT = \underline{\$169.04}$
The payments are \$501.07 quarterly or \$169.04 monthly.

51. At a focal date 7 years from now,
$$FV \text{ of the \$10,000 lump investment} = PV \text{ of withdrawals}$$
Viewed from the focal date, the withdrawals form a simple annuity due.
The future value of the \$10,000 is

$$FV = PV(1+i)^n = \$10,000(1.00\overline{6})^{84} = \$17,474.22$$

With PV(due) = \$17,474.22, $PMT = \$500$, $i = 0.\overline{6}\,\%$,

$$n = -\frac{\ln\left[1 - \dfrac{i \times PV\text{(due)}}{PMT(1+i)}\right]}{\ln(1+i)} = -\frac{\ln\left(1 - \dfrac{0.00\overline{6} \times \$17,474.22}{\$500(1.00\overline{6})}\right)}{\ln(1.00\overline{6})} = 39.62$$

There can be 40 withdrawals with the last one being less than \$500. The last payment will occur 39 months <u>(3 years and 3 months) after the grandson starts college</u>.

53. The future value of the regular $12,000 "draws" is $1,000,000. Hence,
$$FV\text{(due)} = \$1,000,000, \ PMT = \$12,000, \ i = \tfrac{8.2\%}{4} = 2.05\%, \ c = \tfrac{4}{12} = 0.\overline{3}$$

$$i_2 = (1+i)^c - 1 = (1.0205)^{0.\overline{3}} - 1 = 0.0067871635$$

The number of draws will be

$$n = \frac{\ln\left[1 + \dfrac{i \times FV\text{(due)}}{PMT\,(1+i)}\right]}{\ln(1+i)} = \frac{\ln\left(1 + \dfrac{0.0067871635 \times \$1,000,000}{\$12,000(1.0067871635)}\right)}{\ln(1.0067871635)} = 65.91$$

The credit limit will be reached in the 66th month. That is, it will take <u>5 years and 6 months</u> to reach the credit limit.

55. The four quarterly payments form an annuity due. The interest rate being charged by the golf club is the discount rate that makes the present value of the payments equal to the single membership payment of $1714.
Substitute $PV\text{(due)} = \$1714$, $PMT = \$449.40$ and $n = 4$ into formula (13-2).
Solve for i using the trial-and-error method of Appendix 11B.
We obtain $i = 3.2703\%$ per quarter. Therefore,

$$f = (1+i)^m - 1 = (1.032703)^4 - 1 = \underline{13.74\%}$$

57. By paying $159.80 now, the subscriber avoids paying $63.80 at the beginning of each of the next 3 years. The "return on investment" is the discount rate that makes the present value of $n = 3$ payments of $PMT = \$63.80$ equal to $PV\text{(due)} = \$159.80$. Substitute into formula (13-2). Solve for i using the trial-and-error method of Appendix 11B. We obtain $i = 21.26\%$ per year. Hence,
$$j = i = \underline{21.26\% \text{ compounded annually}}$$

59. In each case, the interest rate being charged is the discount rate that makes the present value of 1 year's premium payments equal to $PV\text{(due)} = \$666.96$.
a. For $PMT = \$341.32$ and $n = 2$, solving formula (13-2) for i gives
$i = 4.815\%$ per half year. Hence,
$$f = (1+i)^m - 1 = (1.04815)^2 - 1 = \underline{9.86\%}$$

b. For $PMT = \$173.62$ and $n = 4$, we similarly obtain
$$i = 2.764\% \text{ per quarter and } f = (1+i)^m - 1 = (1.02764)^4 - 1 = \underline{11.52\%}$$

c. For $PMT = \$58.85$ and $n = 12$, we similarly obtain
$$i = 1.057\% \text{ per month and } f = (1+i)^m - 1 = (1.01057)^{12} - 1 = \underline{13.45\%}$$

61. With today as the focal date,
FV of RRSP contributions = PV of the RRIF withdrawals
The amount in the RRSP 10 years ago was

$$FV\text{(due)} = PMT\left[\frac{(1+i)^n - 1}{i}\right](1+i) = \$500\left(\frac{1.025^{40} - 1}{0.025}\right)(1.025) = \$34,543.81$$

The amount in the RRSP today is

$$\$34,543.81\,(1.03)^{40} + \$500\left(\frac{1.03^{40} - 1}{0.03}\right)(1.03) = \$151,514.86$$

(continued)

Exercise 13.3 *(continued)*

61. *(continued)*
    For the RRIF withdrawals,
    $$PV\text{(due)} = \$151{,}514.86,\ n = 12(15) = 180,\ i = \tfrac{8.25\%}{12} = 0.6875\%$$

    The maximum beginning-of-month withdrawals is the value of PMT satisfying

    $$\$151{,}514.86 = PMT\left(\frac{1-1.006875^{-180}}{0.006875}\right)(1.006875)$$

    $$PMT = \underline{\$1459.87}$$

63. At a focal date on the purchase date of the annuity,
    $$FV \text{ of RRSP contributions} = PV \text{ of annuity payments}$$

    For the PV calculation, $PMT = \$3509,\ n = 12(25) = 300,\ i = \tfrac{8\%}{2} = 4\%,\ c = \tfrac{2}{12} = 0.1\overline{6}$.

    $$i_2 = (1+i)^c - 1 = (1.04)^{0.1\overline{6}} - 1 = 0.006558197$$

    $$PV\text{(due)} = \$3509\left(\frac{1-1.006558197^{-300}}{0.006558197}\right)(1.006558197) = \$462{,}781.77$$

    On the left side of the word equation, $FV\text{(due)} = \$462{,}781.77$, $PMT = \$2500$, $i = 8\%$,
    $c = \tfrac{1}{2} = 0.5$, and $i_2 = (1+i)^c - 1 = (1.08)^{0.5} - 1 = 0.039230485$. Hence,

    $$n = \frac{\ln\left[1+\dfrac{i \times FV\text{(due)}}{PMT\,(1+i)}\right]}{\ln(1+i)} = \frac{\ln\left(1+\dfrac{0.039230485 \times \$462{,}781.77}{\$2500(1.039230485)}\right)}{\ln(1.039230485)} = 54.00$$

    Therefore, Mr. van der Linden contributed to his RRSP for 54 half years = __27 years__.

Exercise 13.4

1. *Step 1:* Calculate the original payment size using the idea that the original loan equals the present value of the payments.
   Substitute $PV = \$20{,}000$, $n = 120$, and $i = \tfrac{9\%}{12} = 0.75\%$ into formula (10-2).

   $$\$20{,}000 = PMT\left(\frac{1-1.0075^{-120}}{0.0075}\right)$$

   $$PMT = \$253.35$$

   Step 2: Calculate the balance after 1 year using the idea that the original loan equals the combined present value of the remaining 108 payments. That is,

   $$\$20{,}000 = \$253.35\left(\frac{1-1.0075^{-108}}{0.0075}\right)$$

   Balance = $\$18{,}707.24$

   Step 3: Calculate the number of monthly payments of $1.15(\$253.35) = \$291.35$ required to pay off the loan. Their present value is $\$18{,}707.24$.

   $$n = -\frac{\ln\left(1 - \dfrac{i \times PV}{PMT}\right)}{\ln(1+i)} = -\frac{\ln\left(1 - \dfrac{0.0075 \times \$18{,}707.24}{\$291.35}\right)}{\ln(1.0075)} = 87.92$$

   The total time required to pay off the loan will be
   (12 + 88) months = 8 years and 4 months.
   Therefore, the loan will be paid off __1 year and 8 months__ sooner.

Exercise 13.4 *(continued)*

3. The combined future value of the initial \$67,000 and the semiannual contributions is to be \$500,000. The contributions form an ordinary general annuity having
$PMT = \$4000$, $i = \frac{9\%}{4} = 2.25\%$, and $c = \frac{4}{2} = 2$.

$i_2 = (1+i)^c - 1 = (1.0225)^2 - 1 = 0.045506250$ and

$$\$67,000\,(1.04550625)^n + \$4000 \left(\frac{1.04550625^n - 1}{0.04550625} \right) = \$500,000$$

Solve for n using the trial-and-error method of Appendix 11B. We obtain $n = 29.97$. Therefore, Sheila must make 30 contributions requiring <u>15 years</u>.

5. The combined future value, 10 years from now, of the initial \$133,000 and the semiannual contributions is to be \$350,000. At a focal date 7 years from now,
FV of \$133,000 and RRSP contributions = PV of \$350,000
The right side of the equation is

$$PV = FV(1+i)^{-n} = \$350,000\,(1.0825)^{-3} = \$275,920.73$$

The RRSP contributions form an ordinary general annuity having
$n = 2(7) = 14$, $i = 8.25\%$, and $c = \frac{1}{2} = 0.5$

$$i_2 = (1+i)^c - 1 = (1.0825)^{0.5} - 1 = 0.04043260$$

Putting the initial word equation into mathematics,

$$\$133,000\,(1.0404326)^{14} + PMT \left(\frac{1.0404326^{14} - 1}{0.0404326} \right) = \$275,920.73$$

Solving for PMT gives $PMT = \underline{\$2412.64}$
Natalie must contribute \$2412.64 every 6 months to reach her goal.

7. If the economic value, 5 years from now, of today's purchase price plus the annual property taxes is less than the future purchase price, it is better to buy the property now. The annual property taxes form an ordinary general annuity having
$PMT = \$9000$, $n = 5$, $i = \frac{12\%}{2} = 6\%$, $c = \frac{2}{1} = 2$, and

$$i_2 = (1+i)^c - 1 = (1.06)^2 - 1 = 0.1236000$$

The combined future value, 5 years from now, of the purchase price and the property tax payments is

$$\$450,000\,(1.1236)^5 + \$9000 \left(\frac{1.1236^5 - 1}{0.1236} \right) = \underline{\$863,467}$$

The price would have to exceed \$863,467 five years from today for it to be financially advantageous to purchase the property today.

9. The amount in the RRSP after 25 years will be the future value of all contributions. For the first 10 years, the contributions form an ordinary general annuity having

$$PMT = \$1000, \ n = 4(10) = 40, \ i = \frac{8.5\%}{2} = 4.25\%, \ c = \frac{2}{4} = 0.5, \text{ and}$$

$$i_2 = (1+i)^c - 1 = (1.0425)^{0.5} - 1 = 0.021028893.$$

The amount in the RRSP after 10 years will be

$$\$1000 \left(\frac{1.021028893^{40} - 1}{0.021028893} \right) = \$61,767.70$$

For the last 15 years, the contributions form an ordinary general annuity having

$$PMT = \$1000, \ n = 12(15) = 180, \ i = 4.25\%, \ c = \frac{2}{12} = 0.1\overline{6}, \text{ and}$$

$$i_2 = (1+i)^c - 1 = (1.0425)^{0.1\overline{6}} - 1 = 0.006961062.$$

The combined future value, 25 years from now, of these contributions and the \$61,767.70 lump amount will be

$$\$61,767.70 \, (1.006961062)^{180} + \$1000 \left(\frac{1.006961062^{180} - 1}{0.006961062} \right) = \underline{\$572,376.63}$$

Gayle will have \$572,376.63 in her RRSP after 25 years.

11. Sum of the current loan balances = PV of payments on the consolidated loan

    Step 1: Calculate the monthly payment on the \$8500 loan.

    $$PV = \$8500, \ n = 12(3) = 36, \ i = \frac{10.5\%}{12} = 0.875\%$$

    $$\$8500 = PMT \left(\frac{1 - 1.00875^{-36}}{0.00875} \right)$$

    $$PMT = \$276.27$$

    Step 2: Calculate this loan's balance after 11 payments (with 25 payments remaining).

    $$\text{Balance} = \$276.27 \left(\frac{1 - 1.00875^{-25}}{0.00875} \right) = \$6179.37$$

    Step 3: Calculate the balance on the second loan.

    $$PMT = \$313.69, \ n = 38 \text{ payments remain}, \ i = \frac{9.5\%}{2} = 4.75\%, \ c = \frac{2}{12} = 0.1\overline{6}$$

    $$i_2 = (1+i)^c - 1 = (1.0475)^{0.1\overline{6}} - 1 = 0.00776438317$$

    $$\text{Balance} = \$313.69 \left(\frac{1 - 1.00776438317^{-38}}{0.00776438317} \right) = \$10,288.32$$

    Step 4: Calculate the monthly payment on the consolidated loan.
    Initial loan = \$6179.37 + \$10,288.32 = \$16,467.69.
    With $PV = \$16,467.69$, $n = 60$, and $i = 0.6875\%$, solve for PMT in

    $$\$16,467.69 = PMT \left(\frac{1 - 1.006875^{-60}}{0.006875} \right)$$

    $$PMT = \underline{\$335.88}$$

    The monthly payment on the consolidated loan would be \$335.88.

Exercise 13.4 *(continued)*

13. *a.* The total of the nominal costs is

$$6(\$10,500) + 6(\$9600) + 5(\$9000) + 2(\$12,000) = \underline{\$189,600}$$

b. The economic value, at the date of birth, of all costs is their present value.

Years	Monthly cost ($)	No. of months
1- 6	875	72
7-12	800	72
13-17	750	60
18-19	1000	24

The present value, at the beginning of the 18th year, of the last 2 years' costs is

$$PV = PMT\left[\frac{1-(1+i)^{-n}}{i}\right] = \$1000\left(\frac{1-1.005^{-24}}{0.005}\right) = \$22,562.87$$

The present value, at the beginning of the 13th year, of the last 7 years' costs is

$$\$750\left(\frac{1-1.005^{-60}}{0.005}\right) + \frac{\$22,562.87}{1.005^{60}} = \$55,521.66$$

The present value, at the beginning of the 7th year, of the last 13 years' costs is

$$\$800\left(\frac{1-1.005^{-72}}{0.005}\right) + \frac{\$55,521.66}{1.005^{72}} = \$87,042.52$$

The present value, at the birth date, of all the costs is

$$\$875\left(\frac{1-1.005^{-72}}{0.005}\right) + \frac{\$87,042.52}{1.005^{72}} = \underline{\$113,579}.08$$

c. The economic value, at age 19, of the expenditures is the future value of all the expenditures. This is most easily determined by calculating the future value, 19 years later, of the result from part *b.*

$$FV = PV(1+i)^n = \$113,579.08(1.005)^{228} = \underline{\$354,128}$$

15. The price that Afco will pay is the present value, on the date of the sale, of the 6 payments discounted at 18% compounded semiannually.

Step 1: Calculate the customer's monthly payments. Since no interest is charged during the first 6 months, $1800 is owed when the first of the 6 monthly payments is made. Then, $PV(\text{due}) = \$1800$ with $n = 6$ and $i = \frac{15\%}{12} = 1.25\%$.

$$\$1800 = PMT\left(\frac{1-1.0125^{-6}}{0.0125}\right)(1.0125)$$

$$PMT = \$309.39$$

Step 2: Calculate the present value, 6 months from the date of sale, discounting the payments at $i_2 = (1+i)^c - 1 = (1.09)^{0.1\overline{6}} - 1 = 0.014466592$

$$PV(\text{due}) = \$309.39\left(\frac{1-1.014466592^{-6}}{0.014466592}\right)(1.014466592) = \$1791.42$$

Step 3: Calculate the present value, on the date of sale, of the *Step* 2 amount.

$$PV = FV(1+i)^{-n} = \$1792.42(1.09)^{-1} = \underline{\$1643.51}$$

Pioneer will receive $1643.51 from Afco on the sale of the contract.

Exercise 13.4 *(continued)*

17. With the focal date at Reg's 60th birthday,

    $$FV \text{ of RRSP contributions} = PV \text{ of all annuity payments}$$

    The right side can be calculated in two steps.

    Step 1: Calculate the present value at age 68 of the 20-year annuity having $PMT = \$6000$, $n = 12(20) = 240$, and $i = \frac{7.5\%}{12} = 0.625\%$. Then

    $$PV = \$6000\left(\frac{1 - 1.00625^{-240}}{0.00625}\right) = \$744{,}792.79$$

    Step 2: Calculate the PV at age 60 of the 8-year annuity ($n = 96$) and the *Step* 1 result.

    $$PV = \$5000\left(\frac{1 - 1.00625^{-96}}{0.00625}\right) + \frac{\$744{,}792.79}{1.00625^{96}} = \$769{,}645.01$$

    Step 3: For the left side of the initial word equation,

    $$FV(\text{due}) = \$769{,}645.01,\ n = 4(30) = 120,\ i = 0.625\%,\ c = \tfrac{12}{4} = 3, \text{ and}$$

    $$i_2 = (1 + i)^c - 1 = (1.00625)^3 - 1 = 0.0188674316. \text{ Solve for } PMT \text{ in}$$

    $$\$769{,}645.01 = PMT\left(\frac{1.0188674316^{120} - 1}{0.0188674316}\right)(1.0188674316)$$

    $$PMT = \underline{\$1692.37}$$

    The quarterly RRSP contributions must be $1692.37.

19. The car buyer will be indifferent between the alternatives if the payments during the 4-year term of each loan are the same.

    Step 1: Calculate the monthly payment on $25,000 financed at 1.9% compounded monthly for 4 years.

    Solve for PMT when $PV = \$25{,}000$, $n = 48$, and $i = \frac{1.9\%}{12} = 0.158\overline{3}\%$.

    $$\$25{,}000 = PMT\left(\frac{1 - 1.001583^{-48}}{0.00158\overline{3}}\right)$$

    $$PMT = \$541.29$$

    Step 2: Calculate the initial 4-year loan at 6.6% compounded monthly that would have the same payments. This amount is the present value of the payments discounted at $i = \frac{6.6\%}{12} = 0.55\%$.

    $$\text{Initial loan} = \$541.29\left(\frac{1 - 1.0055^{-48}}{0.0055}\right) = \$22{,}780.51$$

    Step 3: Calculate the cash rebate. For indifference, the rebate must reduce the net price to $22,780.51.

    $$\text{Rebate} = \$25{,}000 - \$22{,}780.51 = \underline{\$2219.49}$$

21. *Step* 1: Calculate the amount in the RRSP at age 58.

$PMT = \$5000$, $n = 2(12) = 24$, $i = \frac{7.5\%}{12} = 0.625\%$, $c = \frac{12}{2} = 6$, and

$i_2 = (1+i)^c - 1 = (1.00625)^6 - 1 = 0.0380908432$

The combined FV of the initial $\$97,000$ and subsequent contributions will be

$$FV = \$97,000\,(1.0380908432)^{24} + \$5000\left(\frac{1.0380908432^{24} - 1}{0.0380908432}\right)1.0380908432$$

$= \$237,914.21 + \$197,955.62$
$= \$435,869.83$

Step 2: Calculate the amount in the RRSP at age 63 (just before the purchase of the second annuity). This will be the future value, after a further 5 years, of half the *Step* 1 result. That is,

$$FV = PV(1+i)^n = \$217,934.91\,(1.00625)^{60} = \$316,723.59$$

Step 3: Calculate the amount available at age 68 to purchase the third annuity. This will be the future value, after a further 5 years, of half the *Step* 2 result. That is,

$$FV = PV(1+i)^n = \$158,361.80\,(1.00625)^{60} = \$230,146.31$$

Step 4: Calculate the payments in the first annuity purchased for $\$217,934.91$. Solve for PMT_1 in

$$\$217,934.91 = PMT_1\left(\frac{1 - 1.00625^{-240}}{0.00625}\right)$$

$PMT_1 = \$1755.67$ per month

Step 5: Calculate the payments in the second annuity purchased for $\$158,361.80$. Solve for PMT_2 in

$$\$158,361.80 = PMT_2\left(\frac{1 - 1.00625^{-240}}{0.00625}\right)$$

$PMT_2 = \$1275.75$

Step 6: Calculate the payments in the third annuity purchased for $\$230,146.31$. Solve for PMT_3 in

$$\$230,146.31 = PMT_3\left(\frac{1 - 1.00625^{-240}}{0.00625}\right)$$

$PMT_3 = \$1854.04$

Step 7: Calculate the total monthly incomes at ages 65 and 70.

Monthly income at age 65 $= PMT_1 + PMT_2 = \underline{\$3031.42}$

Monthly income at age 70 $= PMT_1 + PMT_2 + PMT_3 = \underline{\$4885.46}$.

Review Problems

1. *a.* Initial liability = Present value of all lease payments

   With $PMT = \$1900$, $i = \frac{8.25\%}{12} = 0.6875\%$, $n = 12(5) = 60$

   $$\text{Initial liability} = \$1900\left(\frac{1-1.006875^{-60}}{0.006875}\right)(1.006875) = \underline{\$93,794.81}$$

   b. Liability after the first year = Present value of the remaining 48 payments

   $$= \$1900\left(\frac{1-1.006875^{-48}}{0.006875}\right)(1.006875)$$

   $$= \$77,987.28$$

   The reduction in the liability during the first year will be
   $$\$93,794.81 - \$77,987.28 = \underline{\$15,807.53}$$

3. The $300,000 in the fund represents the present value of the withdrawals.

   a. Given: $PV\text{(due)} = \$300,000$, $n = 25$, $i = 7.75\%$
   Substitute into formula (13-2) and solve for PMT.

   $$\$300,000 = PMT\left(\frac{1-1.0775^{-25}}{0.0775}\right)(1.0775)$$

   $$PMT = \underline{\$25,527.54}$$

   b. $PV = \$300,000$, $n = 25$, $i = 7.75\%$
   Substitute into formula (10-2) and solve for PMT.

   $$\$300,000 = PMT\left(\frac{1-1.0775^{-25}}{0.0775}\right)$$

   $$PMT = \underline{\$27,505.93}$$

5. The contributions form an annuity due having
   $$FV\text{(due)} = \$316,000, \quad PMT = \$3500, \quad n = 2(17) = 34$$
   Either solve for j using the financial calculator functions, or solve formula (13-1) for i using the trial-and-error method of Appendix 11B. We obtain either
   $j = 10.1026\%$ compounded semiannually, or $i = 5.0513\%$ per half year.

   Then $f = (1+i)^m - 1 = (1.050513)^2 - 1 = \underline{10.36\%}$

7. The interest rate being charged is the discount rate that makes the present value of four quarterly payments equal to the annual dues payment.
   Given: $PV\text{(due)} = \$2820$, $PMT = \$736.56$, and $n = 4$
   Either solve for j using the financial calculator functions, or solve formula (13-2) for i using the trial-and-error method of Appendix 11B. We obtain either
   $j = 12.00\%$ compounded quarterly, or $i = 3.00\%$ per quarter.

   Then $f = (1+i)^m - 1 = (1.03)^4 - 1 = \underline{12.55\%}$

Review Problems *(continued)*

9. The contributions form a simple annuity due having FV(due) = $200,000 and PMT = $300.
   If $i = \frac{7.5\%}{12} = 0.625\%$,

$$n = \frac{\ln\left[1 + \dfrac{i \times FV(\text{due})}{PMT(1+i)}\right]}{\ln(1+i)} = \frac{\ln\left(1 + \dfrac{0.00625 \times \$200{,}000}{\$300(1.00625)}\right)}{\ln(1.00625)} = 262.77$$

That is, 263 contributions will be required.

If $i = \frac{8.5\%}{12} = 0.708\overline{3}\%$, we similarly obtain $n = 246.31$.

That is, 247 contributions will be required. Therefore, at the lower rate of return,
263 − 247 = <u>16 more contributions</u> will be required.

11. The interest rate being charged is the discount rate that makes the present value
   of the payments equal to the purchase price. The payments form an annuity due having
   PV(due) = $1395, n = 12, and PMT = $125.
   Using the calculator's financial functions to obtain j = 16.176% compounded monthly.
   Alternatively, substitute into formula (13-2) and solve for i using the trial-and-error
   method of Appendix 11B to obtain i = 1.348% per month.

   Then $\quad f = (1+i)^m - 1 = (1.01348)^{12} - 1 = \underline{17.43\%}$

13. *a.* The contributions form a simple annuity due having
   FV(due) = $1,000,000, n = 31, i = 8%
   Substitute into formula (13-1) and solve for PMT.

$$\$1{,}000{,}000 = PMT\left(\frac{1.08^{31} - 1}{0.08}\right)(1.08)$$

$$PMT = \underline{\$7506.74} \text{ on each birthday}$$

   b. If instead, n = 26, we similarly obtain PMT = <u>$11,580.67</u>

15. The total amount in the RRSP after 30 years will be the future value of all contributions.
   The future value, 10 years from now, of the $4000 contributions will be

$$FV(\text{due}) = \$4000\left(\frac{1.0825^{10} - 1}{0.0825}\right)(1.0825) = \$63{,}476.43$$

   The future value, 30 years from now (an additional n = 20 years), of this amount
   and the $6000 contributions will be

$$\$63{,}476.43\,(1.0825)^{20} + 6000\left(\frac{1.0825^{20} - 1}{0.0825}\right)(1.0825) = \underline{\$615{,}447.79}$$

17. Amount in the RRSP from contributions in the first 5 years
   = FV of all 25 years' contributions − FV of last 20 years' contributions

$$= \$5000\left(\frac{1.08^{25} - 1}{0.08}\right)(1.08) - \$5000\left(\frac{1.08^{20} - 1}{0.08}\right)(1.08)$$

   $= \$394{,}772.08 - \$247{,}114.61$
   $= \$147{,}657.47$

   This difference is

$$\frac{\$147{,}657.47}{\$394{,}772.08} \times 100\% = \underline{37.4\%}$$

   of the value of the RRSP after 25 years.

Review Problems *(continued)*

19. With $PMT = \$5000$, $n = 25$, and $i = 10\%$,

$$FV(\text{due}) = \$5000\left(\frac{1.10^{25}-1}{0.10}\right)(1.10) = \$540,908.83$$

To have the same future value with $i = 8\%$,

$$\$540,908.83 = PMT\left(\frac{1.08^{25}-1}{0.08}\right)(1.08)$$

$$PMT = \$6850.90$$

The annual contributions must, therefore, be increased by

$$\frac{\$6850.90 - \$5000}{\$5000} \times 100\% = \underline{37.0\%}$$

to offset the 2% per annum lower rate of return.

21. The present value of the lease payments discounted at the required rate of return must equal the capital cost of the leased equipment.

a. The lease payments form a general annuity due having

$$PV(\text{due}) = \$35,000, \; n = 12(5) = 60, \; i = \tfrac{12\%}{2} = 6\%, \; c = \tfrac{2}{12} = 0.1\overline{6}, \text{ and}$$

$$i_2 = (1+i)^c - 1 = (1.06)^{0.1\overline{6}} - 1 = 0.00975879418$$

Substitute into formula (13-2) and solve for PMT.

$$\$35,000 = PMT\left(\frac{1 - 1.00975879418^{-60}}{0.00975879418}\right)(1.00975879418)$$

$$PMT = \underline{\$765.97}$$

b. The lease payments now form a simple annuity due having

$$PV(\text{due}) = \$35,000, \; n = 2(5) = 10, \text{ and } i = 6\%$$

$$\$35,000 = PMT\left(\frac{1 - 1.06^{-10}}{0.06}\right)(1.06)$$

$$PMT = \underline{\$4486.21}$$

Self-Test Exercise

1. a. The payments form an annuity due having

$$PMT = \$1000, \; n = 2(20) = 40, \text{ and } i = \tfrac{8.5\%}{2} = 4.25\%$$

$$FV(\text{due}) = \$1000\left(\frac{1.0425^{40}-1}{0.0425}\right)(1.0425) = \underline{\$105,107.80}$$

b. With $PMT = \$2000$, $n = 20$, and $i = 8.5\%$

$$FV(\text{due}) = \$2000\left(\frac{1.085^{20}-1}{0.085}\right)(1.085) = \underline{\$104,978.12}$$

2. Choose the payment plan with the lower economic value.
   For the monthly premiums, $PMT = \$33.71$, $n = 12$, and $i = \frac{7.5\%}{12} = 0.625\%$

   $$PV(\text{due}) = \$33.71\left(\frac{1-1.00625^{-12}}{0.00625}\right)(1.00625) = \$390.88$$

   This is $3.48 more than the single payment falling on the focal date.
   Therefore, choose the <u>single payment plan</u>.

3. a. Initial long-term lease liability = Present value of all lease payments

   $$= \$200,000\left(\frac{1-1.037^{-14}}{0.037}\right)(1.037)$$

   $$= \underline{\$2,234,826.87}$$

   b. Liability = Present value of the remaining 7 payments

   $$= \$200,000\left(\frac{1-1.037^{-7}}{0.037}\right)(1.037)$$

   $$= \underline{\$1,258,744.78}$$

4. For the first 30 months, the payments form a simple annuity due having
   $PMT = \$800$, $n = \frac{30}{3} = 10$, and $i = \frac{8\%}{4} = 2\%$

   For the next 4.5 years, the payments form a general annuity due having
   $PMT = \$800$, $n = 4(4.5) = 18$, $i = \frac{7\%}{2} = 3.5\%$, $c = \frac{2}{4} = 0.5$, and

   $$i_2 = (1+i)^c - 1 = (1.035)^{0.5} - 1 = 0.0173494975$$

   The future value, 30 months from now, of the first 10 payments is

   $$FV(\text{due}) = \$800\left(\frac{1.02^{10}-1}{0.02}\right)(1.02) = \$8934.97$$

   The future value, 7 years from now, of this amount and the remaining 18 payments is

   $$FV = \$8934.97\,(1.035)^9 + \$800\left(\frac{1.0173494975^{18}-1}{0.0173494975}\right)(1.0173494975)$$

   $$= \$12,177.45 + \$17,023.82$$
   $$= \underline{\$29,201.27}$$

5. The present value of the lease payments discounted at the required rate of return must
   equal the capital cost of the equipment. The proposed lease payments form a general
   annuity due having

   $$PV(\text{due}) = \$7650, n = 12(4) = 48, i = \frac{15\%}{4} = 3.75\%, c = \frac{4}{12} = 0.\overline{3}$$

   $$i_2 = (1+i)^c - 1 = (1.0375)^{0.\overline{3}} - 1 = 0.012346926$$

   Substitute into formula (13-2) and solve for PMT.

   $$\$7650 = PMT\left(\frac{1-1.012346926^{-48}}{0.012346926}\right)1.012346926)$$

   $$PMT = \underline{\$209.61}$$

   The beginning-of-month lease payment should be $209.61.

6. With the focal date at Ms. Bowers 62nd birthday,

   FV of RRSP contributions = PV of the annuity payments

   Viewed from the focal date, both payment streams form simple annuities due.
   For the PV calculation,

   $$PMT = \$3500, \; n = 12(20) = 240, \; i = \frac{4.8\%}{12} = 0.4\%$$

   $$PV(\text{due}) = \$3500\left(\frac{1-1.004^{-240}}{0.004}\right)(1.004) = \$541{,}483.87$$

   For the RRSP contributions, $FV(\text{due}) = \$541{,}483.87$, $n = 4(27) = 108$, and $i = \frac{8\%}{4} = 2\%$.

   Substitute into formula (13-1) and solve for PMT.

   $$\$541{,}483.87 = PMT\left(\frac{1.02^{108}-1}{0.02}\right)(1.02)$$

   $$PMT = \underline{\$1417.86}$$

   Each quarterly contribution should be $1417.86.

7. With the focal date set at the date Jeff entered college,

   FV of RESP contributions = PV of withdrawals

   Both payment streams form simple annuities due.
   For the RESP contributions, $PMT = \$50$, $n = 12(14) + 5 = 173$, and $i = \frac{8.25\%}{12} = 0.6875\%$.

   $$FV(\text{due}) = \$50\left(\frac{1.006875^{173}-1}{0.006875}\right)(1.006875) = \$16{,}634.93$$

   For the monthly withdrawals, $PV(\text{due}) = \$16{,}634.93$, $PMT = \$500$, and $i = 0.6875\%$.

   $$n = -\frac{\ln\left[1 - \dfrac{i \times PV(\text{due})}{PMT(1+i)}\right]}{\ln(1+i)} = -\frac{\ln\left(1 - \dfrac{0.006875 \times \$16{,}634.93}{\$500(1.006875)}\right)}{\ln(1.006875)} = 37.61$$

   The payments will run for 38 months or <u>3 years and 2 months</u>.

8. The implied interest rate is the discount rate that makes the present value of four
   3-month memberships equal to the price of a 1-year membership.
   Substitute $PV(\text{due}) = \$250$, $n = 4$, and $PMT = \$80$ into formula (13-2). Solve for i using
   the trial-and-error method of Appendix 11B. We obtain $I = 19.443\%$ per quarter. Then

   $$f = (1+i)^m - 1 = (1.19443)^4 - 1 = \underline{103.54\%}$$

9. To impound an interest rate of 16% compounded semiannually, the present value of
   12 monthly premium payments discounted at this rate equals the annual premium.
   The monthly payments form a general annuity due having

   $$PV(\text{due}) = \$100, \; n = 12, \; I = \frac{10\%}{2} = 5\%, \text{ and } c = \frac{2}{12} = 0.1\overline{6}$$

   $$i_2 = (1+i)^c - 1 = (1.05)^{0.1\overline{6}} - 1 = 0.00816484605$$

   Substitute into formula (13-2) and solve for PMT.

   $$\$100 = PMT\left(\frac{1-1.00816484605^{-12}}{0.00816484605}\right)(1.00816484605)$$

   $$PMT = \underline{\$8.71}$$

   The monthly premium per $100 of annual premium should be $8.71.

14 Loan Amortization; Mortgages

Exercise 14.1

1. Given: $PV = \$1000$, $n = 6$, $i = \frac{15\%}{12} = 1.25\%$

    Substitute into formula (10-2) and solve for PMT.

    $$\$1000 = PMT\left(\frac{1-1.0125^{-6}}{0.0125}\right)$$

    $PMT = \$174.03$

Payment number	Payment	Interest portion	Principal portion	Principal balance
0	--	--	--	$1000.00
1	$174.03	$12.50	$161.53	838.47
2	174.03	10.48	163.55	674.92
3	174.03	8.44	165.59	509.33
4	174.03	6.37	167.66	341.67
5	174.03	4.27	169.76	171.91
6	174.06	2.15	171.91	0.00
	Total:	$44.21		

3. Given: $PV = \$9000$, $n = 6$. $i = 9\%$, $c = \frac{1}{2} = 0.5$

    $$i_2 = (1+i)^c - 1 = (1.09)^{0.5} - 1 = 0.044030651$$

    Solve for PMT in

    $$\$9000 = PMT\left(\frac{1-1.044030651^{-6}}{0.044030651}\right)$$

    $PMT = \$1739.45$

Payment number	Payment	Interest portion	Principal portion	Principal balance
0	--	--	--	$9000.00
1	$1739.45	$396.28	$1343.17	7656.83
2	1739.45	337.14	1402.31	6254.52
3	1739.45	275.39	1464.06	4790.46
4	1739.45	210.93	1528.52	3261.94
5	1739.45	143.63	1595.82	1666.12
6	1739.48	73.36	1666.12	0.00

Exercise 14.1 *(continued)*

5. Given: $PV = \$8000$, $n = 8$, $i = \frac{8\%}{4} = 2\%$

   Substitute into formula (10-2) and solve for PMT.

   $$\$8000 = PMT\left(\frac{1-1.02^{-8}}{0.02}\right)$$

   $$PMT = \$1092.08$$

Payment number	Payment	Interest portion	Principal portion	Principal balance
0	--	--	--	$8000.00
1	$1092.08	$160.00	$932.08	7067.92
2	1092.08	141.36	950.72	6117.20
3	2592.08	122.34	2469.74	3647.46
4	1092.08	72.95	1019.13	2628.33
5	1092.08	52.57	1039.51	1588.82
6	1092.08	31.78	1060.30	528.52
7	539.09	10.57	528.52	0.00
	Total:	$591.57		

7. Given: $PV = \$60{,}000$, $n = 12(6) = 72$, $i = \frac{7.5\%}{12} = 0.625\%$

   Substitute into formula (10-2) and solve for PMT.

   $$\$60{,}000 = PMT\left(\frac{1-1.00625^{-72}}{0.00625}\right)$$

   $$PMT = \$1037.41$$

Payment number	Payment	Interest portion	Principal portion	Principal balance
0	--	--	--	$60,000.00
1	$1037.41	$375.00	$662.41	59,337.59
2	1037.41	370.86	666.55	58,671.04
|	|	|	|	|
42	--	--	--	28,298.14
43	1037.41	176.86	860.55	27,437.59
44	1037.41	171.48	865.93	26,571.66
|	|	|	|	|
70	--	--	--	2055.24
71	1037.41	12.85	1024.56	1030.68
72	1037.12	6.44	1030.68	0.00

9. Given: $PV = \$1000$, $PMT = \$200$, $i = \frac{15\%}{12} = 1.25\%$

Payment number	Payment	Interest portion	Principal portion	Principal balance
0				$1000.00
1	$200.00	$12.50	$187.50	812.50
2	200.00	10.16	189.84	622.66
3	200.00	7.78	192.22	430.44
4	200.00	5.38	194.62	235.82
5	200.00	2.95	197.05	38.77
6	39.25	0.48	38.77	0.00
	Total:	$39.25		

11. Given: $PV = \$9000$, $PMT = \$1800$, $i = 9\%$, $c = \frac{1}{2} = 0.5$

$$i_2 = (1+i)^c - 1 = (1.09)^{0.5} - 1 = 0.044030651$$

Payment number	Payment	Interest portion	Principal portion	Principal balance
0	--	--	--	$9000.00
1	$1800.00	$396.28	$1403.72	7596.28
2	1800.00	334.47	1465.53	6130.75
3	1800.00	269.94	1530.06	4600.69
4	1800.00	202.57	1597.43	3003.26
5	1800.00	132.24	1667.76	1335.50
6	1394.30	58.80	1335.50	0.00

13. Given: $PV = \$8000$, $PMT = \$1000$, $i = \frac{8\%}{4} = 2\%$

Payment number	Payment	Interest portion	Principal portion	Principal balance
0	--	--	--	$8000.00
1	$1000.00	$160.00	$840.00	7160.00
2	1000.00	143.20	856.80	6303.20
3	2000.00	126.06	1873.94	4429.26
4	1000.00	88.59	911.41	3517.85
5	1000.00	70.36	929.64	2588.21
6	1000.00	51.76	948.24	1639.97
7	1000.00	32.80	967.20	672.77
8	686.23	13.46	672.77	0.00
	Total:	$686.23		

15. Given: $PV = \$60,000$, $PMT = \$1000$, $i = \frac{7.5\%}{12} = 0.625\%$

Payment number	Payment	Interest portion	Principal portion	Principal balance
0	--	--	--	$60,000.00
1	$1000.00	$375.00	$625.00	59,375.00
2	1000.00	371.09	628.91	58,746.09
|	|	|	|	|
55	--	--	--	19,128.18
56	1000.00	119.55	880.45	18,247.73
57	1000.00	114.05	885.95	17,361.78
|	|	|	|	|
74	--	--	--	1424.49
75	1000.00	8.90	991.10	433.39
76	436.10	2.71	433.39	0.00

Concept Questions (Section 14.2)

1. a. <u>Yes</u>. The $100,000 loan is effectively two concurrent $50,000 loans. You will pay the same total interest per month (at a given i and n) on two $50,000 loans as you will pay on a single $100,000 loan. Therefore, the monthly payment on a $100,000 loan will be double the monthly payment on a $50,000 loan.

   b. <u>Yes</u>. Again think of the $100,000 loan as two concurrent $50,000 loans. On a $100,000 loan, the payment size, the interest and principal components of each payment, and the balance after any particular payment will be double the corresponding amounts for a $50,000 loan (at the same i and n).

3. <u>Yes</u>. With each successive payment, the interest component becomes smaller and the principal component becomes larger. Therefore, the total principal repaid in the first half of the amortization period will be less than the total principal repaid in the second half of the amortization period. It follows that: (1) less than half of the original principal will be repaid in the first half of the amortization period; and (2) it will take more than half of the amortization period to reduce the balance to half the original principal.

5. a. Each regular payment represents an *under*payment of 0.3¢. Therefore, the adjusted final payment will be <u>more</u> than the regular payment.

   b. The increase in the final payment will be the future value of the 120 underpayments of 0.3¢. This will be <u>(i) more than 120(0.3¢) = 36¢</u>.

7. The interest paid in the 4th year will be <u>(ii) less than</u> the interest paid in the 2nd year. With each successive payment, the interest component becomes smaller and the principal component becomes larger. Therefore, the total interest paid in each successive year will decrease.

Exercise 14.2

1. Given: $PV = \$40,000$, $n = 12(10) = 120$, $i = \frac{6.6\%}{12} = 0.55\%$

   Substitute into formula (10-2) and solve for PMT.

   $$\$40,000 = PMT\left(\frac{1-1.0055^{-120}}{0.0055}\right)$$

   $$PMT = \$456.23$$

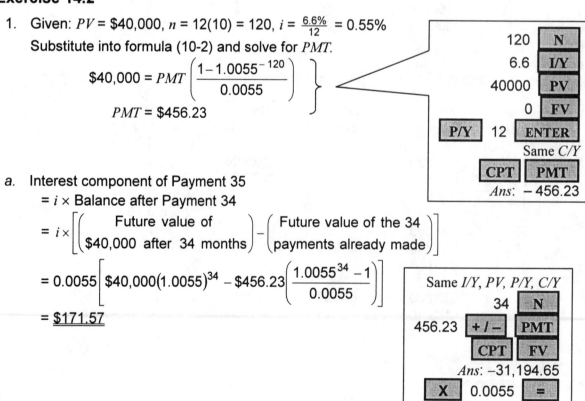

a. Interest component of Payment 35

   $= i \times$ Balance after Payment 34

   $= i \times \left[\left(\begin{array}{c}\text{Future value of}\\ \$40,000 \text{ after } 34 \text{ months}\end{array}\right) - \left(\begin{array}{c}\text{Future value of the } 34\\ \text{payments already made}\end{array}\right)\right]$

   $= 0.0055\left[\$40,000(1.0055)^{34} - \$456.23\left(\frac{1.0055^{34}-1}{0.0055}\right)\right]$

   $= \underline{\$171.57}$

266   *Business Mathematics in Canada, 5/e*

1. *b.* Principal component of Payment 63
   = Balance after Payment 62 − Balance after Payment 63

$$= \left(\begin{array}{c} \text{Future value of} \\ \$40{,}000 \text{ after 62 months} \end{array} \right) - \left(\begin{array}{c} \text{Future value of the 62} \\ \text{payments already made} \end{array} \right)$$

$$\quad - \left(\begin{array}{c} \text{Future value of} \\ \$40{,}000 \text{ after 63 months} \end{array} \right) - \left(\begin{array}{c} \text{Future value of the 63} \\ \text{payments already made} \end{array} \right)$$

$$= \left[\$40{,}000(1.0055)^{62} - \$456.23\left(\frac{1.0055^{62} - 1}{0.0055} \right) \right]$$

$$\quad - \left[\$40{,}000(1.0055)^{63} - \$456.23\left(\frac{1.0055^{63} - 1}{0.0055} \right) \right]$$

= $22,603.17 − $22,271.26
= **$331.91**

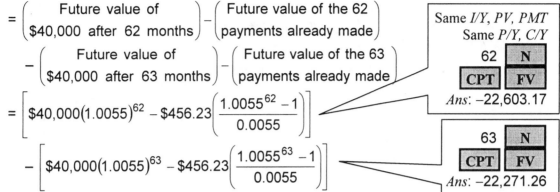

Same I/Y, PV, PMT
Same P/Y, C/Y

| 62 | **N** |

| **CPT** | **FV** |

Ans: −22,603.17

| 63 | **N** |

| **CPT** | **FV** |

Ans: −22,271.26

c. Principal reduction in Year 1
   = $40,000 − Balance after Year 1
   = $40,000 − Balance after Payment 12
   = $40,000 − $37,077.90
   = **$2922.10**

Same I/Y, PV, PMT
Same P/Y, C/Y

| 12 | **N** |

| **CPT** | **FV** |

Ans: −37,077.90

d. Principal reduction in Year 10
   = Balance after Year 9 − Balance after Year 10
   = Balance after Payment 108 − Balance after Payment 120
   = $5283.92 − $0
   = **$5283.92**

Same I/Y, PV, PMT
Same P/Y, C/Y

| 108 | **N** |

| **CPT** | **FV** |

Ans: −5283.92

3. Given: $PV = \$14{,}000$, $n = 2(7) = 14$, $i = \frac{8.4\%}{2} = 4.2\%$

   Substitute into formula (10-2) and solve for *PMT*.

$$\$14{,}000 = PMT\left(\frac{1 - 1.042^{-14}}{0.042} \right)$$

$$PMT = \$1342.92$$

14	**N**
8.4	**I/Y**
14000	**PV**
0	**FV**

| **P/Y** | 2 | **ENTER** |

Same C/Y

| **CPT** | **PMT** |

Ans: − 1342.92

a. Interest component of Payment 10
   = $i \times$ Balance after Payment 9

$$= i \times \left[\left(\begin{array}{c} \text{Future value of} \\ \$14{,}000 \text{ after 4.5 years} \end{array} \right) - \left(\begin{array}{c} \text{Future value of the 9} \\ \text{payments already made} \end{array} \right) \right]$$

$$= 0.042\left[\$14{,}000(1.042)^{9} - \$1342.92\left(\frac{1.042^{9} - 1}{0.042} \right) \right]$$

= **$249.69**

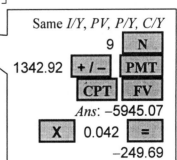

Same I/Y, PV, P/Y, C/Y

| 9 | **N** |

| 1342.92 | **+ / −** | **PMT** |

| **CPT** | **FV** |

Ans: −5945.07

| **X** | 0.042 | **=** |

−249.69

3. *b.* Principal component of Payment 3

= Balance after Payment 2 − Balance after Payment 3

$= \left(\begin{array}{c} \text{Future value of} \\ \$14{,}000 \text{ after 1 year} \end{array} \right) - \left(\begin{array}{c} \text{Future value of the 2} \\ \text{payments already made} \end{array} \right)$

$\quad - \left(\begin{array}{c} \text{Future value of} \\ \$14{,}000 \text{ after 1.5 months} \end{array} \right) - \left(\begin{array}{c} \text{Future value of the 3} \\ \text{payments already made} \end{array} \right)$

$= \left[\$14{,}000(1.042)^2 - \$1342.92\left(\dfrac{1.042^2 - 1}{0.042} \right) \right]$

$\quad - \left[\$14{,}000(1.042)^3 - \$1342.92\left(\dfrac{1.042^3 - 1}{0.042} \right) \right]$

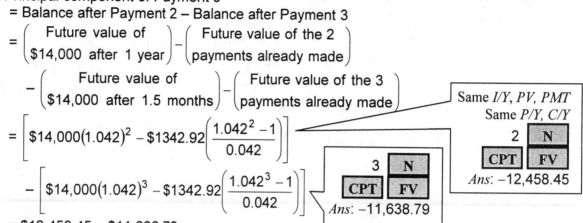

Same *I/Y, PV, PMT*
Same *P/Y, C/Y*

| 2 | N |
| CPT | FV |

Ans: −12,458.45

| 3 | N |
| CPT | FV |

Ans: −11,638.79

= \$12,458.45 − \$11,638.79

= <u>\$819.66</u>

c. Interest paid in Year 6 = Total payments in Year 6 − Principal paid in Year 6

= 2*PMT* − (Balance after Year 5 − Balance after Year 6)

= 2(\$1342.92) − (Balance after Payment 10 − Balance after Payment 12)

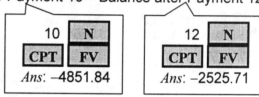

| 10 | N |
| CPT | FV |

Ans: −4851.84

| 12 | N |
| CPT | FV |

Ans: −2525.71

= 2(\$1342.92) − (\$4851.84 − \$2525.71)

= <u>\$359.71</u>

d. Principal reduction by Payments 3 to 6 inclusive

= Balance after Payment 2 − Balance after Payment 6

| 2 | N |
| CPT | FV |

Ans: −12,458.45

| 6 | N |
| CPT | FV |

Ans: −8967.39

= \$12,458.45 − \$8967.39

= <u>\$3491.06</u>

5. Given: *PV* = \$125,000, *n* = 12(20) = 240,

$i = \frac{6\%}{2} = 3\%, c = \frac{2}{12} = 0.1\overline{6}$

$i_2 = (1+i)^c - 1 = (1.03)^{0.1\overline{6}} - 1 = 0.00493862203$

Substitute into formula (10-2) and solve for *PMT*.

$\$125{,}000 = PMT\left(\dfrac{1 - 1.00493862203^{-240}}{0.00493862203} \right)$

PMT = \$890.24

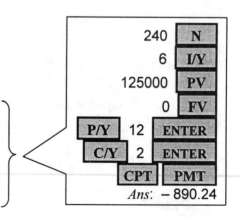

240	N
6	I/Y
125000	PV
0	FV
P/Y	12	ENTER
C/Y	2	ENTER
CPT	PMT

Ans: − 890.24

5. *a.* Interest component of Payment 188

   $\qquad = i \times$ Balance after Payment 187

   $\qquad = 0.00493862203 \times \$41,422.04$

   $\qquad = \underline{\$204.57}$

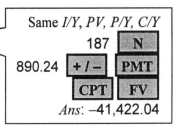

Same *I/Y, PV, P/Y, C/Y*

187   N

890.24   +/−   PMT

CPT   FV

Ans: −41,422.04

b. Principal component of Payment 101

$\qquad$ = Balance after Payment 100 − Balance after Payment 101

$$= \left[\$125,000(1.004938622)^{100} - \$890.24\left(\frac{1.004938622^{100}-1}{0.004938622}\right) \right]$$

$$- \left[\$125,000(1.004938622)^{101} - \$890.24\left(\frac{1.004938622^{101}-1}{0.004938622}\right) \right]$$

$\qquad = \$89,818.64 - \$89,371.98$

$\qquad = \underline{\$446.66}$

Same *I/Y, PV, PMT*
Same *P/Y, C/Y*

100   N

CPT   FV

Ans: −89,818.64

Same *I/Y, PV, PMT*
Same *P/Y, C/Y*

101   N

CPT   FV

Ans: −89,371.98

c. Principal reduction in Year 1

$\qquad = \$125,000 -$ Balance after Year 1

$\qquad = \$125,000 -$ Balance after Payment 12

$\qquad = \$125,000 - \$121,634.62$

$\qquad = \underline{\$3365.38}$

Same *I/Y, PV, PMT*
Same *P/Y, C/Y*

12   N

CPT   FV

Ans: −121,634.62

d. Principal reduction in Year 20

$\qquad$ = Balance after Year 19 − Balance after Year 20

$\qquad$ = Balance after Payment 228

$\qquad\qquad$ − Balance after Payment 240

$\qquad = \$10,345.79 - \$0$

$\qquad = \underline{\$10,345.79}$

Same *I/Y, PV, PMT*
Same *P/Y, C/Y*

228   N

CPT   FV

Ans: −10,345.79

7. Given: $PV = \$50,000$, $n = 4(10) = 40$, $i = \frac{7.6\%}{2} = 3.8\%$, $c = \frac{2}{4} = 0.5$

$\qquad i_2 = (1+i)^c - 1 = (1.038)^{0.5} - 1 = 0.01882285016$

Substitute into formula (10-2) and solve for *PMT.*

$$\$50,000 = PMT\left(\frac{1 - 1.01882285016^{-40}}{0.01882285016}\right)$$

$\qquad PMT = \$1790.26$

a. Interest component of Payment 8 $= i \times$ Balance after Payment 7

$\qquad\qquad\qquad\qquad\qquad\qquad = 0.01882285016\,(\$43,709.81)$

$\qquad\qquad\qquad\qquad\qquad\qquad = \underline{\$822.74}$

b. Principal component of Payment 33

$\qquad$ = Balance after Payment 32 − Balance after Payment 33

$\qquad = \$13,181.541 - \$11,639.395$

$\qquad = \underline{\$1542.15}$

c. Total interest in Payments 21 to 30 inclusive

$\qquad$ = Sum of Payments 21 to 30 − Total principal in Payments 21 to 30

$\qquad = 10PMT -$ (Balance after Payment 20 − Balance after Payment 30)

$\qquad = 10(\$1790.26) - (\$29,608.787 - \$16,180.885)$

$\qquad = \underline{\$4474.70}$

7. *d.* Principal paid in Year 3 = Balance after Year 2 – Balance after Year 3
   = Balance after Payment 8 – Balance after Payment 12
   = $42,742.29 – $38,686.65
   = <u>$4055.64</u>

9. Given: PV = $15,000, PMT = $275, $i = \frac{6\%}{12}$ = 0.5%

   a. Interest component of Payment 13
   = i × Balance after Payment 12
   Balance after Payment 12

   $$= \left[\$15,000(1.005)^{12} - \$275\left(\frac{1.005^{12} - 1}{0.005} \right) \right]$$

   = $12,532.89
   Interest component of Payment 13 = 0.005($12,532.89)
   = <u>$62.66</u>

   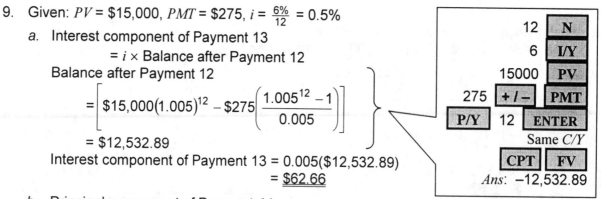

   b. Principal component of Payment 44
   = Balance after Payment 43 – Balance after Payment 44

   = $5432.086 – $5184.246
   = <u>$247.84</u>

   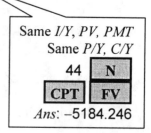
   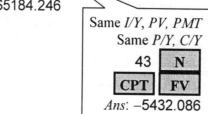

   c. The total number of payments is

   $$n = -\frac{\ln\left(1 - \frac{i \times PV}{PMT}\right)}{\ln(1+i)}$$

   $$= -\frac{\ln\left(1 - \frac{0.005 \times \$15,000}{\$275}\right)}{\ln(1.005)}$$

   = 63.84984

   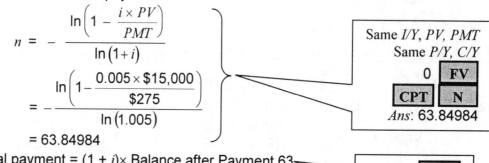

   Final payment = (1 + i)× Balance after Payment 63
   = 1.005($232.63)
   = <u>$233.79</u>

   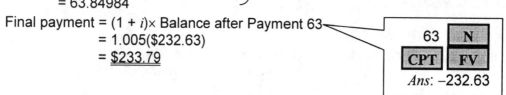

Exercise 14.2 *(continued)*

11. Given: $PV = \$100,000$, $PMT = \$700$, $i = \frac{7.2\%}{2} = 3.6\%$

Then $c = \frac{2}{12} = 0.1\overline{6}$ and

$$i_2 = (1+i)^c - 1 = (1.036)^{0.1\overline{6}} - 1 = 0.00591193086$$

a. Interest component of Payment 221 = $i \times$ Balance after Payment 220

Balance after Payment 220

$$= \left[\$100,000(1.00591193086)^{220} - \$700\left(\frac{1.00591193086^{220} - 1}{0.00591193086} \right) \right]$$

$$= \$51,088.65$$

Interest component of Payment 13 = 0.00591193086($51,088.65)
$$= \underline{\$302.03}$$

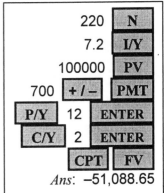

220	N
7.2	I/Y
100000	PV
700 +/−	PMT
P/Y 12	ENTER
C/Y 2	ENTER
CPT	FV

Ans: −51,088.65

b. Principal component of Payment 156
= Balance after Payment 155 − Balance after Payment 156

$$= \$72,514.34 - \$72,243.04$$
$$= \underline{\$271.30}$$

Same I/Y, PV, PMT
Same P/Y, C/Y
155 **N**
CPT **FV**
Ans: −72,514.34

Same I/Y, PV, PMT
Same P/Y, C/Y
156 **N**
CPT **FV**
Ans: −72,243.04

11. c. The total number of payments is

$$n = -\frac{\ln\left(1 - \frac{i \times PV}{PMT}\right)}{\ln(1+i)}$$

$$= -\frac{\ln\left(1 - \frac{0.00591193086 \times \$100,000}{\$700}\right)}{\ln(1.00591193086)}$$

$$= 315.80251$$

Same I/Y, PV, PMT
Same P/Y, C/Y
0 **FV**
CPT **N**
Ans: 315.80251

Final payment = (1 + i) × Balance after Payment 315
$$= 1.00591193086(\$558.78)$$
$$= \underline{\$562.08}$$

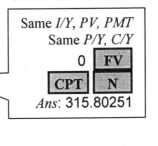

Same I/Y, PV, PMT
Same P/Y, C/Y
315 **N**
CPT **FV**
Ans: −558.78

13. Given: $PV = \$37,000$, $i = \frac{8.2\%}{2} = 4.1\%$, $n = 2(10) = 20$

Substitute into formula (10-2) and solve for *PMT*.

$$\$37,000 = PMT\left(\frac{1 - 1.041^{-20}}{0.041} \right)$$

$$PMT = \$2746.69$$

a. Principal part of Payment 6 = Balance after Payment 5 − Balance after Payment 6
$$= \$30,326.28 - \$28,822.97$$
$$= \underline{\$1503.31}$$

b. Interest part of Payment 16 = $i \times$ Balance after Payment 15
$$= 0.041(\$12,193.43)$$
$$= \underline{\$499.93}$$

Exercise 14.2 *(continued)*

13. *c.* Principal paid by Payments 6 to 15 inclusive
          = Balance after Payment 5 − Balance after Payment 15
          = \$30,326.28 − \$12,193.43
          = <u>\$18,132.85</u>

    d. Interest paid in year 3 = $2PMT$ − (Balance after Payment 4 − Balance after Payment 6)
          = 2(\$2746.69) − (\$31,770.383 − \$28,822.966)
          = <u>\$2545.96</u>

    e. Final payment = $(1 + i) \times$ Balance after Payment 19 = 1.041(\$2913.14) = <u>\$2746.60</u>

15. Given: $PV = \$6000$, $i = \frac{12.75\%}{12} = 1.0625\%$, $n = 4(4) = 16$, $c = \frac{12}{4} = 3$

$$i_2 = (1+i)^c - 1 = (1.010625)^3 - 1 = 0.032214871$$

Substitute into formula (10-2) and solve for PMT.

$$\$6000 = PMT \left(\frac{1 - 1.032214871^{-16}}{0.032214871} \right)$$

$$PMT = \$485.79$$

    a. Interest in Payment 5 = $i_2 \times$ Balance after Payment 4
          = 0.032214871(\$4772.24)
          = <u>\$153.74</u>

    b. Principal in Payment 11 = Balance after Payment 10 − Balance after Payment 11
          = \$2612.40 − \$2210.77
          = <u>\$401.63</u>

    c. Interest paid by Payments 5 to 12 inclusive
          = $8PMT$ − (Balance after Payment 4 − Balance after Payment 12)
          = 8(\$485.79) − (\$4772.24 − \$1796.20)
          = <u>\$910.28</u>

    d. Principal paid in Year 2 = Balance after Payment 4 − Balance after Payment 8
          = \$4772.236 − \$3378.452
          = <u>\$1393.78</u>

    e. Final payment = $(1 + i_2) \times$ Balance after Payment 15 = 1.032215(\$470.62) = <u>\$485.78</u>

17. Given: $PV = \$37,000$, $i = \frac{8.2\%}{2} = 4.1\%$, $PMT = \$2500$

    a. Principal in Payment 16 = Balance after Payment 15 − Balance after Payment 16
          = \$17,169.91 − \$15,373.88
          = <u>\$1796.03</u>

    b. Interest in Payment 6 = $i \times$ Balance after Payment 5
          = 0.041(\$31,665.10)
          = <u>\$1298.27</u>

    c. Principal reduction by Payments 8 to 14 inclusive
          = Balance after Payment 7 − Balance after Payment 14
          = \$29,212.37 − \$18,895.21
          = <u>\$10,317.16</u>

    d. Interest in Year 5 = $2PMT$ − (Principal in Year 5)
          = $2PMT$ − (Balance after Payment 8 − Balance after Payment 10)
          = 2(\$2500) − (\$27,910.08 − \$25,143.12)
          = <u>\$2233.04</u>

17. e. The total number of payments is

$$n = -\frac{\ln\left(1 - \dfrac{i \times PV}{PMT}\right)}{\ln(1+i)} = -\frac{\ln\left(1 - \dfrac{0.041 \times \$37,000}{\$2500}\right)}{\ln(1.041)} = 23.230346$$

Final payment = $(1 + i) \times$ Balance after Payment 23 = 1.041(\$561.77) = <u>\$584.80</u>

19. Given: $PV = \$6000$, $PMT = \$500$, $i = \dfrac{12.75\%}{12} = 1.0625\%$, $c = \dfrac{12}{4} = 3$

$$i_2 = (1+i)^c - 1 = (1.010625)^3 - 1 = 0.032214871$$

a. Interest in Payment 11 = $i_2 \times$ Balance after Payment 10
= 0.032214871(\$2447.83)
= <u>\$78.86</u>

b. Principal in Payment 6 = Balance after Payment 5 – Balance after Payment 6
= \$4364.40 – \$4005.00
= <u>\$359.40</u>

c. Interest paid by Payments 3 to 9 inclusive
= $7PMT$ – (Principal in Payments 3 to 9 inclusive)
= $7PMT$ – (Balance after Payment 2 – Balance after Payment 9)
= 7(\$500) – (\$5376.70 – \$2855.83)
= <u>\$979.13</u>

d. Principal paid in Year 3 = Balance after Payment 8 – Balance after Payment 12
= \$3251.09 – \$1591.97
= <u>\$1659.12</u>

e. The total number of payments is

$$n = -\frac{\ln\left(1 - \dfrac{i_2 \times PV}{PMT}\right)}{\ln(1+i_2)} = -\frac{\ln\left(1 - \dfrac{0.032214871 \times \$6000}{\$500}\right)}{\ln(1.032214871)} = 15.4131627$$

Final payment = $(1 + i_2) \times$ Balance after Payment 15 = 1.0322149(\$202.00) = <u>\$208.51</u>

21. Given: $PV = \$40,000$, $n = 12(15) = 180$, $i = \dfrac{7.5\%}{12} = 0.625\%$

a. Substitute into formula (10-2) and solve for PMT.

$$\$40,000 = PMT\left(\frac{1 - 1.00625^{-180}}{0.00625}\right)$$

$$PMT = \underline{\$370.80}$$

b. Interest part of Payment 60 = $i \times$ Balance after Payment 59
= 0.00625(\$31,413.19)
= <u>\$196.33</u>

Principal part of Payment 60 = PMT – Interest part of Payment 60
= \$370.80 – \$196.33
= <u>\$174.47</u>

c. Balance after Payment 60 = <u>\$31,238.73</u>

d. Interest paid in Year 5 = $12PMT$ – Principal paid in Year 5
= $12PMT$ – (Balance after Pymt 48 – Balance after Pymt 60)
= 12(\$370.80) – (\$33,262.28 – \$31,238.73)
= <u>\$2426.05</u>

23. a. Given: $PV = \$12,000$, Balance after Payment 24 = $\$10,000$, $i = \frac{9\%}{2} = 4.5\%$, $c = 0.1\overline{6}$

$$i_2 = (1+i)^c - 1 = (1.045)^{0.1\overline{6}} - 1 = 0.007363123$$

The initial loan equals the combined present value of 24 payments and the $10,000 balance. That is,

$$\$12,000 = PMT\left(\frac{1-1.007363123^{-24}}{0.007363123}\right) + \left(\frac{\$10,000}{1.007363123^{24}}\right)$$

$$PMT = \underline{\$164.85}$$

b. Interest part of Payment 9 = $i_2 \times$ Balance after Payment 8
$$= 0.007363123(\$11,372.06)$$
$$= \underline{\$83.73}$$

c. Principal in Payment 16 = Balance after Payment 15 – Balance after Payment 16
$$= \$10,791.54 - \$10,706.15$$
$$= \underline{\$85.39}$$

Exercise 14.3

1. The principal reduction in any 5-year period equals the decrease in the loan balance during the period.
    Step 1: Calculate the monthly payment.
    Step 2: Calculate the balance owed at the end of each 5-year interval.
    Step 3: Calculate the principal reduction in each 5-year interval using
    Principal reduction = Beginning balance – Ending balance
    Step 4: Calculate the interest paid in each 5-year interval using
    Interest paid = $60PMT$ – Principal reduction
    (Note: Adjust the last interval's amount for the differing final payment.)

Step 1: $PV = \$100,000$, $n = 12(25) = 300$, $i = \frac{7.2\%}{2} = 3.6\%$, $c = \frac{2}{12} = 0.1\overline{6}$

$$i_2 = (1+i)^c - 1 = (1.036)^{0.1\overline{6}} - 1 = 0.0059113085$$

Substitute into formula (10-2) and solve for PMT.

$$\$100,000 = PMT\left(\frac{1-1.0059113085^{-300}}{0.0059113085}\right)$$

$$PMT = \$712.81$$

Interval	Balance at end (Step 2)	Principal reduction (Step 3)	Interest paid (Step 4)
0 – 5 years	$91,271.80	$ 8728.20	$34,040.40
6 – 10 years	78,840.35	12,431.45	30,337.15
11 – 15 years	61,134.38	17,705.97	25,062.63
16 – 20 years	35,916.00	25,218.38	17,550.22
21 – 25 years	0	35,916.00	6850.39 ①

① Final payment = $(1 + i_2)\times$ Balance after payment 299
$$= 1.0059113085(\$706.42)$$
$$= \$710.60$$
Total interest = $59(\$712.81) + \$710.60 - \$35,916.00 = \$6850.39$

3. Given: $PV = \$100{,}000$, $n = 12(25) = 300$, $c = \frac{2}{12} = 0.1\overline{6}$

   a. For each of $i = \frac{6\%}{2} = 3\%$, $i = \frac{7\%}{2} = 3.5\%$, and $i = \frac{8\%}{2} = 4\%$, calculate i_2 and PMT

$i(\%)$	$i_2\,(\%)$	$PMT(\$)$
3	0.493862203	$\underline{\$639.81}$
3.5	0.575003950	$\underline{700.42}$
4	0.655819694	$\underline{763.21}$

   b. Percent difference $= \dfrac{\$763.21 - \$700.42}{\$700.42} \times 100\% = \underline{8.96\%}$

   c.
$i\,(\%\ csa)$	Total interest paid
6	$300(\$639.81) - \$100{,}000 = \underline{\$91{,}943}$
7	$300(\$700.42) - \$100{,}000 = \underline{\$110{,}126}$
8	$300(\$763.21) - \$100{,}000 = \underline{\$128{,}963}$

   (These answers assume the 300th payment does not differ from the others.)

5. The maximum loan equals the present value of the $1000 payments discounted at the interest rate on the loan.

   Given: $PMT = \$1000$, $n = 12(25) = 300$, $c = \frac{2}{12} = 0.1\overline{6}$

	i	i	$i_2\,(\%)$	Maximum loan
a.	6.5% csa	3.25%	0.534474007%	$PV = \underline{\$149{,}293.00}$
b.	7.5% csa	3.75%	0.615452392%	$PV = \underline{\$136{,}695.14}$

7. *Step* 1: Calculate the payment size for the first 5-year term.
   Step 2: Calculate the balance after 5 years.
   Step 3: Calculate the payment upon renewal.
   Step 4: Calculate the difference between the *Step* 1 and *Step* 3 results.

   Step 1: Given: $PV = \$100{,}000$, $n = 12(25) = 300$, $i = \frac{6.5\%}{2} = 3.25\%$, $c = \frac{2}{12} = 0.1\overline{6}$

   $$i_2 = (1+i)^c - 1 = (1.0325)^{0.1\overline{6}} - 1 = 0.00534474008$$

   Substitute into formula (10-2) and solve for PMT.

   $$\$100{,}000 = PMT\left(\frac{1 - 1.00534474008^{-300}}{0.00534474008}\right)$$

   $$PMT = \$669.82$$

   Step 2: Balance after payment 60 $= \$90{,}455.83$

   Step 3: Now $PV = \$90{,}455.83$, $n = 12(20) = 240$, $i = \frac{7.5\%}{2} = 3.75\%$, $c = \frac{2}{12} = 0.1\overline{6}$

   $$i_2 = (1+i)^c - 1 = (1.0375)^{0.1\overline{6}} - 1 = 0.00615452392$$

   Substitute into formula (10-2) and solve for PMT giving $PMT = \$722.38$

   Step 4: Increase in payment size $= \$722.38 - \$669.82 = \underline{\$52.56}$

Exercise 14.3 (*continued*)

9. a. Given: $PV = \$80,000$, $i = \frac{7.4\%}{2} = 3.7\%$, $n = 12(25) = 300$, $c = \frac{2}{12} = 0.1\overline{6}$

$$i_2 = (1+i)^c - 1 = (1.037)^{0.1\overline{6}} - 1 = 0.00607369206$$

Substitute into formula (10-2) and solve for *PMT*.

$$\$80,000 = PMT\left(\frac{1-1.00607369206^{-300}}{0.00607369206}\right)$$

$PMT = \$580.23$

Balance after payment 36 = $\underline{\$76,216.85}$

b. Now $PV = \$77,587.44$; $i = \frac{6.8\%}{2} = 3.4\%$; $n = 300 - 36 = 264$; $c = \frac{2}{12} = 0.1\overline{6}$

$$i_2 = (1.034)^{0.1\overline{6}} - 1 = 0.00558801773$$

Substitute into formula (10-2) and solve for *PMT* giving $PMT = \underline{\$552.88}$.

11. a. Given: $PV = \$40,000$; $i = \frac{6.6\%}{12} = 0.55\%$; $n = 12(15) = 180$

Substitute into formula (10-2) and solve for *PMT*.

$$\$40,000 = PMT\left(\frac{1-1.0055^{-180}}{0.0055}\right)$$

$PMT = \$350.65$

Rounded monthly payment = $\$360$

Balance after 4 years = Balance after 48 payments of $\$360 = \underline{\$32,333.43}$

b. On renewal, $PV = \$33,333.43$; $n = 12(11) = 132$; $i = \frac{7.2\%}{12} = 0.6\%$

Substitute into formula (10-2) and solve for *PMT*.

$$\$32,333.43 = PMT\left(\frac{1-1.006^{-132}}{0.006}\right)$$

$PMT = \$355.32$

Rounded monthly payment = $\underline{\$360.00}$

13. a. Given: $PV = \$27,000$; $i = \frac{7.25\%}{2} = 3.625\%$; $n = 12(10) = 120$; $c = \frac{2}{12} = 0.1\overline{6}$

$$i_2 = (1+i)^c - 1 = (1.03625)^{0.1\overline{6}} - 1 = 0.00595238336$$

Substitute into formula (10-2) and solve for *PMT*.

$$\$27,000 = PMT\left(\frac{1-1.00595238336^{-120}}{0.00595238336}\right)$$

$PMT = \$315.48$

Rounded payment = $\$320.00$

Balance after 60 payments of $\$320 = \underline{\$15,554.01}$

13. *b.* For the second 5-year term,

$PV = \$15,554.01$; $i = \frac{6.75\%}{2} = 3.375\%$; $n = 60$; $c = \frac{2}{12} = 0.1\overline{6}$ and

$i_2 = (1.03375)^{0.1\overline{6}} - 1 = 0.00554749189$

Solve for *PMT* giving *PMT* = $305.48

Rounded monthly payment = $310.00

The number of monthly payments of $310 needed to pay off the balance owed is

$$n = -\frac{\ln\left(1 - \dfrac{i_2 \times PV}{PMT}\right)}{\ln(1 + i_2)} = -\frac{\ln\left(1 - \dfrac{0.00554749189 \times \$15,554.01}{\$310}\right)}{\ln(1.00554749189)} = 58.9648$$

Final payment = $(1 + i_2) \times$ Balance after 58 payments

= 1.00554749189 ($297.46)

= $\underline{\$299.11}$

15. *a.* GDS ratio must be $\leq 32\%$. Let *PMT* represent the monthly mortgage payment.

Then   GDS ratio = $\dfrac{PMT + \$150 + \$200}{\$5000} \leq 0.32$

That is,

$PMT + \$150 + \$200 \leq 0.32(\$5000)$

$PMT \leq 0.32(\$5000) - \$350 = \$1250$

The TDS ratio must be $\leq 40\%$. That is,

TDS ratio = $\dfrac{PMT + \$600 + \$150 + \$200}{\$5000} \leq 0.40$

Therefore,

$PMT \leq 0.40(\$5000) - \$950 = \$1050$

The TDS ratio is the more restrictive ratio for the Archibalds.

With $PMT = \$1050$, $n = 12(25) = 300$, $i = \frac{6.6\%}{2} = 3.3\%$, and $c = \frac{2}{12} = 0.1\overline{6}$

$i_2 = (1 + i)^c - 1 = (1.033)^{0.1\overline{6}} - 1 = 0.00542586533$

The maximum mortgage loan is

$$PV = \$1050\left(\frac{1 - 1.00542586533^{-300}}{0.00542586533}\right) = \$155,349$$

Rounded to the nearest $100, the maximum mortgage loan (based on income) is $\underline{\$155,300}$.

b. For the maximum CMHC-insured mortgage loan and minimum down payment,

$\$155,300 = 0.95$(Maximum home price)

Maximum home price = $\dfrac{\$155,300}{0.95} = \$163,474$

Rounded to the nearest $100, the maximum price they can pay is $\underline{\$163,500}$.

17. *a.* Given: $PV = \$100,000$; $i = \frac{7\%}{2} = 3.5\%$; $n = 12(25) = 300$; $c = \frac{2}{12} = 0.1\overline{6}$

$i_2 = (1 + i)^c - 1 = (1.035)^{0.1\overline{6}} - 1 = 0.00575003950$

Substitute into formula (10-2) and solve for *PMT*.

$$\$100,000 = PMT\left(\frac{1 - 1.00575003950^{-300}}{0.00575003950}\right)$$

$PMT = \underline{\$700.42}$

Exercise 14.3 (continued)

17. b. The weekly payment is $PMT = 0.25(\$700.42) = \$175.11$.

$PV = \$100,000$; $i = 3.5\%$; and $c = \frac{2}{52} = 0.038461538$.

$$i_2 = (1+i)^c - 1 = (1.035)^{0.038461538} - 1 = 0.00132400752$$

Substituting into formula (10-2n), we obtain

$$n = -\frac{\ln\left(1 - \dfrac{i_2 \times PV}{PMT}\right)}{\ln(1+i_2)} = -\frac{\ln\left(1 - \dfrac{0.00132400752 \times \$100,000}{\$175.11}\right)}{\ln(1.00132400752)} = 1066.41$$

Therefore, 1067 weekly payments will be required. The loan will be paid off after <u>20 years and 27 weeks</u>. The amortization period is reduced by almost 4½ years.

19. This problem is the same as problem 18 except that the initial amortization period is now 20 years. A briefer solution will be presented in this case.

Given: $PV = \$100,000$; $i = \frac{7.2\%}{2} = 3.6\%$; $n = 12(20) = 240$; $c = \frac{2}{12} = 0.1\overline{6}$

$$i_2 = (1+i)^c - 1 = 0.00591193086$$

Solve for PMT giving $PMT = \$780.97$
Balance after 12 payments = $97,647.15.

a. Balance after the $5000 prepayment = $92,647.15
   Solve for n giving $n = 205.01$.
   A total of 206 + 12 = 218 payments (months) will be required to pay off the loan.
   The amortization period will be reduced by
   240 – 218 = 22 months = <u>1 year and 10 months</u>

b. Balance after the $10,000 prepayment = $87,647.15
   Solve for n giving $n = 184.77$
   A total of 185 + 12 = 197 payments (months) will be required to pay off the loan.
   The amortization period will be reduced by
   240 – 197 = 43 months = <u>3 years and 7 months</u>

21. Given: $PV = \$100,000$, $i = \frac{6.9\%}{2} = 3.45\%$, $n = 12(20) = 240$, $c = \frac{2}{12} = 0.1\overline{6}$

$$i_2 = (1+i)^c - 1 = (1.0345)^{0.1\overline{6}} - 1 = 0.00566904493$$

Solve for PMT giving $PMT = \$763.51$
Balance after 12 payments = $97,565.76
Increased payment = 1.10($763.51) = $839.86
Balance after 12 more payments = $94,015.35
Payment after second increase = 1.10($839.86) = $923.85
Solve for the remaining n giving $n = 152.16$
Total time to pay off loan = 153 + 12 + 12 = 177 months
Reduction of the amortization period = (240 – 177) months
$$= 63 \text{ months}$$
$$= \underline{5 \text{ years and 3 months}}$$

23. Given: $PV = \$100{,}000$, $i = \frac{6.8\%}{2} = 3.4\%$, $n = 12(20) = 240$, $c = \frac{2}{12} = 0.1\overline{6}$

$$i_2 = (1+i)^c - 1 = (1.034)^{0.1\overline{6}} - 1 = 0.00558801773$$

Solve for PMT giving $PMT = \$757.73$
Balance after the 8th payment = \$98,377.10
Balance after the extra payment = \$98, 377.10 − \$757.73 = \$97,619.37
Solve for the remaining n giving $n = 228.38$
Total time to pay off loan = 229 + 8 = 237 months
Amortization period will be shortened by 240 − 237 = <u>3 months</u>.

25. Given: $PV = \$100{,}000$; $i = \frac{7.3\%}{2} = 3.65\%$; $n = 12(25) = 300$; $c = \frac{2}{12} = 0.1\overline{6}$

$$i_2 = (1+i)^c - 1 = (1.0365)^{0.1\overline{6}} - 1 = 0.00599282772$$

Solve for PMT giving $PMT = \$719.04$
Balance after the 11th payment = \$98,642.48
Interest for the 12th month = 0.00599282772(\$98,642.48) = \$591.15
Balance after the 12th month = \$98,642.48 + \$591.15 = \$99,233.63
Substitute into formula (10-2n) to obtain the remaining n giving $n = 293.70$
Total time to pay off loan = 294 + 12 = 306 months
The amortization period will be lengthened by <u>6 months</u>.

27. Given: $PV = \$100{,}000$; $i = \frac{6.8\%}{2} = 3.4\%$; $n = 12(25) = 300$; $c = \frac{2}{12} = 0.1\overline{6}$

$$i_2 = (1+i)^c - 1 = (1.034)^{0.1\overline{6}} - 1 = 0.00558801773$$

Solve for PMT giving $PMT = \$688.11$
Balance after 12 payments = \$98,399.71
Monthly payments beginning in the 2nd year = 1.1(\$688.11) = \$756.92
Balance after 12 more payments = \$95,837.18
Balance after the lump payment = \$85,837.18
Substitute into formula (10-2n) to obtain the remaining n giving $n = 180.23$
Total time to pay off the loan = 181 + 24 = 205 months
The amortization period will be reduced by (300 − 205) months = 95 months
or <u>7 years and 11 months</u>.

29. Given: $PV = \$120{,}000$; $i = \frac{7\%}{2} = 3.5\%$; $n = 12(25) = 300$; $c = \frac{2}{12} = 0.1\overline{6}$

$$i_2 = (1+i)^c - 1 = (1.035)^{0.1\overline{6}} - 1 = 0.00575003950$$

Solve for PMT giving $PMT = \$840.50$
Balance after 2 years = Balance after 24 payments = \$116,138.89
Balance after the \$5000 prepayment = \$111,138.89

   a. Solve for the remaining n using formula (10-2n) giving $n = 249.14$
   Total time to repay loan = 250 + 24 = 274 months
   The amortization period will be shortened by
   (300 − 274) months = 26 months = <u>2 years and 2 months</u>

   b. Balance after 5 years = Balance 3 years after the \$5000 prepayment
   = <u>\$103,107.15</u>

Exercise 14.3 (*continued*)

31. Given: $PV = \$100,000$; $i = \frac{6.3\%}{2} = 3.15\%$; $n = 12(20) = 240$; $c = \frac{2}{12} = 0.1\overline{6}$

$$i_2 = (1+i)^c - 1 = (1.0315)^{0.1\overline{6}} - 1 = 0.0051823913$$

Solve for PMT giving $PMT = \$729.11$
Balance after 3 years = Balance after 36 payments = $91,677.95
Payment size beginning in year 4 = 1.10($729.11) = $802.02

a. Use formula (10-2n) to obtain the number of payments of $802.02 required to pay off $91,677.95. We obtain $n = 173.62$.
Total time to pay off the loan = 174 + 36 = 210 months
Reduction in amortization period = 240 − 210 = 30 months or <u>2 years and 6 months</u>.

b. Balance after 5 years
= Balance 24 payments after the balance reaches $91,677.95
= <u>$83,346.28</u>

33. Originally, $PV = \$83,000$; $n = 12(25) = 300$; $i = \frac{7\%}{2} = 3.5\%$; $c = \frac{2}{12} = 0.1\overline{6}$

$$i_2 = (1+i)^c - 1 = (1.035)^{0.1\overline{6}} - 1 = 0.00575003950$$

Substitute into formula (10-2) to obtain $PMT = \$581.35$
Balance after 2 years = $80,329.29
Monthly payment starting in year 3 = $581.35 + $50 = $631.85
With $PV = \$80,329.29$ and $PMT = \$631.85$,
Balance an additional 24 payments later = $75,981.79
Balance after $5000 prepayment = $70,981.79

a. Number of payments of $631.35 to pay off the $70,981.79 balance is

$$n = -\frac{\ln\left(1 - \dfrac{i_2 \times PV}{PMT}\right)}{\ln(1+i_2)} = -\frac{\ln\left(1 - \dfrac{0.00575003950 \times \$70,981.79}{\$631.35}\right)}{\ln(1.00575003950)} = 181.35$$

Overall, the amortization period has been reduced by
300 − (182 + 24 + 24) = 70 months = <u>5 years and 10 months</u>

b. Balance after 5 years = Balance 12 payments after balance reached $70,981.79
= <u>$68,217.02</u>

Exercise 14.4

1. The monthly payments are based on
$PV = \$21,500$, $n = 60$, and $i = \frac{6.5\%}{12} = 0.541\overline{6}$.

Substitute into formula (10-2) and solve for PMT giving $PMT = \$420.67$
Since the borrower receives only $20,000, the effective interest rate per payment interval is the value of i satisfying

$$\$20,000 = \$420.67\left[\frac{1-(1+i)^{-60}}{i}\right]$$

The solution is $i = 0.00797059$ per month.
The effective cost of borrowing is

$$f = (1+i)^m - 1 = (1.00797059)^{12} - 1 = 0.099953 = \underline{9.995\%}$$

Exercise 14.4 (continued)

3. Monthly payments are based on

$$PV = \$105,000, \; n = 12(15) = 180, \; i = \frac{10.8\%}{2} = 5.4\%, \text{ and } c = \frac{2}{12} = 0.1\overline{6},$$

$$i_2 = (1+i)^c - 1 = (1.054)^{0.1\overline{6}} - 1 = 0.0088039370$$

Substitute into formula (10-2) and solve for PMT giving $PMT = \$1164.89$.

a. Balance after $n = 60$ payments is $\$86,097.64$

   The effective interest rate per payment interval is the value of i satisfying

$$\$100,000 = \$1164.89 \left[\frac{1-(1+i)^{-60}}{i} \right] + \$86,097.64(1+i)^{-60}$$

   The solution is $i = 0.00994354$ per month
   The effective annual cost of borrowing is

$$f = (1+i)^m - 1 = (1.00994354)^{12} - 1 = \underline{12.607\%}$$

b. Balance after $n = 120$ payments $= \$54,114.42$
   Solve for i in

$$\$100,000 = \$1164.89 \left[\frac{1-(1+i)^{-120}}{i} \right] + \$54,114.42(1+i)^{-120}$$

   The solution is $i = 0.00959692$ per month
   The effective cost of borrowing is

$$f = (1.00959692)^{12} - 1 = \underline{12.144\%}.$$

c. Solve for i in

$$\$100,000 = \$1164.89 \left[\frac{1-(1+i)^{-180}}{i} \right]$$

   The solution is $i = 0.00954005$ per month
   The effective cost of borrowing is

$$f = (1.00954005)^{12} - 1 = \underline{12.068\%}$$

5. The payments on the loan from the mortgage broker are based on

$$PV = \$82,200, \; i = \frac{10.25\%}{2} = 5.125\%, \; n = 120, \text{ and } c = \frac{2}{12} = 0.1\overline{6}$$

$$i_2 = (1+i)^c - 1 = (1.05125)^{0.1\overline{6}} - 1 = 0.0083647796$$

Substitute into formula (10-2) and solve for PMT giving $PMT = \$1088.00$

a. Balance after 60 payments $= \$51,162.08$
   The effective rate per payment interval on the brokered loan is the solution to

$$\$80,000 = \$1088.00 \left[\frac{1-(1+i)^{-60}}{i} \right] + \$51,162.08(1+i)^{-60}$$

   The solution is $i = 0.009049832$.
   The effective cost of borrowing on the brokered loan is

$$f = (1+i)^m - 1 = (1.009049832)^{12} - 1 = 11.417\%$$

   The effective annual rate on the trust company loan ($i = \frac{10.75\%}{2} = 5.375\%$) is

$$f = (1.05375)^2 - 1 = 11.039\%$$

   The <u>trust company loan's effective rate is 0.378% lower</u>.

---

5. *b.* The effective rate per payment interval on the brokered loan is the solution to

$$\$80{,}000 = \$1088.00\left[\frac{1-(1+i)^{-120}}{i}\right]$$

The solution is $i = 0.00890817$.
The effective cost of borrowing is

$$f = (1.00890817)^{12} - 1 = 11.229\%$$

compared to $f = 11.039\%$ for the trust company loan.
The <u>effective cost of borrowing from the trust company is 0.190% lower</u>.

7. With $PV = \$40{,}000$, $n = 4(10) = 40$, $i = \frac{7\%}{2} = 3.5\%$, $c = \frac{2}{4} = 0.5$, and

$$i_2 = (1+i)^c - 1 = (1.035)^{0.5} - 1 = 0.017349497,$$

Substitute into formula (10-2) and solve for *PMT* giving $PMT = \$1395.12$.

a. The fair market value (FMV) of the mortgage equals the present value of the 40 payments discounted at the prevailing market rate of interest.
With $i = \frac{10.5\%}{2} = 5.25\%$, the market rate per payment interval is

$$i_2 = (1+i)^c - 1 = (1.0525)^{0.5} - 1 = 0.025914226$$

$$FMV = PV = \$1395.12\left(\frac{1-1.025914226^{-40}}{0.025914226}\right) = \underline{\$34{,}488.28}$$

b. With $i = \frac{9\%}{2} = 4.5\%$, the market rate per payment interval is

$$i_2 = (1+i)^c - 1 = (1.045)^{0.5} - 1 = 0.022252415$$

$$FMV = PV = \$1395.12\left(\frac{1-1.022252415^{-40}}{0.022252415}\right) = \underline{\$36{,}699.09}$$

9. The fair market value (FMV) of a mortgage equals the present value of the remaining cash flows discounted at the prevailing market rate.
Step 1: Calculate the payments on the mortgage having

$$PV = \$60{,}000, \; i = \frac{6.8\%}{2} = 3.4\%, \; n = 12(20) = 240, \text{ and } c = \frac{2}{12} = 0.1\overline{6}$$

$$i_2 = (1+i)^c - 1 = (1.034)^{0.1\overline{6}} - 1 = 0.00558801773$$

Substitute into formula (10-2) and solve for *PMT* giving $PMT = \$454.64$
Step 2: Calculate the balance at the end of the 5-year term.
Balance after $n = 60$ payments is $\$51{,}519.54$.
Step 3: Calculate the combined present value of the *Step* 2 balance and the remaining $n = 39$ payments discounted at the prevailing market rate.

a. At a market rate of $i = 3\%$, $i_2 = (1.03)^{0.1\overline{6}} - 1 = 0.004938622$

$$FMV = \$648.58\left(\frac{1-1.004938622^{-39}}{0.004938622}\right) + \frac{\$51{,}519.54}{1.004938622}(1+i)^{-39}$$

$$= \underline{\$58{,}605.77}$$

b. Similarly, at a market rate of $i = \frac{6.8\%}{2} = 3.4\%$,

$$i_2 = (1.034)^{0.1\overline{6}} - 1 = 0.0055880177 \text{ and FMV} = \underline{\$57{,}348.31}$$

c. Similarly, at a market rate of $i = \frac{7.5\%}{2} = 3.75\%$,

$$i_2 = (1.0375)^{0.1\overline{6}} - 1 = 0.0061545239 \text{ and FMV} = \underline{\$56{,}276.22}$$

Exercise 14.4 (*continued*)

11. Equivalent cash value = Cash payment + Fair market value of vendor take-back mortgage
    Step 1: Calculate the monthly payment on the take-back mortgage.

    $PV = \$95,000$, $n = 120$, $i = \frac{8\%}{2} = 4\%$, $c = \frac{2}{12} = 0.1\overline{6}$

    $i_2 = (1+i)^c - 1 = (1.04)^{0.1\overline{6}} - 1 = 0.0065581969$

    Substitute into formula (10-2) and solve for *PMT* giving *PMT* = \$1146.09.

    Step 2: Calculate the present value of these payments discounted at the prevailing market rate (10.25% compounded semiannually).

    $i_2 = (1.05125)^{0.1\overline{6}} - 1 = 0.0083647796$

    $$PV = \$1146.09\left(\frac{1 - 1.0083647796^{-120}}{0.0083647796}\right) = \$86,588.89$$

    Equivalent cash value = \$75,000 + \$86,588.89 = $\underline{\$161,588.89}$

13. Equivalent cash value = Cash payment + FMV of the vendor take-back mortgage
    Step 1: Calculate the balance at the end of the 5-year term.

    $PV = \$100,000$, $i = \frac{8\%}{2} = 4\%$, $PMT = \$750$, $c = \frac{2}{12} = 0.1\overline{6}$

    $i_2 = (1+i)^c - 1 = (1.04)^{0.1\overline{6}} - 1 = 0.0065581969$

    Balance after $n = 60$ payments is \$93,103.36

    Step 2: Calculate the combined present value of the *Step* 1 balance and the first

    60 payments discounted at $i_2 = (1.05125)^{0.1\overline{6}} - 1 = 0.0083647796$

    $$FMV = \$750\left(\frac{1 - 1.0083647796^{-60}}{0.0083647796}\right) + \frac{\$93,103.36}{1.0083647796^{60}} = \$91,749.57$$

    Equivalent cash value = \$50,000 + \$91,749.57 = $\underline{\$141,749.57}$
    Offer M is worth \$1749.50 more (in current dollars).

15. *Step* 1: Calculate the size of the mortgage payments.

    $PV = \$80,000$, $n = 300$, $i = \frac{7.5\%}{2} = 3.75\%$, and $c = \frac{2}{12} = 0.1\overline{6}$

    $i_2 = (1+i)^c - 1 = (1.0375)^{0.1\overline{6}} - 1 = 0.0061545239$

    Substitute into formula (10-2) and solve for *PMT* giving *PMT* = \$585.24

    Step 2: Calculate the balance after 2 years.
    Balance after $n = 24$ payments is \$77,605.80.

    Step 3: a. Calculate 3 months' interest on the *Step* 2 balance.
    Penalty = 3(0.0061545239)\$77,605.80 = \$1432.88

    Step 4: b. Calculate the current market value of the mortgage by discounting the remaining 36 payments and the end-of-term balance at

    $i_2 = (1.03)^{0.1\overline{6}} - 1 = 0.00493862203$

    Balance at the end of the 5-year term ($n = 60$) will be \$73,283.83

    $$FMV = \$585.24\left(\frac{1 - 1.00493862203^{-36}}{0.00493862203}\right) + \frac{\$73,283.83}{1.004938622033^{36}} = \$80,632.61$$

    Step 5: Calculate the part *b* prepayment penalty.
    Penalty = \$80,632.61 − \$77,605.80 = \$3026.81
    The larger of the alternative penalties is $\underline{\$3026.81}$.

Review Problems

1. Amount to be paid off = $1150(1 − 0.25) = $862.50.
    The present value of the six payments is $862.50.

    Given: $PV = 862.50, $n = 6$, $i = \frac{11.25\%}{12} = 0.9375\%$

    Substitute into formula (10-2) to obtain $PMT = 148.50.

Payment number	Payment	Interest portion	Principal portion	Principal balance
0				$862.50
1	$148.50	$8.09	$140.41	722.09
2	148.50	6.77	141.73	580.36
3	148.50	5.44	143.06	437.30
4	148.50	4.10	144.40	292.90
5	148.50	2.75	145.75	147.15
6	148.53	1.38	147.15	0.00
	Total:	$28.53		

3. Given: $PV = $28,000$, $i = \frac{8\%}{4} = 2\%$, $n = 4(7) = 28$

    Substitute into formula (10-2) to obtain $PMT = 1315.71

    a. Principal part of Payment 6 = Balance after Payment 5 − Balance after Payment 6
    $$= $24,067.25 − $23,232.89$$
    $$= \underline{$834.36}$$

    b. Interest part of Payment 22 = $i \times$ Balance after Payment 21
    $$= 0.02($8515.29)$$
    $$= \underline{$170.31}$$

    c. Principal paid by Payment 10 to Payment 15 inclusive
    $$= \text{Balance after Payment 9} − \text{Balance after Payment 15}$$
    $$= $20,628.33 − $14,931.19$$
    $$= \underline{$5697.14}$$

    d. Interest paid in Year 2 = $4PMT$ − (Balance after Payment 4 − Balance after Payment 8)
    $$= 4($1315.71) − ($24,885.26 − $21,513.76)$$
    $$= \underline{$1891.34}$$

5. Given: $PV = $60,000$, $i = \frac{10.5\%}{2} = 5.25\%$, $PMT = $10,000$

Payment number	Payment	Interest portion	Principal portion	Principal balance
0				$60,000.00
1	$10,000.00	$3150.00	$6850.00	53,150.00
2	10,000.00	2790.38	7209.62	45,940.38
3	10,000.00	2411.87	7588.13	38,352.25
4	10,000.00	2013.49	7986.51	30,365.74
5	10,000.00	1594.20	8405.80	21,959.94
6	10,000.00	1152.90	8847.10	13,112.84
7	10,000.00	688.42	9311.58	3801.26
8	4000.83	199.57	3801.26	0.00
	Total:	$14,000.83		

Review Problems (*continued*)

7. Given: $PV = \$45,000$, $i = \frac{4.8\%}{12} = 0.4\%$, $PMT = \$400$

   a. Interest in Payment 37 $= i \times$ Balance after Payment 36
   $$= 0.004(\$36,499.62)$$
   $$= \underline{\$146.00}$$

   b. Principal part of Payment 92 = Balance after Payment 91 − Balance after Payment 92
   $$= \$20,908.36 - \$20,592.00$$
   $$= \underline{\$316.37}$$

   c. Interest paid by Payment 85 to Payment 96 inclusive
   $$= 12PMT - (\text{Balance after Payment 84} - \text{Balance after Payment 96})$$
   $$= 12(\$400) - (\$23,087.92 - \$19,313.83)$$
   $$= \underline{\$1025.91}$$

   d. Principal paid in Year 5 = Balance after Payment 48 − Balance after Payment 60
   $$= \$33,383.64 - \$30,114.76$$
   $$= \underline{\$3268.88}$$

   e. The total number of payments is
   $$n = -\frac{\ln\left(1 - \dfrac{i \times PV}{PMT}\right)}{\ln(1+i)} = -\frac{\ln\left(1 - \dfrac{0.004 \times \$45,000}{\$400}\right)}{\ln(1.004)} = 149.75797$$
   Final payment $= (1 + i) \times$ Balance after Payment 149 $= 1.004(\$302.13) = \underline{\$303.33}$

9. Given: $PV = \$90,000$, $i = \frac{7.25\%}{2} = 3.625\%$, $n = 12(20) = 240$, $c = \frac{2}{12} = 0.1\overline{6}$
   $$i_2 = (1+i)^c - 1 = (1.03625)^{0.1\overline{6}} - 1 = 0.00595238336$$
   Substitute into formula (10-2) to obtain $PMT = \$705.51$.
   a. Balance after 5 years = Balance after Payment 60 = $\underline{\$77,798.79}$

   b. For renewal of the loan after 5 years,
   $PV = \$77,798.79$, $n = 12(15) = 180$, $i = \frac{6.5\%}{2} = 3.25\%$, $c = 0.1\overline{6}$
   $$i_2 = (1.0325)^{0.1\overline{6}} - 1 = 0.0053447401$$
   Substitute into formula (10-2) to obtain $PMT = \underline{\$674.02}$

11. Given: $PV = \$25,000$, $i = \frac{6.6\%}{12} = 0.55\%$, $n = 12(10) = 120$
    Substitute into formula (10-2) to obtain $PMT = \$285.14$.
    The "rounded" payment is $\$290$.
    Balance after 36 payments of $\$290 = \underline{\$18,947.10}$

Review Problems (continued)

13. Given: $PV = \$110{,}000$; $n = 12(25) = 300$; $i = \frac{6.7\%}{2} = 3.35\%$; $c = \frac{2}{12} = 0.1\overline{6}$

$$i_2 = (1+i)^c - 1 = (1.0335)^{0.1\overline{6}} - 1 = 0.00550695788$$

a. Substitute into formula (10-2) to obtain $PMT = \$750.19$.
Balance after 24 payments = \$106,305.17
Monthly payment after 10% increase = 1.1(\$750.19) = \$825.21
The number of these payments required to pay off the balance is

$$n = -\frac{\ln\left(1 - \dfrac{i_2 \times PV}{PMT}\right)}{\ln(1+i_2)} = -\frac{\ln\left(1 - \dfrac{0.00550695788 \times \$106{,}305.17}{\$825.21}\right)}{\ln(1.00550695788)} = 225.04$$

The total time required to pay off the loan is
226 + 24 = 250 months.
Hence, the larger payments reduce the amortization period by
(300 − 250) months = 50 months or <u>4 years and 2 months</u>

b. Balance at end of the 5-year term = Balance 3 years after the payment increase
= Balance after 36 payments of \$1102.75
= <u>\$96,786.36</u>

Self-Test Exercise

1. Given: $PV = \$16{,}000$; $n = 12(5) = 60$; $i = \frac{10.8\%}{12} = 0.9\%$

Substitute into formula (10-2) to obtain $PMT = \$346.29$.

a. Interest in Payment 29 = $i \times$ Balance after Payment 28
= 0.009(\$9590.86)
= <u>\$86.32</u>

b. Principal part of Payment 46 = Balance after Payment 45 − Balance after Payment 46
= \$4838.34 − \$4535.59
= <u>\$302.75</u>

c. Principal paid in Year 2 = Balance after Payment 12 − Balance after Payment 24
= \$13,448.68 − \$10,607.76
= <u>\$2840.92</u>

d. Interest paid in Year 3 = $12PMT$ − (Balance after Pymnt 24 − Balance after Pymnt 36)
= 12(\$346.29) − (\$10,607.76 − \$7444.37)
= <u>\$992.09</u>

Self-Test Exercise (continued)

2. Given: $PV = \$6400$, $i = \frac{10\%}{2} = 5\%$, $n = 12(4) = 48$, $c = \frac{2}{12} = 0.1\overline{6}$

$$i_2 = (1+i)^c - 1 = (1.05)^{0.1\overline{6}} - 1 = 0.0081648460$$

Substitute into formula (10-2) to obtain $PMT = \$161.70$

Payment number	Payment	Interest portion	Principal portion	Principal balance
0				$6400.00
1	$161.70	$52.26	$109.44	6290.56
2	161.70	51.36	110.34	6180.22
33				2274.13
34	161.70	18.57	143.13	2131.00
35	161.70	17.40	144.30	1986.70
46				319.47
47	161.70	2.61	159.09	160.38
48	161.69	1.31	160.38	0.00

3. Given: $PV = \$255,000$; $PMT = \$6000$; $i = 6\%$; $c = \frac{1}{4} = 0.25$

$$i_2 = (1+i)^c - 1 = (1.06)^{0.25} - 1 = 0.014673846$$

a. The number of payments needed to pay off the loan is

$$n = -\frac{\ln\left(1 - \dfrac{i_2 \times PV}{PMT}\right)}{\ln(1 + i_2)} = -\frac{\ln\left(1 - \dfrac{0.014673846 \times \$255,000}{\$6000}\right)}{\ln(1.014673846)} = 67.08243496$$

Final payment $= (1 + i_2) \times$ Balance after Payment 67
$= 1.014673846(\$490.72)$
$= \underline{\$497.92}$

b. Interest in Payment 27 $= i_2 \times$ Balance after Payment 26
$= 0.014673846(\$184,120.26)$
$= \underline{\$2702.05}$

c. Principal part of Payment 53 $=$ Balance after Payment 52 $-$ Balance after Payment 53
$= \$80,652.82 - \$75,836.30$
$= \underline{\$4816.52}$

d. Principal paid by Payments 14 to 20 inclusive
$=$ Balance after Payment 13 $-$ Balance after Payment 20
$= \$222,914.89 - \$202,950.21$
$= \underline{\$19,964.68}$

e. Interest paid in Year 6 $= 4PMT - ($Balance after Pymnt 20 $-$ Balance after Payment 24$)$
$= 4(\$6000) - (\$202,950.21 - \$190,593.78)$
$= \underline{\$11,643.57}$

4. Initially, $PV = \$45,000$; $n = 12(25) = 300$; $i = \frac{8\%}{2} = 4\%$; and $c = \frac{2}{12} = 0.1\overline{6}$.

$$i_2 = (1+i)^c - 1 = (1.04)^{0.1\overline{6}} - 1 = 0.00655819694$$

Substitute into formula (10-2) to obtain $PMT = \$343.45$
Balance after 60 payments = $\$41,460.80$
At the first renewal,

$$PV = \$41,460.80; \ n = 12(20) = 240; \ i = \frac{7\%}{2} = 3.5\%; \ c = 0.1\overline{6},$$

$$i_2 = (1.035)^{0.1\overline{6}} - 1 = 0.0057500395$$

Solving for PMT again gives $PMT = \$318.96$
Balance after a further 60 payments (of $318.96) = $\underline{\$35,708.26}$

5. $PV = \$87,000$; $i = \frac{7.4\%}{2} = 3.7\%$; $n = 12(20) = 240$; $c = \frac{2}{12} = 0.1\overline{6}$

$$i_2 = (1+i)^c - 1 = (1.037)^{0.1\overline{6}} - 1 = 0.00607369206$$

Substitute into formula (10-2) to obtain $PMT = \$689.65$
   a. Balance after 16 payments = $\$84,299.26$
       Balance after $4000 prepayment = $\$80,299.26$
       The number of additional payments required to pay off this balance is

$$n = -\frac{\ln\left(1 - \frac{i_2 \times PV}{PMT}\right)}{\ln(1 + i_2)} = -\frac{\ln\left(1 - \frac{0.00607369206 \times \$80,299.26}{\$689.65}\right)}{\ln(1.00607369206)} = 202.83$$

Total time to pay off loan = 203 + 16 = 219 months. Hence, the $4000 prepayment
shortens the amortization period by 240 − 219 = 21 months or <u>1 year and 9 months</u>.
   b. Balance after 3 years = Balance 20 months after the $4000 prepayment = $\underline{\$76,018.77}$

www.Exercise.com (Chapter 14)

1. a. After 15 months of a 30-month loan, about 48% of the original principal is paid off.
       After 15 years of a 30-year loan, only 22% of the original principal is paid off.
    b.

Term (years)	Total interest
5	$2022.27
10	4244.27
15	6686.49
20	9334.07
25	12,169.49
30	15,173.35

    c. (i) 254 months
        (ii) 357 months

15   Bonds and Sinking Funds

Concept Questions (Section 15.2)

1. Four variables affecting a bond's price are:
   - the face value of the bond
   - the bond's coupon rate
   - the prevailing market rate of return on bonds
   - the time remaining until maturity of the bond

   Only the prevailing market rate of return *always* has an inverse effect on the bond's price.

3. <u>Yes</u>. If, during the holding period, the capital loss (due to a rise in the prevailing market rate of return) exceeds the coupon interest paid on the bond, you will suffer a net loss on the bond investment.

5. If prevailing interest rates decline, the prices of all bonds will rise. However, the prices of long-term bonds will rise more than the prices of short-term bonds. Therefore, you will improve the portfolio's capital gain if, prior to the interest rate decline, you <u>increase the relative weighting of long-term bonds</u> (by selling short-term bonds and using the proceeds to purchase long-term bonds).

Exercise 15.2

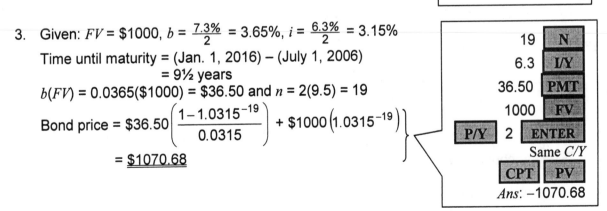

1. Given: $FV = \$1000$, $b = \frac{8.2\%}{2} = 4.1\%$, $i = \frac{6.8\%}{2} = 3.4\%$

   Time until maturity = (June 1, 2017) – (June 1, 2006)
   $$= 11 \text{ years}$$
   $b(FV) = 0.041(\$1000) = \$41$ and $n = 2(11) = 22$

   Bond price $= \$41\left(\dfrac{1-1.034^{-22}}{0.034}\right) + \$1000\left(1.034^{-22}\right)$

   $$= \$1107.22$$

22	**N**
6.8	**I/Y**
41	**PMT**
1000	**FV**
P/Y 2	**ENTER**

   Same *C/Y*

   CPT   **PV**

   Ans: –1107.22

3. Given: $FV = \$1000$, $b = \frac{7.3\%}{2} = 3.65\%$, $i = \frac{6.3\%}{2} = 3.15\%$

   Time until maturity = (Jan. 1, 2016) – (July 1, 2006)
   $$= 9\tfrac{1}{2} \text{ years}$$
   $b(FV) = 0.0365(\$1000) = \$36.50$ and $n = 2(9.5) = 19$

   Bond price $= \$36.50\left(\dfrac{1-1.0315^{-19}}{0.0315}\right) + \$1000\left(1.0315^{-19}\right)$

   $$= \$1070.68$$

19	**N**
6.3	**I/Y**
36.50	**PMT**
1000	**FV**
P/Y 2	**ENTER**

   Same *C/Y*

   CPT   **PV**

   Ans: –1070.68

5. Given: $FV = \$1000$, $b = \frac{5.9\%}{2} = 2.95\%$, $i = \frac{6.2\%}{2} = 3.1\%$

 Time until maturity = (Aug. 1, 2032) − (Aug. 1, 2004)
 $= 28$ years
 $b(FV) = 0.0295(\$1000) = \$29.50$ and $n = 2(28) = 56$

 Bond price $= \$29.50\left(\dfrac{1-1.031^{-56}}{0.031}\right) + \$1000\left(1.031^{-56}\right)$

 $\qquad\quad = \underline{\$960.37}$

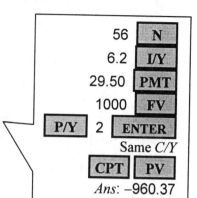

Same *C/Y*

Ans: −960.37

7. Given: $FV = \$1000$, $b = \frac{6.6\%}{2} = 3.3\%$, $i = \frac{6\%}{2} = 3\%$

 Time until maturity = (June 1, 2023) − (June 1, 2002) = 21 years
 $b(FV) = 0.033(\$1000) = \$33$ and $n = 2(21) = 42$

 Bond price $= \$33\left(\dfrac{1-1.03^{-42}}{0.03}\right) + \$1000\left(1.03^{-42}\right) = \underline{\$1071.10}$

9. Given: $FV = \$1000$, $b = \frac{6.5\%}{2} = 3.25\%$, $i = \frac{5.5\%}{2} = 2.75\%$

 $b(FV) = 0.0325(\$1000) = \$332.50$ and $n = 2(13.5) = 27$

 Bond price $= \$32.50\left(\dfrac{1-1.0275^{-27}}{0.0275}\right) + \$1000\left(1.0275^{-27}\right)$

 $\qquad\quad = \$1094.41$
 Bond premium $= \$1094.41 - \$1000 = \underline{\$94.41}$

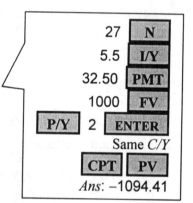

Same *C/Y*

Ans: −1094.41

11. Given: $FV = \$1000$, $b = \frac{5.75\%}{2} = 2.875\%$, $i = \frac{6.5\%}{2} = 3.25\%$

 $b(FV) = 0.02875(\$1000) = \$28.75$ and $n = 2(16) = 32$

 Bond price $= \$28.75\left(\dfrac{1-1.0325^{-32}}{0.0325}\right) + \$1000\left(1.0325^{-32}\right) = \$926.08$

 Bond discount $= \$1000 - \$926.08 = \underline{\$73.92}$

13. Given: $FV = \$1000$, $b = \frac{7\%}{2} = 3.5\%$, $i = \frac{5.75\%}{2} = 2.875\%$, $n = 2(15) = 30$

 Bond price $= \$35\left(\dfrac{1-1.02875^{-30}}{0.0285}\right) + \$1000\left(1.02875^{-30}\right) = \underline{\$1124.51}$

15. Given: $FV = \$20,000$, $b = \frac{8\%}{2} = 4\%$, $i = \frac{6.5\%}{2} = 3.25\%$, $n = 2(15-8) = 14$

 Regular coupon payment $= b(FV) = 0.04(\$20,000) = \$800$

 Bond price $= \$800\left(\dfrac{1-1.0325^{-14}}{0.0325}\right) + \$20,000\left(1.0325^{-14}\right) = \underline{\$21,665.89}$

Exercise 15.2 *(continued)*

17. For all four bonds, $FV = \$1000$, $b = \frac{7\%}{2} = 3.5\%$,

and $i = \frac{6\%}{2} = 3\%$. $n = 10, 20, 30,$ and 50 for

bonds A, B, C, and D, respectively.

Price of A $= \$35\left(\dfrac{1-1.03^{-10}}{0.03}\right) + \$1000\left(1.03^{-10}\right) = \underline{\$1042.65}$

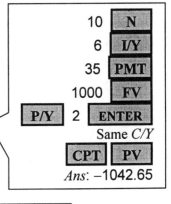

Price of B $= \$35\left(\dfrac{1-1.03^{-20}}{0.03}\right) + \$1000\left(1.03^{-20}\right) = \underline{\$1074.39}$

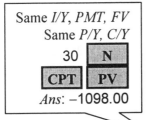 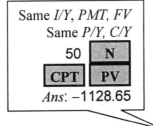 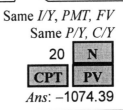

Similarly, price of C = $\underline{\$1098.00}$ and price of D = $\underline{\$1128.65}$
The results demonstrate that, for the same spread of the
market rate *below* the coupon rate, *longer* maturity
bonds have a *larger premium*.

19. For all three bonds, $FV = \$1000$, $n = 2(20) = 40$, and $i = \frac{5\%}{2} = 2.5\%$

$b = 3\%, 3.5\%,$ and 4% for bonds J, K, and L, respectively.
Coupon payments = $30, $35, and $40 for bonds J, K, and L, respectively.

Price of J $= \$30\left(\dfrac{1-1.025^{-40}}{0.025}\right) + \$1000\left(1.025^{-40}\right) = \underline{\$1125.51}$

Price of K $= \$35\left(\dfrac{1-1.025^{-40}}{0.025}\right) + \$1000\left(1.025^{-40}\right) = \underline{\$1251.03}$

Price of L $= \$40\left(\dfrac{1-1.025^{-40}}{0.025}\right) + \$1000\left(1.025^{-40}\right) = \underline{\$1376.54}$

The results demonstrate that, for bonds having the same time to maturity, a *larger*
spread of the coupon rate *above* the market rate results in a greater bond premium.

21. For both bonds, $FV = \$1000$, $n = 2(12) = 24$, and $i = \frac{7\%}{2} = 3.5\%$

$b = 3\%$ and 4% for bonds E and F, respectively.
Coupon payments = $30 and $40 for bonds E and F, respectively.

Price of E $= \$30\left(\dfrac{1-1.035^{-24}}{0.035}\right) + \$1000\left(1.035^{-24}\right) = \underline{\$919.71}$

Price of F $= \$40\left(\dfrac{1-1.035^{-24}}{0.035}\right) + \$1000\left(1.035^{-24}\right) = \underline{\$1080.29}$

23. All three bonds have $FV = \$1000$ and $b = \frac{6\%}{2} = 3\%$.

    $n = 10, 20,$ and 50 for bonds G, H, and J, respectively.

    When $i = \frac{6\%}{2} = 3\%$ $(= b)$, all bonds will be priced at par ($1000).

    If i becomes $\frac{7\%}{2} = 3.5\%$,

$$\text{Price of G} = \$30\left(\frac{1-1.035^{-10}}{0.035}\right) + \$1000\left(1.035^{-10}\right) = \$958.42$$

$$\text{Price of H} = \$30\left(\frac{1-1.035^{-20}}{0.035}\right) + \$1000\left(1.035^{-20}\right) = \$928.94$$

$$\text{Price of J} = \$30\left(\frac{1-1.035^{-30}}{0.035}\right) + \$1000\left(1.035^{-30}\right) = \$882.72$$

The prices of bonds G, H, and J <u>drop by $41.58, $71.06, and $117.28</u>, respectively. The longer the maturity of a bond, the more sensitive its price is to a given change in the market rate of return.

25. Given: $FV = \$10,000$, $b = \frac{6.5\%}{2} = 3.25\%$, $n = 2(25 - 3) = 44$, $i = \frac{5.6\%}{2} = 2.8\%$

    a. Coupon payment $= b(FV) = 0.0325(\$10,000) = \$325.00$

$$\text{Price} = \$325\left(\frac{1-1.028^{-44}}{0.028}\right) + \$10,000\left(1.028^{-44}\right) = \underline{\$11,130.32}$$

    b. Percent capital gain $= \dfrac{\text{Selling price} - \text{Purchase price}}{\text{Purchase price}} \times 100\%$

$$= \frac{\$1130.32}{\$10,000} \times 100\%$$

$$= \underline{11.30\%}$$

27. Given: $b = \frac{6.5\%}{2} = 3.25\%$, $n = 2(20 - 3) = 34$

    The percent capital gain will be the same for all bond denominations. Use $FV = \$1000$.

    a. If $i = \frac{5.5\%}{2} = 2.75\%$,

$$\text{Price} = \$32.50\left(\frac{1-1.0275^{-34}}{0.0275}\right) + \$1000\left(1.0275^{-34}\right) = \$1109.53$$

$$\text{Percent capital gain} = \frac{\$1109.53 - \$1000}{\$1000} \times 100\% = \underline{10.95\%}$$

    b. If $i = \frac{6.5\%}{2} = 3.25\%$ $(= b)$, the bond's price will be its face value $(FV = \$1000)$.

    Then, percent capital gain $= \underline{0\%}$

    c. If $i = \frac{7.5\%}{2} = 3.75\%$,

$$\text{Price} = \$32.50\left(\frac{1-1.0375^{-34}}{0.0375}\right) + \$1000\left(1.0375^{-34}\right) = \$904.80$$

$$\text{Percent capital gain} = \frac{\$904.80 - \$1000}{\$1000} \times 100\% = \underline{-9.52\%}$$

Exercise 15.2 *(continued)*

29. The answer will not depend on the bond's face value. Use $FV = \$1000$.
    When the bond was purchased, $b = \frac{10\%}{2} = 5\%$, $n = 2(20) = 40$, and $i = \frac{18.5\%}{2} = 9.25\%$.

$$\text{Purchase price} = \$50\left(\frac{1-1.0925^{-40}}{0.0925}\right) + \$1000\left(1.0925^{-40}\right) = \$553.89$$

When the bond was sold, $i = \frac{9.7\%}{2} = 4.85\%$ and $n = 2(15.5) = 31$.

$$\text{Selling price} = \$50\left(\frac{1-1.0485^{-31}}{0.0485}\right) + \$1000\left(1.0485^{-31}\right) = \$1023.80$$

In effect, the initial \$553.89 investment purchased an annuity paying \$50 every 6 months for 4½ years plus a lump amount of \$1023.80 at the end of the 4½ years. The rate of total return is the discount rate that makes \$553.89 equal to the present value of the payments received.
Solve for i in

$$\$553.89 = \$50\left[\frac{1-(1+i)^{-9}}{i}\right] + \$1023.80(1+i)^{-9}$$

The solution is $i = 14.246\%$ per 6 months.
The nominal annual rate of total return was
$\quad j = 2i = \underline{28.49\%\ compounded\ semiannually}$.

Exercise 15.3

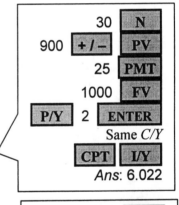

1. Given: $FV = \$1000$, $n = 2(15) = 30$,
   $\quad b = \frac{5\%}{2} = 2.5\%$, and Price = \$900
   The yield to maturity (YTM) is $2i$ where i is the solution to

$$\$900 = \$25\left[\frac{1-(1+i)^{-30}}{i}\right] + \$1000(1+i)^{-30}$$

   The solution is $i = 3.011\%$ per 6 months
   $\quad$ YTM $= 2i = \underline{6.02\%\ compounded\ semiannually}$.

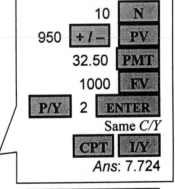

3. For both bonds, $FV = \$1000$, $b = \frac{6.5\%}{2} = 3.25\%$, Price = \$950.
   For bond A, $n = 2(5) = 10$ and

$$\$950 = \$32.50\left[\frac{1-(1+i)^{-10}}{i}\right] + \$1000(1+i)^{-10}$$

   Solving for i gives $i = 3.862\%$ per 6 months. Then
   $\quad$ YTM $= 2i = \underline{7.72\%\ compounded\ semiannually}$.

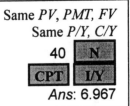

   For bond C, $n = 2(20) = 40$ and

$$\$950 = \$32.50\left[\frac{1-(1+i)^{-40}}{i}\right] + \$1000(1+i)^{-40}$$

   Solving for i gives $i = 3.484\%$ per 6 months. Then
   $\quad$ YTM $= 2i = \underline{6.97\%\ compounded\ semiannually}$.

Exercise 15.3 *(continued)*

5. Currently, $i = b$. Consequently, the bond currently trades at par ($1000).

a. If the price rises to $1020 with $n = 2(3) = 6$, $b = \frac{6\%}{2} = 3\%$, and $FV = \$1000$,

Then, YTM = $2i$ where

$$\$1020 = \$30\left[\frac{1-(1+i)^{-6}}{i}\right] + \$1000(1+i)^{-6}$$

Solving for i gives $i = 2.635\%$ and
YTM = $2i$ = 5.27% compounded semiannually.
Therefore, the YTM <u>decreased by</u> 6.00% − 5.27% = <u>0.73% compounded semiannually</u>.

b. If the price rises to $1020 with $n = 2(15) = 30$, $b = \frac{10\%}{2} = 5\%$ and $FV = \$1000$,

Then, YTM = $2i$ where

$$\$1020 = \$30\left[\frac{1-(1+i)^{-30}}{i}\right] + \$1000(1+i)^{-30}$$

Solving for i gives $i = 2.899\%$ and
YTM = $2i$ = 5.80% compounded semiannually.
The YTM <u>decreased by</u> 6.00% − 5.80% = <u>0.20% compounded semiannually</u>.

7. Given: $FV = \$1000$, $b = \frac{11.25\%}{2} = 5.625\%$, $n = 2(6.5) = 13$, price = $761.50.

The YTM was $2i$ where i is the solution to

$$\$761.50 = \$56.25\left[\frac{1-(1+i)^{-13}}{i}\right] + \$1000(1+i)^{-13}$$

Solving for i gives $i = 8.772\%$
Hence, the YTM was $2i$ = <u>17.54% compounded semiannually</u>.

Exercise 15.4

1. Given: $FV = \$1000$, $b = \frac{10\%}{2} = 5\%$, $i = \frac{9.75\%}{2} = 4.875\%$

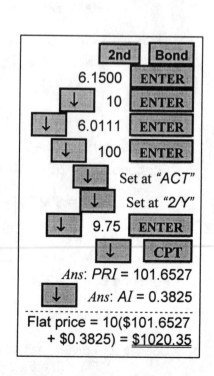

2nd Bond
6.1500 ENTER
↓ 10 ENTER
↓ 6.0111 ENTER
↓ 100 ENTER
↓ Set at "ACT"
↓ Set at "2/Y"
↓ 9.75 ENTER
↓ CPT
Ans: PRI = 101.6527
↓ *Ans:* AI = 0.3825
- - - - - - - - - - - - - - -
Flat price = 10($101.6527
+ $0.3825) = <u>$1020.35</u>

Time from preceding interest payment date to maturity
= (June 1, 2011) − (June 1, 2000)
= 11 years = 22 half-years
Price (on June 1, 2000)

$$= \$50\left(\frac{1-1.04875^{-22}}{0.04875}\right) + \$1000\left(1.04875^{-22}\right)$$

= $1016.64
Time from preceding interest payment to purchase date
= (June 15, 2000) − (June 1, 2000) = 14 days
Number of days in current interest payment interval
= (Dec. 1, 2000) − (June 1, 2000) = 183 days
Price (on June 15, 2000) = $1016.64 $(1.04875)^{14/183}$
= <u>$1020.35</u>

Exercise 15.4 (continued)

3. Given: $FV = \$1000$, $b = \frac{6.2\%}{2} = 3.1\%$, $i = \frac{6.4\%}{2} = 3.2\%$

    Time from preceding interest payment date to maturity
    $$= (\text{Jan. 1, 2017}) - (\text{Jan. 1, 2002}) = 30 \text{ half-years}$$
    Price (on Jan. 1, 2002)

    $$= \$31\left(\frac{1-1.032^{-30}}{0.032}\right) + \$1000\left(1.032^{-30}\right) = \$980.90$$

    Time from preceding interest payment date to purchase date
    $$= (\text{Apr. 15, 2002}) - (\text{Jan. 1, 2002}) = 104 \text{ days}$$
    Number of days in current interest payment interval
    $$= (\text{July 1, 2002}) - (\text{Jan. 1, 2002}) = 181 \text{ days}$$
    Price (on Apr. 15, 2002) $= \$980.90\,(1.032)^{104/181} = \underline{\$998.81}$

5. Given: $FV = \$1000$, $b = \frac{9.5\%}{2} = 4.750\%$, $i = \frac{5.4\%}{2} = 2.7\%$

    Time from preceding interest payment date to maturity
    $$= (\text{Aug. 1, 2014}) - (\text{Aug. 1, 1998}) = 32 \text{ half-years}$$

    Price (on Aug. 1, 1998) $= \$47.50\left(\dfrac{1-1.027^{-32}}{0.027}\right) + \$1000\left(1.027^{-32}\right) = \$1435.56$

    Time from preceding interest payment date to purchase date
    $$= (\text{Dec. 15, 1998}) - (\text{Aug. 1, 1998}) = 136 \text{ days}$$
    Number of days in current interest payment interval
    $$= (\text{Feb. 1, 1999}) - (\text{Aug. 1, 1998}) = 184 \text{ days}$$
    Price (on Dec. 15, 1998) $= \$1435.56\,(1.027)^{136/184} = \underline{\$1464.11}$

7. Given: $FV = \$1000$, $b = \frac{5.2\%}{2} = 2.6\%$, $i = \frac{5.7\%}{2} = 2.85\%$

    Time from preceding interest payment date to maturity
    $$= (\text{Dec. 1, 2018}) - (\text{Dec. 1, 1999}) = 38 \text{ half-years}$$

    Price (on Dec. 1, 1999) $= \$26\left(\dfrac{1-1.0285^{-38}}{0.0285}\right) + \$1000\left(1.0285^{-38}\right) = \$942.43$

    Time from preceding interest payment date to purchase date
    $$= (\text{March 25, 2000}) - (\text{Dec. 1, 1999}) = 115 \text{ days}$$
    Number of days in current interest payment interval
    $$= (\text{June 1, 2000}) - (\text{Dec. 1, 1999}) = 183 \text{ days}$$
    Price (on March 25, 2000) $= \$942.43\,(1.0285)^{115/183} = \underline{\$959.22}$

9. Given: $FV = \$1000$, $b = \frac{11\%}{2} = 5.5\%$, $i = \frac{9.9\%}{2} = 4.95\%$

    Time from preceding interest payment date to maturity
    $$= (\text{Oct. 15, 2011}) - (\text{Apr. 15, 1992}) = 39 \text{ half-years}$$

    Price (on Apr. 15, 1992) $= \$55\left(\dfrac{1-1.0495^{-39}}{0.0495}\right) + \$1000\left(1.0495^{-39}\right) = \$1094.23$

    Time from preceding interest payment date to purchase date
    $$= (\text{June 11, 1992}) - (\text{Apr. 15, 1992}) = 57 \text{ days}$$
    Number of days in current interest payment interval
    $$= (\text{Oct. 15, 1992}) - (\text{Apr. 15, 1992}) = 183 \text{ days}$$
    Price (on June 11, 1992) $= \$1094.23\,(1.0495)^{57/183} = \underline{\$1110.82}$

	2nd	Bond
	4.1502	ENTER
↓	6.2	ENTER
↓	1.0117	ENTER
↓	100	ENTER
↓	Set at "ACT"	
↓	Set at "2/Y"	
↓	6.4	ENTER
↓	CPT	

Ans: PRI = 98.0999

↓   *Ans:* AI = 1.7812

Flat price = 10($98.0999 + $1.7812) = $\underline{\$998.81}$

11. Given: $FV = \$1000$, $b = \frac{10\%}{2} = 5\%$, $i = \frac{5.5\%}{2} = 2.75\%$

   Time from preceding interest payment date to maturity
   $= $ (July 15, 2019) – (January 15, 2003)
   $= 33$ half-years
   Price (on Jan. 15, 2003)

   $$= \$50\left(\frac{1-1.0275^{-33}}{0.0275}\right) + \$1000\left(1.0275^{-33}\right)$$

   $= \$1483.95$

   Time from preceding interest payment to purchase date
   $= $ (June 1, 2003) – (January 15, 2003)
   $= 33$ days
   Number of days in current interest payment interval
   $= $ (July 15, 2003) – (January 15, 2003)
   $= 137$ days

   Price (on Aug. 8, 1981) $= \$1483.95\left(1.0275\right)^{137/181}$
   $\qquad\qquad = \underline{\$1514.74}$

2nd	**Bond**	
6.0103	**ENTER**	
↓ 10	**ENTER**	
↓ 7.1519	**ENTER**	
↓ 100	**ENTER**	
↓	Set at *"ACT"*	
↓	Set at *"2/Y"*	
↓ 5.5	**ENTER**	
↓	**CPT**	

   Ans: $PRI = 147.6890$

   ↓ *Ans*: $AI = 3.7845$

   Flat price $= 10(\$147.6890 + \$3.7845) = \underline{\$1514.74}$

13. Given: $FV = \$1000$, $b = \frac{9\%}{2} = 4.5\%$, $i = \frac{10\%}{2} = 5\%$

   Time from preceding interest payment date to maturity
   $= $ (Mar. 15, 2012) – (Mar. 15, 1993) $= 38$ half-years

   Price (on Mar. 15, 1993) $= \$45\left(\dfrac{1-1.05^{-38}}{0.05}\right) + \$1000\left(1.05^{-38}\right) = \underline{\$915.66}$

   Number of days in current interest payment interval
   $= $ (Sept. 15, 1993) – (Mar. 15, 1993) $= 184$ days

Date	No. days since Mar. 15, 1993	Price
Apr. 15, 1993	31	$\$915.66\left(1.05\right)^{31/184} = \underline{\$923.22}$
May 15, 1993	61	$\$915.66\left(1.05\right)^{61/184} = \underline{\$930.59}$
June 15, 1993	92	$\$915.66\left(1.05\right)^{92/184} = \underline{\$938.27}$
July 15, 1993	122	$\$915.66\left(1.05\right)^{122/184} = \underline{\$945.77}$
Aug. 15, 1993	153	$\$915.66\left(1.05\right)^{153/184} = \underline{\$953.57}$

   Price after interest payment on Sept. 15, 1993

   $$= \$45\left(\frac{1-1.05^{-37}}{0.05}\right) + \$1000\left(1.05^{-37}\right)$$

   $= \underline{\$916.44}$

Exercise 15.4 *(continued)*

15. Given: $FV = \$5000$, $b = \frac{7\%}{2} = 3.5\%$, Maturity date = January 21, 2014

On the date of purchase (January 25, 1995), $i = \frac{9.5\%}{2} = 4.75\%$

On the date of sale (January 13, 1996), $i = \frac{7.4\%}{2} = 3.7\%$

a. *Step 1*: Determine the purchase price.
Time from preceding interest payment date to maturity
$\qquad$ = (January 21, 2014) − (January 21, 1995)
$\qquad$ = 38 half-years
Price (Jan. 21, 1995)

$$= \$175\left(\frac{1-1.0475^{-38}}{0.0475}\right) + \$5000\left(1.0475^{-38}\right)$$

$\qquad$ = \$3909.81
Time from preceding interest payment to purchase date
$\qquad$ = (January 25, 1995) − (January 21, 1995)
$\qquad$ = 4 days
Number of days in current interest payment interval
$\qquad$ = (July 21, 1995) − (January 21, 1995)
$\qquad$ = 181 days
Price (January 25, 1995) = $\$3909.81\,(1.0475)^{4/181}$
$\qquad\qquad\qquad\qquad$ = \$3913.82

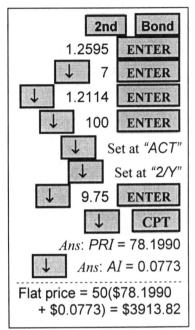

Ans: PRI = 78.1990

Ans: AI = 0.0773

Flat price = 50(\$78.1990
+ \$0.0773) = \$3913.82

Step 2: Determine the selling price.
Time from preceding interest payment date to maturity
$\qquad$ = (January 21, 2014) − (July 21, 1995)
$\qquad$ = 37 half-years
Price (July 21, 1995)

$$= \$175\left(\frac{1-1.037^{-37}}{0.037}\right) + \$5000\left(1.037^{-37}\right)$$

$\qquad$ = \$4800.20
Time from preceding interest payment date to date of sale
$\qquad$ = (Jan. 13, 1996) − (July 21, 1995)
$\qquad$ = 176 days
Number of days in current interest payment interval
$\qquad$ = (Jan. 21, 1996) − (July 21, 1995)
$\qquad$ = 184 days
Price (Jan. 13, 1996) = $\$4800.20\,(1.037)^{176/184}$
$\qquad\qquad\qquad\qquad$ = \$4969.95
Step 3: Calculate the capital gain.
$\qquad$ Capital gain = \$4969.95 − \$3913.82 = <u>\$1056.13</u>

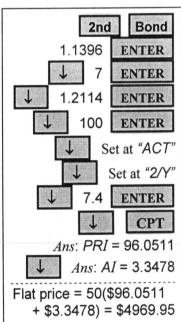

Ans: PRI = 96.0511

Ans: AI = 3.3478

Flat price = 50(\$96.0511
+ \$3.3478) = \$4969.95

b. Percent capital gain = $\dfrac{\$1056.13}{\$3913.82} \times 100\% = \underline{26.98\%}$

17. Quoted price = Flat price – Accrued interest = $1065.50 – Accrued interest
Time from preceding interest payment date to quotation date
= August 1 – May 15 = 78 days
Number of days in current interest payment interval
= November 15 – May 15 = 184 days

Accrued interest = $Prt = (FV)bt$ = $1000(0.038)$$\frac{78}{184}$ = $16.11

Quoted price = $1065.50 – $16.11 = $1049.39
The quoted price is <u>104.94% of face value</u>.

19. Given: Quoted price (on Oct. 23) = 108.50% of face value
FV = $1000, $b = \frac{7.2\%}{2}$ = 3.6% paid on Mar. 1 and Sept. 1

Time from preceding interest payment date to quotation date
= October 23 – September 1 = 52 days
Number of days in current interest payment interval
= March 1 – September 1 = 181 days
Accrued interest = (Coupon payment) × (Fraction of payment interval that has elapsed)
= $36$$\left(\frac{52}{181}\right)$
= $10.34

Flat price = Quoted price + Accrued interest = $1085.00 + $10.34 = <u>$1095.34</u>

21. In the solution to Problem 4, it was determined that the flat price on June 1, 1997
was $1239.47, and that 73 days of the 184-day interest payment interval had
elapsed. Hence,
Accrued interest = $45$$\left(\frac{73}{184}\right)$ = $17.85

Quoted price = Flat price – Accrued interest = $1239.47 – $17.85 = <u>$1221.62</u>

22. **Note: Bond yields in Table 15.2 (and in most sources of financial news) are rounded
to 4 figures. Therefore, we can expect bond prices calculated using these yields to
have no better than 4-figure accuracy. Keep this in mind when comparing the
"quoted prices" calculated in this problem to the "quoted prices" presented in
Table 15.2.**

   a. Given: Purchase date = March 8, 2004
       Coupon rate = 4.25%, FV = $100,
       Maturity date = September 1, 2009
       YTM = 3.601%
   The computed price agrees with the given
   quoted price.

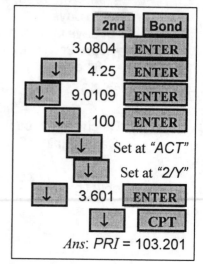

Exercise 15.4 (continued)

22. b. Given: Purchase date = March 8, 2004
       Coupon rate = 10.25%, FV = $100,
       Maturity date = March 15, 2014
       YTM = 4.245%
   The computed price agrees with the given quoted price.

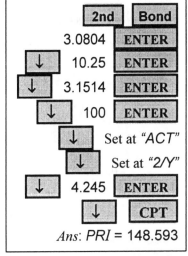

2nd Bond
3.0804 ENTER
↓ 10.25 ENTER
↓ 3.1514 ENTER
↓ 100 ENTER
↓ Set at "ACT"
↓ Set at "2/Y"
↓ 4.245 ENTER
↓ CPT
Ans: PRI = 148.593

   c. Given: Purchase date = March 8, 2004
       Coupon rate = 7.75%, FV = $100,
       Maturity date = December 22, 2025
       YTM = 5.295%
   The computed price agrees with the given quoted price.

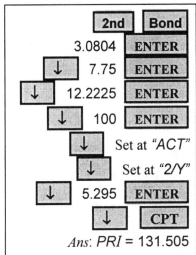

2nd Bond
3.0804 ENTER
↓ 7.75 ENTER
↓ 12.2225 ENTER
↓ 100 ENTER
↓ Set at "ACT"
↓ Set at "2/Y"
↓ 5.295 ENTER
↓ CPT
Ans: PRI = 131.505

Exercise 15.5

1. Given: FV = $12,000,000, n = 2(10) = 20, $i = \frac{7\%}{2} = 3.5\%$

   a. Substitute into formula (10-1) and solve for PMT.

   $$\$12,000,000 = PMT\left(\frac{1.035^{20} - 1}{0.035}\right)$$

   $PMT = \underline{\$424,333}$

   b. The balance after the 12th interval (and payment) will be

   $$FV = \$424,333\left(\frac{1.035^{12} - 1}{0.035}\right) = \underline{\$6,196,094}$$

3. Given: FV = $15,000,000, n = 15, i = 6.5%

   a. Substitute into formula (10-1) and solve for PMT.

   $$\$15,000,000 = PMT\left(\frac{1.065^{15} - 1}{0.065}\right)$$

   $PMT = \underline{\$620,292}$

   b. The balance after the 11th interval will be

   $$FV = \$620,292\left(\frac{1.065^{11} - 1}{0.065}\right) = \underline{\$9,534,856}$$

---

5. Given: FV(due) = \$6,000,000, $i = \frac{5.25\%}{12} = 0.4375\%$, $n = 12(5) = 60$

   a. Substitute into formula (13-1) and solve for PMT.

   $$\$6,000,000 = PMT\left(\frac{1.004375^{60} - 1}{0.004375}\right)(1.004375)$$

   $$PMT = \underline{\$87,284}$$

   b. The balance at the end of the 27th interval will be

   $$FV\text{(due)} = \$87,284\left(\frac{1.004375^{27} - 1}{0.004375}\right)(1.004375) = \underline{\$2,506,640}$$

7. Given: FV(due) = \$18,000,000, $n = 2(15) = 30$, $i = \frac{6.75\%}{2} = 3.375\%$

   a. Substitute into formula (13-1) and solve for PMT.

   $$\$18,000,000 = PMT\left(\frac{1.03375^{30} - 1}{0.03375}\right)(1.03375)$$

   $$PMT = \underline{\$344,297}$$

   b. The balance at the end of the 19th interval will be

   $$FV\text{(due)} = \$344,297\left(\frac{1.03375^{19} - 1}{0.03375}\right)(1.03375) = \underline{\$9,268,208}$$

9. Given: $FV = \$10,000,000$, $n = 2(10) = 20$, $i = \frac{7\%}{2} = 3.5\%$, $2b = 10\%$

   a. Substitute into formula (10-1) and solve for PMT.

   $$\$10,000,000 = PMT\left(\frac{1.035^{20} - 1}{0.035}\right)$$

   $$PMT = \underline{\$353,611}$$

   b. Annual cost of the debt = $2PMT + (2b)\$10,000,000$

   $$= 2(\$353,611) + \$1,000,000$$

   $$= \underline{\$1,707,222}$$

   c. Balance after 12th interval = $FV = \$353,611\left(\frac{1.035^{12} - 1}{0.035}\right) = \$5,163,414$

   Book value of debt = $\$10,000,000 - \$5,163,414 = \underline{\$4,836,586}$

11. Given: $FV = \$15,000,000$, $n = 2(15) = 30$, $i = \frac{6.5\%}{2} = 3.25\%$, $2b = 9\%$

    a. Substitute into formula (10-1) and solve for PMT.

    $$\$15,000,000 = PMT\left(\frac{1.0325^{30} - 1}{0.0325}\right)$$

    $$PMT = \underline{\$302,726}$$

    b. Annual cost of the debt = $2PMT + (2b)(\$15,000,000)$

    $$= 2(\$302,726) + 0.09(\$15,000,000)$$

    $$= \underline{\$1,955,452}$$

    c. Book value of debt after the 21st interval = $\$15,000,000 - \$302,726\left(\frac{1.0325^{21} - 1}{0.0325}\right)$

    $$= \underline{\$6,081,667}$$

Exercise 15.5 *(continued)*

13. Given: $FV = \$7,000,000$, $n = 2(5) = 10$, $i = \frac{5.75\%}{2} = 2.875\%$, $2b = 8\%$

   a. Substitute into formula (10-1) and solve for PMT.

   $$\$7,000,000 = PMT\left(\frac{1.02875^{10} - 1}{0.02875}\right)$$

   $PMT = \underline{\$614,137}$

   b. Annual cost of the debt $= 2PMT + 2b(\$7,000,000)$
   $$= 2(\$614,137) + 0.08(\$7,000,000)$$
   $$= \underline{\$1,788,274}$$

   c. Book value of debt after the 7th interval $= \$7,000,000 - \$614,137\left(\frac{1.02875^{7} - 1}{0.02875}\right)$
   $$= \underline{\$2,311,969}$$

15. Given: $FV = \$11,000,000$, $n = 2(15) = 30$, $i = \frac{7.5\%}{2} = 3.75\%$, $2b = 10.25\%$

   a. Substitute into formula (10-1) and solve for PMT.

   $$\$11,000,000 = PMT\left(\frac{1.0375^{30} - 1}{0.0375}\right)$$

   $PMT = \underline{\$204,464}$

   b. Annual cost of the debt $= 2PMT + 2b(\$11,000,000)$
   $$= 2(\$204,464) + 0.1025(\$11,000,000)$$
   $$= \underline{\$1,536,428}$$

   c. Book value of debt after the 19th interval $= \$11,000,000 - \$204,464\left(\frac{1.0375^{19} - 1}{0.0375}\right)$
   $$= \underline{\$5,478,509}$$

17. Given: $FV = \$800,000$, $n = 2(3) = 6$, $i = \frac{7\%}{2} = 3.5\%$

   Substitute into formula (10-1) and solve for PMT.

   $$\$800,000 = PMT\left(\frac{1.035^{6} - 1}{0.035}\right)$$

   $PMT = \$122,135$

Payment interval number	Payment (at end)	Interest earned	Increase in the fund	Balance in fund (end of interval)
0	—	—	—	$0
1	$122,135	$0	$122,135	122,135
2	122,135	4275	126,410	248,545
3	122,135	8699	130,834	379,379
4	122,135	13,278	135,413	514,792
5	122,135	18,018	140,153	654,945
6	122,135	22,923	145,058	800,003
	Total:	$67,193	$800,003	

Total interest $= \$800,003 - 6(\$122,135) = \underline{\$67,193}$

Exercise 15.5 (continued)

19. Given: FV(due) = $1,000,000, $n = 5$, $i = 6.75\%$
     Substitute into formula (13-1) and solve for PMT

$$\$1,000,000 = PMT\left(\frac{1.0675^5 - 1}{0.0675}\right)(1.0675)$$

$$PMT = \$163,710$$

Payment interval number	Payment (at start)	Interest earned	Increase in the fund	Balance in fund (end of interval)
0	—	—	—	$0
1	$163,710	$11,050	$174,760	174,760
2	163,710	22,847	186,557	361,317
3	163,710	35,439	199,149	560,466
4	163,710	48,882	212,592	773,058
5	163,710	63,232	226,942	1,000,000
	Total:	$181,450	$1,000,000	

Total interest = $1,000,000 – 5($163,710) = $181,450

21. From the solution to Problem 2,
     $PMT = \$302,720$, $n = 4(5) = 20$, $i = 3\%/2 = 1.5\%$

Payment interval number	Payment (at end)	Interest earned	Increase in the fund	Balance in fund (end of interval)
0	—	—	—	$0
1	$302,720	$0	$302,720	302,720
2	302,720	4541	307,261	609,981
|	|	|	|	|
10				3,239,928
11	302,720	48,559	351,319	3,591,247
12	302,720	53,869	356,589	3,947,836
|	|	|	|	|
18				6,202,544
19	302,720	93,038	395,758	6,598,302
20	302,720	98,975	401,695	6,999,997

23. From the solution to Problem 9,
     $PMT = \$353,611$, $n = 2(10) = 20$, $i = 7\%/2 = 3.5\%$

Payment interval number	Payment	Interest earned	Increase in the fund	Balance in fund (end of interval)	Book value of the debt
0	—	—	—	$0	$10,000,000
1	$353,611	$0	$353,611	353,611	9,646,389
2	353,611	12,376	365,987	719,598	9,280,402
|	|	|	|	|	|
18				8,663,360	1,336,640
19	353,611	303,218	656,829	9,320,189	679,811
20	353,611	326,207	679,818	10,000,007	(7)

Exercise 15.5 *(continued)*

25. *a.* Given: $FV(\text{due}) = \$600,000$, $n = 12(5) = 60$, $i = \frac{7.5\%}{12} = 0.625\%$

$$\$600,000 = PMT\left(\frac{1.00625^{60} - 1}{0.00625}\right)(1.00625)$$

$PMT = \underline{\$8221}$

b. Interest earned in Year 4
   = Balance after Year 4 − Balance after Year 3 − 12PMT

$$= \$8221\left(\frac{1.00625^{48} - 1}{0.00625}\right)(1.00625) - \$8221\left(\frac{1.00625^{36} - 1}{0.00625}\right)(1.00625) - 12(\$8221)$$

= \$461,399 − \$332,809 − \$98,652
= $\underline{\$29,938}$

c. Solve for n in

$$\$300,000 = \$8221\left(\frac{1.00625^{n} - 1}{0.00625}\right)(1.00625)$$

$n = 32.79$
Hence, the fund will pass the halfway point in the <u>33rd month</u>.

d. Interest earned in the 35th month
   = $i \times$ (Balance after the 34th month + PMT)

$$= 0.00625\left[\$8221\left(\frac{1.00625^{34} - 1}{0.00625}\right)(1.00625) + \$8221\right]$$

= 0.00625(\$312,297 + \$8221)
= $\underline{\$2003}$

27. Given: $FV = \$20,000,000$, $n = 2(20) = 40$, $i = \frac{4.5\%}{2} = 2.25\%$

a. $$\$20,000,000 = PMT\left(\frac{1.0225^{40} - 1}{0.0225}\right)$$

$PMT = \underline{\$313,548}$

b. Interest earned in Year 6
   = Balance after Year 6 − Balance after Year 5 − 2PMT

$$= \$313,548\left(\frac{1.0225^{12} - 1}{0.0225}\right) - \$313,548\left(\frac{1.0225^{10} - 1}{0.0225}\right) - 2(\$313,548)$$

= \$4,264,949 − \$3,472,766 − \$627,096
= $\underline{\$165,087}$

c. Increase in the fund during Interval 27
   = Balance after Interval 27 − Balance after Interval 26

$$= \$313,548\left(\frac{1.0225^{27} - 1}{0.0225}\right) - \$313,548\left(\frac{1.0225^{26} - 1}{0.0225}\right)$$

= $\underline{\$559,178}$

Exercise 15.5 (continued)

27. d.

Payment interval number	Payment (at end)	Interest earned	Increase in the fund	Balance in fund (end of interval)	Book value of the debt
0	---	---	---	$0	$20,000,000
1	$313,548	$0	$313,548	313,548	19,686,452
2	313,548	7,055	320,603	634,151	19,365,849
|	|	|	|	|	|
38	---	---	---	18,522,966	1,477,034
39	313,548	416,767	730,315	19,253,281	746,719
40	313,548	<u>433,199</u>	746,747	20,000,028	(28)
	Total:	<u>$7,458,108</u>			

Total Interest = $20,000,028 – 40($313,548) = <u>$7,458,108</u>

29. Given: FV(due) = $800,000, $n = 4(10) = 40$, $i = \frac{7\%}{4} = 1.75\%$

a. $\qquad$ $800,000 = PMT\left(\dfrac{1.0175^{40} - 1}{0.0175}\right)(1.0175)$

$\qquad\qquad$ $PMT =$ <u>$13,737</u>

b.

Payment interval number	Payment	Interest earned	Increase in the fund	Balance in fund (end of interval)	Book value of the debt
0	—	—	—	$0	$800,000
1	$13,737	$240	$13,977	13,977	786,023
2	13,737	485	14,222	28,199	771,801
|	|	|	|	|	|
38				745,465	54,535
39	13,737	13,286	27,023	772,488	27,512
40	13,737	<u>13,759</u>	27,496	799,984	16
	Total:	<u>$250,504</u>			

Total interest = $799,984 – 40($13,737) = <u>$250,504</u>

Review Problems

1. Given: $FV = 1000, $n = 2(19.5) = 39$, $b = \frac{7.5\%}{2} = 3.75\%$, $i = \frac{8.6\%}{2} = 4.3\%$

Bond price = $37.50\left(\dfrac{1 - 1.043^{-39}}{0.043}\right) + $1000\,(1.043)^{-39} = 896.86

Bond discount = $1000 – $896.86 = <u>$103.14</u>

Review Problems (*continued*)

3. Given: For each bond, $FV = \$1000$ and $b = \frac{8.5\%}{2} = 4.25\%$

At the time the bonds were purchased, $n = 2(18) = 36$ and $i = \frac{9.8\%}{2} = 4.9\%$

$$\text{Purchase price} = \$42.50\left(\frac{1-1.049^{-36}}{0.049}\right) + \$1000(1.049)^{-36} = \$891.05$$

Now, $n = 2(13.5) = 27$ and $i = \frac{8\%}{2} = 4.0\%$

$$\text{Current price} = \$42.50\left(\frac{1-1.04^{-27}}{0.04}\right) + \$1000(1.04)^{-27} = \$1040.82$$

Capital gain $= 15(\$1040.82 - \$891.05) = \underline{\$2246.55}$

5. Given: $FV = \$1000$, $b = \frac{9.5\%}{2} = 4.75\%$, $i = \frac{5.2\%}{2} = 2.6\%$

Time from preceding interest payment date to maturity
$$= \text{(June 15, 2014)} - \text{(June 15, 1998)} = 32 \text{ half-years}$$

$$\text{Price (on June 15, 1998)} = \$47.50\left(\frac{1-1.026^{-32}}{0.026}\right) + \$1000(1.026)^{-32} = \$1463.22$$

Time from preceding interest payment date to purchase date
$$= \text{(Dec. 10, 1998)} - \text{(June 15, 1998)} = 178 \text{ days}$$
Number of days in current interest payment interval
$$= \text{(Dec. 15, 1998)} - \text{(June 15, 1998)} = 183 \text{ days}$$
Price (on Dec. 10, 1989) $= \$1463.22(1.026)^{178/183} = \underline{\$1500.21}$

7. Given: $FV\text{(due)} = \$750,000$, $n = 2(3) = 6$, $i = \frac{6\%}{2} = 3\%$

Substitute into formula (13-1) and solve for PMT.

$$\$750,000 = PMT\left(\frac{1.03^6 - 1}{0.03}\right)(1.03)$$

$$PMT = \$112,571$$

Payment interval number	Payment (at start)	Interest earned	Increase in the fund	Balance in fund (end of interval)
0	—	—	—	$0
1	$112,571	$3377	$115,948	115,948
2	112,571	6856	119,427	235,375
3	112,571	10,438	123,009	358,384
4	112,571	14,129	126,700	485,084
5	112,571	17,930	130,501	615,585
6	112,571	21,845	134,416	750,001
	Total: $74,575		$750,001	

Self-Test Exercise

1. Given: $FV = \$1000$, $b = \frac{6.8\%}{2} = 3.4\%$, $n = 2(18) = 36$, $i = \frac{6.5\%}{2} = 3.25\%$

   Bond price $= \$34\left(\dfrac{1-1.0325^{-36}}{0.0325}\right) + \$1000(1.0325)^{-36} = \$1031.56$

   In order that YTM $= 2i = 7\%$ compounded semiannually,

   Price $= \$34\left(\dfrac{1-1.035^{-36}}{0.035}\right) + \$1000(1.035)^{-36} = \$979.71$

   Therefore, the bond price will have to be
   $\$1031.56 - \$979.71 = \underline{\$51.85}$
   lower for the yield to maturity to be 0.5% higher.

2. The answer will be the same for any face value. Use $FV = \$1000$.
   Currently, $n = 2(22.5) = 45$, $b = \frac{8\%}{2} = 4\%$, and $i = \frac{6.9\%}{2} = 3.45\%$.

   Current price $= \$40\left(\dfrac{1-1.0345^{-45}}{0.0345}\right) + \$1000(1.0345)^{-45} = \$1124.77$

   Percent capital gain $= \dfrac{\$1124.77 - \$1000}{\$1000} \times 100\% = \underline{12.48\%}$

3. Given: $FV = \$1000$, $b = \frac{7.9\%}{2} = 3.95\%$, $n = 2(8.5) = 17$, Price $= \$1034.50$
   The YTM is $2i$ where i is the solution to

   $$\$1034.50 = \$39.50\left[\dfrac{1-(1+i)^{-17}}{i}\right] + \$1000(1+i)^{-17}$$

   The solution is $i = 3.6735\%$
   Therefore, YTM $= 2i = \underline{7.35\% \text{ compounded semiannually}}$

4. Given: $FV = \$1000$, $b = \frac{7.6\%}{2} = 3.8\%$, $i = \frac{5.9\%}{2} = 2.95\%$
   Time from preceding interest payment date to maturity
   $\qquad = $ (Nov. 1, 2012) $-$ (May 1, 2000) $= 12\frac{1}{2}$ years $= 25$ half-years

   Price (on May 1, 2000) $= \$38\left(\dfrac{1-1.0295^{-25}}{0.0295}\right) + \$1000(1.0295)^{-25} = \$1148.84$

   Time from preceding interest payment date to June 10, 2000
   $\qquad = $ (June 10, 2000) $-$ (May 1, 2000) $= 40$ days
   Number of days in current interest payment interval
   $\qquad = $ (Nov. 1, 2000) $-$ (May 1, 2000) $= 184$ days
   Price (on June 10, 2000) $= \$1148.84(1.0295)^{40/184} = \underline{\$1156.12}$

5. Quoted price $=$ Flat price $-$ Accrued interest
   $\qquad = \$1156.12 - \$38\left(\frac{40}{184}\right)$
   $\qquad = \underline{\$1147.86}$

Self-Test Exercise (continued)

6. Given: $FV = \$500,000$, $n = 2(7) = 14$, $i = 7\%/2 = 3.5\%$

Substitute into formula (10-1) and solve for *PMT*.

$$\$500,000 = PMT\left(\frac{1.035^{14} - 1}{0.035}\right)$$

$$PMT = \$28,285$$

Payment interval number	Payment	Interest earned	Increase in the fund	Balance in fund (end of interval)	Book value of the debt
0	—	—	—	$0	$500,000
1	$28,285	$0	$28,285	28,285	471,715
2	28,285	990	29,275	57,560	442,440
|	|	|	|	|	|
12				413,016	86,984
13	28,285	14,456	42,741	455,757	44,243
14	28,285	15,951	44,236	499,993	7

Exercise 15A

1. Given: $FV = \$1000$, $b = \frac{9\%}{2} = 4.5\%$, $n = 2(3) = 6$, $i = \frac{8\%}{2} = 4\%$

$$\text{Bond price} = \$45\left(\frac{1 - 1.04^{-6}}{0.04}\right) + \$1000(1.04)^{-6} = \underline{\$1026.21}$$

Coupon number	Coupon payment	Interest on book value	Premium amortized	Book value of bond	Unamortized premium
0	—	—	—	$1026.21	$26.21
1	$45.00	$41.05	$3.95	1022.26	22.26
2	45.00	40.89	4.11	1018.15	18.15
3	45.00	40.73	4.27	1013.88	13.88
4	45.00	40.56	4.44	1009.44	9.44
5	45.00	40.38	4.62	1004.82	4.82
6	45.00	40.18	4.82	1000.00	0.00
	$270.00	$243.79	$26.21		

Exercise 15A *(continued)*

3. Given: $FV = \$1000$, $b = 10\%/2 = 5\%$, $n = 2(12) = 24$, $i = 8.8\%/2 = 4.4\%$

Purchase price = $\$50\left(\dfrac{1-1.044^{-24}}{0.044}\right) + \$1000\,(1.044)^{-24} = \underline{\$1087.85}$

Coupon number	Coupon payment	Interest on book value	Premium amortized	Book value of bond	Unamortized premium
0	—	—	—	$1087.85	$87.85
1	$50.00	$47.87	$2.13	1085.72	85.72
2	50.00	47.77	2.23	1083.49	83.49
3	50.00	47.67	2.33	1081.16	81.16
				1016.52	16.52
22	50.00	44.73	5.27	1011.25	11.25
23	50.00	44.50	5.50	1005.75	5.75
24	50.00	44.25	5.75	1000.00	0.00
	$1200.00	$1112.15	$87.85		

5. Given: $FV = \$1000$, $b = \dfrac{8\%}{2} = 4\%$, $n = 2(3) = 6$, $i = \dfrac{9.5\%}{2} = 4.75\%$

Purchase price = $\$40\left(\dfrac{1-1.0475^{-6}}{0.0475}\right) + \$1000\,(1.0475)^{-6} = \underline{\$961.63}$

Coupon number	Coupon payment	Interest on book value	Discount amortized	Book value of bond	Unamortized discount
0	—	—	—	$961.63	$38.37
1	$40.00	$45.68	$5.68	967.31	32.69
2	40.00	45.95	5.95	973.26	26.74
3	40.00	46.23	6.23	979.49	20.51
4	40.00	46.53	6.53	986.02	13.98
5	40.00	46.84	6.84	992.86	7.14
6	40.00	47.14	7.14	1000.00	0.00
	$240.00	$278.37	$38.37		

7. Given: $FV = \$1000$, $b = \dfrac{8.5\%}{2} = 4.25\%$, $n = 2(11) = 22$, $i = \dfrac{10.4\%}{2} = 5.2\%$

Purchase price = $\$42.50\left(\dfrac{1-1.052^{-22}}{0.052}\right) + \$1000\,(1.052)^{-22} = \underline{\$877.20}$

Coupon number	Coupon payment	Interest on book value	Discount amortized	Book value of bond	Unamortized discount
0	—	—	—	$877.20	$122.80
1	$42.50	$45.61	$3.11	880.31	119.69
2	42.50	45.78	3.28	883.59	116.41
3	42.50	45.95	3.45	887.04	112.96
				974.23	25.77
20	42.50	50.66	8.16	982.39	17.61
21	42.50	51.08	8.58	990.97	9.03
22	42.50	51.53	9.03	1000.00	0.00
	$935.00	$1057.80	$122.80		

16   Business Investment Decisions

Exercise 16.1

1. *a.* Fair market value of the future cash flows (discounted at Vencap's cost of capital)

$$= \frac{(-\$30,000)}{1.12} + \frac{(-\$10,000)}{1.12^2} + \frac{\$20,000}{1.12^3} + \frac{\$60,000}{1.12^4} + \frac{\$40,000}{1.12^5}$$

$$= -\$26,785.7 - \$7971.9 + \$14,235.6 + \$38,131.1 + \$22,697.1$$

$$= \$40,306$$

Since the purchase price is less than the present value of the future cash flows, <u>the investment should be made</u>.

b. The economic value, in current dollars, of Vencap will be increased by

(Present value of the expected cash flows) – (Purchase price)

<u>The increase in economic value is</u> $40,306 – $37,000 = <u>$3306</u>

3. If Vencap requires a 17% rate of return on investment, it should offer an amount equal to the present value of the future cash flows discounted at 17%.

$$\text{Price} = \frac{(-\$30,000)}{1.17} + \frac{(-\$10,000)}{1.17^2} + \frac{\$20,000}{1.17^3} + \frac{\$60,000}{1.17^4} + \frac{\$40,000}{1.17^5} = \underline{\$29,805}$$

5. *a.* If Arrowsmith's cost of capital is 12.5%, the present value of the forecast cash flows is

$$\frac{\$90,000}{1.125} + \frac{\$90,000}{1.125^2} + \frac{(-\$30,000)}{1.125^3} + \frac{\$90,000}{1.125^4} + \frac{\$90,000}{1.125^5} + \frac{(-\$30,000)}{1.125^6}$$

$$= \$221,373$$

The present value of the expected cash flows is larger than the price of the timber rights. Arrowsmith should still <u>buy the timber rights</u> if its cost of capital is 12.5%.

b. The economic value of Arrowsmith Lumber would be increased by

$221,373 – $220,000 = <u>$1373</u>

7. The lower cost alternative should be selected. This will be the alternative having the lower present value of costs (net of any salvage or resale value).

a. The lease payments form a simple annuity due having

$PMT = \$1000$, $n = 48$, and $i = 0.55\%$. Then

$$PV(\text{lease}) = PV(\text{due}) = \$1000 \left(\frac{1 - 1.055^{-48}}{0.055} \right) 1.055 = \$42,317$$

$$PV(\text{purchase}) = \$45,000 - \$5000 \, (1.055)^{-48} = \$41,157$$

The <u>machine should be purchased</u> since the current economic value of the lifetime costs is $1160 less than if the machine is leased.

b. If the firm's cost of borrowing is $i = 0.75\%$ per month,

$$PV(\text{lease}) = \$1000 \left(\frac{1 - 1.0075^{-48}}{0.0075} \right) 1.0075 = \$40,486$$

$$PV(\text{purchase}) = \$45,000 - \$5000 \, (1.0075)^{-48} = \$41,507$$

The <u>machine should be leased</u> since the current economic value of the lifetime costs is $1021 less than if the machine is purchased.

Exercise 16.1 (*continued*)

9. a. The alternative having the lower present value of costs should be chosen. Since the college will continue to own the telephone system after 5 years, the fair comparison is purchasing the system versus leasing for 5 years followed by exercising the purchase option. For the lease, $PMT = \$1500$, $n = 20$, and $i = 2.5\%$.

$$PV(\text{lease}) = \$3000 + PV(\text{due}) + \$3000\,(1.025)^{-20}$$

$$= \$3000 + \$1500\left(\frac{1-1.025^{-20}}{0.025}\right)1.025 + \$1830.81$$

$$= \$28,799$$

The college should choose to <u>lease the system</u>.

   b. Leasing will save $\$30,000 - \$28,799 = \underline{\$1201}$ in current dollars.

11. The alternative having the lower present value of costs should be chosen. The rental payments form a simple annuity due having $PMT = \$1000$ per month and $n = 60$.

   a. If $i = \frac{7\%}{12} = 0.58\overline{3}\,\%$,

$$PV(\text{rent}) = \$1000\left(\frac{1-1.0058\overline{3}^{-60}}{0.0058\overline{3}}\right)1.0058\overline{3} = \$50,797$$

$$PV(\text{purchase payments}) = \$180,000 + \$300\left(\frac{1-1.0058\overline{3}^{-60}}{0.0058\overline{3}}\right) - \frac{\$200,000}{1.0058\overline{3}^{60}}$$

$$= \$180,000 + \$15,151 - \$141,081$$
$$= \$54,070$$

Mr. Harder <u>should rent, thereby saving</u> $\$54.070 - 50,797 = \underline{\$3273}$ in current dollars.

   b. If $i = \frac{6\%}{12} = 0.5\%$,

$$PV(\text{rent}) = \$1000\left(\frac{1-1.005^{-60}}{0.005}\right)1.005 = \$51,984$$

$$PV(\text{purchase payments}) = \$180,000 + \$300\left(\frac{1-1.005^{-60}}{0.005}\right) - \frac{\$200,000}{1.005^{60}}$$

$$= \$180,000 + \$15,518 - \$148,274$$
$$= \$47,244$$

Mr. Harder <u>should buy, thereby saving</u> $\$51,984 - \$47,244 = \underline{\$4740}$.

Exercise 16.2

1. a. $$NPV = \$70,000\left(\frac{1-1.12^{-7}}{0.12}\right) + \frac{\$80,000}{1.12^7} - \$333,000$$

$$= \$319,463.0 + \$36,187.3 - \$333,000$$
$$= \$22,651$$

Since the investment has a positive NPV, St. Lawrence Bus Lines <u>should sign the contract</u>.

Exercise 16.2 (*continued*)

1. *b.* $\text{NPV} = \$70,000\left(\dfrac{1-1.14^{-7}}{0.14}\right) + \dfrac{\$80,000}{1.14^7} - \$333,000 = -\$848$

   At a 14% cost of capital, the investment's NPV is a small negative amount. <u>The contract should not be signed</u>. (The small magnitude of the NPV in relation to the amounts involved means that the future profits and resale value would be nearly sufficient to pay back the $333,000 financing along with a 14% rate of return to the providers of the financing.)

   c. As the discount rate (cost of capital) increases beyond 14%, the NPV will remain negative and grow in magnitude. At a 16% cost of capital, the NPV is $-\$21,994$. The investment <u>should be rejected</u> at any cost of capital above 14%.

3.

Time (years)	Cash flow	Present value
0	−$150,000	−$150,000
1	−50,000	− 43,478
2	−50,000	− 37,807
3	200,000	131,503
4	300,000	171,526
	Total (NPV):	$ 71,744

The economic value, at the start of planting, of the 20-hectare ginseng crop is $71,744.

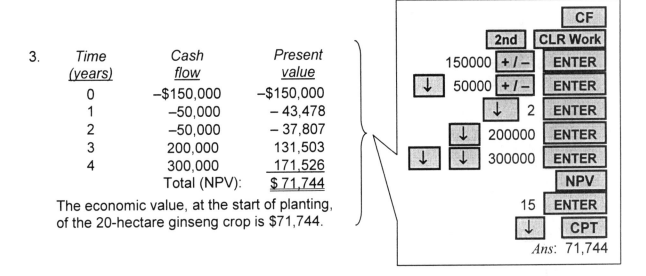

5.

Time (years)	Capital cash flow	Operating profit	Net cash flow
0	−$150,000		−$150,000
1	−150,000	0	−150,000
2	−150,000	0	−150,000
3	0	0	0
4 to 9	0	$90,000	90,000
10	100,000	90,000	190,000

$$\text{NPV} = \dfrac{\$90,000\left(\dfrac{1-1.14^{-6}}{0.14}\right)}{1.14^3} + \dfrac{\$190,000}{1.14^{10}}$$

$$- 150,000\left(\dfrac{1-1.14^{-3}}{0.14}\right)(1.14)$$

$$= \$236,226.6 + \$51,251.3 - \$396,999.1$$

$$= -\$109,521$$

Since the NPV of the new project is negative, <u>it should be rejected</u>.

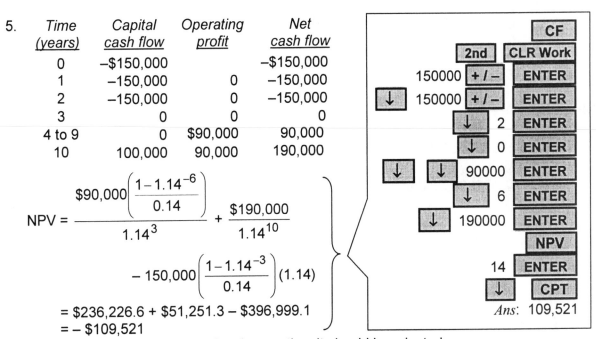

7.

Time (years)	Capital cash flow	Operating profit	Net cash flow
0	–$ 900,000		–$900,000
1	–3,800,000		–3,800,000
2 to 5		$600,000	600,000
6 to 12		1,000,000	1,000,000
13	800,000	1,000,000	1,800,000

$$NPV = \frac{\$600,000\left(\dfrac{1-1.14^{-4}}{0.14}\right)}{1.14} + \frac{\$1,000,000\left(\dfrac{1-1.14^{-7}}{0.14}\right)}{1.14^5}$$

$$+ \frac{\$1,800,000}{1.14^{13}} - \frac{\$3,800,000}{1.14} - \$900,000$$

$$= \$1,533,533 + \$2,227,211$$
$$+ \$327,725 - \$3,333,333 - \$900,000$$
$$= -\$144,864$$

Since the project has a negative NPV at a discount rate of 14%, the rate of return on the investment will be below 14% and Jasper <u>should not proceed</u> with the project.

		CF
	2nd	CLR Work
900000	+/–	ENTER
↓ 3800000	+/–	ENTER
↓ ↓	600000	ENTER
	↓ 4	ENTER
↓	1000000	ENTER
	↓ 7	ENTER
↓	1800000	ENTER
		NPV
	14	ENTER
	↓	CPT

Ans: –144,864

9.

Time (years)	Capital cash flow	Operating profit	Net cash flow
0	–$275,000		–$275,000
1 to 2		$75,000	75,000
3	–40,000	75,000	35,000
4		75,000	75,000
5	–40,000	55,000	15,000
6		55,000	55,000
7	30,000	55,000	85,000

$$NPV = \$75,000\left(\frac{1-1.14^{-2}}{0.14}\right) + \frac{\$35,000}{1.14^3} + \frac{\$75,000}{1.14^4} + \frac{\$15,000}{1.14^5} + \frac{\$55,000}{1.14^6} + \frac{\$85,000}{1.14^7} - \$275,000$$

$$= \$123,499.5 + \$23,624.0 + \$44,406.0 + \$7790.5 + \$25,057.3 + \$33,959.2 - \$275,000$$
$$= -\$16,653$$

<u>The product should not be manufactured</u> since the investment has a negative NPV.

Exercise 16.2 (*continued*)

11.

Time (years)	Capital cash flow	Operating profit	Net cash flow
0	–$12,000,000		–$12,000,000
1		$2,000,000	2,000,000
2		2,200,000	2,200,000
3		2,420,000	2,420,000
4		2,662,000	2,662,000
5		2,928,200	2,928,200
6		3,221,020	3,221,020
7	2,000,000	3,543,122	5,543,122

Since the NPV ($295,258) is positive, Wildcat Drilling should acquire the new drilling rig.

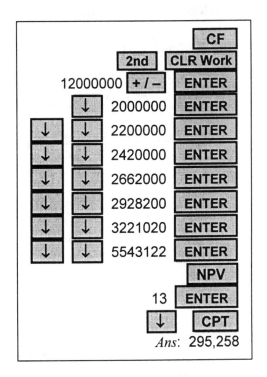

Exercise 16.3

1. Rank the projects in descending order of NPV per invested dollar.

Project	Initial investment	Project NPV	NPV per invested dollar	Cumulative investment
B	$60,000	$40,000	$0.67	$60,000
D	200,000	110,000	0.55	260,000
C	130,000	60,000	0.46	390,000
A	100,000	25,000	0.25	490,000

Now find the combination of projects having the largest aggregate NPV subject to the $300,000 constraint on total investment.

Combination of projects	Combined NPV	Total investment
B, D	$150,000	$260,000
B, C, A	125,000	290,000

Projects B and D have the highest NPV subject to the capital budgeting constraint.

3. Calculate each project's NPV and rank the projects in descending order of NPV per invested dollar.

Project	Initial investment	Project NPV	NPV per invested dollar	Cumulative investment
F	$20,000	$3375	$0.17	$20,000
E	28,000	4329	0.15	48,000
A	30,000	3935	0.13	78,000
C	18,000	2131	0.12	96,000
B	36,000	1188	0.03	132,000
D	22,000	– 456	–0.02	154,000

Projects F, E, and A should be selected (requiring a combined investment of $78,000).

Exercise 16.3 (*continued*)

5. $\text{NPV(Massey)} = \$77{,}000\left(\dfrac{1-1.11^{-6}}{0.11}\right) + \dfrac{\$50{,}000}{1.11^6} - \$190{,}000 = \$162{,}483$

   $\text{NPV(Deere)} = \$70{,}000\left(\dfrac{1-1.10^{-6}}{0.10}\right) + \dfrac{\$40{,}000}{1.10^6} - \$156{,}000 = \$171{,}447$

   Carl should <u>purchase the Deere</u> combine. In current dollars, its NPV is
   $$\$171{,}447 - \$162{,}483 = \underline{\$8964}$$
   larger than the NPV for the purchase of the Massey combine.

7.

Investment C			Investment D		
Time (years)	Capital cash flow	Operating profit	Time (years)	Capital cash flow	Operating profit
0	−$50,000		0	−$25,000	
1		$16,000	1 to 3	−25,000	
2	−30,000	16,000	4 to 9		$35,000
3 to 9		16,000	10	20,000	35,000
10	30,000	16,000			

   $\text{NPV(C)} = \$16{,}000\left(\dfrac{1-1.15^{-10}}{0.15}\right) + \dfrac{\$30{,}000}{1.15^{10}} - \dfrac{\$30{,}000}{1.15^2} - \$50{,}000$

   $\qquad\qquad = \$15{,}031$

   $\text{NPV(D)} = \dfrac{\$35{,}000\left(\dfrac{1-1.15^{-7}}{0.15}\right)}{1.15^3} + \dfrac{\$20{,}000}{1.15^{10}} - \$25{,}000\left(\dfrac{1.15^3-1}{0.15}\right) - \$25{,}000$

   $\qquad\qquad = \$95{,}744 + \$4944 - \$57{,}081 - \$25{,}000$
   $\qquad\qquad = \$18{,}607$

   The company should <u>choose investment D</u> whose current economic value
   is <u>$3576 more</u> than C's economic value.

9. We will use the Equivalent Annual Cash Flow Method.

   $\text{NPV(H, 3 years)} = \$55{,}000\left(\dfrac{1-1.13^{-3}}{0.13}\right) - \$119{,}000 = \$10{,}863$

   H's equivalent annual cash flow is the value of *PMT* in

   $\$10{,}863 = PMT\left(\dfrac{1-1.13^{-3}}{0.13}\right)$

   $PMT = \$4601$

   $\text{NPV(J, 4 years)} = \$58{,}000\left(\dfrac{1-1.13^{-4}}{0.13}\right) - \$160{,}000 = \$12{,}519$

   J's equivalent annual cash flow is the value of *PMT* in

   $\$12{,}519 = PMT\left(\dfrac{1-1.13^{-4}}{0.13}\right)$

   $PMT = \$4209$

   <u>Model H should be purchased</u> because it has the larger equivalent annual cash flow.

11. The truck that generates the larger equivalent annual cash flow (EACF) should be purchased.

$$\text{NPV(15-ton, 7 years)} = \$35,000\left(\frac{1-1.09^{-7}}{0.09}\right) + \frac{\$30,000}{1.09^7} - \$150,000 = \$42,564$$

This truck's EACF is the value of *PMT* in

$$\$42,564 = PMT\left(\frac{1-1.09^{-7}}{0.09}\right)$$

$$PMT = \$8457$$

$$\text{NPV(25-ton, 6 years)} = \$48,000\left(\frac{1-1.09^{-6}}{0.09}\right) + \frac{\$40,000}{1.09^6} - \$200,000 = \$39,175$$

The 25-ton truck's EACF is the value of *PMT* in

$$\$39,175 = PMT\left(\frac{1-1.09^{-6}}{0.09}\right)$$

$$PMT = \$8733$$

The 25-ton truck should be purchased. It will generate a
$8733 – $8457 = $276 larger
annual economic benefit to the owner than the 15-ton truck.

13. $$\text{NPV(Hawk, 5 years)} = \frac{\$60,000}{1.065^5} - \$60,000\left(\frac{1-1.065^{-5}}{0.065}\right) - \$240,000$$

$$= \$43,792.9 - \$249,340.8 - \$240,000$$
$$= -\$445,548$$

The equivalent annual cost (EAC) is the value of *PMT* in

$$-\$445,548 = PMT\left(\frac{1-1.065^{-5}}{0.065}\right) \quad \text{giving} \quad PMT = -\$107,214$$

(The negative sign is interpreted as a cash outflow or cost.)

$$\text{NPV(Falcon, 7 years)} = \frac{\$80,000}{1.065^7} - \$80,000\left(\frac{1-1.065^{-7}}{0.065}\right) - \$190,000$$

$$= \$51,480.5 - \$438,761.6 - \$190,000$$
$$= -\$577,281$$

The Falcon's EAC is the value of *PMT* in

$$-\$577,281 = PMT\left(\frac{1-1.065^{-7}}{0.065}\right) \quad \text{giving} \quad PMT = -\$105,256$$

The Falcon has a lower (by $1958) equivalent annual cost.

15. The present value of the costs for 8 years with the Caterpillar is

$$\frac{\$20,000}{1.12^8} - \frac{\$30,000}{1.12^6} - \frac{\$30,000}{1.12^4} - \frac{\$30,000}{1.12^2} - \$160,000$$

$$= \$8077.7 - \$15,198.9 - \$19,065.5 - \$23,915.8 - \$160,000$$
$$= -\$210,103$$

The equivalent annual cost (EAC) of the Caterpillar is the value of *PMT* in

$$-\$210,103 = PMT\left(\frac{1-1.12^{-8}}{0.12}\right) \quad \text{giving} \quad PMT = -\$42,294$$

(*continued*)

Exercise 16.3 (*continued*)

15. (*continued*)

The present value of the costs for 12 years with the International is

$$\frac{\$20,000}{1.12^{12}} - \frac{\$20,000}{1.12^9} - \frac{\$20,000}{1.12^6} - \frac{\$20,000}{1.12^3} - \$210,000$$

$$= \$5133.5 - \$7212.2 - \$10,132.6 - \$14,235.6 - \$210,000$$

$$= -\$236,447$$

The EAC of the International is the value of *PMT* in

$$-\$236,447 = PMT\left(\frac{1-1.12^{-12}}{0.12}\right) \quad \text{giving} \quad PMT = -\$38,171$$

The <u>International model should be purchased</u> since its equivalent annual cost is
$42,294 − $38,171 = $4123 lower.

Exercise 16.4

1. The NPV of the license at the discount rate *i* is

$$NPV = \$10,000\left[\frac{1-(1+i)^{-10}}{i}\right] - \$50,000$$

The IRR is the value for *i* that makes the NPV = 0.
The value is *i* = 15.1% (to the nearest 0.1%).
The investment's IRR is <u>15.1%</u>.

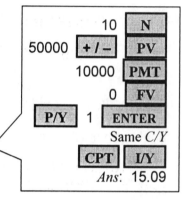

3. For the first stage, the IRR is the value of *i* satisfying

$$\$30,000\left[\frac{1-(1+i)^{-10}}{i}\right] - \$100,000 = 0$$

The solution is *i* = <u>27.3% = IRR for Stage 1</u>.
Similarly, for Stage 2, solve for *i* in

$$\$27,000\left[\frac{1-(1+i)^{-9}}{i}\right] - \$100,000 = 0$$

The solution is *i* = <u>22.7% = IRR for Stage 2</u>.
For Stage 3, solve for *i* in

$$\$22,000\left[\frac{1-(1+i)^{-8}}{i}\right] - \$100,000 = 0$$

The solution is *i* = <u>14.6% = IRR for Stage 3</u>.
For Stage 4, solve for *i* in

$$\$22,000\left[\frac{1-(1+i)^{-7}}{i}\right] - \$100,000 = 0$$

The solution is *i* = <u>12.1 % = IRR for Stage 4</u>.
<u>Stages 1, 2, and 3 should be approved</u> since their IRR's exceed the cost of capital (14%).

5. The investment's IRR is the value of i satisfying

$$NPV = 0 = \$16,000\left[\frac{1-(1+i)^{-10}}{i}\right] + \frac{\$25,000}{(1+i)^{10}} - \$100,000$$

The solution is $i = \underline{11.7\%}$ = IRR of the investment. The <u>investment should be not be made</u> since the IRR (11.7%) is less than the cost of capital (12%).

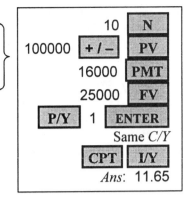

7. The investment's IRR is the value of i satisfying

$$NPV = 0 = \$20,000\left[\frac{1-(1+i)^{-5}}{i}\right]$$

$$+ \frac{\$15,000\left[\frac{1-(1+i)^{-5}}{i}\right]}{(1+i)^5} - \$100,000$$

The solution is $i = \underline{12.7\%}$ = IRR of the investment. The investment <u>should be undertaken</u> since its IRR exceeds the cost of capital (12%).

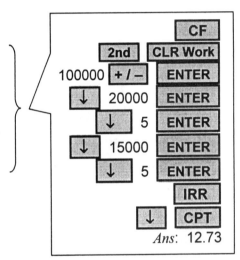

9. The investment's IRR is the value of i satisfying

$$NPV = 0 = \frac{\$25,000}{(1+i)} + \frac{\$60,000}{(1+i)^2}$$

$$+ \frac{\$50,000}{(1+i)^3} + \frac{\$35,000}{(1+i)^4} - \$120,000$$

The solution is $i = \underline{15.0\%}$ = IRR of the investment. The investment just meets the minimum requirement for acceptance since its IRR equals the firm's cost of capital (15%). <u>The product should</u>, therefore, <u>be introduced</u>.

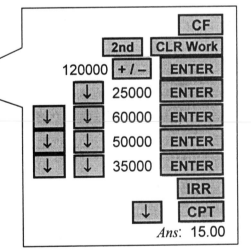

Exercise 16.4 (*continued*)

11. Note that the Year 11 operating profit will be exactly offset by the $1,000,000 expenditure for environmental restoration. The project's IRR is the value of i satisfying

$$\text{NPV} = 0 = \frac{\$1,000,000\left[\dfrac{1-(1+i)^{-9}}{i}\right]}{1+i} - \frac{\$3,000,000}{1+i} - \$2,000,000$$

The solution is $i = \underline{12.4\%}$ = IRR of the project. The mine <u>should not be developed</u> because the IRR is less than the company's cost of capital.

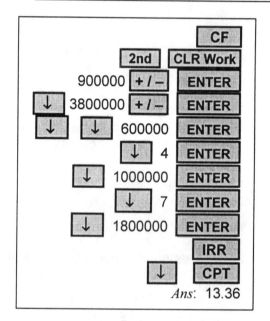

Time (years)	Capital cash flow	Operating profit	Net cash flow
0	–$ 900,000		–$900,000
1	–3,800,000		–3,800,000
2 to 5		$600,000	600,000
6 to 12		1,000,000	1,000,000
13	800,000	1,000,000	1,800,000

13.

The project's IRR is <u>13.4%</u>. Since the IRR is less than the required rate of return (14%), <u>Jasper should not undertake the expansion</u>.

Exercise 16.5

1 a. The IRR on project C is the value i satisfying

$$NPV = 0 = \$43,000 \left[\frac{1-(1+i)^{-6}}{i} \right] - \$150,000$$

The solution is $i =$ <u>18.1% = IRR of project C</u>.
The IRR on project D is the value of i satisfying

$$NPV = 0 = \$30,000 \left[\frac{1-(1+i)^{-6}}{i} \right] - \$100,000$$

The solution is $i =$ <u>19.9% = IRR of project D</u>.
<u>Project D</u> should be selected on the basis of having the larger IRR.

b. $NPV(C) = \$43,000 \left(\dfrac{1-1.15^{-6}}{0.15} \right) - \$150,000 = \$12,733$

$NPV(D) = \$30,000 \left(\dfrac{1-1.15^{-6}}{0.15} \right) - \$100,000 = \$13,534$

<u>Project D</u> has the larger NPV if the firm's cost of capital is 15%.

c. $NPV(C) = \$43,000 \left(\dfrac{1-1.12^{-6}}{0.12} \right) - \$150,000 = \$26,791$

$NPV(D) = \$30,000 \left(\dfrac{1-1.12^{-6}}{0.12} \right) - \$100,000 = \$23,342$

<u>Project C</u> has the higher NPV if the firm's cost of capital is 12%.

3. a. The IRR on Project X is the value of i satisfying

$$NPV = 0 = \frac{\$400,000}{1+i} + \frac{\$300,000}{(1+i)^2} + \frac{\$200,000}{(1+i)^3} - \$650,000$$

The solution is $i =$ <u>20.8% = IRR on Project X</u>.
The IRR on Project Y is the value of i satisfying

$$NPV = 0 = \frac{\$1,050,000}{(1+i)^3} - \$650,000$$

The solution is $i =$ <u>17.3% = IRR on Project Y</u>.
Based on an IRR ranking, <u>Project X should be selected</u>.

b. $NPV(X) = \dfrac{\$400,000}{1.14} + \dfrac{\$300,000}{1.14^2} + \dfrac{\$200,000}{1.14^3} - \$650,000 = \$66,712$

$NPV(Y) = \dfrac{\$1,050,000}{1.14^3} - \$650,000 = \$58,720$

At a cost of capital of 14%, <u>Project X</u> has the larger NPV and <u>should be selected</u>.

c. $NPV(X) = \dfrac{\$400,000}{1.11} + \dfrac{\$300,000}{1.11^2} + \dfrac{\$200,000}{1.11^3} - \$650,000 = \$100,085$

$NPV(Y) = \dfrac{\$1,050,000}{1.11^3} - \$650,000 = \$117,751$

At a cost of capital of 11%, <u>Project Y</u> has the larger NPV and <u>should be selected</u>.

Exercise 16.5 (*continued*)

5. a. The IRR on Project X is the value of i satisfying

$$NPV = 0 = \frac{\$60,000 \left[\dfrac{1-(1+i)^{-3}}{i}\right]}{(1+i)^2} - \$100,000$$

The solution is i = <u>16.0% = IRR on project X</u>.

The IRR on Project Y is the value of i satisfying

$$NPV = 0 = \frac{\$40,000 \left[\dfrac{1-(1+i)^{-4}}{i}\right]}{1+i} - \frac{\$50,000}{1+i} - \$50,000$$

The solution is i = <u>17.5% = IRR on Project Y</u>.
<u>Project Y is preferred</u> on an IRR basis.

b. $$NPV(\text{Project X}) = \frac{\$60,000 \left(\dfrac{1-1.15^{-3}}{0.15}\right)}{1.15^2} - \$100,000 = \$3587$$

$$NPV(\text{Project Y}) = \frac{\$40,000 \left(\dfrac{1-1.15^{-4}}{0.15}\right)}{1.15} - \frac{\$50,000}{1.15} - \$50,000 = \$5825$$

At a cost of capital of 15%, <u>Project Y</u> has the larger NPV and <u>should be selected</u>.

c. Similarly, at a cost of capital of 12%,
NPV(Project X) = $14,884
NPV(Project Y) = $13,834
<u>Project X</u> now has the higher NPV and <u>should be selected</u>.

Exercise 16.6

1. a.

Year	Cumulative profit
1	$ 8000
2	20,000
3	32,000
4	44,000
5	56,000

Payback period = $4 + \dfrac{\$52,000 - \$44,000}{\$56,000 - \$44,000}$ years

= <u>4.67 years</u>

b. Since it will take longer than 4 years to recover the initial investment from profits, the firm <u>would not make the investment</u>.

Exercise 16.6 (*continued*)

3.

	Cumulative profit		
Year	Project X	Project Y	
1	$25,000	0	
2	50,000	$25,000	
3	75,000	50,000	
4	100,000	75,000	
5	125,000	100,000	
6	150,000	125,000	
7		150,000	
8		175,000	

Payback period(Project X) = 4 years
Payback period(Project Y) = 5 years

NPV(Project X)

$$= \$25,000\left(\frac{1-1.1^{-6}}{0.1}\right) - \$100,000$$

$$= \$8882$$

$$NPV(Project\ Y) = \frac{\$25,000\left(\dfrac{1-1.1^{-7}}{0.1}\right)}{1.1} - \$100,000 = \$10,646$$

Project X would be <u>preferred on the basis</u> of its shorter <u>payback</u> but Project Y would be <u>preferred on the basis of</u> its larger <u>NPV</u>.

5.

	Proposal A		Proposal B	
Year	Profit	Cumulative profit	Profit	Cumulative profit
1	$16,250	$16,250	$12,500	$12,500
2	17,500	33,750	12,500	25,000
3	17,500	51,250	15,000	40,000
4	17,500	68,750	15,000	55,000

a. $$NPV(A) = \frac{\$16,250}{1.14} + \frac{\$17,500\left(\dfrac{1-1.14^{-3}}{0.14}\right)}{1.14} - \$45,000 = \$4893$$

$$NPV(B) = \$12,500\left(\frac{1-1.14^{-2}}{0.14}\right) + \frac{\$15,000\left(\dfrac{1-1.14^{-2}}{0.14}\right)}{1.14^2} - \$35,000 = \$4589$$

<u>Proposal A is preferred</u> on the basis of its larger NPV.

b. The IRR on Proposal A is the value of i satisfying

$$NPV = 0 = \frac{\$16,250}{1+i} + \frac{\$17,500\left[\dfrac{1-(1+i)^{-3}}{i}\right]}{1+i} - \$45,000$$

The solution is i = 19.1% = IRR on proposal A.
The IRR on proposal B is the value of i satisfying

$$NPV = 0 = \$12,500\left[\frac{1-(1+i)^{-2}}{i}\right] + \frac{\$15,000\left[\dfrac{1-(1+i)^{-2}}{i}\right]}{(1+i)^2} - \$35,000$$

The solution i = 20.0% = IRR on proposal B.
<u>Proposal B is preferred</u> on the basis of its larger IRR.

Exercise 16.6 (*continued*)

5. *c.* Payback period(A) $= 2 + \dfrac{\$45{,}000 - \$33{,}750}{\$17{,}500} = 2.64$ years

Payback period(B) $= 2 + \dfrac{\$35{,}000 - \$25{,}000}{\$15{,}000} = 2.67$ years

There is a weak <u>preference for proposal A</u> based on its slightly shorter payback period.

Review Problems

1. *a.* For the lease alternative,

$PMT = \$385$, $n = 60$, $i = 0.75\%$

$$PV(\text{lease}) = PV(\text{due}) = \$385\left(\frac{1 - 1.0075^{-60}}{0.0075}\right)(1.0075) = \$18{,}686$$

$$PV(\text{purchase}) = \$22{,}500 - \frac{\$5000}{1.0075^{60}} = \$19{,}307$$

The <u>car should be leased</u> because the economic value of the net cash outflows is $621 lower.

b. If the trade-in value after 5 years is $7000,

$$PV(\text{purchase}) = \$22{,}500 - \frac{\$7000}{1.0075^{60}} = \$18{,}029$$

In this case, the car should be <u>purchased</u> (a $657 advantage over leasing).

3.

Time (years)	Capital cash flow	Operating profit	Net cash flow
0	-$2,000,000		-$2,000,000
1	-1,000,000		-1,000,000
2 to 8		$750,000	750,000
9	-1,000,000	750,000	-250,000

$$NPV = \frac{\$750{,}000\left(\dfrac{1 - 1.14^{7}}{0.14}\right)}{1.14} - \$2{,}000{,}000 - \frac{\$1{,}000{,}000}{1.14} - \frac{\$250{,}000}{1.14^{9}}$$

$$= \$2{,}821{,}253 - \$2{,}000{,}000 - \$877{,}193 - \$76{,}877$$

$$= -\$132{,}817$$

Since the NPV is negative when the cash flows are discounted at 14%, the <u>project will not provide</u> the company with <u>a rate of return exceeding 14%</u>.

Review Problems (*continued*)

5.

Time (years)	Capital cash flow	Operating profit	Net cash flow
0	−$60,000		−$60,000
1 to 4		$16,500	16,500
5 to 7		15,500	15,500
8	10,000	15,500	25,500

$$\text{NPV} = \$16,500\left(\frac{1-1.15^{-4}}{0.15}\right) + \frac{\$15,500\left(\dfrac{1-1.15^{-3}}{0.15}\right)}{1.15^4} + \frac{\$25,500}{1.15^8} - \$60,000$$

$$= \$47,107.1 + \$20,234.3 + \$8336.0 - \$60,000$$
$$= \$15,677$$

The machine should be acquired since the investment has a positive NPV.

7. Choose the machine having the larger equivalent annual cash flow (EACF).

$$\text{NPV(X, 5 years)} = \$16,000\left(\frac{1-1.14^{-5}}{0.14}\right) + \frac{\$10,000}{1.14^5} - \$50,000 = \$10,123$$

X's EACF is the value of PMT satisfying

$$\$10,123 = PMT\left(\frac{1-1.14^{-5}}{0.14}\right) \qquad \text{giving} \qquad PMT = \$2949$$

$$\text{NPV(Y, 10 years)} = \$16,000\left(\frac{1-1.14^{-10}}{0.14}\right) + \frac{\$10,000}{1.14^{10}} - \$72,000 = \$14,155$$

Y's EACF is the value of PMT satisfying

$$\$14,155 = PMT\left(\frac{1-1.14^{-10}}{0.14}\right) \qquad \text{giving} \qquad PMT = \$2714$$

Machine X should be selected because its equivalent annual cash flow is $235 larger.

9. Choose the alternative having the lower equivalent annual cost. The present value of the net costs of a Songster for 5 years is

$$\frac{\$20,000}{1.065^5} - \$10,000\left(\frac{1-1.065^{-5}}{0.065}\right) - \$90,000 = -\$116,959$$

The Songster's equivalent annual cost (EAC) is the value of PMT in

$$\$116,959 = PMT\left(\frac{1-1.065^{-5}}{0.065}\right) \qquad \text{giving} \qquad PMT = \$28,144$$

The present value of the net costs of a Boston Wailer for 7 years is

$$\frac{\$40,000}{1.065^7} - \$8000\left(\frac{1-1.065^{-7}}{0.065}\right) - \$110,000 = -\$128,136$$

The Boston Wailer's EAC is the value of PMT in

$$\$128,136 = PMT\left(\frac{1-1.065^{-7}}{0.065}\right) \qquad \text{giving} \qquad PMT = \$23,363$$

The Boston Wailer's equivalent annual cost is $28,144 − $23,363 = $4781 lower.

Review Problems (*continued*)

11. The investment's IRR is the value of i satisfying

$$NPV = 0 = \$55,000 \left[\frac{1-(1+i)^{-8}}{i} \right] + \frac{\$125,000}{(1+i)^8} - \$300,000$$

The solution is $i = \underline{13.9\%}$ = IRR of the investment.
<u>The investment should not be made</u> since its IRR is less than the cost of capital (15%).

13. *a.* The IRR on project P is the value of i satisfying

$$NPV = 0 = \frac{\$120,000 \left[\dfrac{1-(1+i)^{-4}}{i} \right]}{(1+i)^3} - \$225,000$$

The solution is $i = \underline{15.0\%}$ = IRR <u>on project P</u>.
The IRR on project Q is the value of i satisfying

$$NPV = 0 = \$55,000 \left[\frac{1-(1+i)^{-7}}{i} \right] - \$225,000$$

The solution is $i = \underline{15.6\%}$ = IRR <u>on project Q</u>.
On the basis of their IRR ranking, <u>project Q is preferred</u>.

b. $NPV(\text{project P}) = \dfrac{\$120,000 \left(\dfrac{1-1.16^{-4}}{0.16} \right)}{1.16^3} - \$225,000 = -\$9879$

$NPV(\text{project Q}) = \$55,000 \left(\dfrac{1-1.16^{-7}}{0.16} \right) - \$225,000 = -\$2879$

<u>Neither project should be selected</u> because they both have a negative NPV.

c. $NPV(\text{project P}) = \dfrac{\$120,000 \left(\dfrac{1-1.13^{-4}}{0.13} \right)}{1.13^3} - \$225,000 = \$22,375$

$NPV(\text{project Q}) = \$55,000 \left(\dfrac{1-1.13^{-7}}{0.13} \right) - \$225,000 = \$18,244$

<u>Project P</u> has the larger NPV and <u>should be selected</u>.

Self-Test Exercises

1. If the plane is leased,
    $$PMT = \$5600, \ n = 60, \ i = \tfrac{7.5\%}{12} = 0.625\%$$

    $$PV(\text{lease}) = PV(\text{due}) = \$5600\left(\frac{1-1.00625^{-60}}{0.00625}\right)(1.00625) = \$281,216$$

    If the plane is purchased,
    $$PV(\text{purchase}) = \$360,000 - \frac{\$140,000}{1.00625^{60}} = \$263,667$$

    Rainbow Aviation <u>should purchase the plane</u> and thereby gain an economic advantage (in current dollars) of
    $$\$281,216 - \$263,667 = \underline{\$17,549}$$

2.

Time (years)	Capital cash flow	Operating profit	Net cash flow
0	−$100,000		−$100,000
1	−60,000	$24,000	−36,000
2 to 4		24,000	24,000
5	−16,000	24,000	8000
6 to 9		15,000	15,000
10	60,000	15,000	75,000

$$NPV = \$24,000\left(\frac{1-1.13^{-5}}{0.13}\right) + \frac{\$15,000\left(\frac{1-1.13^{-5}}{0.13}\right)}{1.13^{5}}$$

$$+ \frac{\$60,000}{1.13^{10}} - \frac{\$16,000}{1.13^{5}} - \frac{\$60,000}{1.13} - \$100,000$$

$$= \$84,413.6 + \$28,635.2 + \$17,675.3 - \$8684.2 - \$53,097.3 - \$100,000$$

$$= -\$31,057$$

<u>Huron should not purchase the boat</u> because the investment has a negative NPV.

3. Rank the projects in descending order of NPV per invested dollar.

Project	Initial investment	Project NPV	NPV per invested dollar	Cumulative investment
A	$200,000	$63,000	$0.32	$200,000
D	250,000	75,000	0.30	450,000
C	350,000	90,000	0.26	800,000
B	400,000	100,000	0.25	1,200,000
E	100,000	20,000	0.20	1,300,000

<u>Projects A, D, and C</u> give the highest aggregate NPV within the $800,000 capital budget constraint.

4. Choose the project having the larger NPV.
    $$NPV(A) = \$6000\left(\frac{1-1.15^{-8}}{0.15}\right) + \frac{\$5000}{1.15^{8}} - \$25,000 = \$3558$$

    $$NPV(B) = \frac{\$15,000}{1.15} + \frac{\$19,000}{1.15^{5}} + \frac{\$24,000}{1.15^{8}} - \$25,000 = \$5335$$

    <u>Choose Project B</u> because its NPV is $1777 larger.

Self-Test Exercises (*continued*)

5. Choose the alternative possessing the larger equivalent annual cash flow (EACF).

$$\text{NPV(C, 3 years)} = \$30,000 \left(\frac{1-1.16^{-3}}{0.16} \right) + \frac{\$10,000}{1.16^3} - \$55,000 = \$18,783$$

C's EACF is the value of *PMT* satisfying

$$\$18,783 = PMT \left(\frac{1-1.16^{-3}}{0.16} \right) \quad \text{giving} \quad PMT = \$8363$$

$$\text{NPV(D, 5 years)} = \$35,000 \left(\frac{1-1.16^{-5}}{0.16} \right) + \frac{\$20,000}{1.16^5} - \$100,000 = \$24,123$$

D's EACF is the value of *PMT* satisfying

$$\$24,123 = PMT \left(\frac{1-1.16^{-5}}{0.16} \right) \quad \text{giving} \quad PMT = \$7367$$

The firm should <u>purchase Machine C</u> because it has a $996 larger annual economic advantage.

6. Buy the harvester having the lower equivalent annual cost (EAC). The present value of the Spud Finder's net costs for 5 years is $140,000. Its EAC is the value of *PMT* satisfying

$$\$140,000 = PMT \left(\frac{1-1.13^{-5}}{0.13} \right) \quad \text{giving} \quad PMT = \$39,804$$

The present value of the Tater Taker's net costs for 7 years is

$$\$20,000 \left(\frac{1-1.13^{-7}}{0.13} \right) - \$80,000 = \$168,452$$

The Tater Taker's EAC is the value of *PMT* in

$$\$168,452 = PMT \left(\frac{1-1.13^{-7}}{0.13} \right) \quad \text{giving} \quad PMT = \$38,089$$

The farmer should <u>buy the Tater Taker</u> because its equivalent annual cost is $1715 lower.

7. Since the investment's NPV is $20,850, the initial investment is the value of C satisfying

$$\$20,850 = \frac{\$74,000}{1.12} + \frac{\$84,000}{1.12^2} + \frac{\$96,000}{1.12^3} + \frac{\$70,000}{1.12^4} - C$$
$$= \$66,071.4 + \$66,964.3 + \$68,330.9 + \$44,486.3 - C$$
$$C = \$225,003$$

Cumulative profit after 2 years = $158,000
Cumulative profit after 3 years = $254,000

$$\text{Payback period} = 2 + \frac{\$225,003 - \$158,000}{\$254,000 - \$158,000} = \underline{2.7 \text{ years}}$$

Self-Test Exercises (*continued*)

8. The investment's IRR is the value of i satisfying

$$NPV = 0 = \$100,000\left[\frac{1-(1+i)^{-4}}{i}\right] + \frac{\$50,000\left[\frac{1-(1+i)^{-4}}{i}\right]}{(1+i)^4} - \$400,000$$

The solution is $i = \underline{12.0\% = IRR}$ of the investment.
<u>The new product should not be introduced</u> because the IRR is less than the firm's cost of capital (13%).

9. a. The IRR on Investment A is the value of i satisfying

$$NPV = 0 = \frac{\$30,000}{1+i} + \frac{\$80,000}{(1+i)^2} - \$70,000$$

The solution is $i = \underline{30.5\% = IRR \text{ on Investment A}}$.
The IRR on Investment B is the value of i satisfying

$$NPV = 0 = \frac{\$50,000}{1+i} + \frac{\$50,000}{(1+i)^2} - \$65,000$$

The solution is $i = \underline{34.2\% = IRR \text{ on Investment B}}$.
<u>Investment B</u> would be selected on the basis on an IRR ranking.

b. $$NPV(\text{Investment A}) = \frac{\$30,000}{1.14} + \frac{\$80,000}{1.14^2} - \$70,000 = \$17,873$$

$$NPV(\text{Investment B}) = \frac{\$50,000}{1.14} + \frac{\$50,000}{1.14^2} - \$65,000 = \$17,333$$

With the cost of capital at 14%, <u>Investment A</u> has the larger NPV and should be chosen.

c. Similarly, at a cost of capital of 17%,
$$NPV(\text{Investment A}) = \$14,082$$
$$NPV(\text{Investment B}) = \$14,261$$
<u>Investment B</u> now has the higher NPV and should be chosen.